T0312969

Sustainability in Fashion and Textiles
Values, Design, Production and Consumption

Sustainability in Fashion and Textiles

VALUES, DESIGN, PRODUCTION AND CONSUMPTION

EDITED BY MIGUEL ANGEL GARDETTI AND ANA LAURA TORRES

Taylor & Francis Group

LONDON AND NEW YORK

First published in paperback 2024

First published 2013 by Greenleaf Publishing

Published 2017 by Routledge
4 Park Square, Milton Park, Abingdon, Oxon OX14 4RN

and by Routledge
605 Third Avenue, New York, NY 10158

Routledge is an imprint of the Taylor & Francis Group, an informa business

© 2013, 2017, 2024 Taylor & Francis

Publisher's Note
The publisher has gone to great lengths to ensure the quality of this reprint but points out that some imperfections in the original copies may be apparent.

British Library Cataloguing in Publication Data:
A catalogue record for this book is available from the British Library.

ISBN: 978-1-906093-78-5 (hbk)
ISBN: 978-1-03-292026-9 (pbk)
ISBN: 978-1-351-27760-0 (ebk)

DOI: 10.4324/9781351277600

Cover by LaliAbril.com

Contents

Foreword

Kate Fletcher

Things are often not exactly as they seem. Hidden behind prevailing ways of doing things and conventional assumptions about our societies, our cultural norms, our economics and our industries is a burgeoning and blossoming array of alternatives. These alternative ways of seeing the world and taking action are indispensable for sustainability; and it is our job to nurture them. They are a requisite for an engaged process of 'flourishing' (to borrow John Ehrenfeld's (2008) evocative description of sustainability); that is of enhanced connectedness with our sense of ethics, with each other and the natural world.

For me the fostering of alternatives to the status quo in fashion and textiles is essential if we are to deeply engage with the process of sustainability and respond with resilience, cooperation and practical skills to sector-wide challenges ranging from water shortages, fractured communities and loss of biodiversity. Such 'big pic-ture' themes are an intrinsic part of the fashion, textiles and sustainability dynamic. For fibre, fabric, garment, fashion are a fundament of being alive (meeting the basic need for protection) and, at one and the same time, at the heart of human culture. And yet a fabric or garment's creation, use and disposal is also implacably making the planet less habitable. Such tensions pervade the fashion, textiles and sustainabil-ity space—and we must learn to understand how to engage, critique and transform them. Managing this process well could lead to important change. For the currency of fashion is global and is disseminated rapidly, having potential to quickly ignite alternative behaviours, patterns of thinking and ways of wearing clothes.

As is obvious from a quick glance at the pages of this wide-ranging edited volume, the fashion and textile supply chain is complex—involving more production steps than many others—and is distributed internationally. Likewise the sustainability impacts implicated in the production and use of fashion and textiles are multi-farious and interrelated. They reach beyond the boundaries of individual compa-nies, supply chains, academic disciplines and as such are whole system issues.

An elemental web of interconnectedness ties the activities of a farmer growing fibre crops for commodity markets, a designer in his or her studio conceiving of a new season's collection, a supplier factory working to supply a global brand, fashion buyers, retailers, marketing specialists and of course the users of those clothes— 'people'—you and me—so often faceless, but critical to the whole.

It is into this terrain of connections and linkages that this book steps. Its very existence is evidence, if indeed any more were needed, that the field of fashion, textiles and sustainability is maturing. It now has its own language and dynamics and as an area of scholarship, it is advancing apace. Experts in this area are developing new skills, those of inter-disciplinarians. The disciplinary divisions that so typified past approaches to fashion and textiles—the splits between technologists and creatives, between craft and design, between natural science and social science—are now being knitted together by a new breed of thinkers and practitioners. Such experts are now succeeding in both corralling and opening up the broad and inclusive framework of sustainability and drawing on multiple academic traditions and methodologies to understand better what this means for fashion and textiles. The broad range of contributions from across the spectrum of scholarly exploration and analysis reflected in the pages that follow are complete with a sense of the lively, ethical and reflective nature of the subject. They show many threads in the web of relationships at play. For me they touch on the emergence of key themes that show the increasing sophistication of the debate: that systemic change is an essential part of the dialogue; that consumption must be grappled with head on; and that solutions are not only technological in nature.

It is also a sign of hope to me that the editors of this volume hail from Latin America. For too long, initiators of sustainability debates in fashion and textiles have been from the mature economies of the rich North, perhaps reflecting the idea that sustainability is something to be concerned about when other needs have been met. Yet as has been convincingly shown by numerous research studies (such as those reported on by Offer 2006), wealth is a poor proxy for welfare. While it is certainly true that economic growth provides high welfare payoffs as basic needs are met; beyond this fairly basic level, economic growth provides diminishing or even negative returns. The insight is that ecological and social 'richness' has little to do with economic development; that sustainability themes are shared and universal. Yet just as this realisation of joint potential dawns, sustainability perhaps seems more remote than ever; beating a fast retreat as ideas and institutions of consumerist materialism further dominate global aspirations and hyper-individualism sees people choosing to invest more directly in themselves and less in commitment to others and the next generation. This prioritisation of the 'I' over the 'we', of individual self-seeking over the common good, is limiting dramatically any improvements that can be made. Sustainability in fashion and textiles requires that, as well as a deep engagement with the detail of the fashion sector's day-to-day resource flows, we also grapple with some of the most challenging systemic, global themes of human culture.

It is fitting therefore that this book—with its South American connections—is brought together in a year where that continent is (again) the epicentre of major systemic scrutiny of planetary boundaries and future ways of living. The Rio+20 Summit, which starts the very week I am writing this Foreword, marks the point 20 years on from the Rio Earth Summit which influenced me so greatly at the time. It reflects on and records progress on themes which are still at the heart of sustainability debates today: intergenerational equity; over-consumption in rich countries; poverty reduction in poor ones; ecosystem limits; biodiversity; access and use of resources. Many of these themes are played out in this volume. All of them are part of the fashion and textile industry's future success. When we work with them we will learn to recognise finitude and abundance; longevity and beauty; fashion and sustainability.

To all engaging in this area of practice and study I evoke the call to action of the late and great ecologist, Ernest Callenbach: Onwards!

Kate Fletcher
London, June 2012
www.katefletcher.com
@katetfletcher

References

Ehrenfeld, J.R. (2008) *Sustainability by Design* (New Haven, CT: Yale University Press).
Offer, A. (2006) *The Challenge of Affluence* (Oxford, UK: Oxford University Press).

Introduction*

Miguel Angel Gardetti and Ana Laura Torres
The Sustainable Textile Centre, Argentina

In 2000 the world's consumers spent around US$1 trillion on clothing—split roughly one-third in Western Europe, one-third in North America and one-quarter in Asia (Make Trade Fair and Oxfam International 2004). Seven per cent of total world exports are in clothing and textiles. Significant parts of the sector are dominated by developing countries, particularly in Asia, and above all by China. Industrialised countries are still important exporters of clothing and textiles, especially Germany, Italy in clothing and the United States in textiles. According to Allwood *et al.* (2006), the developing countries now account for half of world textile exports and almost three-quarters of world clothing exports.

Because of the size of the sector and the historical dependence of clothing manufacture on cheap labour, the clothing and textile industry is subject to intense political interest and has been significantly shaped by international trading agreements.

Estimating the number of people working in these sectors is extremely difficult because of the number of small firms and subcontractors active in the area and the difficulty of drawing boundaries between sectors (Allwood *et al.* 2006). According to statistics from the UNIDO (United Nations Industrial Development Organisation) Industrial Statistics Database (INDSTAT), around 26.5 million people work within the clothing and textiles sector worldwide (ILO 2006).

Also the same report indicates that of these 26.5 million employees, 13 million are employed in the clothing sector and 13.5 million in the textiles sector. These figures are only people employed in manufacturing—not retail or other supporting sectors (Allwood *et al.* 2006).

---

* Our special thanks go to the review panel for their outstanding work. This book would not have been possible without their dedication and commitment.

Around 70% of clothing workers are women (Hernández 2006). In the garment industry, women typically sew, finish and pack clothes. Supervisors, machine operators and technicians tend to be men—who earn more. In the past five to ten years, employment in the sector has increasingly been concentrated in China, Pakistan, Bangladesh, India, Mexico, Romania, Cambodia and Turkey. All of these countries, apart from India, have shown increases in clothing and textile employment from 1997 to 2002 (Allwood *et al.* 2006).

However, for many smaller developing countries, which are small exporters on a global scale, clothing and textiles exports are their dominant form of external earnings. In Bangladesh, Haiti and Cambodia, clothing and textiles account for more than 80% of total exports. Similar high figures apply to the proportion of the country's manufacturing workers employed within the clothing and textiles sector.

Setup and switch-over times and costs have traditionally led to large batch manufacture of clothing with long lead times—fashion shows for summer clothing are held in the autumn to allow six months for manufacture. However, this pattern is rapidly changing—with customer demand for so-called 'fast fashion' where stores change the designs on show every few weeks, rather than twice per year. This emphasis on speeding up production has led to concentration in the industry with fewer larger suppliers—to take advantage of economies of scale (for instance in purchasing) and to simplify the number of relationships that must be maintained by retailers.

This trend is now more noticeable in the clothing sector with the growth of 'full package' companies that are able to supply quick time delivery orders to big retailers (Allwood *et al.* 2006). Downstream textile finishing and dyeing processes are being integrated into textile weaving factories and further integrated with clothing manufacture and the distribution networks. Such integration supports rapid servicing of the demand for 'fast fashion' by avoiding the build up of stock characteristic of long supply chains and providing shorter lead times. There is also a trend towards investing in increased capacity and introducing 'new industrial robotics': substituting expensive labour with novel technologies. A variant of such single company vertical integration also in evidence is the development of clusters of businesses supporting each other through regional integration (FIAS 2006).

Given this panorama, there is no doubt that the textile (and fashion) industry is significant to our economy. However, within the context of sustainability, this industry commonly operates to the detriment of environmental and social factors (Gardetti and Torres 2011).

Understanding sustainable textiles and fashion

Given the complexities that exist in the textile and fashion industry, and the importance of our cultural and emotional connection with clothes, some issues that will contribute to a better understanding of this book are presented below.

What is sustainable development and sustainability?

Sustainable development is a problematic expression, and few people agree on what it means. One can take the term and 'reinvent' it considering one's own needs. It is a concept that continuously leads us to change objectives and priorities since it is an open process and as such, it cannot be reached definitively. However, one of the most widely accepted definitions of sustainable development, though diffuse and non-operating, is the one proposed by the World Commission on Environment and Development (WCED 1987) report, *Our Common Future*, also known as the Brundtland Report, which defines sustainable development as the development model that allows us to meet present needs, without compromising the ability of future generations to meet their own needs. The essential objective of this development model is to raise the quality of life by long-term maximisation of the productive potential of ecosystems, through the appropriate technologies for this purpose (Gardetti 2005).

While achieving sustainability is the goal of sustainable development (Doppelt 2010), the word 'sustainability' has several meanings nowadays, and is frequently reduced by associating it with 'environment'. Some authors, such as Frankel (1998) and Elkington (1998), define sustainability as the balance between three elements: economy, environment and social equity. Though this definition is closely linked to *organisations*, it can also be applied at the *societal* level. But not everybody agrees with Frankel and Elkington: Paul Gilding (2000) argues that much of the 'complexity' of sustainability is lost when considering only the three mentioned aspects. Sustainable development is not only a new concept, but also a new paradigm, and this requires us to look at things differently. It is a notion of the world deeply different from the one that dominates our current thinking and includes satisfying basic human needs such as justice, freedom and dignity (Ehrenfeld 1999). It is the vision through which we can build a way of being.[1] Also, Suzuki and Dressel (2002) define sustainability, at the *individual level*, as the assessment of all human behaviours with the vision of reformulating those that contradict the development of a sustainable future.

What is understood by textile and clothing industry?

According to the European Commission, the textile and clothing industry is a diverse and heterogeneous industry covering a large range of activities from the transformation of fibres to yarns and fabrics and from these to clothing, which may be either fashion or non-fashion clothes.[2]

---

1 'Sustainability by Choice', unpublished document, J.R. Ehrenfeld 2002.
2 European Commission Enterprise and Industry 'Textiles and Clothing: External Dimension', www.ec.europa.eu/enterprise/sectors/textiles/external-dimension/index_en.htm, accessed 28 March 2012.

The clothing industry is intensive and offers basic level jobs for unskilled labour in developed as well as developing countries. Job creation in the sector has been particularly strong for women in poor countries, who previously had no income opportunities other than the household or the informal sector. Moreover, it is a sector where relatively modern technology can be adopted, even in poor countries, at relatively low investment costs. These technological features of the industry have made it suitable as the first rung on the industrialisation ladder in poor countries, some of which have experienced a very high output growth rate in the sector (Nordås 2004).

At the same time, the textile and clothing (and fashion) industry has high-value added segments where design, research and development are important competitive factors. The high end of the fashion industry uses human capital intensively in design and marketing. The same applies to market segments such as sportswear where both design and material technology are important.

Textiles provide the major input to the clothing industry, creating vertical linkages between the two. At the micro level, the two sectors are increasingly integrated through vertical supply chains that also involve the distribution and sales activities. Indeed, the retailers in the clothing sector increasingly manage the supply chain of the clothing and textiles sectors.

The textile and clothing industry includes:

- Obtaining and processing raw materials, i.e. the preparation and production of textile fibres. 'Natural' fibres include, among others, cotton, wool, silk, flax and hemp. 'Manufactured' fibres include fibres resulting from the transformation of natural polymers (cellulosic fibres such as viscose, modal, Lyocell) or synthetic polymers (fibres from organic material such as oil, i.e. polyester, nylon, acrylic, polypropylene) and fibres from inorganic materials (such as glass)

- Production of yarns

- Production of fabrics

- Finishing activities which give textiles visual, physical and aesthetic properties that consumers demand, such as bleaching, printing, dyeing and coating.

- Transformation of textiles into garments that can be either fashion or non-fashion garments (the so-called 'clothing industry')

Figure 1 **Textile, clothing and fashion industry**

Source: authors

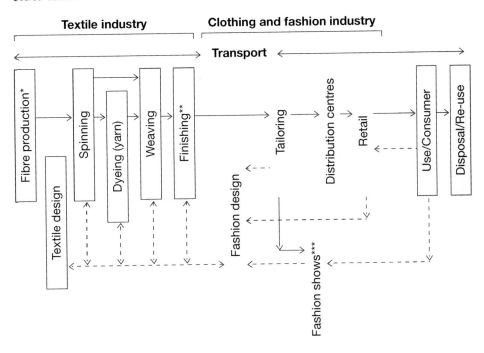

* For some particular fibres that includes dismounting and cleaning
** includes dry-cleaning and printing
*** includes other events

⟶ Material flow

· – – > Information flow

Figure 1 graphically summarises the above-mentioned processes. In this figure the dotted lines represent information flow, while continuous lines represent goods and services flow. The direction of the arrows indicates a system driven by demand. Information flow begins with the consumer and set the base for what and when is being produced. It is also worth mentioning that, in many cases, information flows directly from retailers to textiles facilities.

The relationship between fashion and sustainability: History and contradictions

Linda Welters, in her work 'The Fashion of Sustainability' (2008), presents the connection points between sustainability—as understood today—and fashion since the year 1600. Welters highlights that sustainability is not a new concept in the history of fashion but it has been part of its repertoire.

Basically, fashion is the way in which our clothes reflect and communicate our individual vision within society, linking us to time and space (Fletcher 2008).

Clothing is the material thing that gives fashion a contextual vision in society (Cataldi *et al.* 2010).

Fashion is something that always changes, while its meaning remains unaltered. Fashion, which is a deep cultural expression and aims directly at who we are and how we connect to other people, frequently suggests a passing trend, something transient and superficial.

As Walker (2006) points out, these negative connotations of fashion pertain only to the way in which it is manifested and used. Change itself is inherently neither positive nor negative—it is the nature of the change that matters. Sustainability, by contrast, has to do with long-term perspective. Fashion can be defined as the discarding of clothes that are fully functional for purely semiotic or symbolic reasons (Koefoed and Skov undated). The fact that the production and use of fashion garments generate a great amount of waste, would make it appear as an impediment for sustainability.

But, beyond these contradictions, fashion should not necessarily come into conflict with sustainable principles. Indeed, it has a role in the promotion and achievement of sustainability and it may even be a key element in working towards more sustainable ways of living (Walker 2006)

According to Hethorn and Ulasewicz (2008), fashion is a process, is expressed and worn by people, and as a material object, has a direct link to environment. It is embedded in everyday life. So, sustainability within fashion means that through the development and use of a thing or a process, there is no harm done to the people or the planet, and that thing or process, once put into action, can enhance the well-being of the people who interact with it and the environment it is developed and used within.

Textiles and fashion impacts

Several authors and organisations have analysed textiles and clothing industry impacts. Some of them are Slater (2000), Allwood *et al.* (2006), Fletcher (2008), Defra (2008), Ross (2009), Dickson *et al.* (2009) and Gwilt and Rissanen (2011).

One specific study is *Fashioning Sustainability: A Review of Sustainability Impacts of the Clothing Industry*, which Stephanie Draper, Vicky Murray and Ilka Weissbrod conducted in 2007 for WWF, financed by Marks & Spencer.

Figure 2 shows, schematically, environmental and social impacts of the textile, clothing and fashion industry.

Figure 2 Environmental and social impacts of the textile, clothing and fashion industry

Source: authors

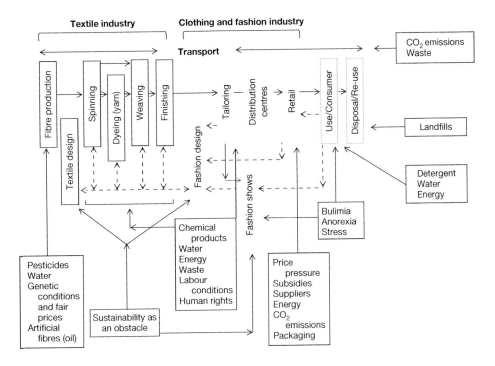

Regarding the **obtaining of fibre as raw material**, the use of pesticides during this process leads to health problems for workers, causes soil degradation and the loss of biodiversity. Water is such a necessary element in the processing of cotton in particular, that this crop has been called the 'thirsty crop'. While the use of agrochemicals tends to be reduced, the use of genetically modified organisms for such purposes could lead to another type of impact.

Abuses of working conditions are also commonly seen in other stages of these industries; many times, human rights are violated in so-called sweatshops which are characterised by low wages and excessive working time. The risks are even greater if health and safety systems are not appropriate.

In turn, many of the synthetic fibres are derived from a non-renewable resource such as oil. In general, environmental abuse combines with ethical issues when there is an excessive use of water and when land for food production is usurped.

Considering the whole **textile chain, from spinning to finishing**, it cannot be ignored that the use of chemicals may have carcinogenic and neurological effects, may cause allergies and may affect fertility. During these processes, large amounts of water and energy are used and, in general, non-biodegradable wastes are produced.

In the **marketing and sales processes**, subsidies and quotas with great impact on developing countries arise. The lack of international regulation on these issues creates a 'win–lose' scenario. In addition, prices should allow a fair distribution of profit throughout the supply chain. These stages also involve the use of energy and lots of packaging as well as the generation of carbon emissions (CO_2). The paradox, in this case, is that for its survival, the workforce depends on a system that seems to be destroying the world's capacity to withstand such a force. In both textile and fashion **design**, sustainability is, in general, perceived as an obstacle. Finally, major impacts derived from **transport**, are carbon emissions and waste generation.

The consumer (use and disposal)

Impacts generated by consumers deserve a special mention. It is not only Ehrenfeld (1999 and 2002) and Suzuki and Dressel (2002) who place sustainability at the *individual level*. Previously, D. Early, in the work 'What is Sustainable Design' from 1993, defined sustainability as the integration of natural systems to human behaviour patterns. While Vieira—also in 1993—maintains that sustainability identifies a concept and a developing attitude that observes the land, water and energy resources as integral aspects of development. Teresa Presas, in her work 'Interdependence and Partnership: Building Blocks to Sustainable Development' (2001), claims that a real transition towards sustainable development requires a new way of thinking. It requires the use of a collective learning mechanism for all types of environments and stakeholders and the creation of the necessary space for a structure of dialogue on what our vision of sustainable society is. But a sustainable society is not possible without sustainable individuals (Cavagnaro and Curiel 2012). That is, individual capacities seem to be at the heart of the issue.

These definitions should lead to a more responsible attitude from the consumer. They refer not only to reducing water and energy consumption and chemicals and detergent use, but also—and according to Fletcher (2008)—to material consumption patterns. While, during the production phase, material choice and efficiency are very important issues when considering social and environmental impacts, the benefits derived from this are often lost if laundry practices by consumers are not influenced. Several authors (Easter 2007; Fletcher 2008; Dombek-Keith and Loker 2011) agree that, for frequently washed garments, the effects of reducing water and energy use during washing, drying and ironing processes are greater than the possible effects of modifying production methods.

Annie Sherburne, designer from Kingston University, UK, in a work from 2009 titled 'Achieving Sustainable Textiles: A Designer's Perspective', points out:

> The biggest impacts of textiles and garments occur when they are being used by the consumer (estimated at 75–95% of the total environmental impact) and is mainly explained by the use of electricity, hot water and washing and drying processes. This contributes to the generation of greenhouse gases and global warming.

It is also important to consider the large amount of waste caused through consumption.

According to Kate Fletcher (2008), the process of transforming the industry into something more sustainable—and more sensitive to our needs—takes time. It is a long-term commitment to a new way of producing and consuming that requires widespread personal, social and institutional change. In the shorter term, there exist other, more easily won, opportunities to tackle consumers' patterns, such as those that come from subverting well-recognised social and psychological mechanisms that induce blind consumption such as: the pressure to compare themselves to others, such as through the accumulation and display of possessions; the continuous replacing of things with their 'updated' versions; the cultural obligation to experience everything and buy things accordingly; and the constant consumption as part of a continuous process of identity formation.

The need for a wider vision in the textile sector

For Kate Fletcher (2008, 2009), though little recognised, deep issues such as consumption patterns, globalisation of fashion, physical and mental health associated with fashion trends (each one of these reflecting cultural visions and social norms that influence the textile industry), should be part of the *substantive* debate of sustainability in textiles, which is frequently reduced to technical aspects.

Sustainability issues in textiles require taking into account the influences emerging from outside the boundaries of the conventional textile industry. These 'external' influences—ranging from agricultural practices to international energy policies, passing through consumption patterns and levels of ecological notions of society—have a great influence on the sustainability of the sector as a whole. Ecological and social systems extend beyond the boundaries of companies and individual industries; therefore to develop a more sustainable textile industry we need to commit ourselves with these issues *at the level they correspond to* and connect with other disciplines, industries, communities and international groups, beyond their own boundaries.

The timeline and the now...'the design of a journey'

The appearance of the first books in the field of textiles, fashion and sustainability is very recent. The 'journey' begins in 1998, when A.R. Horrocks, as editor, published *Ecotextiles '98 Sustainable Development: Proceedings of the Conference Ecotextile '98*, a book in which he presents a selection of woks presented at the Eco-Textile Conference held at the University of Bolton, UK. Then, in 2000, Keith Slater published *Environmental Impact of Textiles: Production, Processes and Protection*.

Some years later, in 2005, R.S. Blackburn as editor, published *Biodegradable and Sustainable Fibres*, while in 2006, Youjiang Wang published *Recycling in Textiles*. In 2007, M. Miraftab and A.R. Horrocks, both as editors, published *Ecotextiles: The Way Forward for Sustainable Development in Textiles*, which presents a selection of 23 works, submitted at the EcoTextile 2004 Conference (University of Bolton, UK) while in the same year, the publishing house Earth Pledge released *Future Fashion: White Papers*, which was the first book to integrate the issue of fashion in relation to sustainability.

In January 2008, Kate Fletcher published *Sustainable Fashion and Textiles: Design Journeys*, a work in which she presents information about sustainable impacts of fashion and textiles, alternative practices for global sustainability, design and social innovation concepts. Fletcher challenges—holistically—existing ideas about the essence of sustainability in the fashion and textile industry. Also at the beginning of 2008, more precisely in February, two books were published: *Eco-Chic: The Fashion Paradox* by Sandy Black, who shows the relationship between fashion and the environment, and *Sustainable Fashion, Why Now? A Conversation about Issues, Practices, and Possibilities*, edited by Janet Hethorn and Connie Ulasewicz.

By 2009, R.S. Blackburn, again as editor, presented *Sustainable Textiles: Life Cycle and Environmental Impact*, a book which reviews the different path to obtain more sustainable textile materials and technologies, and Liz Parker and Marsha A. Dickson published *Sustainable Fashion: A Handbook for Educators*, which presents practical ideas on how to teach and integrate environment and social aspects in the fashion industry. Also in the same year, V. Ann Paulins and Julie L. Hillery presented *Ethics in the Fashion Industry*, which addresses the complex aspects of the fashion industry, and Marsha A. Dickson, Suzzanne Loker and Molly Eckman presented *Social Responsibility in the Global Apparel Industry*, which introduces the reader to the social and environmental aspects of the clothing industry accompanied by an analysis of how enterprises can improve their (social) responsibility across their value chain. A year later, in 2010, Sass Brown presented those companies that are making the difference in the field of sustainable fashion design in her book *Eco-Fashion*.

Alison Gwilt and Timo Rissanen published, in 2011, *Shaping Sustainable Fashion: Changing the Way We Make and Use Clothes*, which illustrates—divided into four areas—creative solutions along the life-cycle of garments, while Marion I. Tobler-Rohr, also in 2011, presented the *Handbook of Sustainable Textile Production*, which contains an important compilation of economic, technical and environmental data in the manufacturing textile chain, becoming a key piece to integrate sustainable development into textiles.

In 2012, *Fashion & Sustainability: Design for Change* was published by Kate Fletcher and Lynda Grose, a book which examines how sustainability has the potential to transform the fashion system and introduces innovative people that work on it. Also in the same year, Gardetti and Torres were guest editors for a special issue of *The Journal of Corporate Citizenship* on 'Textiles, Fashion and Sustainability', which presents six academic works on the subject.

Sectoral initiative in the Global Compact and the Principles for Responsible Management Education

The Nordic Fashion Association and the Nordic Initiative Clean and Ethical (NICE) have developed a code of conduct for the fashion industry, named *The NICE Manual*, released in 2009, which contains 13 principles that provide ethical, responsible and sustainable guidelines for facing the great challenges of the industry and links them to the United Nations Global Compact principles.[3] This code has given rise to *the first initiative of the Global Compact in this sector*. This initiative concerns a (new) code of conduct, this time jointly developed between the Nordic Fashion Association, NICE and the Global Compact, which was publicly presented at the Copenhagen Fashion Summit on 3 May 2012, known as the *NICE Code of Conduct and Manual for the Fashion and Textile Industry*. In the words of Georg Kell, Executive Director of the United Nations Global Compact:

> As an industry facing serious and widely publicized social and environmental challenges, the fashion and textile industry is uniquely positioned to launch a sectoral initiative under the umbrella of the UN Global Compact... We are very excited about this effort and look forward to collaborating with NICE and its partners (Kell 2012).

The Global Compact is a joint initiative of the United Nations Development Programme (UNDP), the Economic Commission for Latin America and the Caribbean (ECLAC) and the International Labour Organisation (ILO), aimed at fostering the development of corporate social responsibility, promoting human rights, labour standards, environmental stewardship and anti-corruption. The main objective of the Global Compact is to facilitate the alignment of business operations and strategies with ethical objectives universally agreed and internationally applicable, in order to achieve a global and inclusive economy (Kell 2003). This process allows the United Nations to know in which way to work with other sectors, particularly the private sector (Annan 2004).

Table 1 shows the UN Global Compact's ten principles and the application areas. The principles are inspired by the Universal Declaration of Human Rights, the International Labour Organisation's Declaration on Fundamental Principles and Rights at Work, the Rio Declaration on Environment and Development and the United Nations Convention against Corruption.

---

3 For further information: www.unglobalcompact.org

Table 1 **United Nations Global Compact principles and application areas**
Source: Fuertes *et al.* 2004; United Nations 2004

Areas	Principles
Human rights	1. Businesses should support and respect the protection of internationally proclaimed human rights
	2. Business should make sure that they are not complicit in human rights abuses
Labour	3. Businesses should uphold the freedom of association and the effective recognition of the right to collective bargaining
	4. The elimination of all forms of forced and compulsory labour
	5. The effective abolition of child labour
	6. The elimination of discrimination in respect of employment and occupation
Environment	7. Business should support a precautionary approach to environmental challenges
	8. Undertake initiatives to promote greater environmental responsibility
	9. Encourage the development and diffusion of environmentally friendly technologies
Anti-corruption	10. Businesses should work against corruption in all its forms, including extortion and bribery

Miguel Angel Gardetti and Ana Laura Torres have been founders and are currently coordinators of the Sustainable Textile Centre,[4] which is the first initiative with an academic and research profile in Latin America promoting a holistic, multidimensional and more sustainable vision of the textile and fashion sector, through knowledge generation and transfer, education and capacity building, and the development of strategic partnerships. The Centre adheres to the Principles for Responsible Management Education,[5] principles that have been agreed with different schools of business and academic associations from around the world, which are intended to be a guiding framework on which the bases of a common and integrated education settle, within an increasingly globalised society, which requires new values for a more sustainable development of the world. These principles are shown in Table 2.

4 For further information: www.ctextilsustentable.org.ar
5 For further information: www.unprme.org. Within this frame—and based on a mailing exchange between Jonas Haertle, Head of the Principles for Responsible Management Education (PRME) secretariat of the United Nations Global Compact Office, and Miguel Angel Gardetti from the Sustainable Textile Centre—there exists an initiative for the creation of a working group on 'textiles, fashion and sustainability', that could be pursued if the Schools of Business adhering to the Principles express interest in this and if financial resources to sustain the activities are obtained.

Table 2 **Principles for Responsible Management Education (PRME) of the United Nations Global Compact**

Source: Principles for Responsible Management Education (www.unprme.org)

Principle 1	**Purpose**: We will develop the capabilities of students to be future generators of sustainable value for business and society at large and to work for an inclusive and sustainable global economy
Principle 2	**Values**: We will incorporate into our academic activities and curricula the values of global social responsibility as portrayed in international initiatives such as the United Nations Global Compact
Principle 3	**Method**: We will create educational frameworks, materials, processes and environments that enable effective learning experiences for responsible leadership
Principle 4	**Research**: We will engage in conceptual and empirical research that advances our understanding about the role, dynamics and impact of corporations in the creation of sustainable social, environmental and economic value
Principle 5	**Partnership**: We will interact with managers of business corporations to extend our knowledge of their challenges in meeting social and environmental responsibilities and to explore jointly effective approaches to meeting these challenges
Principle 6	**Dialogue**: We will facilitate and support dialogue and debate among educators, business, government, consumers, media, civil society organisations and other interested groups and stakeholders on critical issues related to global social responsibility and sustainability

The book

This book is a complement to the special issue of *The Journal of Corporate Citizenship* on 'Textiles, Fashion and Sustainability'. As with the call for papers for the special issue, the call for papers for this book intended to explore the different dimensions of the textile, clothing and fashion industry. This call attracted 60 submissions, 53 of which were invited to the second round for full manuscript review. Finally, and with the help of the review panel throughout this process, 23 top-quality papers were selected which deal with the essential aspects in these areas.

For a better understanding, the book has been divided into four sections, which are presented below:

1. **The systemic vision and the value chain in the textile and fashion industry**, which includes chapters dealing with a broad vision of the industry, the supply chain, processes, design and the disposition phase.

2. **Marketing, brands and regulatory aspects in the textile and fashion industry**, involves chapters about brands, retailers, communication strategies and regulatory aspects.

3. **The practice in textiles and fashion**, section in which several cases related to the industry are presented.

4. **Consumer: purchase, identity, use and care of clothing and textiles**

The first section, **The systemic vision and the value chain in the textile and fashion industry**, begins with a chapter by Carlotta Cataldi, Crystal Grover and Maureen Dickson called 'Slow fashion: Tailoring a strategic approach for sustainability' which explores a strategic approach to move the fashion industry towards sustainability. Instead of focusing on the unsustainable mainstream fast fashion model, the authors took an appreciative look at the Slow Fashion movement. Further on, Lynda Grose, in her chapter 'Wisdoms from the fashion trenches', gives voice to the insights of individuals working in the fashion trenches. She maintains that, as a collective, they quietly challenge fashion industry norms and open up more opportunities to inspire change for sustainability.

The next chapter, 'From principle to practice: Embedding sustainability in clothing supply chain strategies', by Alison Ashby, Melanie Hudson Smith and Rory Shand, undertakes to understand how firms can address their responsibilities across the supply chain.

Kristin Fransson, Yuntao Zhang, Birgit Brunklaus and Sverker Molander then present a chapter describing the information flows regarding chemicals in textile supply chains, entitled 'Managing chemical risk information: The case of Swedish retailers and Chinese suppliers in textile supply chains'. Harrie W.M. van Bommel, in his chapter based on quantitative research among fashion/clothing companies in the Netherlands, 'Innovation power of fashion focal companies and participation in sustainability activities in their supply network', poses the question of the extent to which the innovation characteristics of the 'focal' company (the innovation power) itself and the cooperation characteristics of its supply network can explain the sustainability strategy in its supply network. The sixth chapter that composes this first part bears the title 'Sustainable colour forecasting: The benefits of creating a better colour trend forecasting system for consumers, the fashion industry and the environment', written by Tracy Diane Cassidy. Her chapter refers to the benefits of changing the colour forecasting process and the implications that this proposal has for the industry. It sets out the theory of planned obsolescence and explains how the current process contributes to product waste within the fashion retail sector. A better system is then given with an overview of how this could promote style rivalry to provide a longer-term solution.

In relation to design, two chapters are presented. One of them, 'Fashioning use: A polemic to provoke pro-environmental garment maintenance' by Tullia Jack, argues that a consideration of the way clothes are used allows designers to embed pro-environmental practices in garments with vast resource conservation potential, and this is supported by examples of garment design that shape the way people wash clothes. The second one, by Lynda Grose, focuses on the educational aspect. She wonders how a designer of material goods is to practise responsibly. The author looks reflectively and critically at the undergraduate Sustainable Fashion

Design classes taught at California College of the Arts. The chapter, entitled 'Fashion design education for sustainability practice: Reflections on undergraduate level teaching', aims to note successes and continued challenges, including institutional inflexibility, society's perception of design and mounting economic pressures on students.

Closing this first section, two chapters dealing with the disposal phase are presented. The first one, 'Upcycling fashion for mass production', is written by Tracy Diane Cassidy and Sara Li-Chou Han. Here, the authors explore the concept of upcycling fashion on a mass industrial scale as a potential long-term solution to the textile waste issue. The upcycling process is then described in a fashion context. The challenges that the industry would need to address are highlighted and some suggestions for a way forward are given. The second one, 'Creating new from that which is discarded: The collaborative San Francisco Tablecloth Repurposing Project', is by Connie Ulasewicz and Gail Baugh. This chapter chronicles the challenges and innovations of industry professionals in the San Francisco Bay Area sewn products trade association, PeopleWearSF as they design, manufacture and market new products from the repurposed tablecloths.

The second part of the book, **Marketing, brands and regulatory aspects in the textile and fashion industry**, opens with a chapter written by Ines Weller called 'Sustainable consumption and production patterns in the clothing sector: Is green the new black?' This chapter first presents the way in which supply and demand in ecological clothing has developed over the last 20 to 30 years in Germany. It then goes on to give an overview of the important ecological and social hot spots in the textile chain and presents the requirements for sustainable consumption and production patterns in the clothing sector based on the ecological hot spots identified.

Later, Cameron Neil, Eloise Bishop and Kirsten Simpson present the chapter 'Redefining "Made in Australia": A "fair go" for people and planet'. This chapter discusses the challenge (and opportunities) for Australian fashion brands of becoming 'ethical and green' and also the authors briefly discuss the state of the Australian fashion industry, the local and global context of ethical and sustainable fashion, and introduce Ethical Clothing Australia. The third chapter presented in this part of the book is by Iain A. Davies and Carla-Maria Streit, and is titled '"Sustainability isn't sexy": An exploratory study into luxury fashion'. The authors wonder if there is room for sustainability in the high-end luxury fashion market and discuss the role of ethics in luxury fashion markets.

Ilaria Pasquinelli and Pamela Ravasio then present 'Ethical fashion in Western Europe: A survey of the status quo through the digital communications lens'. The authors argue that from fast fashion to couture, the sustainability agenda can no longer be ignored by the fashion industry. The acknowledgement and reputation of efforts, however, is fully dependent on the style and content of a company's communications. In this chapter the communication strategies of 42 European fashion brands and retailers with respect to their sustainability commitments are analysed.

Closing this part, Claude Meier presents his chapter, 'Effectiveness of standard initiatives: Rules and effective implementation of transnational standard initiatives

(TSI) in the apparel industry: An empirical examination'. Guided by an analytical framework, the contribution empirically examines which elements of the institutional designs of the Fair Wear Foundation (FWF) and the Business Social Compliance Initiative (BSCI) lead to effective implementations of ILO core conventions in the apparel industry in risk countries.

The third part of the book, **The practice in textiles and fashion**, presents five interesting cases. The first contribution, 'Corporate responsibility in the garment industry: Towards shared value' by Anna Larsson, Katarina Buhr and Cecilia Mark-Herbert, is a comparative case study which offers a contextual understanding of conditions for corporate responsibility from a garment retailer perspective. Following that is the chapter by Kim Poldner, entitled 'Zigzag or interlock? The case of the Sustainable Apparel Coalition'. This qualitative case study zooms in on the Sustainable Apparel Coalition, a group of leading apparel companies that work towards a more sustainable global textile industry.

Patsy Perry in her chapter, 'Garments without guilt? A case study of sustainable garment sourcing in Sri Lanka', maintains that the inherent conflict between CSR principles and the characteristics of fashion supply chains may be reconciled by adopting the supply chain management (SCM) philosophy of long-term orientation and shared goals between trading partners. This case study of Sri Lankan export garment manufacturers shows how successful implementation of CSR has enabled the country to compete as a low-risk sourcing destination for global fashion retailers.

The fourth case study, 'Next one, please: Integrating sustainability criteria in the procurement of operating-room textiles: The case of Germany', is by Gabriel Weber, Edeltraud Günther, Holger Hoppe and Julia Hillmann. The authors assess how life-cycle management and, moreover, life-cycle costing could be used for a better integration of sustainability criteria within the setting of the case study hospitals.

Finally, Sarah E. Heidebrecht and Joy M. Kozar, in their chapter, 'Development and the garment industry: Commonwealth of the Northern Mariana Islands', illustrate how the effects of the garment industry in a small, developing island nation, the Commonwealth of the Northern Mariana Islands (CNMI), are dramatically affected by a trade arrangement, the Multi-Fibre Arrangement (MFA). They also expose the effects of dependency when the garment industry is used as the main source of revenue.

The fourth and last section of this book, **Consumer: purchase, identity, use and care of clothing and textiles**, presents three chapters. The first of them, 'Young academic women's clothing practice: Interactions between fast fashion and social expectations in Denmark', is by Charlotte Louise Jensen and Michael Søgaard Jørgensen. The authors investigate how young Danish academic women's clothing practices are shaped. The aim is to analyse environmental impacts, environmental concerns and conditions for 'greener' clothing practices.

Next, Fernando F. Fachin presents 'Connecting meanings and materials: Identity dynamics in sustainable fashion'. In the context of sustainable fashion, the objective of this research is to explore identity constitution processes of entrepreneurial ecodesigners. More specifically, with a sociomaterial approach, this chapter considers the constitutive interaction of meaning and material in processes of identity formation of ecodesigners. Last, Helen Goworek, Tom Fisher, Alex Hiller, Tim Cooper and Sophie Woodward make their contribution with the chapter 'Consumers' attitudes towards sustainable fashion: Clothing usage and disposal', which explores consumers' views in relation to the sustainability of clothing maintenance and divestment and the potential impact of these views on the clothing and textiles industry.

Figure 3 shows the relationship between the chapters in this book and the different components of the textile, clothing and fashion industry.

Figure 3 **Relationship between the chapters in this book and the different components of the textile, clothing and fashion industry**

Note: Chapters written by more than an author are mentioned with '*et al.*' in order to simplify the figure

Source: authors

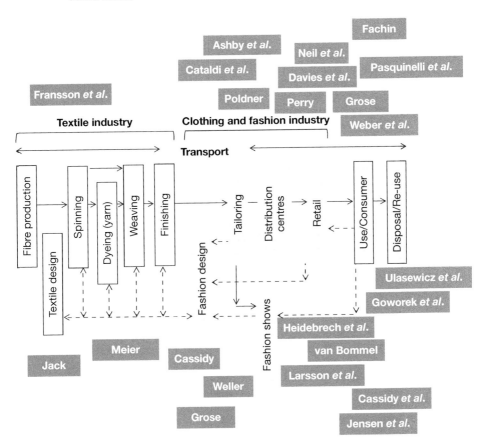

Finally, these diverse contributions represent a major step forward in expanding the knowledge base of this nascent relationship (textiles–fashion and sustainability). It is certainly a wide and representative compilation of writings on the subject. Note that this initiative has received a large international response and we hope it will continue to stimulate further debate.

Bibliography

Allwood, J.M., S.E. Laursen, C. Malvido de Rodríguez and N.M.P. Bocken (2006) *Well Dressed? The Present and Future Sustainability of Clothing and Textiles in the United Kingdom* (Cambridge, UK: University of Cambridge, Institute for Manufacturing).

Annan, K. (2004) 'Prologue', in M. McIntosh, S. Waddock and G. Kell (eds.), *Learning to Talk: Corporate Citizenship and the Development of the UN Global Compact* (Sheffield, UK: Greenleaf Publishing).

Black, S. (2008) *Eco-Chic: The Fashion Paradox* (London: Black Dog Publishing).

Blackburn, R.S. (ed.) (2005) *Biodegradable and Sustainable Fibres* (Cambridge, UK: Woodhead Publishing Limited/The Textile Institute).

Blackburn, R.S. (ed.) (2009) *Sustainable Textiles: Life Cycle and Environmental Impact* (Cambridge, UK: Woodhead Publishing Limited/The Textile Institute).

Brown, S. (2010) *Eco-Fashion* (London: Laurence King Publishing).

Cataldi, C., M. Dickson and C. Grover (2010) *Slow Fashion: Tailoring a Strategic Approach towards Sustainability* (Master's thesis; Karlskrona, Sweden: School of Engineering, Blekinge Institute of Technology).

Cavagnaro, E., and G. Curiel (2012) *The Three Levels of Sustainability* (Sheffield, UK: Greenleaf Publishing).

Defra (UK Department for Environment, Food and Rural Affairs) (2008) *Sustainable Clothing Roadmap Briefing Note December 2007: Sustainability Impacts of Clothing and Current Interventions* (London: Defra).

Dickson, M.A., S. Loker and M. Eckman (2009) *Social Responsibility in the Global Apparel Industry* (New York: Fairchild Books).

Dombek-Keith, K., and S. Loker (2011) 'Sustainable Clothing Care by Design', in A. Gwilt and T. Rissanen (eds.), *Shaping Sustainable Fashion: Changing the Way We Make and Use Clothes* (London: Earthscan).

Doppelt, B. (2010) *Leading Change toward Sustainability* (Sheffield, UK: Greenleaf Publishing).

Draper, S., V. Murray and I. Weissbrod (2007) *Fashioning Sustainability: A Review of Sustainability Impacts of the Clothing Industry* (London: Forum for the Future and Marks & Spencer).

Early, D. (1993) 'What is Sustainable Design', *The Urban Ecologist*, Spring 1993.

Earth Pledge (2007) *Future Fashion: White Papers* (New York: Earth Pledge).

Easter, E. (2007) 'The Environmental Impact of Laundry', in Earth Pledge, *Future Fashion: White Papers* (New York: Earth Pledge).

Ehrenfeld, J.R. (1999) 'Cultural Structure and the Challenge of Sustainability', in K. Sexton, A.A. Marcus, K.W. Easter and T.D. Burkhardt (eds.) *Better Environmental Decisions: Strategies for Governments, Businesses, and Communities* (Washington, DC: Island Press).

Elkington, J. (1998) *Cannibals with Forks* (Gabriola Island, BC: New Society Publishers).

FIAS (2006) 'Lesotho: The Competitiveness of Regional and Vertical Integration of Lesotho's Garment Industry', www.agoatoolkit.com/agoa/English/Select%20Products/Apparel%20 and%20Textile/Apparel%20and%20textiles%20Industry%20profiles/05.pdf, accessed December 2006.

Fletcher, K. (2008) *Sustainable Fashion and Textiles: Design Journeys* (London: Earthscan).

Fletcher, K. (2009) 'Systems Change for Sustainability in Textiles' in R.S. Blackburn (ed.), *Sustainable Textiles: Life Cycle and Environmental Impact* (Cambridge, UK: Woodhead Publishing Limited/The Textile Institute).

Fletcher, K., and L. Grose (2012) *Fashion & Sustainability: Design for Change* (London: Laurence King Publishing).

Frankel, C. (1998) *In Earth's Company* (Gabriola Island, BC: New Society Publishers).

Fuertes, F., A. Iamettyi and M.L. Goyburu (2004) Guía del Pacto Global: Una Forma Práctica de Implementar los Nueve Principios a la Gestión Empresarial (Buenos Aires: Global Compact Office in Argentina).

Gardetti, M.A. (2005) 'Desarrollo Sustentable, Sustentabilidad y Sustentabilidad Corporativa', in M.A. Gardetti (ed.), *Textos en Sustentabilidad Empresarial: Integrando las consideraciones sociales, ambientales y económicas con el corto y largo plazo* (Buenos Aires: LA-BELL).

Gardetti, M.A., and A.L. Torres (2011) 'Gestión Empresarial Sustentable en la Industria Textil y de la Moda', work presented at the *VII Congreso Nacional de Tecnología Textil, 'La sustentabilidad como desafío estratégico'*, Buenos Aires, Argentina, 3–5 August 2011.

Gardetti, M.A., and A.L. Torres (2012) 'Special Issue on Textiles, Fashion and Sustainability', *Journal of Corporate Citizenship* 45 (Spring 2012).

Gilding, P. (2000) 'Sustainability-Doing', in D. Dunphy, J. Benveniste, A. Griffiths and P. Sutton (eds.), *Sustainability: The Corporate Challenge of the 21st Century* (St Leonards, New South Wales: Allen & Unwin).

Gwilt, A., and T. Rissanen (2011) *Shaping Sustainable Fashion: Changing the Way We Make and Use Clothes* (London: Earthscan).

Hernandez, M.P. (2006) *The Outcome of Hong Kong: Reflections from a Gender Perspective* (Geneva: IGTN International Gender and Trade Network and Center of Concern).

Hethorn, J., and C. Ulasewicz (eds.) (2008) *Sustainable Fashion, Why Now? A Conversation about Issues, Practices, and Possibilities* (New York: Fairchild Books).

Horrocks, A.R. (1998) *Ecotextiles '98: Sustainable Development: Proceedings of the Conference Ecotextile* (Cambridge, UK: Woodhead Publishing Limited/The Textile Institute).

ILO (2006) 'Global Employment Trends Brief', www.ilo.org/wcmsp5/groups/public/---ed_emp/---emp_elm/---trends/documents/publication/wcms_114294.pdf, accessed October 2006.

Kell, G. (2003) 'The Global Compact: Origins, Operations, Progress, Challenges', *The Journal of Corporate Citizenship* 11 (Autumn 2003, special issue on The United Nations Global Compact).

Kell, G. (2012) 'Copenhagen Fashion Summit 2012', Nordic Fashion Association, www.nordicfashionassociation.com/40479/UN%20Global%20Compact%20Partnership, accessed April 2012.

Koefoed, O., and L. Skov (undated) 'Sustainability in Fashion', in 'Openwear: Sustainability, Openness and P2P Production in the World of Fashion', research report of the EDUfashion project, www.openwear.org/data/files/Openwear%20e-book%20final.pdf, accessed 9 May 2012.

Make Trade Fair and Oxfam International (2004) *Trading Away Your Rights, Women Working in Global Supply Chains* (Oxford, UK: Oxfam International).

Miraftab, M., and A.R. Horrocks (eds.) (2007) *Ecotextiles: The Way Forward for Sustainable Development in Textiles* (Cambridge, UK: Woodhead Publishing Limited/The Textile Institute).

Nordås, H.K. (2004) *The Global Textile and Clothing Industry post the Agreement on Textiles and Clothing* (Geneva: World Trade Organization).

Nordic Fashion Association (2009) *How to Be NICE: NICE Code of Conduct and Manual* (Copenhagen: Nordic Fashion Association).

Nordic Fashion Association, Nordic Initiative Clean and Ethical (NICE) and Global Compact (2012) *NICE Code of Conduct and Manual for the Fashion and Textile Industry* (Copenhagen: Nordic Fashion Association and Global Compact).

Parker, L., and M.A. Dickson (eds.) (2009) *Sustainable Fashion: A Handbook for Educators* (Bristol, UK: Labour Behind the Label on behalf of Polish Humanitarian Organization, Südwind Agentur, Schone Kleren Campagne and Educators for Socially Responsible Apparel Business).

Paulins, V.A., and J.L. Hillery (2009) *Ethics in the Fashion Industry* (New York: Fairchild Books).

Presas, T. (2001) 'Interdependence and Partnership: Building Blocks to Sustainable Development', *International Journal of Corporate Sustainability: Corporate Environmental Strategy* 8.3: 203-208.

Ross, R.J.S. (2009) *Slaves to Fashion: Poverty and Abuse in the New Sweatshop* (Ann Arbor, MI: The University of Michigan Press).

Sherburne, A. (2009) 'Achieving Sustainable Textiles: A Designer's Perspective', in R.S. Blackburn (ed.), *Sustainable Textiles: Life Cycle and Environmental Impact* (Cambridge, UK: Woodhead Publishing Limited/The Textile Institute).

Slater, K. (2000) *Environmental Impact of Textiles: Production, Processes and Protection* (Cambridge, UK: Woodhead Publishing Limited/The Textile Institute).

Suzuki, D., and H. Dressel (2002) *Good News For A Change: How Everyday People are Helping the Planet* (Toronto, Canada: Stoddart Publishing Co.).

Tobler-Rohr, M.I. (2011) *Handbook of Sustainable Textile Production* (Cambridge, UK: Woodhead Publishing Limited/The Textile Institute).

United Nations (2004) *The Tenth Principle Against Corruption* (New York: United Nations).

Vieira, R. (1993) 'A Checklist for Sustainable Developments', in a resource guide for *Building Connections: Livable, Sustainable Communities* (Washington, DC: American Institute of Architects).

Walker, S. (2006) *Sustainable by Design: Explorations in Theory and Practice* (London: Earthscan).

Wang, Y. (2006) *Recycling in Textiles* (Cambridge, UK: Woodhead Publishing Limited/The Textile Institute).

Welters, L. (2008) 'The Fashion of Sustainability', in J. Hethorn and C. Ulasewicz (eds.), *Sustainable Fashion, Why Now? A Conversation about Issues, Practices, and Possibilities* (New York: Fairchild Books).

WCED (World Commission on Environment and Development) (1987) *Our Common Future* (Oxford, UK: Oxford University Press).

Miguel Angel Gardetti has a degree in textile engineering (Universidad Tecnológica Nacional), specialising in shell and crude fibres, and has worked in both domestic and foreign industries. He also holds a PhD in environmental management (Pacific Western University, CA). He was founder of the Sustainable Textile Centre, which he has coordinated since its beginning. He is also the head of the Instituto de Estudios para la Sustentabilidad Corporativa (Centre for Study of Corporate Sustainability).

Ana Laura Torres holds a BSc in ecology, granted by Universidad Nacional de La Plata, specialising in corporate sustainability at the Centre for Study of Corporate Sustainability. She collaborated in the creation and development of the Sustainable Textile Centre, which she has coordinated since its beginning. She has worked as an environmental consultant for the German Institute of Investment and Development (DEG) in Cologne, Germany, and she has conducted research and teaching activities at Universidad Nacional de La Plata (Argentina).

Part I
The systemic vision and the value chain in the textile and fashion industry

1

Slow fashion
Tailoring a strategic approach for sustainability

Carlotta Cataldi, Maureen Dickson and Crystal Grover
Co-founders, Slow Fashion Forward

Instead of tackling ecological and social issues in the mainstream fashion industry by consulting with established, globalised fashion brands, solutions for sustainable fashion may be found in an alternative sector altogether, the slow fashion movement.

This chapter summarises the thesis 'Slow Fashion: Tailoring a Strategic Approach towards Sustainability' written collaboratively by Carlotta Cataldi, Maureen Dickson and Crystal Grover in 2010 during Master's studies in Strategic Leadership towards Sustainability at the Blekinge Institute of Technology in Sweden. It outlines the strategic planning methods used in the research and proposes a set of recommendations that can serve as guidelines for established or emerging fashion professionals that are embarking on a sustainable business journey.

1.1 How can slow fashion help society to become more sustainable?

> You never change things by fighting the existing reality. To change something, build a new model that makes the existing model obsolete (Richard Buckminster Fuller).

Slow fashion represents a new future vision for the fashion and textile industry, one where natural resources and labour are highly valued and respected. It aims to slow down the rate at which we withdraw materials from nature and acts to satisfy fundamental human needs. In this movement, the people who design, produce and consume garments are reconsidering the impacts of choosing quantity over quality; and redesigning ways to create, consume and relate to fashion.

The slow movements began to emerge in the late 1980s with Slow Food, a movement born in Italy with the purpose of preserving the cultural integrity of cuisine in local regions.[1] The term 'slow fashion' was first coined by Kate Fletcher and shares many characteristics with the Slow Food movement (Fletcher 2007).

The slow approach allows for quality design and production to emerge, with high regard for the garment-making process and its relationship with the human and natural resources on which it depends. Slow fashion includes many diverse business models that maintain profits, while conserving and enhancing our ecological and social systems.

To conserve and protect the natural resources being consumed globally by the fashion industry, the slow fashion movement promotes:

Sustainable innovations in style, textiles and techniques;	Versatile, timeless and multifunctional clothing design;	Upcycling and reusing existing textiles; and,	Strategic and service-based alternatives (i.e. fashion leasing)

For example, Timo Rissanen's 'jigsaw puzzle' method (Fig. 1.1) uses all pieces of the garment pattern in the final design (McQuillan 2011). Upcycling vintage and reclaimed materials is another strategy for slowing down consumption and extending the lifespan of existing materials.

Slow fashion organisations may also support local communities and economies by sourcing materials and labour locally. **Pact**, an underwear brand, ensures that the organic cotton crop, its processing, spinning, knitting, weaving, dyeing, printing and sewing happen within the same 100-mile radius in Turkey. Some initiatives get right to the heart of resourcefulness, such as **Our Social Fabric**, a community-based textile-sourcing initiative in Vancouver. While, **Remade in Leeds** teaches locals sewing skills and makes new clothes from castoffs.[2]

Many brands also invest in communities for the long term and aim to help catalyse social change in locales where operations take place; for example, **Oliberté**, a footwear brand, has set up production in Africa with the goal of providing sustainable employment for the growing middle class (GOOD 2012).

The slow fashion movement is also working to preserve traditional garment-making skills rooted in cultural heritage. The fashion industry can look to the past, and has a responsibility and opportunity to carry forward these traditional techniques into future generations. The **Permacouture Institute** has initiated a fibre and dye mapping project and seed saving to preserve biodiversity in textile fibres and dye plants.

---

1 Slow Food International, Slow Food Philosophy, Mission. Available from www.slowfood.com (accessed September 2012).
2 L. Harrison, interviewed by authors, 24 February 2010, London.

Figure 1.1 **Timo Rissanen's No Waste Hoodie**

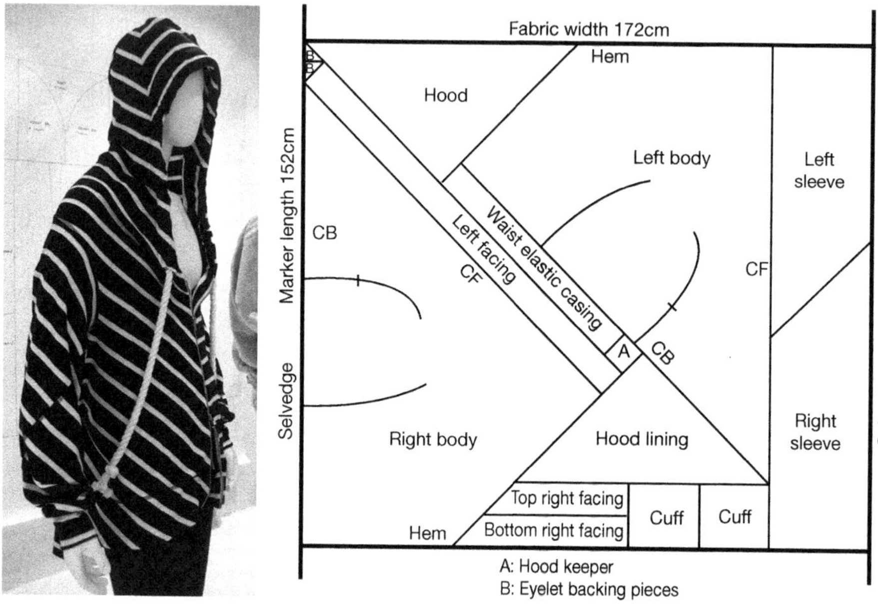

In the slow fashion movement, garment workers are paid a living wage and provided with safe and healthy working conditions. Slow fashion aims to *improve* the quality of life for people in and affected by the fashion industry and examines all aspects of the garment life-cycle: from fibre harvesting to disposal.

A defining trait of the slow fashion movement is that it recognises the evolving fashion needs of 'New Consumers' (BBMG 2011). New Consumers make more conscious choices that support a sustainable future by *slowing down* to discover how and where garments are made, and learn about minimising their consumer impacts. Whenever possible, responsible actions are taken to be creative and skilful, by consuming less, restyling garments, swapping clothing or supporting sustainably sourced and locally made fashion.

Slow fashion has the capacity to support the human needs of every person across the entire supply chain, with more opportunities to participate, express, create and innovate sustainably.

1.2 The fashion industry as a system

We live in a world of complex systems. Organisms, ecosystems, factories, families, cities and even the Earth itself are all complex systems. A system is an organised collection of parts that are highly integrated to accomplish an overall goal.

When making decisions and operating in a complex system, like the fashion industry, it can be useful to imagine that we are birds soaring above it. Gaining perspective of the global fashion system we can see its parts and the connections between them, and understand the greater impacts that fashion production and consumption have on society and ecological systems. From the raw fibres such as cotton, wool and silk, harvested across geographies, the millions of garment workers labouring in factories, to the independent designers cutting patterns, and the final garment that clothes an individual for a lifetime. These connections across the fashion supply chain and beyond to the garment wearer are encompassed in the larger fashion system.

Quality over quantity	Ecological design systems	Satisfying human needs
Traditional craftsmanship	Cultural diversity Fair labour	Enhancing communities
Supporting local economies	Building supply chain relationships	Diverse business models

We can visualise the fashion industry as being composed of smaller systems, such as the mainstream 'fast fashion' industry, the emerging slow fashion movement, and others, such as haute couture (see Fig. 1.2). In this chapter, slow fashion gathers a number of business models and fashion industry terms, such as sustainable new, eco fashion, ethical fashion, locally made, vintage and second-hand, under one unified movement.[3]

Every action carried out collectively by one system, such as fast fashion, or another one, such as slow fashion, will have an impact on the whole. This way of thinking can help understand the overall structure of the fashion system, the patterns and the cycles present in it, and it can facilitate the identification of the root causes of problems, showing the interconnectivity between events, and suggesting the most strategic ways to create solutions.

It also highlights the dependence of our society and the fashion industry on the ecosphere: natural resources such as clean water, land, air, fossil fuels and raw fibres, as well as ecological biodiversity (see Fig. 1.2).

---

3 The slow fashion movement includes designers, brands, suppliers, buyers, manufacturers, retailers and New Consumers, and their collective interactions.

Figure 1.2 **The fashion industry as a system**

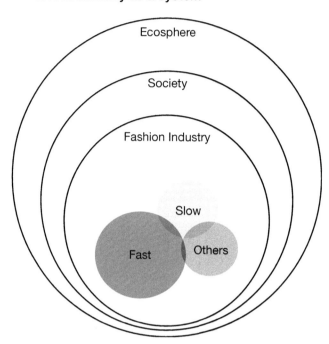

1.3 Fashion and human needs

The use and consumption of material goods, including fashion, is correlated to the attempt of individuals to meet their human needs, which are an intrinsic part of human nature. Satisfying these needs can help people to have emotionally rich, healthy lives (Max-Neef 1991). Several people have proposed different classifications of human needs, but the theory of Chilean economist, Manfred Max-Neef, is the most comprehensive as it considers nine human needs organised in a non-hierarchical way (see Table 1.1). These are the same for everyone, regardless of culture, religion or historical time.

Each person can satisfy their needs in different ways. Max-Neef calls these 'satisfiers'. Fashion can act as a satisfier for the needs of subsistence and protection, which tend to require a minimum level of material input. It also acts as a satisfier for the needs of identity, creation and participation, which could theoretically be satisfied by participatory processes (personal, social and cultural) rather than by consumption of fashion goods (Jackson and Marks 1994).

Table 1.1 **Basic human needs**

Source: Adapted from Max-Neef 1991

9 Human needs		
Subsistence	Protection	Participation
Idleness	Creation	Affection
Understanding	Identity	Freedom

1.4 A closer look at fast fashion

The primary purpose of 'fast fashion' is to accelerate consumption of trend-driven clothing, while maximising profits for a limited number of globalised megabrands. From a positive perspective, fast fashion allows millions of people to purchase clothing at affordable prices, making it possible for low-income families as well as young adults to access the latest runway trends, improving feelings of belonging and well-being. The global fashion industry is also a driver of economic growth and employs 26 million people worldwide (Allwood *et al.* 2006).

This business model has its trade-offs. Garments are being sold at very low retail prices, which encourages consumers to purchase more than they need. The price also discounts the true external environmental and social costs of producing the garment. The news of child labour in the cotton fields of Uzbekistan and Burkina Faso and the extremely low wages and unpaid overtime in thousands of factories in developing countries are making it evident that, as a system, fast fashion is capable of hindering the ability of millions of people worldwide to meet some of their fundamental human needs.

Today's fashion scenario, characterised by mass-produced, throwaway fashion, has also decreased the capacity for consumers to satisfy their human needs. Fast fashion promotes trends that dress consumers all over the world, producing a homogeneous look that is unlikely to satisfy, for example, the needs of identity and creativity. As a society, we are also losing the most basic garment-making and repair skills, since skills are decreasing in value in a world where garments are cheap and disposable. Above all, it disconnects the consumer from the process of garment making, limiting the feeling of participation. In this way, we can say that mainstream fast fashion is a pseudo-satisfier to a number of human needs.

1.5 Today's sustainability challenge and the fashion industry

The mainstream fashion industry is contributing to today's sustainability challenge in a number of ways. Thanks to the many publications released by research centres and NGOs, and the increasing visibility these topics are gaining in media, the industry is more aware of the important impacts that fashion production and consumption have on ecological and social systems.

Due to increasing consumer demand for fast fashion, the fashion industry currently uses a constant flow of natural resources to supply this demand. The current operation of the fashion industry is consistently contributing to the depletion of fossil fuels in textile and garment production and transportation (Allwood *et al.* 2006). Fresh water reservoirs are also being increasingly diminished for cotton crop irrigation; one significant example is the depletion of the Aral Sea (Draper *et al.* 2007; Environmental Justice Foundation 2010). The fashion industry is introducing in a systematic way, and in greater amounts, man-made compounds such as pesticides and synthetic fibres, which have a persistent presence in nature (Claudio 2007). The textile industry is also a major source of toxic wastewater pollution, threatening ecosystems and human health (Greenpeace International 2011). As a result, natural resources are in jeopardy, leading to issues such as biodiversity loss, desertification and, not least, climate change, which affects society at large.

To visualise the sustainability challenge of today's fashion industry, the funnel metaphor (see Fig. 1.3) is used to illustrate that if the consumptive behaviour of

Figure 1.3 **The funnel metaphor**
Source: Holmberg and Robèrt 2000

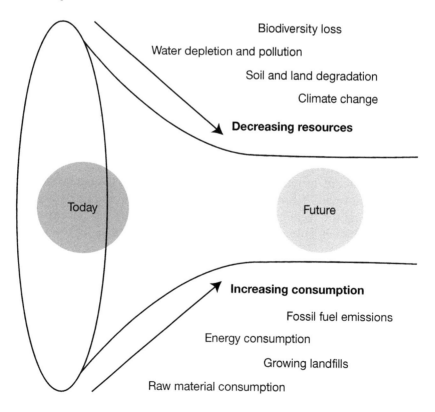

the fashion industry, including consumers, keeps increasing at the current rate, the adverse impacts on society and the ecological environment will also increase. This leads to a progressively limited space for the industry to handle these impacts in the future and to resolve the issues humanity is facing today (symbolised by the sloping walls of the funnel).

Using this metaphor we can conclude that if we do not want to 'hit the narrowing walls of the funnel', we must redesign the current unsustainable practices in society, including the fashion industry. This change, if achieved, is likely to result in a gradual return to equilibrium, where the fashion industry can operate without compromising the health of the Earth and of people.

1.6 Taking a strategic, systems-based approach

The slow fashion movement is an alternative for creating a truly sustainable fashion system. By taking a strategic, systems-thinking approach, slow fashion can become a robust, widely accepted fashion model. Both the Framework for Strategic Sustainable Development (FSSD) and leverage points are powerful tools to help organisations, and in this case, individual fashion designers, businesses and the industry at large, to achieve sustainability.

1.6.1 Framework for Strategic Sustainable Development

The Framework for Strategic Sustainable Development (FSSD) is a strategic planning tool that can be particularly useful in any given system that aims to move towards sustainability (see Fig. 1.4). Its main purpose is to provide clarity, insight and structure in scenarios that present complex problems.

Figure 1.4 **Framework for Strategic Sustainable Development**
Source: Adapted from Robèrt *et al.* 2002

The five level framework builds on an understanding of what makes life possible, how our biosphere functions and how society is connected to and reliant on the Earth's natural systems. Rather than get lost in abstract definitions and causes, it builds on a platform of basic science and is designed to allow true interdisciplinary, cross-sector cooperation for concrete and measurable change towards sustainability (Robèrt et al. 2002). After all, if the fashion industry wants to achieve 'success', we have to first understand what this means in real terms before an individual or organisation can take strategic steps to achieve it.

Success corresponds to achieving a more sustainable society, and in this case, slow fashion is a viable avenue for the fashion industry to get there. Sustainability, which represents the ultimate vision of success for society and for the fashion industry, has been defined in many different ways by various organisations, but the four sustainability principles developed by Dr Karl-Henrik Robèrt, Dr John Holmberg and Dr Göran Broman, are the most comprehensive and have been peer reviewed by a network of scientists (The Natural Step 2012).

To craft a sustainable fashion industry, each one of our actions as individuals, fashion designers, brands and organisations, should move towards following these basic principles (see Fig. 1.5).

During 2010, 46 slow and sustainable fashion designers, brands, buyers and manufacturers from Canada, the United States, UK, Denmark, Sweden and other European countries were surveyed. Taking advantage of the FSSD as an organising tool, and systems thinking as an overarching model, the slow fashion movement

Figure 1.5 **Basic principles for sustainability adapted for the fashion industry**

Source: Adapted from The Natural Step 2012

4 Sustainability Principles

The Slow Fashion movement will work to contribute to a sustainable society by ensuring that it will not subject nature to the systematic increase in:

SP1 Concentrations of substances extracted from the earth – These are finite and scarce materials such as fossil fuels for energy production or heavy metals for dyeing fabric. Their systematic accumulation in the ecosphere contributes to global-scale issues such as climate change and air, water and soil pollution.

SP2 Concentrations of substances produced by the textile industry – These are man-made materials such as synthetic fibres (polyester, nylon, acrylic, etc.) or toxic chemicals used in textile processing and manufacturing which are not kept in closed cradle to cradle loops. At their end of life they do not fully decompose leading to an accumulation in the soil and landfills, leaching into waterways and compromising human, wildlife and overall ecological well-being.

SP3 Degradation of nature – Many human activities can undermine the health of the earth. They include relying on monoculture conventional cotton crops causing biodiversity loss, removing forests to harvest wool and agricultural crops for fibres, or polluting waterways with factory effluents.

And in this society...

SP4 People are not subject to conditions that systemically undermine their ability to meet their needs. There are currently many issues in the fashion industry that do not support an equal quality of life for all workers in the supply chain by failing to address fair wages and work place health and safety issues properly. Also, by neglecting the above three principles, the industry is undermining the ability of future generations to meet their own needs as they will not have enough resources to sustain themselves.

is just starting to organise itself as a system, but it is not being strategic in its actions.

At the **system level**, many of the slow fashion stakeholders are aware of the ecological boundaries that they operate within. Many designers practise environmental stewardship by choosing to work with organic cotton and wool, modal, tencel, peace silk, hemp and others.

There is also a greater social awareness of business operations and their effect on people in all facets of the supply chain. Many companies are having a positive impact by participating in fair trade initiatives, establishing cooperatives and employing codes of conduct, to secure the fair treatment of fashion workers.

Some brands have joined the **Asian Floor Wage Alliance, Ethical Trading Initiative** and the **Fair Wear Foundation**, among others. By paying a living wage, and having garment prices reflect this cost, they are positively supporting organic farmers, textile mills and garment producers.

At the **success level**, many respondents provided a definition of what sustainability means for their business and these definitions incorporated environmental and/or social goals (see Fig. 1.6). But, the businesses do not share a common definition of sustainability and currently have no common vision of success for the future. Rather, the slow fashion movement is a collection of fragmented initiatives that are working independently.

At the **strategy level**, with no shared vision of a sustainable future, the slow fashion movement is not able to 'backcast' from success. Consequently, slow fashion players are not being strategic in their individual or collective actions. Additionally, there is no evidence that the movement is using a prioritised approach for determining strategic actions or a long-term strategy for attaining sustainability.

The **action level** describes what can be tangibly done by one organisation or company in a way that supports an overall strategy to attain success (Robèrt *et al.* 2002). Fashion brands and individual designers are already undertaking numerous sustainability actions:

Figure 1.6 **Industry sustainability quotes**
Source: Cataldi *et al.* 2010

Using eco-friendly materials and natural fibres that support the green economy.

Trying to make the smallest impact on the environment while still running business and making money.

Providing a framework and network between people in which fashion is valued and enjoyed and the stories behind the production or manufacture are shared and transparent.

Having garments made in a production house that has fair wages and has flexible working hours; this creates a more quality made garment. Being environmentally conscious in all aspects of sourcing, from fabrics to office supplies, etc.

The direction everything in our earth needs to go... consuming only what you must, buying what you need, and creating with an awareness that everything we eat, wear and buy has an impact.

- Promoting organic fibres and vegetable dyes locally by educating the suppliers

- Remaking existing vintage fabrics into unique garments

- Offering lifetime repair or redesign assistance

- Engaging the garment wearer in issues around sustainable fashion

- Using biodegradable packaging

- Offsetting carbon emissions by purchasing offsets which are invested in alternative energy projects

A number of sustainable fashion research and education centres have been cropping up, such as the **Centre for Sustainable Fashion** in the UK, the **Sustainable Textile Centre** in Argentina and the **Textile Arts Center** in New York. This is leading to more cohesive sustainability actions within the fashion industry, and for fashion designers specifically. But, across the supply chain, not all actors—especially consumers—see their interconnectivity with others in the slow fashion movement and sustainability at large.

At the **tools level**, designers and brands are using some sustainability tools in their business operations. For example, life-cycle thinking and ecodesign is being used as a tool by a number of designers in the movement. Also, many brands are using textile and garment labels such as Certified Organic Cotton, Fair Trade, OEKO TEX STANDARD 100, Made-By label, Organic Exchange 100 (OE 100) and the Global Organic Textile Standard (GOTS).

1.6.2 Discovering leverage points in the fashion industry

In 1997, scientist and system thinker, Donella Meadows, developed the concept of leverage points to help identify places to intervene strategically to create change in any system (see Fig. 1.7) (Meadows 1999). They can be applied to any organisation or business sector, and they help stakeholders understand how a system can grow or evolve in a positive direction. By looking at specific leverage points across the complex fashion industry, selected areas can be pinpointed to propel the fashion system towards sustainability.

Many leverage points in the fashion industry, if used strategically by fashion stakeholders, can work to help slow fashion grow stronger as a movement. At the same time, there are many barriers rooted in the larger fashion system that are difficult to remove, preventing an established slow fashion movement. Each leverage point is a snapshot of the actions, tools and initiatives within the fashion industry that are helping or hindering the slow fashion movement.[4]

---

4 Note: There are many leverage points in a system and, knowing this, this chapter emphasises the issues that are most relevant at this time.

Figure 1.7 **Leverage points**

Source: Meadows 1999

12 Constants, parameters & numbers
11 The size of buffers relative to flows
10 Structure of material stocks & flows
9 Lengths of delays
8 Negative feedback loops
7 Positive feedback loops
6 Flow of information
5 Rules of the system
4 Power to self-organise
3 Goals of the system
2 Paradigm the system arises from
1 Transcend paradigms

At leverage point 12, efficiency standards for textile and garment manufacturing processes are quite widely used by the movement and not hard to attain. As a result, water consumption is often being reduced and wastewater is being filtered from dyehouses (Fletcher 2008: 61). One barrier to using this leverage point effectively is that certifications can be costly, making it often inaccessible to small producers and designers.

Buffers of sustainable materials such as organic cotton, linen, hemp and modal are being created to supply increasing demand (leverage point 11). Organic cotton represents less than 1% of the cotton market, but on a positive note, the demand grew by 20% in 2010 (Textile Exchange 2011). Many designers are interested in sourcing more sustainable textiles in the future, but they are generally more expensive. There is also a delay in increasing the supply of renewable fibres and developing natural dyes caused by a lack of technologies and skills.[5]

Localised supply chains in addition to textile upcycling, is supporting material flows (leverage point 10). **Goodone** (Fig. 1.8) specialises in upcycling and sources reclaimed materials locally from London. But, in most cases, it is still more cost-effective to source new sustainable textiles from developing countries, and creating

5 Noon Design Studio, www.noondesignstudio.com (accessed September 2012).

Figure 1.8 **Goodone**

new supply chain structures can be very challenging and time consuming.[6] Platforms such as **Ethical Fashion Forum, Source4Style, Offset Warehouse, C.L.A.S.S.** and **Shared Talent India** are helping remove sourcing barriers for fashion designers, as they offer a reliable place for designers to share knowledge and purchase sustainable fabrics and textiles.

Positive feedback loops drive the system behaviour towards growth. In any system, there can be many of these self-reinforcing cycles. The larger fashion industry benefits from the presence of a negative feedback loop created by slow fashion that *slows down* the growth of the entire system and acts as a stabiliser (leverage point 8). Positive feedback loops, even in a system that needs to grow, such as slow fashion, must be watched because they can easily become unstoppable and do more harm than good (leverage point 7).

More media coverage and marketing is required to help increase visibility, fuel awareness and demand for slow fashion garments (see Fig. 1.9). However, this positive feedback loop could constantly increase demand, and could neutralise the desired effect of slowing down total production. It is recommended that consumer awareness campaigns are in place to educate about the values of 'New Consumerism' to help keep slow fashion demand at a sustainable rate, rather than spiralling

6 Jason Kibbey, PACT Organic Underwear, interview by authors, 27 April 2010, Karlskrona, Sweden (hand-written notes via Skype). L. Chenoweth, interview by Maureen Dickson, January 2012, Ottawa, Canada (hand-written notes via Skype).

Figure 1.9 **Positive reinforcing loop for the slow fashion movement**

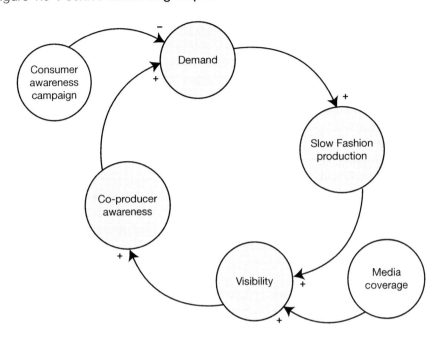

towards over-consumption. For example, the **NICE Consumer Project** has been launched in the EU to create a sustainable framework for fashion consumption (Eder-Hansen *et al.* 2012).

If new information on sustainability and the benefits of slow fashion is communicated both within the supply chain and to consumers, this flow of information can be a very effective point of intervention (leverage point 6). Within the fashion supply chain, there is a limited amount of information on the sustainability impacts, and it is also difficult to compare the impacts of fibres and dyeing processes.

Some organisations are helping to educate fashion designers about ecological and social aspects, for example **Forum for the Future** Fashion Futures programme, **London College of Fashion** MA in Fashion & the Environment, **California Collage of the Arts** Fashion Sustainability Workshop Series, **Slow Fashion Forward** and **Social Alterations**.

Slow fashion designers are improving consumer engagement by offering information on how and where the garments are made. In recent years, sustainable fashion has graced the runways, bringing more mainstream media coverage to the subject, such as **Aesthetica** in London, **GreenShows** at NY Fashion Week, **WHITE Milano** and **Eco Fashion Week** Vancouver. In addition, an array of online magazines and blogs are showcasing to consumers how sustainable and ethical clothing can be stylish and widely accessible: **Eco Fashion World, Six Magazine, Ef Magazine** and many others. But the overall consumer awareness of sustainable fashion and the slow fashion movement is concentrated within the early adopters.

There are not enough rules and legislation to limit pollution in the fashion supply chain, and enforcement in some jurisdictions is weak—resulting in lower retail prices for fast fashion companies (leverage point 5). Slow fashion producers are going above and beyond environmental standards, thus for many their garment prices are more expensive and not as competitive. Also, organic and Fair Trade certifications and labelling schemes are too expensive and time consuming for small fashion brands, and the public's awareness of these eco-labels is limited.

At the most influential leverage points, the slow fashion movement is beginning to self-organise from grass-roots initiatives and innovative, forward-thinking small brands, but it still needs strategic organisation to succeed as an officially recognised movement (leverage point 4).

Slow fashion brands have a wide variety of business goals that involve directly or indirectly the desire to achieve ecological, social and economic sustainability (leverage point 3). The diversity of goals within the slow fashion movement that are creative and unique, together address an expansive area of needs that will help the movement move towards sustainability. This also leads to a more resilient movement, by having many groups working towards the same end: sustainability, from a multitude of angles.

The slow fashion mind-set is based on conscious 'reflective consumption', while the fast fashion mind-set is based on trend-driven consumerism. At leverage point 2, slow fashion is establishing a new mind-set altogether by shifting consumer attitudes from being passive in society to playing an active, participatory role in the fashion production process. Here, the human experience is heightened by being more engaged in the creative process by co-creating with designers or by finding meaningful experiences to consume fashion.

The **IOU Project** (Fig. 1.10) creates a personal connection between consumers and the textile weavers and garment makers in India,[7] while **The Uniform Project**

Figure 1.10 **IOU Project**

7 I OWE YOU Project website: www.iouproject.com

and **Six Items or Less** experiment are examples of creating a shift in the mind-set of consumers.[8] On Black Friday 2011, **Patagonia** also introduced the 'Don't Buy This Jacket' campaign to encourage consumers to rethink their purchases and consume less. Using this highly effective leverage point can tip the slow fashion movement from early adoption to widespread diffusion in society.

To create the systematic change needed to move towards sustainability in the fashion industry, slow fashion presents an alternative paradigm to the current fast fashion model. By establishing new values in the fashion industry that satisfy fundamental human needs, instead of market wants, slow fashion can allow for the Earth's natural regeneration to occur.

1.7 Strategic recommendations

A number of short, medium and long-term recommendations have been suggested to strengthen the slow fashion movement and to move it towards sustainability (see Appendix). Each recommendation is targeted at a specific group of stakeholders, is viewed through the FSSD and activates one or more of the leverage points discussed above. Three key recommendations are discussed below in detail.

1.7.1 Co-create slow fashion values as a vision of success

> At the heart of building a shared vision is the task of designing and evolving ongoing processes in which people at every level of the organisation, in every role, can speak from the heart about what really matters to them and be heard…by each other. The quality of this process, especially the amount of openness and genuine caring, determines the quality and power of the results. The (vision) can only emerge from a coherent process of reflection and conversation (Peter Senge).

Slow fashion values should be co-created from within the movement to provide inspiration and guidance for designers and others working in the movement. To become the predominant fashion model in a sustainable society, these values could be co-created to form a shared mental model that represents collective goals and aspirations, and to provide a focal point for self-organisation.

These values, similarly to the principles of Slow Food, Slow Design and Permaculture, can be unique to the movement by representing a shared vision of success, and form the basis for future actions. It will be understood that the main goal of the movement is to contribute to a more 'sustainable society', as defined by the four science-based Sustainability Principles outlined earlier in this chapter. Individual designers, brands and organisations can further customise these values for their business.

---

8 The Uniform Project, www.theuniformproject.com (accessed September 2012).

By co-creating shared values, the slow fashion movement can start to become more strategic in its development. In fact, by sharing the same values and an overall vision, people in the movement will feel a stronger connection between their businesses and this can strengthen their relationships to create a community of support. These values can naturally reflect in the work carried out by people in the slow fashion movement and will send a clear message to other fashion designers and New Consumers, providing inspiration for both.

1.7.2 Establish a slow fashion network

A slow fashion network should be established to create trusting, local relationships and foster global interconnectedness. A unique global slow fashion organisation can be formed to represent and promote the slow fashion values, encourage collaboration, and spur mobilisation between stakeholders across the entire supply chain, and to engage New Consumers. This recommendation is based on the opportunities raised by leverage point 4 (the power to self-organise) and leverage point 6, relative to the flow of information within the supply chain.

Decentralised local hubs are a key aspect of the slow fashion network to ensure flexibility, preserve local cultures and traditional garment-making skills, sustain local economies and build trusting relationships. Local chapters allow members to meet in person, to keep their relationships alive and to find solutions to shared problems.

Startups and small brands will be able to benefit from the visibility that the whole organisation has on a global and local level. This includes having access to business support such as educational, research and consultancy services, marketing tools and media coverage.

The network can work to build a stronger industry, by facilitating collaboration, sharing information, encouraging transparency and improving producer relationships. It would allow the slow fashion movement to increase its visibility in the market, by spreading the ideals of sustainable development and the values of slow fashion within the larger fashion industry. This will trigger an increase in the demand for slow fashion, sparking future growth of the movement, positively influencing society as a whole.

1.7.3 Develop a slow fashion garment label

A garment label unique to slow fashion should be developed to distinguish the movement within the larger fashion market and to add credibility. This labelling scheme would build on and incorporate current fibre and production process standards, such as Organic Exchange 100, Fair Trade and the Global Organic Textile Standard (GOTS). The slow fashion label would be certified by an independent third-party organisation, and would be globally accessible and easily recognised by consumers. It would also need to be financially affordable for small brands and designers (i.e. fee structure would reflect company profits or market share).

A garment label can help increase visibility of smaller brands and designers that are part of the network and could use shared communication and media channels, cutting down individual marketing and advertising costs. It would lead to a greater awareness of the industry and allow for a starting point to build more trusting and long-lasting relationships with New Consumers. By identifying the label with a credible and globally recognised organisation, people will trust the label and will want to support designers and brands through their purchases or individual actions. Overall, it will help to secure profits to sustain slow fashion businesses over time.

1.8 Final thoughts

Many slow fashion initiatives have cropped up that, if strategically organised, may represent a sustainable alternative to the mainstream fashion model. Brands and small-scale fashion designers working with a social and ecological purpose in mind, NGOs dedicated to safeguarding workers' rights or distributing organic textiles, and even one-off creative projects, give life to this diverse fashion movement.

Our analysis through the lens of the FSSD indicates that the slow fashion movement exists and is quickly flourishing, but at the same time its activities are highly disorganised and scattered around the globe, concentrating in only a few countries. With no common vision of sustainable fashion in the future, or a shared definition of what sustainability means for the industry, the slow fashion movement, and the fashion industry at large, is unable to operate strategically using a backcasting strategy.

Using leverage points, many small points of intervention, where a strategic move in the right direction could produce a big change in the whole fashion system, were identified to strengthen the movement and guide it towards success. Several short, medium and long-term recommendations were suggested as first steps in creating a stronger slow fashion movement.

The authors recognise that bringing the recommendations to life will require the utmost collaboration between individual designers, educators, global supply chain networks, certification bodies and governments. As such, there are a number of challenges that need to be overcome to move the recommendations forward and to strengthen the slow fashion movement.

At the same time, slow fashion presents a world of opportunities for establishing new sustainable business models, creating fulfilling and creative employment, and building lasting relationships. By taking a strategic, systems-based approach, slow fashion can grow from a grass-roots movement to a mainstream model for fashion production and consumption. Overall, we hope that this chapter has inspired the slow fashion movement and allowed individuals to see their importance within the larger fashion industry and their role in helping shape a more sustainable society.

References

Allwood, J., S. Laursen, C. Rodríguez and N. Bocken (2006) *Well Dressed? The Present and Future Sustainability of Clothing and Textiles* (Cambridge, UK: University of Cambridge, Institute for Manufacturing, www.ifm.eng.cam.ac.uk/sustainability/projects/mass/UK_textiles.pdf).

BBMG (2011) *Unleashed: How New Consumers Will Revolutionize Brands and Scale Sustainability* (New York: BBMG).

Cataldi, C., M. Dickson and C. Grover (2010) *Slow Fashion: Tailoring a Strategic Approach towards Sustainability* (Sweden: Blekinge Institute of Technology).

Claudio, L. (2007) 'Waste Couture: The Environmental Impact of the Clothing Industry', *Environmental Health Perspectives* 115.9 (September 2007, www.ehp.niehs.nih.gov/members/2007/11-9/EHP115pa449PDF).

Delano, R. (2007) 'The Low Down on Bamboo', in *Future Fashions White Papers* (New York: Earth Pledge): 160-67.

Draper, S., V. Murray and I. Weissbrod (2007) *Fashioning Sustainability: A Review of the Sustainability Impacts of the Clothing Industry* (London: Forum for the Future).

Eder-Hansen, J., J. Kryger, J. Morris and C. Sisco (2012) *The NICE Consumer Research Summary and Discussion Paper: Toward a Framework for Sustainable Fashion Consumption in the EU* (Copenhagen: Danish Fashion Institute).

Environmental Justice Foundation (2010) 'The Aral Sea Crisis', www.ejfoundation.org/page146.html, accessed 12 September 2012.

Fletcher, K. (2007) 'Slow Fashion', *The Ecologist*, 1 June 2007 (www.theecologist.org/green_green_living/clothing/269245/slow_fashion.html).

Fletcher, K. (2008) *Sustainable Fashion and Textiles: Design Journeys* (London: Earthscan).

Greenpeace International (2011) *Dirty Laundry: Unravelling the Corporate Connections to Toxic Water Pollution in China* (The Netherlands: Greenpeace International).

GOOD (2012) 'How Oliberté, the Anti-TOMS, Makes Shoes and Jobs in Africa', www.good.is/posts/how-oliberte-the-anti-toms-makes-shoes-and-jobs-in-africa, accessed 11 October 2012.

Holmberg, J., and K.-H. Robèrt (2000) 'Backcasting: A Framework for Strategic Planning', *International Journal of Sustainable Development and World Ecology* 7.4: 291-308 (www.naturalstep.org/sites/all/files/3b-Backcasting.pdf).

Jackson, T., and N. Marks (1994) *Consumption, Sustainable Welfare and Human Needs with Reference to the UK Expenditure Patterns between 1954 and 1994* (Guildford, UK: Centre for Environmental Strategy, University of Surrey).

Max-Neef, M. (1991) *Human Scale Development: Conception, Application and Further Reflections* (New York: Apex Press).

McQuillan, H. (2011) 'Zero Waste Design Practice: Strategies and Risk Taking for Garment Design', in A. Gwilt and T. Rissanen (eds.), *Shaping Sustainable Fashion: Changing the Way we Make and Use Clothes* (London: Earthscan).

Meadows, D. (1999) 'Leverage Points: Places to Intervene in a System', Donella Meadows Institute, www.donellameadows.org/archives/leverage-points-places-to-intervene-in-a-system, accessed 22 October 2012.

Robèrt, K.-H., B. Schmidt-Bleek, J. Aloisi de Larderel, G. Basile, L. Jansen, R. Kuehr, P. Price Thomas, M. Suzuki, P. Hawken and M. Wackernagel (2002) 'Strategic Sustainable Development: Selection, Design and Synergies of Applied Tools', *Journal of Cleaner Production* 10.3: 197-214.

Sanfilippo, D. (2007) 'A Fair Deal for Farmers', in *Future Fashions White Papers* (New York: Earth Pledge): 137-49.

Textile Exchange (2011) *Global Organic Cotton Market Grows 20%, Hits $5.61 Billion in 2010, Textile Exchange Report Shows* (Lubbock, TX: Textile Exchange, 6 September 2011).

The Natural Step (2012) 'The Four System Conditions', www.naturalstep.org/en/the-system-conditions, accessed 12 September 2012.

Bibliography

Birtwistle, G., and C.M. Moore (2006) 'Fashion Adoption in the UK: A Replication Study', paper presented at the *Anzmac Conference*, Brisbane.

Clean Clothes Campaign (2006) 'Improving Working Conditions in the Global Garment', www.cleanclothes.org, accessed 18 January 2010.

Davidson, C. (2008) 'Cutting Your Cloth Twice Over', BBC News, www.news.bbc.co.uk/2/hi/business/6248796.stm, accessed February 2010.

Defra (2007) 'Sustainable Clothing Roadmap Briefing Note December 2007: Sustainability Impacts of Clothing and Current Interventions', Department for Environment, Food and Rural Affairs, www.archive.defra.gov.uk/environment/business/products/roadmaps/clothing/documents/clothing-briefing-Dec07.pdf, accessed 11 October 2012.

Defra (2008) 'Public Understanding of Sustainable Clothing', Department for Environment, Food and Rural Affairs, www.randd.defra.gov.uk/Document.aspx?Document = EV0405_7666_FRP.pdf, accessed 11 October 2012.

Ducas, C. (2010) Interview by authors, 6 April 2010, Karlskrona, Sweden (hand-written notes via Skype).

Ernest, C., A.H. Ferrer and D. Zult (2005) *The End of the Multi-Fibre Arrangement and its Implication for Trade and Employment* (Geneva, Switzerland: International Labour Organization [ILO], www.ilo.org/wcmsp5/groups/public/---ed_emp/---emp_elm/documents/publication/wcms_114030.pdf).

European Commission (2009) 'Enterprise and Industry: Textiles and Clothing', www.ec.europa.eu/enterprise/sectors/textiles/environment, accessed 12 September 2012.

Fox, S. (2007) 'Cleaner Cotton Grown in Color', in *Future Fashions White Papers* (New York: Earth Pledge): 128-36.

Friedman, V. (2010) 'Sustainable Fashion: What Does Green Mean?' *Financial Times*, 5 February 2010 (www.ft.com/cms/s/2/2b27447e-11e4-11df-b6e3-00144feab49a.html).

Gagnon, S., and Y. Gagnon (2007) 'Eco-Fabrics: Balancing Fashion and Ideals', in *Future Fashions White Papers* (New York: Earth Pledge): 36-45.

Haraldsson, H.V. (2004) *Introduction to System Thinking and Causal Loop Diagrams* (Lund, Sweden: Institute of Chemical Engineering, Lund University).

Hethorn, J., and C. Ulasewicz (2008) *Sustainable Fashion: Why Now: A Conversation about Issues, Practices, and Possibilities* (New York: Fairchild Books & Visuals).

Honoré, C. (2004) *In Praise of Slowness, Challenging the Cult of Speed* (New York: Harper Collins Publishers).

Karus, M. (2005) *European Hemp Industry 2001 till 2004: Cultivation, Raw Materials, Markets and Trends* (Germany: European Industrial Hemp Association).

Kolander, C. (2007) 'In Defence of Truth and Beauty', in *Future Fashions White Papers* (New York: Earth Pledge): 160-67.

Kolander, C. (2010) Interview by authors, 14 April 2010, Karlskrona, Sweden (hand-written notes via Skype).

Maxwell, J.A. (2005) *Qualitative Research Design: An Interactive Approach* (Thousand Oaks, CA: Sage Publications).

McGrew, L., and C. Charet (2010) Interview by authors, 10 May 2010, Karlskrona, Sweden (via email).

Meadows, D. (2008) *Thinking in Systems: A Primer* (White River Junction, VT: Chelsea Green Publishing Company).

Morgan, L., and G. Birtwistle (2009) 'An Investigation of Young Fashion Consumers' Disposal Habits', *International Journal of Consumer Studies* 33: 190-98.

PACT (2010) www.wearpact.com, accessed April 2010.

Richards, M., R. Gabrielle and S. Shepp (2007) 'Leather for Life', in *Future Fashions White Papers* (New York:Earth Pledge): 53-62.

Senge, P. (1990) *The Fifth Discipline: The Art & Practice of the Learning Organization* (London: Century Business).

Serbin, L. (2007) 'Hemp Goes Straight', in *Future Fashions White Papers* (New York: Earth Pledge): 46-52.

Slow+Design International Seminar (2006) 'Slow+Design, Manifesto+Abstracts', www.experientia.com/blog/uploads/2006/10/slow_design_background.pdf, accessed 11 October 2012.

Social Alterations (2010) 'Student Education', www.socialalterations.com, accessed 11 October 2012.

Staemanns, M., and G. Hanness (2009) 'Latest Trends in Organic Cotton from the World Congress "From Fashion to Sustainability" in Switzerland', www.organiccotton.org/oc/News/News.php, accessed April 2010.

Textile Exchange (2010) 'Making Informed Choices', www.textileexchange.org/content/making-informed-choices, accessed 11 October 2012.

TNS Worldpanel (2008) *Consumers' Ethical Concerns over Fashion Reach Record High* (Press Release: 18 October 2008; London: TNS Worldpanel).

Von Busch, O. 'Self-Passage 2010', www.kulturservern.se/wronsov/selfpassage/index2.htm, accessed September 2012.

Waste Online (2010) www.wasteonline.org.uk/index.aspx, accessed September 2012.

Wilson, E. (2003) *Adorned in Dreams, Fashion and Modernity* (New Brunswick, NJ: Rutgers University Press).

Carlotta Cataldi studied Public Relations and Fashion at the IULM University in Milan and has a Master's degree in Strategic Leadership towards Sustainability attained at the Blekinge Institute of Technology in Sweden. She lives between Italy and Barcelona, where she works as a Project Assistant at Textile Exchange and collaborates with like-minded people, moving sustainable fashion forward.

Maureen Dickson builds on a Master's degree in Strategic Leadership towards Sustainability from the Blekinge Institute of Technology in Sweden, a BSc in Environmental Science, and four years of experience in the non-profit sector, where she led a number of sustainability projects to provide insights to Canadian business leaders, investors and policy-makers. She is currently leading projects and collaborating with organisations to host sustainable fashion workshops and community events.

Crystal Grover is a LEED AP, has attained a BFA from Columbia College Chicago in Interior Architecture, and an MSc in Strategic Leadership towards Sustainability from the Blekinge Institute of Technology in Sweden. She is also a co-founder of INDO, a design duo that takes materials from the waste and recycling streams, and breathes new purpose into them as artistic installations.

Appendix I **Strategic recommendations**

Recommendation	Timeframe	Players	Leverage point(s)
Industry collaboration and communication			
Co-create slow fashion values	**Short-term**	**Slow fashion producers**	**2,3,4**
Backcast from slow fashion values	Short-term	Slow fashion producers	2,3,4
Establish a slow fashion network	**Short-term**	**Slow fashion producers**	**4,6**
Create partnerships with fashion colleges, Blekinge Institute of Technology (BTH), The Natural Step and the Real Change programme to educate on the Sustainability Principles and strategic sustainable development	Short-term and ongoing	BTH, sustainability practitioners and fashion design colleges	3,6
Offer sustainability workshops for slow fashion producers. Workshops can provide producers with a background on the core concepts of strategic sustainable development and sustainability	Short-term and ongoing	Slow fashion producers, sustainability practitioners	3,6
Create a social marketing campaign to inform consumers about the benefits of the slow fashion movement to generate awareness, excitement and interest for sustainable fashion consumption, sewing and repair skills, clothes swapping, and responsible care and disposal	Short-term	Sustainability practitioners	2,3,6
Increase communication between designers, retailers and consumers to facilitate flow of information on the details of garment production and material sourcing	Short-term and ongoing	Fashion designers, brands, retailers and consumers	6
Create an online mapping tool connected to the slow fashion network that displays slow fashion designers and retailers by city/country for easy consumer access	Short-term and ongoing	Online network, brands, retailers	4,6
Increase educational programmes among consumers with regard to sustainable fashion consumption, sewing and repair skills, and the end of life of clothing and textiles	Short-term	Schools, NGOs, fashion designers	2,6

Recommendation	Timeframe	Players	Leverage point(s)
Sourcing materials and textiles			
Provide bank loans for farmers of more sustainable fibres such as rain-fed cotton, hemp, bamboo	Short-term	Banking sector	7,11
Educate banks about the investment benefits vs. investment risks for rain-fed cotton farming to increase support (Sanfilippo 2007)	Short-term	Sustainability practitioners, farmers	7,11
A commitment to buying an upcoming harvest of a rain-fed cotton crop (at least 30% buy in but 60% is preferred); this could help facilitate access to credits and give financial institutions the insurance they need to grant less expensive loans to these farmers (Sanfilippo 2007)	Short-term	Brands, textile manufacturers	7,11
Local textile manufacturers should add small overruns to their production to give small designers the opportunity to grow their business so that, in time, they will also be able to order an entire run, which in turn will boost production for the textile mills (Schiffrin 2010)*	Short-term	Textile mills, designers, brands	7,10
Create networks of collaborating designers/brands by region; with the idea that they could buy a minimum quantity of organic/fair trade/dead stock/or other new crops and textiles therefore allowing them to meet minimum orders and be able to support farmers growing new 'higher risk' materials (Schiffrin 2010)	Short-term	Online textile/ fibre platforms	7,11
Make dead stock and surplus fabrics/overruns from larger textile/ garment manufacturers accessible to smaller designers. Get this connected to the market via a web database (Schiffrin 2010)	Short-term	Textile and garment manufactures, small designers	7,10,11
Encourage collaboration between online marketplaces and databases such as Source4Style, Textile Exchange and others to make the comparing and buying of organic fabrics easier (Schiffrin 2010)	Short-term	Online networks	4,6

Recommendation	Timeframe	Players	Leverage point(s)
Invest in R&D to start developing technologies to allow for treatment of new sustainable fibres such as hemp, nettle, bamboo and others	Short-term	Research centres, universities, national governments	7,9,11
Invest in recycling mills, implement residential textile recycling programmes and increase community 'recycling banks' for textiles	Short-term	Municipalities, NGOs, charities and textile brokers	7,9,10
Expand organic certification for bamboo to all countries globally to create awareness around the difference processes and impacts of the fibre (Delano 2007)	Medium-term	GOTS and other organic certification bodies	6,5
R&D for the natural dyeing process	Medium-term	Research centres, universities, national governments	7,9,11
Conduct market research to determine the viability of growing raw material (plants, trees) for natural dyes	Medium-term	Governments, universities, farmers	7,9,11
Garment design			
Increased education for fashion designers on life-cycle garment impacts and ecodesign practices such as using recycled textiles, compostable fabrics and remaking existing garments	Short-term and ongoing	Fashion colleges, designers, sustainability practitioners	2,6,7
Brand and retail			
Conduct market research on the viability of starting a take-back programme for used garments	Short-term	Brands and retailers	8,10
Collaborate with existing garment recycling initiatives to expand their use (i.e. ECO CIRCLE)	Short-term	Brands and retailers	10
Implement a 'lifetime' policy for garments, by offering repair or restyling services for the garment, educating the consumer on how to extend the life-span of the garments (handing down the garment to other consumers), or through multi-functional, versatile and classic design	Short-term	Designers, brands and retailers	6,8

Recommendation	Timeframe	Players	Leverage point(s)
Regulations, codes of conduct and labelling			
To ensure a stable stock of recycled textiles, there could be legislation for all textile producers to support or have their own take-back programme similar to the electronics industry	Short-term	National governments, EU	5,10
Provide subsides or tax credits to domestic textile producers (in Canada, US and European countries) to support a local textile industry	Short-term	National governments	5,10
Improve social marketing of existing eco-labels such as GOTS, certified organic and Fair Trade so that consumers are educated on the meaning of the labels	Short-term	GOTS, certified organic and other eco-labelling schemes	5,6
Create a slow fashion garment label	**Medium-term**	**Textile and garment labelling certification entities, slow fashion producers**	**5,6**
Remove subsidies to conventional cotton production and provide subsidies and tax credits to local material producers of emerging sustainable materials	Medium-term	National governments	5

* Magdalena Schiffrin, email interview by authors, 8 April 2010, Karlskrona, Sweden.

Wisdoms from the fashion trenches

Lynda Grose

Fashion Design for Sustainability, California College of the Arts, USA

In fashion, sustainability initiatives have so far been led by industry, specifically by companies working together with their suppliers to improve sustainability performance in the supply chain. As a result, people in the technical areas and in corporate social responsibility (CSR) departments of these companies hold significantly more knowledge about the ecological and social impacts of garments than those working at more operational levels. Yet rarely is this deep knowledge communicated more broadly within the company. For the scientific and technical language of textile processing and standards is particular and not easy to explain or digest in the scope of a busy fashion industry workday. When it is communicated, what is discussed is always contextualised against the organisation's corporate culture, its customer, its image and not least by its imperative to sell more products.

Few companies charge their employees to deeply question how businesses might limit or slow the flow of ecological throughput in the fashion system, or how businesses might be reconfigured to connect to nature's capacities and limits or how our industry might adapt so that it preserves and restores its own natural support systems. Fewer still encourage employees to question the underpinning beliefs or mind-set that shape our industry and society (Fletcher and Grose 2012). These deeper issues remain invisible in the commercial and cultural worlds in which most of us live and work. Yet we humans are 'not closed off from the natural world, but rather integral components of it' (Macy 1995: 242) and many of us have an 'inkling' or sense that the fashion industry in which we work is somehow misshaped or misaligned with the fundamental values we all share.

The following statements or 'wisdoms' have been offered spontaneously by professionals working in the fashion sector or associated industries—often at a time of reflection or during conversations that extended beyond the immediate business responsibilities and tasks at hand. Some comments note a point of cognisance on the part of the speaker; others are used by the author to reflect or to shed light on the working logic of the current fashion industry and how it influences, or directs, the misshaping. As a collective, these 'wisdoms' expand the context for discussing sustainability in the fashion sector and help highlight additional opportunities for change.

2.1 Knowing what to optimise

> We have to do more with less...[and] increase yield of cotton per acre.
> (Cotton industry professionals, reviewing long-term climate
> change impact and human population trends)

Cotton has made an enormous contribution to the fashion and sustainability movement over the last few decades. As arguably the most scrutinised fibre on the planet, it has helped define a lens through which the fashion industry has been able look at all other fibres and to develop a 'playing field' for textiles and sustainability as a whole. Yet cotton has an even greater contribution to make to further change, not only through the detail of its cultivation, but as a magnifier of a prevalent mind-set in the fashion industry and in our culture as a whole.

In California, for example, cotton is grown in one of the most highly productive agricultural systems on the planet. Since labour in California is expensive, all crops are managed using chemicals and technology to minimise handwork. Chemicals are applied using state-of-the-art equipment—spray rigs for ground applications and crop dusters for applications by air; mechanical harvesters ensure the maximum amount of fibre is picked in a day; hydraulic module makers compact the fibre into solid, flat-bed-truck-sized bricks to ensure efficient transportation to gins; global positioning satellite (GPS) systems and plant and soil temperature monitoring devices direct the grower's actions to a particular part of the field (otherwise known as precision agriculture); and 68% of California's cotton crop is genetically modified. Even the land is laser levelled to ensure optimum irrigation water flow from one side of the field to the other. These combined technologies have enabled California farmers to yield 3.5 bales or 1,882 kilos per hectare, more than three times the yield achieved by a typical smallholder farmer in India.[1]

---

1 Based on an estimate of 576 kilos per hectare as cited in Osakwe 2009.

Yet, California is a miner's canary for cotton growing and farming in general, for despite these superlative fibre yields, and decades of access to the best available technologies, many farmers still struggle to stay on the land. Over the last 20 years, cotton farms in the US have doubled in size and halved in number (Freese 2007), as medium-sized farms have been unable to compete with efficiencies of scale. The land in this area is now so highly optimised that farmers carefully weigh the expense of further inputs against the potential financial return, and often hold back on additional applications of water, for example, if the cost is not likely to be offset by increased yields.[2] In other words, California farmers have reached a point of diminishing returns—peak cotton. Increasing the volume of production is no longer the imperative. Economic viability and stability is.

Striking parallels can be drawn between industrialised cotton cultivation and the industrialised fashion design process. For commercial designers also maximise efficiencies—driving designs from studio idea-to-spec sheet-to-producer as fast as possible and stretching an 8-hour working day into 12 and 15 hours as deadlines demand; producer factories maximise speed and volume of product throughput at minimal cost; and corporate advertising pushes shoppers (mostly women) to buy and discard more and more products to trigger additional purchases and ensure perpetual growth in sales. Indeed, studies show that, by 2005, the average American consumer purchased one piece of clothing every five and a half days (Mooallem 2009) and now discards 30 kg of garments a year—the equivalent of 30 pairs of jeans or 90 short-sleeved T-shirts. And garments that aren't thrown away are hoarded! The fastest growing real estate category in the US is self-storage, now a $22 billion per annum industry (Botsman and Rogers 2010: 13).

Any designer, witnessing the massive mobilisation of natural resources for commercial fashion use on the one hand, and the speed with which those resources are processed, delivered and disposed on the other hand, cannot help but reflect on their own practice and question the conventional logic of 'producing more': for what purpose?

'Companies need more stuff because that's the business model they are working with' (Adams 2009). The logic of this model provides a 'mechanical order' (L. Mumford, cited in Glendenning 1995), which 'socialises' all who work in the textile supply chain and in associated industries—it directs the structure of the fashion industry itself as well as the way people think and behave on a daily basis. As a result, highly qualified and well-intentioned individuals become isolated in their specialities and blind to everything but the imperative of producing 'more'; unable to see the whole system, 'we optimise the wrong things' (Core 77 2001).

---

2 D. Munk, Crop Advisor, University of California Agricultural Extension, in conversation, Firebaugh, CA, 20 October 2011.

2.2 Questioning industry norms

> The company has an incinerator on site, which they use to burn goods that come in faulty or with the logo damaged. They are quite proud to show this off because it demonstrates how concerned they are about maintaining the quality of their products.
>
> (Intern working at a large company)

As the fashion industry works to improve its sustainability performance, its primary focus has been on terms of engagement for workers, fibre procurement and processing of materials and in particular, lowering a garment's sustainability impact profile. Great efforts have been put to this goal: cross-industry matrices have been developed through the long and arduous processes of data collection, normalisation and consensus building;[3] and alliances have been forged to facilitate unprecedented transparency for product development. These initiatives are important, for they foster empathy between companies and individuals working in an otherwise ruthlessly competitive industry and they raise environmental performance parameters across the entire clothing sector. But the sustainability profile of a single garment is only a small part of the picture.

For in meeting the prime directive of economic efficiency, individual garments are designed for maximum speed and ease of production and maximum broad-based appeal to consumers, resulting in a ubiquitous aesthetic at retail. With individual pieces varying very little from one company to the next, garments are utterly dependent on advertising to differentiate one brand of clothing from another and to compete for customer attention and loyalty. From the photo shoot setting to product styling and store atmosphere, companies surround the product with an aspirational image and lure consumers to buy into it. In short, companies don't sell products; they sell brands (Klein 1999).

The brand, then, is the most highly prized and protected asset of any company for it is considered a product's 'main attraction' (Klein 1999: 29) and is the primary means by which to ensure higher sales and greater profits. So it is that when products are received at the warehouse with a damaged brand logo, that the accepted norm is to destroy the garments altogether rather than mark them down for sale into outlet stores. For secondary lower-price retail channels dilute the consumer's retail 'experience' and the associated 'value' of the brand.

The sustainability ramifications of this behaviour are obvious. All the natural resources and the superlative human intelligence that has been applied to their optimisation—the inputs to fibre cultivation, wild water diverted to flow through textile mills, mountain tops removed to access coal to generate electricity to run production facilities—all this embodied energy or 'hidden history' (Hawken *et al.* 1999: 88) goes to waste in the incinerator.

---

3 Sustainable Apparel Coalition, www.apparelcoalition.org, accessed 13 January 2012; Leather Working Group, www.leatherworkinggroup.com, accessed 13 January 2012; Global Organic Textile Standards, www.global-standard.org, accessed 13 January 2012, to name a few.

Seconds are just one of many points in a garment's journey through the fashion system where waste is generated; nonetheless, they emphasise the importance of looking beyond the materiality of products when considering sustainability to include the broader underpinnings that direct social and cultural behaviours. For reducing the water footprint and increasing the organic content or physical durability of a single garment are all misplaced strategies if the ultimate use and wear of those garments are not also considered and ensured.

2.3 Acting on personal values

> Our company wouldn't take a stand one way or the other on genetically modified (GM) cotton, but personally, I am really happy that that cotton is non-GM.
>
> (Employee at a large global company)

Cotton is grown in over one hundred countries, each with its particular farming systems, ecological conditions and pressures. Though the use of chemicals on cotton has been the fashion industry's main focus over the last two decades, there are a number of additional issues associated with cotton cultivation. Fresh water resources, for example, are of increasing concern worldwide and this has focused attention on Uzbekistan, where the Aral Sea has been depleted to a fraction of its former size because water from inflowing rivers is being diverted to use for the irrigation of nearby cotton crops (Fletcher and Grose 2012: 22). This particular case has earned cotton a reputation as a 'thirsty' crop. However, in West Texas, where cotton is dry-farmed, and in West Africa, where tropical rainfall is high, water use is less of an issue. Differences such as these demand regional cotton cultivation strategies that respond to the specific ecologies and needs in each area. But diverse cotton strategies challenge the fashion industry, for its structures have been built on centralised commodity fibre systems and economies of scale driven by the imperatives of speed and low cost.

The most well-known strategy for chemical use on cotton is organic, which allows only approved substances to be used on the crop and employs a range of biological controls in place of the most toxic chemicals. Additional routes include biological integrated pest management (IPM) systems, which use biological means as a first resort and then chemicals to control pests and pathogens—a system that reportedly reduces chemical use by at least 50% (Gibbs and Grose 2008)—and genetically modified (GM) cotton, which uses biotechnology to resist pest infestations and make weed management simpler.

There are two main types of GM cotton: Bt (abbreviation of the bacterial toxin, *Bacillus thuringiensis*) and Ht (abbreviation of herbicide tolerant) cotton. Bt cotton is engineered so that *Bacillus thuringiensis* (which is poisonous to pests) is embedded into the genetic code of the plant so when the crop comes under attack, pests die and the need for pesticide sprays is eliminated. Ht cotton is adapted to survive the application of a broad-spectrum herbicide that would otherwise kill the crop.

This allows farmers to spray the herbicide freely to control weeds, without having to shield the cotton plant from exposure to the chemical, thereby simplifying weed management and reducing labour costs.

2.3.1 Problems with Bt cotton

Though peer-reviewed papers suggest that Bt has been most successful at achieving chemical reductions, these findings are hotly debated by experts looking at the systemic and unintended consequences of GM technology. Many questions remain unanswered—not least of which is the long-term efficacy of GM technology itself.

Unlike broad-spectrum insecticides, Bt affects quite a narrow range of insects (the bollworm family specifically) and so the negative effects on beneficial insects have been rare (Gould and Tabashnik 1998). It can therefore be used in combination with biological controls, which has helped to establish Bt sprays as a staple of organic farming systems, and as a highly valuable complement to IPM systems. Besides toxicity benefits, Bt sprays are also degraded by sunlight in hours or days, so they tend not to persist in the environment. In contrast, incorporating Bt genes into the plants' genomes causes the toxin to be present throughout the season, and GM crops planted over millions of acres increase the space over which pests are exposed (ESI 2002). This double time/space exposure of the pest to the Bt toxin fosters genetic resistance, which would enable the pest to re-infest the crop and require heavier and stronger sprays for control over the long term. This, it is argued, would not only undermine the efficacy of GM, but also threatens organic and the more widespread IPM systems. All sectors of the cotton industry, including pesticide companies and biotech technology owners, agree that it is only a matter of time before cotton pests evolve resistance to the Bt toxin (ICAC 2005).

To combat insect resistance, experts acknowledge that 'some level of pre-emptive resistant management is required' (ICAC 2004). However, this is challenging to administer. For, nature is complex and no single plan can be optimally suited for all pests in all regions. One resistance management strategy recommended by the US Department of Agriculture (USDA) calls for 'refuge areas' to be planted alongside conventional cotton and sprayed using an insecticide other than Bt to provide a habitat where pests not exposed to Bt are then available to mate with those that have been exposed, thereby reducing the probability of genetic resistance. But this approach has limitations, not least of which is the variable compliance by farmers (Ronald 2011), and is particularly challenging in developing countries, where smallholder farmers have difficulty even grasping the concept (Fitt *et al.* 2004).

GM cotton has grown rapidly since it was first introduced commercially in 1996. It now accounts for almost 50% of all conventional cotton produced in the world, and experts warn (Jayaraman *et al.* cited in ICAC 2005: 12) that with the expanding area of Bt cotton, poor refuge practices call for serious attention. Yet 85% of the adoption of Bt transgenic cotton is in developing countries, with further growth planned, and biosafety plans are clearly impossible to administer.

2.3.2 Problems with herbicide-tolerant cotton

Ht cotton initially benefited farmers by reducing labour costs for weeding. However, with the widespread use of a single herbicide, Monsanto's Roundup (representing 96% of the Ht market), genetic resistance to the active ingredient, glyphosate, has rapidly developed and there are now 12 herbicide-resistant weeds across several states in the US (Allen 2008). The immediate response from farmers faced with resistant weeds is to spray more herbicide, resulting in an increased volume of glyphosate on cotton. In California, for example, where Ht represents 61% of the cotton crop, glyphosate volume increased 200% between 1996 and 2005 (PANNA 2008). In light of evident resistance, the cotton industry now recommends that a range of methods and techniques for weeding be employed, rather than a single technology (ICAC 2004). In short, to ensure its long-term effectiveness, GM requires the variety of techniques that integrated pest management already offers.

An individual studying these issues, guided by their own values and discursive reasoning may come to the common sense conclusion to err on the side of caution and avoid the use of GM cotton. Yet GM cottonseed is already co-mingled with conventional cottonseed, and given the global reach, complexity and opacity of the fashion and textile system, companies simply do not know where the majority of their cotton fibre, let alone the seeds, originates. Furthermore, there has been little public debate about GM technology, so the general public, especially in the US, is unaware of the short-term benefits or the long-term risks of the technology. And without immediate marketing gains, companies are unwilling to take the time and expense to root out GM cottonseed, even if it were practicable.

This kind of dilemma, where an employee feels a moral obligation and yet 'finds their choices constrained...by physical infrastructure and...institutional channels' (Thein Durning 1995: 75) creates an emotional tension; a situation where, as Joanna Macy puts it: 'we immunize...or anesthetize...ourselves against the demands of the situation by narrowing our awareness' (Macy 1995: 249) in order to continue a day's work, as normal. Robert Lifton refers to this as 'leading a double life' (cited in Macy 1995: 243). Yet despite this apparent clash of values, common ground can be found. For example, if the threat of evolving genetic resistance is 'real and acknowledged by everybody' (ICAC 2005), then it is only logical that a variety of strategies be implemented by companies to mitigate the consequences of an unexpected infestation in GM cotton production. A large-scale failed cotton crop has wide-ranging economic ramifications, not only for farmers, but also for the whole industry, since everyone depends on a steady flow of cotton fibre to process into goods for sale. Including non-GM IPM cotton and organic cotton in a company's 'cotton portfolio' therefore become a prudent business strategy, providing a practical 'safety net' for if and when GM undermines its own efficacy. Moreover, this strategy is a multi-satisfier, for it aligns ecological goals with business benefits and one's own personal values.

2.4 Using our common sense(s)

> It's not even about consumption any more... It's about sales!
> (Designer, former business owner)

Most young designers enter the fashion industry because they enjoy combining clothes together in new and innovative ways and/or make their own garments. At college, they learn the craft of practice—build a deep knowledge of historical and contemporary influences on fashion, and develop making and patterning skills that enable the manipulation of these sociocultural influences to be successfully expressed as something 'new'.

For a designer, the ultimate reward for the enormous creative and physical effort that goes into realising a well-crafted concept and garment is to see one's own designs appreciated and worn. But as fundamental as it is, this core motivation can often be at odds with those of the fashion industry. For with its narrow focus on economic efficiency, the industrial fashion process tends to drive the speed and volume of product development up while simultaneously driving product innovation down (Fletcher and Grose 2012), streamlining the creative process and decoupling designers from making altogether. Draping has all but disappeared from the industrial fashion studio; patternmaking has been relegated to the technical (Rissanen 2011) and often to the computer; the process of 'thinking by hand' is therefore inhibited, and the hand of the designer in the product, absent. Creative ideas become an intellectual exercise rather than being rooted in the intelligence and acquired wisdom of iterative making and construction. Moreover, to ensure that ideas are delivered at top volume and speed on a daily basis, companies subscribe to trend services, which 'prop up' the creative process with ready-made styling ideas for rapid implementation; designers become facilitators, pushing spec packages along at ever increasing speeds. The ultimate measure of success in the industrialised fashion industry is the number of units sold to the retail store—an abstracted measure which edits out all immaterial values—the sensual, poetic, social and cultural qualities of clothes—that all of us, designers and wearers alike, recognise and appreciate when they are allowed to be present.

The fashion industry's focus on optimising speed, efficiency and volume, then, not only pushes natural resources beyond tolerable thresholds, but also pushes against the creative and often ethical thresholds of the designer, creating an emotional 'burden' or lingering sense of dis-ease. But as uncomfortable as this state of dis-ease can be, it can also be a tipping point for agency. For, 'every designer at some point (reaches) a limit in terms of restrictions they choose to adhere to' (McQuillan 2010). Designer, Nathalie Chanin, for example, decided to start her own company, Alabama Chanin, after working in industry and witnessing buyers relentlessly negotiating poor workers down on the cost of a garment, penny-by-penny. The clothing she now designs reflects the culture and place and people she works with; production volume is restrained by the speed of handwork. It is fairness, loyalty, community, friendship, locality and craft that are optimised in her business model and set at the heart of her practice. And Dutch designer, Monique van Heist, who was the winner of the Mercedes-Benz Dutch Fashion Award in 2008, redesigned the very structure of fashion development cycles with her Hello Fashion concept. Starting from a base collection, van Heist now adds a limited number of new styles and colours each season, repeating and slowly increasing the offering over time, with the expressed purpose of optimising the embodied *design* energy in each product and supporting her own well-being.[4]

The above examples of designers taking action to align their practice to their own values parallel long-term shifts in wearer lifestyles. Harvard University economist, Juliet Schor, author of *The Overworked American,* found that 'workers in all core regions of the consumer society express(ed) a strong desire for additional leisure time and a willingness to trade pay increases for it' (Thein Durning 1995). Fifty-three per cent of Americans now say that having less stress and more time with their family and friends would make them much more satisfied with their lives (Fletcher and Grose 2012); and an increasing number of people are participating in various forms of collaborative consumption (Botsman and Rogers 2010) by exchanging products through a variety of web-based platforms and leasing long-term through vintage stores and donate-purchase cycles at charity shops. These shifts in the fashion industry and among individual wearers indicate that people are opting for 'lives at once simpler and more satisfying' (McQuillan 2010: 93): collectively and accumulatively forming what Ignacio Valero calls 'sensible communities'.[5]

2.5 Directing fashion practice

> I choose colours and fabrics based on my own ethics and the mission of my company.
>
> (Designer, business owner, with long-term product development experience)

Though most companies today treat sustainability as *part* of their business—added on or attended to as costs, logistics and market interests allow, and dropped when market interest wanes—it is when sustainability is taken on as a constant, that its true potential for design is unleashed. For, there is no innate tension or conflict between business and sustainability, cost and sustainability, or aesthetics and sustainability—they are all in dynamic relationship (Papanek 1985: 7). Designers know very well how to bring out the immaterial qualities of fashion to create resonance and 'value' and, in actuality, this value can be met through the practice of sustainability as much as it can through the multiple qualities that must be balanced in product development.

Colour and fabric, for example, are arguably the most visually stimulating and tactile aspects of fashion. Each season, designers begin creative development with their inspiration and start to build a colour palette and fabric choices around it,

4 M. van Heist, in conversation, Dutch Fashion Week, California College of the Arts, San Francisco.
5 I. Valero, Professor of Humanities and Sciences, in conversation, California College of the Arts, Oakland, CA, 2011.

mulling over and meticulously combining variations in tone and texture to balance patterns and the collection as a whole. Being restricted to certain fabrics, colours and dye processes and working within given ecological limits mimics the parameters imposed by any creative brief. Just as Missoni's or Paul Smith's particular colour preferences and distinct prints form the creative 'signature' of the designer, so designers practising sustainability become proficient and adept at balancing additional demands and the tensions, conflicts and perceived 'limits' give way to an active, integral and poetic capacity for creative advantage.

This directive holds true for all aspects of fashion design. For example, the flat patterns developed by zero waste designers reflect a philosophy, acquired skill and focused execution that is immediately recognised and appreciated by layman and fashion practitioner alike. So masterly and distinct is the aesthetic of zero waste patterns, that they defy comparison to industrial jigsaw and CAD system efficiencies. For, the patterns optimise not only the embedded energy in the fabric, but also the highly creative skills and mind of the designer. Perhaps most importantly of all, then, is that the creative responses by all designers to the challenges of sustainability help bring visual form to a completely different way of seeing clothes, the world of fashion and fashion practice itself.

2.6 Unfreezing old patterns

> I have to do my conventional work, to have credibility when I talk about sustainability.
>
> (Fashion journalist and author)

Individuals wanting to practice fashion for sustainability can often feel quite lonely in trying to do 'good work'. 'Where do I belong?' is a commonly expressed concern, which acknowledges the gap between an individual's shift in cognisance and the inertia of entrenched logic, industry structures and vested interests, which remain difficult to change.

Part of the challenge in finding a place to 'belong' is that we are so unused to seeing things in relationship, that our perceptions about the available options for sustainability practice are similarly narrowed. We have a fractured intellect and are limited in what we imagine we can do tomorrow, by what is available to us today (Fletcher and Grose 2012). But even though typical design positions available in the fashion sector today might not yet provide designers with the opportunity to engage in systemic change, new platforms are nonetheless being created by practitioners themselves. These redirections start to form new professional norms simply by being there and over time will create new ecologies of practice, which will eventually lead to more flexible structures and thinking.

In the meantime, hybrid positions, where individuals work within industry and take on sustainability initiatives on their own volition, can also provide great potential as vehicles for change, for they blur the ideological boundaries between the old dualism, 'sustainable' vs. 'conventional' practice, and they create 'bridges' which enable people to make the shift from being passively aware or overwhelmed by sustainability issues, to becoming active sustainability practitioners. Working in a hybrid position also builds practical wisdom. For, by engaging deeply in the current field of fashion, valuable experience and knowledge is gained and points of leverage for change can be identified, proving the more recent adaptation of an old adage: 'You have to be part of the problem before you can be part of the solution'.

Practical knowledge and experience in the industry builds credibility, which has the potential to make sustainability 'more lively to people who would otherwise be hard-pressed to accept the idea as a theory' (Roszak 1995a). For example, the Sustainable Cotton Project (SCP),[6] a non-profit organisation working in California to help farmers in transition from chemically intensive to biological cultivation systems in cotton, notes that conventional growers are more likely to heed someone with practical experience and demonstrable examples. So, in addition to enlisting growers in their Cleaner Cotton™ programme, the organisation also organises farm days for larger groups of growers and helps facilitate the exchange of information through presentations, demonstrations and workshops, farmer-to-farmer.

Practical industry knowledge also enables individuals to persuade or enable people to change, rather than 'confronting [them] with a task that appears impossible' (Rosak 1995b: 16). For example, an employee of accessory manufacturer, G. Hensler, recently met with resistance when questioning a supplier on the details of processing impacts. Further discussion revealed the suppliers' concern about divulging proprietary and potentially self-incriminating information and a deeper fear of losing orders. Making long-term commitments to normalise business cycles, and enlisting a third party assessment company to document processes under a confidentiality agreement, are just two mechanisms now being considered to enable supply chain transparency while also protecting the supplier's interests. Empathetic relationships, such as those that are forming in the above example, take time to cultivate and therefore rub against the prevalent industrial supply chain imperatives of speed and low price, at whatever cost. But these relationships are at the heart of sustainability, for they foster trust and lead to synergies that would otherwise remain dormant; they open up new opportunities to create change.

2.7 Conclusion

> New values never arrive in the abstract; they come entangled in concrete situations, new realities and new understandings of the world.
> (Thein Durning 1995)

The current fashion industry is built on the principle of limitless growth. This is an outdated model. For, in a world of degraded ecosystems, declining resources

6 www.sustainablecotton.org, accessed 12 January 2012.

and increasing human population and wealth, unchecked growth in the consumption of material goods, including fashion and apparel, cannot be sustained over the long term. The imperatives of daily work rarely call on fashion practitioners to deeply question the nature of business and how the fashion industry may adapt to preserve and restore the ecosystems on which it depends. Yet, each fashion professional has deep knowledge of the fashion system and this practical wisdom often bears witness to the limitations of the industry, prompting personal reflection and insights on how the fashion sector might be better aligned to sustainability.

This chapter brought together a series of statements that start to give voice to the insights of individuals working in the fashion trenches. These insights, frequently based on common sense, intuition and ethical values, call into question the massive mobilisation of natural resources for commercial fashion use; a segmented supply chain that compels us to optimise the wrong things; the drive for immediate marketing gains that run counter to ecological and social gains; and individual product profiles which exclude cultural and social considerations essential to long-term sustainability. As a collective, these 'wisdoms' start to identify an emergent 'coming to our senses' (Valero 2011), and a building sense of agency within the fashion sector itself.

Many fashion practitioners still 'find their choices constrained…by physical infrastructure and…institutional channels' (Thein Durning 1995: 75), while others are nonetheless developing ways to align ecological goals with both business benefits and their personal values. Others, still, are 'taking a stance' (Leerberg *et al*. 2010) to influence business practices even when that position runs contrary to vested interests and industry givens or axioms. As practitioners continue to question the relentless drive to produce more, the inevitability of GM technology, the complicit production of waste, the arbitrary number of retail cycles, and a design process which is decoupled from nature, making and personal well-being, they will also begin to challenge our culture's fetish (Hamilton 2004) for material growth, and over time forge completely different ecologies for practice where 'well-being meets well dressed' (McQuillan 2010: 96).

Bibliography

Adams, B. (2009) 'Sustainability Lead—IDEO', Design Green Now, panel 27 March 2009, California College of the Arts, San Francisco, www.designgreennow.com/2009/03/27/bob-adams-sustainability-lead-ideo, accessed 12 December 2011.

Allen, W. (2008) *War on Bugs* (White River Junction, VT: Chelsea Green Publishing).

Botsman, R., and R. Rogers (2010) *What's Mine is Yours: The Rise of Collaborative Consumption* (New York: Harper Collins Publishers).

Core 77 (2001) 'Material Shortages and Designing a New World', interview with Michael Braungart, Core 77, www.core77.com/blog/articles/dr_michael_braungart_on_material_shortages_and_designing_a_new_material_world_18669.asp, accessed 20 December 2011.

ESI (Essential Science Indicators) (2002) 'Genetically Modified Crops, an Interview with Bruce Tabashnik PhD', ESI, www.esi-topics.com/gmc/interviews/BruceTabashnik.html, accessed 12 December 2012.

Fitt, G.P., K. Hake, C. James, J. Pages, D. Roupakias, J.M. Stewart, P.J. Wakelyn and Y. Zafar (2004) *Report of the Second Expert Panel on Biotechnology of Cotton* (Washington, DC: ICAC): 31.

Fletcher, K., and L. Grose (2012) *Fashion and Sustainability: Design for Change* (London: Laurence King).

Freese, B. (2007) *Cotton Concentration Report* (Washington, DC: Center for Food Safety/ International Center for Technology Assessment).

Gibbs, M., and L. Grose (2008) 'New Cotton Category Comes to Market', *Pesticide News*.

Glendenning, C. (1995) 'Technology, Trauma and the World', in T. Roszak, M.E. Gomes and A.D. Kanner (eds.), *Ecopsychology: Restoring the Earth, Healing the Mind* (San Francisco: Sierra Club Books): 45.

Gould, F., and B. Tabashnik (1998) 'Bt Cotton Resistance Management', in M. Mellon and J. Rissler (eds.), *USA: Now or Never* (Washington, DC: Union of Concerned Scientists).

Hamilton, C. (2004) *Growth Fetish* (London: Pluto Press).

Hawken, P., A. Lovins and L.H. Lovins (1999) *Natural Capitalism: Creating the Next Industrial Revolution* (Boston, MA: Little Brown).

ICAC (International Cotton Advisory Committee) (2004) *Report of the Second Expert Panel on Biotechnology of Cotton* (Washington, DC: ICAC).

ICAC (2005) 'Concerns, Apprehensions and Risks of Biotech Cotton', *ICAC Recorder*, March 2005.

Jayaraman, K.S., J.L. Fox, H. Ji and C. Orellana (2002) 'Indian Bt gene monoculture: Potential Time Bomb', *Nature Biotechnology* 23.2: 158, as cited in ICAC (2005) *The Performance of Bt Cotton Hybrids in India* (March 2005).

Klein, N. (1999) *No Logo: Taking Aim at the Brand Bullies* (New York: Picador).

Leeberg, M., V. Riisberg and J. Boutrup (2010) 'Design Responsibility and Design as Reflective Practice: An Educational Challenge', *Sustainable Development* 18: 306-17.

Macy, J. (1995) 'Working Through Environmental Despair' in T. Roszak, M.E. Gomes and A.D. Kanner (eds.), *Ecopsychology: Restoring the Earth, Healing the Mind* (San Francisco: Sierra Club Books).

McQuillan, H. (2010) 'Zero Waste Design Practice', in T. Rissanen and A. Gwelt (eds.), *Shaping Sustainable Fashion* (London: Earthscan).

Mooallem, J. (2009) 'The Self-Storage Self', New York Times, www.nytimes.com/2009/09/06/magazine/06self-storage-t.html, accessed 4 December 2011.

Osakwe, E. (2009) 'ICAC Cotton Fact Sheet USA', International Cotton Advisory Committee, www.icac.org/econ_stats/country_facts/english.html, accessed 1 August 2011.

PANNA (Pesticide Action Network North America) (2008) 'PAN Pesticide Database', www.pesticideinfo.org, accessed 21 August 2008.

Papanek, V. (1985) *Design for the Real World* (Chicago: Academy Chicago Publishers).

Rissanen, T. (2011) In conversation, in *Fashion Sustainability Workshop Series: Waste*, California College of the Arts, San Francisco, 4–6 August 2011.

Ronald, P. (2011) 'Plant Genetics, Sustainable Agriculture and Global Food Security', *Genetics* 188.1: 11-20 (www.genetics.org/content/188/1/11.full 5/1/11, accessed 25 January 2012).

Roszak, T. (1995a) 'Foreword', in T. Roszak, M.E. Gomes and A.D. Kanner (eds.), *Ecopsychology: Restoring the Earth, Healing the Mind* (San Francisco: Sierra Club Books): xvii.

Roszak, T. (1995b) 'Where Psyche Meets Gaia', in T. Roszak, M.E. Gomes and A.D. Kanner (eds.), *Ecopsychology: Restoring the Earth, Healing the Mind* (San Francisco: Sierra Club Books): 16.

Thein Durning, A. (1995) 'Are We Happy Yet', in T. Roszak, M.E. Gomes and A.D. Kanner (eds.), *Ecopsychology: Restoring the Earth, Healing the Mind* (San Francisco: Sierra Club Books): 73.

Lynda Grose is a designer, consultant and assistant professor at California College of the Arts. She co-founded ESPRIT's ecollection line, the first ecologically responsible clothing line developed by a major corporation. Lynda now advises across private and non-profit sectors and recently co-authored the book, *Fashion and Sustainability: Design for Change* (Laurence King Publishing, 2012).

3

From principle to practice
Embedding sustainability in clothing supply chain strategies

Alison Ashby, Melanie Hudson Smith and Rory Shand
Plymouth Business School, UK

The fashion clothing industry is particularly subject to strong external pressure for sustainable behaviour and the increased outsourcing of manufacturing has created long, globally fragmented supply chains. Supply chain management (SCM) has come to the fore in this industry, as the way a firm designs and manages its supply chain can provide competitive advantage in a market focused on cost, speed and availability. It also provides a relational view of the supply chain that can be used to evaluate and address the environmental, social and economic impacts of products, processes and practices.

Building on sustainability theory and supply chain strategy, this chapter attempts to provide an integrated understanding of how supply chains can be managed in practice to effectively address the dimensions of sustainability. It analyses all stages within the clothing supply chain and assesses the different environmental and social impacts that can occur throughout the product life-cycle. It considers the value of long-term, collaborative relationships in providing a coordinated supply chain strategy which addresses these serious, increasingly high profile issues, and in turn generates competitive advantage.

The chapter will address the following research questions:

1. How is sustainability interpreted academically and how does this translate into practice?

2. How is sustainability addressed in supply chains and what role does SCM play?

3. How does the clothing industry address environmental and social impacts within supply chains and how can this inform sustainable supply chain management (SSCM)?

The chapter commences with a discussion of the definitions and interpretations of sustainability followed by a review of the SCM literature. The two fields are then aligned, with a focus on the models/tools that can be applied to enable sustainable supply chains. The application of these models within the clothing industry is investigated and insights which can inform both theory development and supply chain practice identified and discussed.

3.1 Defining sustainability

The idea of sustainability was verbalised by Schumacher in 1972, as 'permanence', where 'nothing makes economic sense unless its continuance for a long time can be projected without running into absurdities' (Grinde and Khare 2008: 129). Sustainable as an adjective was institutionalised by the 1992 Rio Earth Summit conference and is seen as an indication of environmental goodness (Appleton 2006) and a long-term perspective (Orians 1990).

In 1983 the World Commission on Environment and Development (WCED) was established and the result of their work formalised in the 1987 Brundtland Report, *Our Common Future*. It defined sustainability as 'development which meets the needs of the present without compromising the ability of future generations to meet their own needs' (WCED 1987: 43), and over 25 years later remains the most often quoted definition of this concept. Its two central tenets are:

- 'the concept of "needs", in particular the essential needs of the world's poor, to which overriding priority should be given'

- 'the idea of limitations imposed by the state of technology and social organisation on the environment's ability to meet present and future needs' (WCED 1987: 43)

Prior to the Brundtland Report, sustainability in the business context was seen as 'a company's ability to increase its earnings steadily' (Werbach 2009), i.e. an emphasis on economic performance. The Brundtland definition however emphasises the importance of environmental and social sustainability, and the literature on this concept recognises that sustainability is multi-dimensional (Orians 1990; Dempsey *et al.* 2009; Udo and Jansson 2009).

The three pillars (Springett 2003; Vachon and Mao 2008; Hutchins and Sutherland 2008) or interconnected rings (Giddings *et al.* 2002) of economy, environment and

Figure 3.1 **Three ring sector view of sustainability**

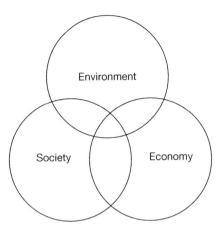

society illustrated in Figure 3.1 are pervasive throughout sustainability literature and offer a holistic view of the concept. However the extent to which they can be fully integrated is frequently questioned and Gladwin *et al.* (1995) challenge the model as they believe it encourages a 'technical fix' approach. As each sector can be treated separately, fundamental connections may be ignored and there is an inherent assumption that trade-offs are permitted. While there is clear academic recognition of the need to integrate economic, environmental and social sustainability, there is limited guidance on how it can be achieved in practice.

3.2 Levels of sustainability

Expanding on the three ring sector view, Inyang (2009), Udo and Jansson (2009), Springett (2003) and Sathiendrakumar (1996) all identify different 'strengths' of sustainability from (very) weak to (very) strong, and align these with the idea of an achievable standard. Weak sustainability/technocentrism views that the stock of capital assets, whether man-made or natural, is perfectly substitutable, with technology replacing resources, while at the strong/ecocentric end of the spectrum natural capital *must* be protected and cannot be substituted.

Figure 3.2 aligns the range of different academic viewpoints into a single spectrum, with each horizontal division representing an individual author's interpretation of the different 'strengths' of sustainability. It illustrates the overlap between viewpoints, as well as emphasising the many different ways of interpreting sustainability. Traditional economists are seen to have a 'relaxed' view of sustainability and measure it in monetary terms with economic growth taking priority, in line with the pre-Brundtland sustainability definition. Environmentalists take a more stringent

Figure 3.2 **Sustainability spectrum**

Weak sustainability		**Strong sustainability**
(Neoclassical economics)		(Ecological economics)
Utility is non-declining over time		Economy and nature complementary and
Substituting one form of capital for another		should **both** be sustained
(Nilson 2010)		

Technocentrism	**Sustaincentrism**	**Ecocentrism**
Right to master natural	Economic and human	Non-human nature should
creation for human benefit	activities inextricably	only be used to satisfy vital
	linked with natural systems	needs of sustenance

(Gladwin *et al.* 1995)

Physical or human capital		Natural capital needs to be
can substitute natural		maintained
capital		Technology not the answer,
Technology provides the		but some substitution
means		possible

(Inyang 2009; Sathiendrakumar 1996)

Status quo	**Reform**	**Transformation**
Need for change	Acceptance of problems but	Social and environmental
acknowledged but economic	belief that shifts in policy	problems rooted in existing
growth is the solution	and lifestyle can be achieved	economic structures
No major environmental or	over time and within present	Strong commitment to
social problems	social and economic	social equity and justice
	structures.	
	(Brundtland Report sits here)	

(Hopwood *et al.* 2005)

Political reality		**Material reality**
Capitalist economy		Economy dependent on
dominates environment		society and environment
and society		

(Giddings *et al.* 2002)

Rationalism	**Communitarianism**	**Ecocentrism**
Society = sum of individuals	Utility should not just apply	Everything on planet
Greatest utility for greatest	at individual level	interconnected and
number – desires not needs	**All** must partake, not just	interdependent
Goal is maximum economic	greatest number	Humanity dependent on
efficiency		natural systems

(Sillanpää 1998)

and potentially extremist view where no growth can occur at the detriment of natural resources (Inyang 2009). This invites the criticism that this position does not adequately consider the needs of poor people, which is key to the Brundtland definition (Appleton 2006).

There is a general perception in the academic literature that weak sustainability is currently the prevailing approach in practice, where economic growth dominates and positive economic outcomes outweigh negative social or environmental impacts (Lamberton 2005). In this model engagement with social and environmental issues is typically kept at a superficial, 'green business as usual' level (Springett 2003). Strong sustainability in contrast emphasises the importance of sustaining the environment and is much more qualitative in its approach (Nilsen 2010).

The clothing industry has traditionally operated at the weak end of the sustainability spectrum with an emphasis on the economic dimension and transactional relationships, and an inherent acceptance of the negative social and environmental impacts that can occur along the supply chain (Allwood *et al.* 2006). Supply chain management (SCM) was used initially to achieve production efficiencies and maximise profit through a 'race to the bottom' outsourcing strategy focused on short-term, low-cost supplier relationships (Bruce *et al.* 2004). However in recent years the focus has shifted because of the growing pressure for supply chains to operate in environmentally and socially responsible ways (Birtwistle and Moore 2007; Goworek 2011), and how a supply chain is designed and managed has become of strategic importance (Bergvall-Forsberg and Towers 2007), as outlined in the following section.

3.3 The role of supply chain management

Most organisations are part of at least one supply chain (Samaranayake 2005) and competition is increasingly based on 'supply chain vs. supply chain' (Gold *et al.* 2009; Soler *et al.* 2010). Globalisation and economic trends have created highly complex supply chains (Varma *et al.* 2006) and the design, organisation, interactions, competences, capabilities and management of supply chains have become key issues (Gold *et al.* 2009). Under these circumstances SCM represents a key discipline for establishing strategies that successfully integrate economic, environmental and social issues and practices.

SCM has been practitioner-led (Burgess *et al.* 2006) and represents an evolutionary step beyond logistics (Samaranayake 2005) by integrating the management of cooperations with that of material and information flows (Handfield and Nichols 1999). The prime driver for the development of SCM has traditionally been economic sustainability, based on the premise that an integrated, efficient supply chain helps to minimise monetary risks and increase profits (Fawcett *et al.* 2008), aligning with the previously highlighted weak, 'business as usual approach' to sustainability. However increased consumer awareness and stakeholder pressure has led to social and environmental sustainability becoming additional drivers in supply chain strategies.

3.4 Making connections: Supply chain relationships

A key strategic contribution of SCM is the development of difficult-to-imitate supplier relationships, and the strategic management of suppliers is linked to collaborative 'partnerships' (Preuss 2005a). When environmental and social sustainability is incorporated in these relationships there are tangible supply chain benefits. These include safer and cleaner facilities across the supply chain, reduced environmental and health risks and improved product quality (Sarkis 1995). They can also offer competitive advantage through positive PR, reduced long-term risks related to product liability, resource depletion and waste management, and the ability to proactively move ahead of regulation (Preuss 2005a).

Traditional supplier interactions have been predominantly 'arms length', focusing on increasing suppliers to economise transaction costs and minimise risk (Lowson 2002), whereas the more recent relational model focuses on sharing of information (Preuss 2005b; Power 2005). Collaborative relationships are characterised by information sharing as well as a long-term approach and mutual advantage (Preuss 2005a) with joint efforts achieving objectives and creating value that could not be realised otherwise (Gattorna and Walters 1996; Nyaga *et al.* 2010). Effective SCM relies on these close, long-term and committed working relationships (Spekman *et al.* 1998) and requires confidence and trust among partners (Varma *et al.* 2006).

Integrated supply chains are inherently strategic (Power 2005) and there has been a defined shift from a tactical focus to a more strategic approach in SCM (Attaran and Attaran 2007). The sharing of meaningful, rare, valuable, not imitable or non-substitutable information (Barney and Hesterley 2008) can create 'distinctive visibility', while relational embeddedness gained through a history of interactions can both improve performance and provide a sustainable competitive advantage (Soler *et al.* 2010; Bernardes 2010).

3.5 Addressing sustainability in supply chains

Building on the SCM principles outlined above, the emerging discipline of sustainable supply chain management (SSCM) explicitly incorporates the ecological and social aspects of business, as well as economic sustainability (Svensson 2007). It represents 'the strategic, transparent integration and achievement of an organisation's social, environmental and economic goals in the systemic coordination of key inter-organisational business processes for improving the long-term economic performance of the individual company and its supply chains' (Carter and Rogers 2008: 368).

A sustainability strategy for managing the supply chain defines the firm's values, how the values will be enforced and the consequences for not achieving them (Mahler 2007). It is necessary to holistically and purposefully identify environmental and social initiatives which support a firm's sustainability strategy and have traceability and visibility into both upstream and downstream operations (Carter and Easton 2011). This is critical for the success of *whole* supply chain management (Ageron *et al.* 2011) and genuine sustainability results from making supply chains more sustainable (Mahler 2007), emphasising the need to apply a holistic model (Stokes and Tohamy 2009) which recognises and manages all three dimensions.

3.5.1 The environment

A firm's impact extends beyond any single process to the complete product life-cycle (Sharfman *et al.* 2009) and firms should be responsible for their products 'from cradle to grave' (Lippman 2001; Kleindorfer *et al.* 2005). Reverse logistics, where a manufacturer accepts previously shipped products or parts for possible recycling, remanufacturing or disposal (Varma *et al.* 2006) is increasingly included in SCM and effectively 'closes the loop'. This final stage is increasingly seen as a competitive necessity and has strong strategic relevance to addressing the environmental dimension in supply chains (Crandall 2006).

Forward and reverse supply chains form a 'closed loop' when managed in a coordinated way and can foster sustainability (Kleindorfer *et al.* 2005). Closed loop supply chains (CLSC) enable the 'cradle-to-cradle' approach by taking back products from customers and recovering added value by re-using the products and/or their components (Guide Jr and Van Wassenhove 2009). They are characterised by the firm's active involvement in the recovery process in order to extend a product's life or manage final disposal (Klassen and Johnson in New and Westbrook 2004). The key goal is to keep all materials within the life-cycle and minimise any flow into the external environment (Sarkis 1995), as illustrated in Figure 3.3. The concept of CLSC is of key importance in addressing the major environmental concern of waste and hazardous materials/processes, as well as generating economic value through extending product life and the re-use/recycling of products (Blumberg 2005).

Waste minimisation and recycling imperatives have placed greater emphasis on product life-cycle approaches (Stokes and Tohamy 2009). Closed loop concepts and life-cycle analysis (LCA) provide an appropriate focus for environmental sustainability research as they apply a more connected and holistic view of supply chains, especially as these approaches have been under-explored to date. A key way to improve sustainability in its true holistic context is to lengthen the life of materials and products. The recycling and re-use of materials can generate additional revenue streams while also reducing the level and cost of waste disposal (Sarkis *et al.* 2010).

Figure 3.3 **Closed loop supply chain**
Source: Sarkis 1995

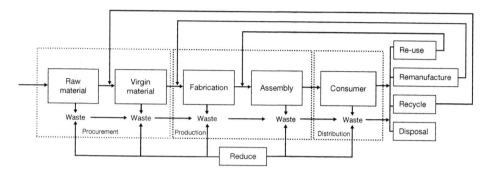

Every product generated, transported, used and discarded within a supply chain has some degree of impact on the environment, and is a function of the material and energy consumed, and wastes released in the product's life-cycle (Tsoulfas and Pappis 2006). A 'green' supply chain is where a firm works with their suppliers to improve the environmental performance of products and processes (Simpson and Power 2005). There are three recognised strategies to managing environmental impact: reactive through minimum 'end of pipe' pollution control; proactive where firms recycle and re-use products and materials within their supply chains and aim to pre-empt new legislation; and value-seeking where environmental behaviour is integrated into the business strategy with a supply network-wide responsibility (van Hoek 1999; Preuss 2005a).

Relationships are key to successful implementation of value-seeking strategies and symmetrical, strategic partnerships focus on long-term, mutually beneficial supply chain alliances with joint goals and knowledge exchange (Forman and Sogaard Jorgensen 2004). This move away from purely transactional relationships produces a stronger and more proactive form of environmental management. Figure 3.4 illustrates the transition from reactive to proactive strategies against different forms of supply chain, and reiterates that a proactive network of committed suppliers is required to achieve sustainability (New and Westbrook 2004). However in line with the sustainability spectrum in Figure 3.2, most current environmental management investment tends to be in 'end-of-pipe' technologies (i.e. a reactive approach) (Vachon and Klassen 2006) as processes and products can remain largely unchanged.

The right supply chain orientation (SCO) can be seen as antecedent to successful SCM, with a firm recognising the systemic and strategic implications of managing the numerous flows in the supply chain (Defee *et al.* 2009). This emphasises that firms applying a systems rather than transactional approach are more likely to successfully address sustainability. SCO also represents a means for firms to compete through the creation of distinctive supply chain capabilities (Mentzer

Figure 3.4 **Approaches to environmental management in supply chains**

Source: UNDERSTANDING SUPPLY CHAINS: CONCEPTS, CRITIQUES AND FUTURES edited by Steve New & Roy Westbrook (2004) Ch. 10 'The Green Supply Chain' by Robert D. Klassen & P. Fraser Johnson pp. 229-251 Figure 10.4 from p. 244. By permission of Oxford University Press, www.oup.com.

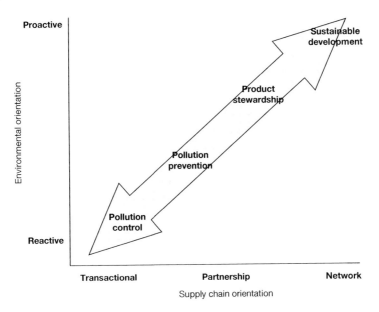

et al. 2001) and strong supplier relationships facilitate the adoption and diffusion of environmentally focused practices (Florida 1996) such as recycling and waste management.

3.5.2 Society

While the environmental dimension focuses on the responsible management of natural resources, social sustainability is concerned with the management of social resources, including people's skills and abilities, institutions, relationships and social values (Sarkis *et al.* 2010). At the business level this requires firms and their suppliers to add value by increasing the human capital of individuals, and the societal capital of communities (Dyllick and Hockerts 2002).

The issue of fair and equitable treatment within supply chains can be addressed through common standards applied by NGOs. The International Labour Organisation (ILO) has an established set of principles, which include aspects of human rights, child and forced labour, employment, wages and training (Leire and Mont 2010). Certification through these bodies is one of the few areas in sustainability research where social issues such as working conditions are explicitly addressed (Pagell and Wu 2009) and can be used to establish a set of social criteria to be applied to the supply chain, with suppliers monitored to ensure compliance (Leire and Mont 2010). Pojasek (2010) specifies the following seven principles of social sustainability which are integral to the ISO 26000 standard for social responsibility: accountability; transparency; ethical behaviour; respect for stakeholder interests; respect for the rule of law; respect for international norms of behaviour; and respect for human rights.

As previously discussed, SCM is of key importance for building strong, long-term relationships with suppliers (Spekman *et al.* 1998) and it also plays an important role in the creation of social capital. Social capital comprises human capital in terms of people's skills, motivation and loyalty, and societal capital which includes education and culture (Dyllick and Hockerts 2002). The relational embeddedness of social capital derived through ongoing interactions with suppliers is increasingly seen as a critical antecedent to firm performance (Bernardes 2010). Sustainable supply chains proactively invest in human capital, for example through HR practices which seek to improve employee well-being and commitment and build a culture that values both people and the environment (Pagell and Wu 2009).

Specific issues that need to be addressed in SSCM include the cooperation and communication between supply chain members which contributes to the required proactive approach highlighted in Figure 3.4; risk management to identify environmental and social problems before they are exposed publicly; and the total life-cycle of a product (Seuring and Muller 2008). This extends to the reconceptualisation of the supply chain by changing what it does, moving towards the closed loop system of Figure 3.3 and thinking differently about who is in the supply chain (Pagell and Wu 2009) and how to interact with them.

While supply chains may be defined as connected systems or networks, academic research to date has focused on the individual stages (Soni and Kodali 2011) with a distinct emphasis on 'hard', measurable processes rather than the less tangible interactions, relationships and flows which are considered key to SSCM (Fabbe-Costes *et al.* 2011). This bias aligns with the weak end of the sustainability spectrum and the transactional form of SCO illustrated in Figure 3.4, and translates to the reactive approach to sustainability which dominates in current practice. While this highlights the difficulty and complexity of managing supply chains sustainably, it also exposes this as an imperative area of research, and the closed loop model (Fig. 3.3) provides a positive means to proactively move towards strong sustainability.

3.6 Sustainability in the clothing industry

The clothing sector is organisationally complex (Forman and Sogaard Jorgensen 2004) and supply chains can be very long with many different parties involved. They are dominated by large, powerful retailers while at the other end are large numbers of small manufacturers with limited power (Bruce *et al.* 2004). The power concentrates in those companies selling products to the end consumers, who increasingly demand customised products within shortening life-cycles (Seuring 2001). Globalisation trends have made supply chains broader and more international (de Brito *et al.* 2008) and the clothing industry has seen the outsourcing of most if not all production activities to overseas suppliers in developing countries (Bergvall-Forsberg and Towers 2007). Traditionally it has been characterised by market coordination on price (Goldbach *et al.* 2003) and this remains a key driver in the selection of suppliers.

There has also been an increasingly 'throwaway' attitude to clothing, especially within the fashion industry, as a result of increased purchase frequency and substantial reductions in pricing (Birtwistle and Moore 2007), which has resulted in an increased rate of garment disposal (Allwood *et al.* 2006). From the estimated 35 kg of clothing and textiles that each UK consumer purchases annually, approximately 75% goes to landfill (de Brito *et al.* 2008) despite the fact that more than 50% of all textiles thrown away are recyclable (Birtwistle and Moore 2007). However there are predictions that there will be a move away from disposable fashion as consumers become increasingly aware of ethical and environmental issues (Goworek 2011), and the economic and environmental benefits of re-use and recycling are increasingly being realised (Birtwistle and Moore 2007).

The clothing industry can be seen as an extreme case for managing environmental issues because of the frequent shifts in product portfolio and its internationally organised product chains that substantially influence and extend the stages where impacts can occur. Suppliers in both developed and developing countries are involved in these extended supply chains adding social and cultural considerations as well as differences between government regulations. Today, not only are environmental standards the focus in clothing supply chains, but also key social issues such as workers' rights, working conditions and child labour (Forman and Sogaard Jorgensen 2004).

3.7 The clothing supply chain

There are seven key clothing supply chain levels: fibre production, which includes growing, harvesting and cleaning of fibres; spinning, where fibres are converted into yarn; weaving or knitting of yarn into fabric; dyeing and finishing of fabric; garment production; and finally the distribution of the finished product to the retailers and then the end customer (Allwood *et al.* 2006). Ecological and social impacts can occur at all of these levels, but at different intensities (Goldbach *et al.* 2003), as illustrated in Figure 3.5.

The greatest environmental impacts in clothing supply chains relate to the use of energy and toxic chemicals, while from the social perspective the concerns are around fair treatment, working conditions, worker rights and child labour (Allwood *et al.* 2006). Clothing production processes make intense use of chemical products and natural resources (land and water), generating a high environmental impact (Fletcher 2008). Furthermore, the search for lower cost production has led to a dramatic relocation of production sites towards the Far East (de Brito *et al.*

Figure 3.5 **Clothing supply chain and its environmental and social impacts**

Fibre production (natural and synthetic)	Spinning Fibre into yarn	Knitting/weaving Yarn into fabric	Wet treatment (washing, dyeing)	Manufacture Finished garments	Distribution To retailer	Consumption By end customer
Land use intensity Water use Resource scarcity Animal welfare Fair pricing	Energy use Waste Labour issues	Energy use Waste Labour issues	Water use Pollution Health and safety	Energy use Waste Labour issues	Carbon emissions/ Greenhouse gases	Product care Product disposal

2008), which brings social and regulation implications. There has been a growing response to many of these supply chain issues and since the 1990s a number of NGOs have been established to actively encourage 'ethical' clothing: for example, the Clean Clothes Campaign, Labour Behind the Label and the Ethical Trading Initiative (Goworek 2011).

In addressing the environmental dimension, organically grown fibres are actively promoted by pro-sustainability organisations (de Brito *et al.* 2008) because of their reduced impact on the environment. Organic cotton became commercially available in the early 1990s (Goworek 2011) and is grown without the use of synthetic pesticides and defoliated by natural means. Interest is increasing in this raw material through the growing awareness of problems of soil toxicity and harmful effects on workers from conventional pesticides. However, despite its positive benefits to the environment and continued growth in the sales of organic cotton products, it still only represents 1% of total world cotton production (Allwood *et al.* 2006).

Fairtrade is a well-developed social practice that, as well as seeking fairer relationships with suppliers, aims to establish more direct relationships between groups of producers and consumers (Barratt Brown 1993). It provides an alternative model of international trade based on better trading conditions and price, as well as educating consumers about the negative effects of traditional trade (Davies and Crane 2010). It has the underlying 'people' principles of good working standards and conditions for workers (Strong 1997); Fairtrade cotton farmers are paid a minimum price plus a premium that contributes to regional development projects (Goworek 2011).

Organic and Fairtrade cotton are the most prominent, recognisable approaches to environmental and social sustainability in the industry, and clear labelling systems exist which communicate these to the consumer. However they relate specifically to the raw material stage of a *natural* fibre and do not explicitly translate their principles along the entire supply chain. The extreme negative impacts of conventional cotton production are well acknowledged and organic and Fairtrade address these issues; however they also echo the current emphasis on the 'greening' of individual processes/products and represent a reactive SCO through the bias towards pollution prevention (see Fig. 3.4). While key environmental problems are being resolved, the lack of coordination means that relationships are still largely transactional in nature, preventing the move towards a more ecocentric approach.

3.8 Are sustainable supply chains achievable?

Recycling and re-use are proactive methods of addressing sustainability and by 'closing the loop' inherently require a more collaborative form of supply chain. They can have a positive impact on a product's life-cycle and address the issue of resource availability which is especially important as virgin resources become scarcer (Sarkis *et al.* 2010). The most well known recycling method utilised in the industry is the conversion of plastic PET bottles into polyester fleece fabric, used by mainstream retailers such as Marks & Spencer. Leading supplier Teijin has extended this technology to allow worn polyester garments to be 100% recycled back into polyester fibre, and they actively promote a closed loop approach.[1] Such life-cycle responsibility aligns with product stewardship and therefore positions Teijin towards a proactive partnership approach to environmental management (Fig. 3.4).

Economies of scale need to be sufficient to make closing the loop viable (Sarkis *et al.* 2010) and the returning of used products by the end consumer is a key issue. It has been effective in the corporate clothing sector as it is feasible for large quantities of used garments to be returned to the fibre producer. However this technology has also extended into the fashion clothing sector with high profile sustainable brand Patagonia operating the Common Threads initiative which encourages re-use, repair and recycling of its products.[2] UK-based Finisterre has built on this closed loop approach offering a repair service for its outdoor clothing customers to ensure maximum product longevity, and will ultimately return garments to Teijin for recycling back into polyester fibre.[3] Both firms have strong brands and a loyal customer base which makes this approach feasible, and involving all supply chain actors through the product life-cycle, including the customer, enables them to achieve a networked ecocentric supply chain strategy.

Finisterre's closed loop model (Fig. 3.6) incorporates all the key clothing supply chain stages, but also recognises the importance of the design function as well as the consumer's role. While recycling and re-use can close the manufacturing loop, the design function is key to making the most responsible and sustainable design decisions *before* the process begins. Design for the Environment (DfE) is a recognised tool which provides an avenue for firms to address the natural environment (Preuss 2005b), and to develop recoverable products which are durable, repeatedly usable, harmlessly recoverable and environmentally compatible in disposal

1 www.teijin.co.jp, accessed 17 September 2012.
2 www.patagonia.com, accessed 17 September 2012.
3 www.finisterreuk.com, accessed 17 September 2012.

Figure 3.6 **Closed loop clothing supply chain**

Source: www.finisterreuk.com

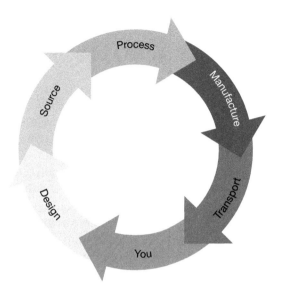

(Tsoulfas and Pappis 2006). The consumer's role is multifaceted as they are responsible for the use, after care and disposal of the finished product, but as Figure 3.6
indicates, their demands and requirements will also influence the design process.

The major challenge in creating sustainable supply chains, especially in such
a complex industry, is not in creating standards or technical measures, but the
management and coordination of all actors (Goldbach *et al.* 2003). Organic cotton, Fairtrade and the recycling of synthetic products into useable raw materials
are all positive recognitions of the importance of operating more responsibly, but
there is a need to move away from changing processes to embedding sustainability
in the relationships that connect the stages and promote supply chain transparency. While collaborative long-term relationships are considered vital for SSCM,
the fashion clothing industry has traditionally been highly transactional in nature
focusing on minimising costs, and while supply chain partnerships exist there
are questions as to whether these are mutually beneficial relationships (Bruce
et al. 2004).

Patagonia was established in the 1970s and grew out of a small company making
tools for climbers. It produces clothing for outdoor sports and activities and is a
recognised industry leader in sustainability. It explicitly puts the planet at the heart
of operations with the mission statement 'build the best product, cause no unnecessary harm, use business to inspire and implement solutions to the environmental
crisis' (Chouinard 2006). It also does business with as few suppliers as possible to
develop long-term, transparent and mutually beneficial relationships. Established
in 2006, Finisterre is a UK surfing lifestyle brand which echoes many of Patagonia's

principles in its approach, aiming to make the best technical apparel with minimal environmental impact. From the beginning, Finisterre has always stood for three points of commitment—product, people and environment—and also focuses on long-term relationships and a fully transparent, traceable supply chain.

Patagonia is a profitable company with sales in excess of $300 million: evidence that all three sustainability dimensions can be balanced. Finisterre is working towards that balance, strongly adhering to its key commitments to establish the brand and product credentials, and will not compromise these for short-term financial benefit. Both firms are particularly committed to the environment, which may contribute to Finisterre's current imbalance, and it positions them towards the ecocentric end of the sustainability spectrum. Their visibility of and commitment to each stage of the product life-cycle and coordinated, committed supplier relationships means they operate at the optimum network SCO necessary for achieving sustainability. However, while both new and long-established clothing brands such as Patagonia and Finisterre show that closed loop chains with strong supplier relationships are achievable, this proactive, responsible supply chain strategy is still far from being the industry norm.

Translating the closed loop model into mainstream, commercial supply chains is an important challenge for the clothing industry and there are signs that the practices of re-use and recycling are becoming sources of added value in supply chains, creating new products from 'waste' (Fletcher 2008). Charitable organisation TRAID Remade[4] reconstructs second-hand clothing into customised one-offs and Junky Styling has applied a similar approach to develop a unique fashion brand from recycled men's suiting.[5] From Somewhere progresses this model from specific customer niches into mainstream retail, transforming 'liability stock', that is, finished fabrics which manufacturers order as a contingency, into affordable fashion clothing which is sold via major retailers. Its recent collaboration with F&F at Tesco has enabled From Somewhere to apply a replicable strategy to a highly commercial supply chain, and illustrates that closed loops can be achieved at a scale to make a tangible impact on the industry as a whole.

3.9 Conclusion

This chapter has set out to review relevant sustainability and supply chain strategy literature to establish current academic viewpoints and has applied these findings to the clothing industry to understand how sustainability and supply chain management (SCM) concepts are being achieved in practice. In today's global marketplace a firm cannot ignore its suppliers' practices and must be acutely aware of stakeholder expectations (Lippman 2001; Handfield *et al.* 2005; Bansal 2005;

---

4 www.traidremade.com, accessed 17 September 2012.
5 www.junkystyling.co.uk, accessed 17 September 2012.

Sharfman *et al.* 2009). Expectations are increasingly focused on environmentally and socially responsible principles and practice which need to extend across the entire supply chain. SCM offers substantial potential for translating sustainability theory into practice, but a persistent gap exists between the diffusion of sustainability discourse and its practical application (Hamdouch and Zuindeau 2010), as well as a lack of impact of research on practice (Ghoshal 2005).

The application of sustainability theory to SCM has only recently started to receive significant academic attention (Sarkis *et al.* 2010), but the alignment of the two concepts offers great potential for gaining a holistic understanding of sustainability in practice. SCM extends organisational boundaries (Frankel *et al.* 2008), and the coordinated, proactive model (Lippman 2001; Kleindorfer *et al.* 2005) that evolves from this aligns strongly with the key principles of sustainability. It requires responsibility for the full life-cycle of a product, and could move the environmental dimension beyond the dominant and reactive 'greening' of supply chain processes.

Closed loop concepts provide a much more appropriate focus for environmental sustainability research as they apply a connected and holistic view of supply chains, and have been under-explored to date in research and practice. The clothing industry is particularly relevant for illustrating the needs, but also the major challenges of closed loop supply chains. In alignment with the research literature, current practice in this industry tends to focus on processes or supply chain stages and therefore only addresses specific environmental or social problems: for example, the use of organic farming methods to address the environmental issues surrounding conventional cotton production. While these are positive actions which can inform practice in other industries, it highlights the difficulty in achieving a coordinated response to sustainability across the supply chain.

The challenge for researchers is to develop appropriate methods and tools to capture the evolving field of sustainable supply chain management (SSCM), and a key research direction is the role and impact of supply chain relationships in achieving sustainability. To fully understand sustainable supply chains there needs to be closer analysis of the relational aspects of SCM and how they can be used to address both environmental *and* social sustainability. SCM literature places emphasis on supplier relationships, but there is limited discussion in the literature on how these can be harnessed to achieve sustainability. This represents a key area for future research; its lack of focus to date suggests the challenge of researching the field from a more holistic viewpoint, but it also offers the greatest potential for progressing SSCM from 'greening' to a 'virtuous circle' that addresses sustainability at all stages and interactions.

Strategically SSCM can provide tangible benefits and value including shorter development cycles, increased revenues and decreased costs, and increased agility and flexibility (Samaranayake 2005; Fawcett *et al.* 2008). There is strategic and competitive advantage in sustainable supply chain behaviours, with the effective management of risk through SCM (Reinhardt 1999) and the tacit knowledge and relational embeddedness from a history of interactions offering the potential of a *sustainable* competitive advantage (Soler *et al.* 2010; Bernardes 2010). Competitive advantage also serves as a powerful driver for organisations moving towards sustainable supply chains/networks (Sharma and Ruud 2003).

The strong relationships with suppliers that can result from SSCM provide the opportunities for environmentally conscious practices: for example redesigning products and processes, reducing waste and controlling pollution (Florida 1996). Long-term relationships also improve a firm's awareness of the social and cultural issues that need to be addressed in a supply chain (Sarkis *et al.* 2010), and can create the level of collaboration, commitment and trust (Varma *et al.* 2006; Attaran and Attaran 2007) required to go beyond the short-termist approaches of prevention and compliance. An emphasis on relationships can enable a shift from the prevailing metaphor of 'greening' to where the holistic nature of sustainability is addressed in the supply chain strategy and concerns the social dimension as much as production and consumption (Preuss 2005a).

There is a major opportunity for future SSCM research to focus on key individual industries such as clothing as sample frames. SSCM can inform clothing supply chain strategy and practice, but how this industry is addressing the multifaceted issues of sustainability can also directly impact how this important research field evolves (Carter and Easton 2011). If social and environmental sustainability can be successfully integrated into clothing supply chains then it will be applicable to practice in other key sectors and industries (Forman and Sogaard Jorgensen 2004). Given the highly inter-disciplinary nature of sustainability it will also inform and develop academic theory beyond supply chain strategy to include governance, legislation and policies, and marketing and branding.

References

Ageron, B., A. Gunasekaran and A. Spalanzani (2011) 'Sustainable Supply Management: An Empirical Study', *International Journal of Production Economics* 111: 2-22.

Allwood, J.M., S.E. Laursen, C. Malvido de Rodriguez and N.M.P. Bocken (2006) *Well-dressed? The Present and Future Sustainability of Clothing and Textiles in the United Kingdom* (Cambridge, UK: Biffaward Programme on Sustainable Resource Reuse, Institute for Manufacturing, University of Cambridge).

Appleton, A.F. (2006) 'Sustainability: A Practitioner's Reflection', *Technology in Society* 28: 3-18.

Attaran, M., and S. Attaran (2007) 'Collaborative Supply Chain Management', *Business Process Management Journal* 13: 390-404.

Bansal (2005) 'Evolving Sustainability: A Longitudinal Study of Corporate Sustainable Development', *Strategic Management Journal* 26: 197-218.

Barney, J.B., and W.S. Hesterley (2008) *Strategic Management and Competitive Advantage: Concepts and Cases* (Upper Saddle River, NJ: Pearson Education Inc).

Barratt Brown, M. (1993) *Fair Trade* (London: Zed Books).

Bergvall-Forsberg, J., and N. Towers (2007) 'Creating Agile Supply Networks in the Fashion Industry: A Pilot Study of the European Textile and Clothing Industry', *Journal of the Textile Institute* 98: 377-85.

Bernardes, E.S. (2010) 'The Effect of Supply Management on Aspects of Social Capital and the Impact on Performance: A Social Network Perspective', *Journal of Supply Chain Management* 46: 45-56.

Birtwistle, G., and C.M. Moore (2007) 'Fashion Clothing: Where Does it All End Up?' *International Journal of Retail and Distribution Management* 35: 210-16.

Blumberg, D.F. (2005) *Introduction to Management of Reverse Logistics and Closed Loop Supply Chain Processes* (Boca Raton, FL: Taylor and Francis).

Bruce, M., L. Daly and N. Towers (2004) 'Lean or Agile: A Solution for Supply Chain Management in the Textiles and Clothing Industry?' *International Journal of Operations & Production Management* 24: 151-70.

Burgess, K., J. Singh and R. Koroglu (2006) 'Supply Chain Management: A Structured Literature Review and Implications for Future Research', *International Journal of Operations & Production Management* 26: 703-29.

Carter, C.R., and P.L. Easton (2011) 'Sustainable Supply Chain Management: Evolution and Future Directions', *International Journal of Physical Distribution & Logistics Management* 41: 46-62.

Carter, C.R., and D.S. Rogers (2008) 'A Framework of Sustainable Supply Chain Management: Moving Toward New Theory', *International Journal of Physical Distribution and Logistics Management* 38: 360-87.

Chouinard, Y. (2006) *Let My People Go Surfing* (New York: Penguin Books).

Crandall, R.E. (2006) 'How Green Are Your Supply Chains?' *Industrial Management* 48: 6-11.

Davies, I.A., and A. Crane (2010) 'Corporate Social Responsibility in Small- and Medium-Sized Enterprises: Investigating Employee Engagement in Fair Trade Companies', *Business Ethics: A European Review* 19: 126-39.

De Brito, M.P., V. Carbone and C.M. Blanquart (2008) 'Towards a Sustainable Fashion Retail Supply Chain in Europe: Organisation and Performance', *International Journal of Production Economics* 114: 534-53.

Defee, C.C., T. Esper and D. Mollenkopf (2009) 'Leveraging Closed-Loop Orientation and Leadership for Environmental Sustainability', *Supply Chain Management: An International Journal* 14: 87-98.

Dempsey, N., G. Bramley, S. Power and C. Brown (2009) 'The Social Dimension of Sustainable Development: Defining Urban Sustainability', *Sustainable Development* 19.5: 289-300.

Dyllick, T., and K. Hockerts (2002) 'Beyond the Business Case for Sustainability', *Business Strategy and the Environment* 11: 130-41.

Fabbe-Costes, N., C. Roussat and J. Colin (2011) 'Future Sustainable Supply Chains: What Should Companies Scan?' *International Journal of Physical Distribution & Logistics Management* 41: 228-52.

Fawcett, S.E., G.M. Magnan and M.W. McCarter (2008) 'Benefits, Barriers, and Bridges to Effective Supply Chain Management', *Supply Chain Management: An International Journal* 13: 35-48.

Fletcher, K. (2008) *Sustainable Fashion and Textiles* (London: Earthscan).

Florida, R. (1996) 'Lean and Green: The Move to Environmentally Conscious Manufacturing', *California Management Review* 39: 80-105.

Forman, M., and M. Sogaard Jorgensen (2004) 'Organising Environmental Supply Chain Management', *Greener Management International* 45: 43-62.

Frankel, R., Y.A. Bolumole, R.A. Eltantawy, A. Paulraj and G.T. Gundlach (2008) 'The Domain and Scope of SCM's Foundational Disciplines: Insights and Issues to Advance Research', *Journal of Business Logistics* 29: 1-30.

Gattorna, J.L., and D.W. Walters (1996) *Managing the Supply Chain: A Strategic Perspective* (Basingstoke, UK: Macmillan Business).

Ghoshal, S. (2005) 'Bad Management Theories are Destroying Good Management Practices', *Academy of Management Learning & Education* 4: 75-91.

Giddings, B., B. Hopwood and G. O'Brien (2002) 'Environment, Economy and Society: Fitting Them Together into Sustainable Development', *Sustainable Development* 10: 187-96.

Gladwin, T.N., J.J. Kennelly and T-S. Krause (1995) 'Shifting Paradigms for Sustainable Development: Implications for Management Theory and Research', *Academy of Management Review* 20: 874-907.

Gold, S., S. Seuring and P. Beske (2009) 'Sustainable Supply Chain Management and Inter-Organisational Resources: A Literature Review', *Corporate Social Responsibility and Environmental Management* 17.4: 230-45.

Goldbach, M., S. Back and S. Seuring (2003) 'Co-ordinating Sustainable Cotton Chains for the Mass Market', *Greener Management International* 43: 65-78.

Goworek, H. (2011) 'Social and Environmental Sustainability in the Clothing Industry: A Case Study of a Fair Trade Retailer', *Social Responsibility Journal* 7: 74-86.

Grinde, J., and A. Khare (2008) 'The Ant, the Grasshopper or Schrodinger's Cat: An Exploration of Concepts of Sustainability', *Journal of Environmental Assessment Policy and Management* 10: 115-41.

Guide Jr, V.D.R., and L.N. van Wassenhove (2009) 'The Evolution of Closed-Loop Supply Chain Research', *Operations Research* 57: 10-18.

Hamdouch, A., and B. Zuindeau (2010) 'Sustainable Development, 20 Years On: Methodological Innovations, Practices and Open Issues', *Journal of Environmental Planning and Management* 53: 427-38.

Handfield, R., and E.L. Nichols (1999) *Introduction to Supply Chain Management* (Upper Saddle River, NJ: Prentice-Hall).

Handfield, R.B., R.P. Sroufe and S. Walton (2005) 'Integrating Environmental Management and Supply Chain Strategies', *Business Strategy and the Environment* 14: 1-19.

Hopwood, B., M. Mellor and G. O'Brien (2005) 'Sustainable Development: Mapping Different Approaches', *Sustainable Development* 13: 38-52.

Hutchins, M.J., and J.W. Sutherland (2008) 'An Exploration of Measures of Social Sustainability and their Application to Supply Chain Decisions', *Journal of Cleaner Production* 16: 1688-98.

Inyang, H.I. (2009) 'Sustaining Sustainability: Approaches and Contexts', *Journal of Environmental Management* 90: 3687-89.

Kleindorfer, R., K. Singhal and L.N. van Wassenhove (2005) 'Sustainable Operations Management', *Production and Operations Management* 14: 482-92.

Lamberton, G. (2005) 'Sustainable Sufficiency: An Internally Consistent Version of Sustainability', *Sustainable Development* 13: 53-68.

Leire, C., and O. Mont (2010) 'The Implementation of Socially Responsible Purchasing', *Corporate Social Responsibility and Environmental Management* 17: 27-39.

Lippman, S. (2001) 'Supply Chain Environmental Management', *Environmental Quality Management*, Winter 2001: 11-14.

Lowson, R.H. (2002) *Strategic Operations Management The New Competitive Advantage* (London: Routledge).

Mahler, D. (2007) 'The Sustainable Supply Chain', *Supply Chain Management Review* 11: 59-60.

Mentzer, J.T., W. Dewitt, J.S. Keebler, M. Soonhoong, N.W. Nix, C.D. Smith and Z.G. Zacharia (2001) 'Defining Supply Chain Management', *Journal of Business Logistics* 22: 1-25.

New, S., and R. Westbrook (2004) *Understanding Supply Chains: Concepts, Critiques and Future* (Oxford, UK: Oxford University Press).

Nilsen, H.R. (2010) 'The Joint Discourse "Reflexive Sustainable Development": From Weak Towards Strong Sustainable Development', *Ecological Economics* 69: 495-501.

Nyaga, G.N., J.M. Whipple and D.F. Lynch (2010) 'Examining Supply Chain Relationships: Do Buyer and Supplier Perspectives on Collaborative Relationships Differ?' *Journal of Operations Management* 28: 101-14.

Orians, G.H. (1990) 'Ecological Concepts of Sustainability', *Environment*, November 1990: 10-39.

Pagell, M., and Z. Wu (2009) 'Building a More Complete Theory of Sustainable Supply Chain Management Using Case Studies of 10 Exemplars', *Journal of Supply Chain Management* 45: 37-56.

Pojasek, R.B. (2010) 'Is Sustainability Becoming a Regulatory Requirement?' *Environmental Quality Management*, Summer 2010: 83-90.

Power, D. (2005) 'Supply Chain Management Integration and Implementation: A Literature Review', *Supply Chain Management: An International Journal* 10: 252-63.

Preuss, L. (2005a) *The Green Multiplier: A Study of Environmental Protection and the Supply Chain* (Basingstoke, UK: Palgrave Macmillan).

Preuss, L. (2005b) 'Rhetoric and Reality of Corporate Greening: A View from the Supply Chain Management Function', *Business Strategy and the Environment* 14: 123-39.

Reinhardt, F.L. (1999) 'Bringing the Environment Down to Earth', *Harvard Business Review* 77: 149-58.

Samaranayake: (2005) 'A Conceptual Framework for Supply Chain Management: A Structural Integration', *Supply Chain Management: An International Journal* 10: 47-59.

Sarkis, J. (1995) 'Manufacturing Strategy and Environmental Consciousness', *Technovation* 15: 79-97.

Sarkis, J., M.M. Helms and A.A. Hervani (2010) 'Reverse Logistics and Social Sustainability', *Corporate Social Responsibility and Environmental Management* 17: 337-54.

Sathiendrakumar, R. (1996) 'Sustainable Development: Passing Fad or Potential Reality?' *International Journal of Social Economics* 23: 151-63.

Seuring, S. (2001) 'Green Supply Chain Costing', *Greener Management International* 33 (Spring 2001): 71-80.

Seuring, S., and M. Muller (2008) 'Core Issues in Sustainable Supply Chain Management: A Delphi Study', *Business Strategy and the Environment* 17: 455-66.

Sharfman, M.P., T.M. Shaft and R.P. Anex Jr (2009) 'The Road to Co-operative Supply-Chain Environmental Management: Trust and Uncertainty Among Pro-Active Firms', *Business Strategy and the Environment* 18: 1-13.

Sharma, S., and A. Ruud (2003) 'On the Path to Sustainability: Integrating Social Dimensions into the Research and Practice of Environmental Management', *Business Strategy and the Environment* 12: 205-14.

Sillanpää, M. (1998) 'A New Deal for Sustainable Development in Business: Taking the Social Dimension Seriously', *Greener Management International* 23: 93-115.

Simpson, D.F., and D. Power (2005) 'Use the Supply Relationship to Develop Lean and Green Suppliers', *Supply Chain Management: An International Journal* 10: 60-68.

Soler, C., K. Bergstrom and H. Shanahan (2010) 'Green Supply Chains and the Missing Link Between Environmental Information and Practice', *Business Strategy and the Environment* 19: 14-25.

Soni, G., and R. Kodali (2011) 'A Critical Analysis of Supply Chain Management Content in Empirical Research', *Business Process Management Journal* 17: 238-66.

Spekman, R.E., J.W. Kamauff Jr and N. Myhr (1998) 'An Empirical Investigation into Supply Chain Management: A Perspective on Partnerships', *Supply Chain Management* 3: 53-67.

Springett, D. (2003) 'Business Conceptions of Sustainable Development: A Perspective from Critical Theory', *Business Strategy and the Environment* 12: 71-86.

Stokes, S., and N. Tohamy (2009) '7 Traits of a Green Supply Chain', *Supply Chain Management Review*, October 2009.

Strong, C. (1997) 'The Role of Fair Trade Principles within Sustainable Development', *Sustainable Development* 5: 1-10.

Svensson, G. (2007) 'Aspects of Sustainable Supply Chain Management (SSCM): Conceptual Framework and Empirical Example', *Supply Chain Management: An International Journal* 12: 262-66.

Tsoulfas, G.T., and C.P. Pappis (2006) 'Environmental Principles Applicable to Supply Chains Design and Operation', *Journal of Cleaner Production* 14: 1,593-1,602.

Udo, V.E., and P.M. Jansson (2009) 'Bridging the Gaps for Global Sustainable Development', *Journal of Environmental Management* 90: 3700-07.

Vachon, S., and R.D. Klassen (2006) 'Green Project Partnership in the Supply Chain: The Case of the Package Printing Industry', *Journal of Cleaner Production* 14: 661-71.

Vachon, S., and Z. Mao (2008) 'Linking Supply Chain Strength to Sustainable Development: A Country Level Analysis', *Journal of Cleaner Production* 16: 1552-60.

Van Hoek, R.I. (1999) 'From Reversed Logistics to Green Supply Chains', *Supply Chain Management* 4: 129-34.

Varma, S., S. Wadhwa and S.G. Deshmukh (2006) 'Implementing Supply Chain Management in a Firm: Issues and Remedies', *Asia Pacific Journal of Marketing and Logistics* 18: 223-43.

WCED (World Commission on Environment and Development) (1987) *Our Common Future* (Oxford, UK: Oxford University Press).

Werbach, A. (2009) 'When Sustainability Means More than Green', *McKinsey Quarterly* 4: 74-79.

With a first degree in Printed Textile Design, **Alison Ashby** has worked in the clothing and textile industry for 18 years in a range of business development and project management roles and has direct experience of implementing sustainability in supply chains. She joined Plymouth Business School in 2009 and is researching a PhD in Sustainable Supply Chains. She has published papers in *Supply Chain Management: An International Journal* and the *International Journal of Environmental, Cultural, Economic and Social Sustainability*.

Mel Hudson Smith is a Lecturer in Operations Management at Plymouth Business School. In addition to teaching operations and supply chain management, her research interests include sustainable supply chains and patient satisfaction in English GP surgeries. She has published in a number of journals including the *International Journal of Operations and Production Management, Production Planning and Control*, the *International Journal of Production Economics* and *Supply Chain Management: An International Journal*.

Rory Shand is Lecturer in Public Policy and Management, and leads on sustainability in teaching on the BSc Public Services, BSc Public Services Management, and in the MSc Public Management. He has recently completed research on the Big Society and Environmental NGOs as well as the governance of regeneration projects in Plymouth, and has published on housing, sustainability and regeneration in the Thames Gateway and in Germany. Rory is Deputy Director of the Sustainability, Leadership, Governance and Policy Research Group (SLGP).

4

Managing chemical risk information

The case of Swedish retailers and Chinese suppliers in textile supply chains*

Kristin Fransson, Birgit Brunklaus and Sverker Molander
Chalmers University of Technology, Sweden

Yuntao Zhang
The Fourth Research and Design Engineering Corporation of CNNC, China

A typical supply chain for textile products is today most likely to be complex and global (Bruce and Daly 2004). According to statistics from the European Union, the value of textiles imported to the EU (€83,000 million) exceeds the value of textiles exported (€33,000 million), and the largest share of textiles imported to the EU comes from China (European Commission 2010). In textile production, a large number of chemicals are used, for instance during cultivation of cotton fibres where herbicides and insecticides are used for plant protection (Rouette 2001). In the wet processing of the cloth, many more or less hazardous substances such as dyestuffs, acids and bases are applied during steps such as dyeing and printing

* This study was financed by the Swedish Research Council for Environment, Agricultural Sciences and Spatial Planning (Formas), which is gratefully acknowledged by the authors. We would also like to thank the companies and organisations participating in this study.

(Lacasse and Baumann 2004). In addition, chemicals can be used to give the cloth specific properties, such as dirt repellence, antibacterial properties, flame retardant properties and crease resistance (Ren 2000). It is thus important for the actors in the supply chain to exchange information about chemicals in order to avoid adverse effects, both in the countries where the textiles are produced and in those where they are used. In general, the flows of information in a supply chain are related to the flows of products and money (Coyle *et al.* 2003), but there are also other flows of information, for instance to and from governments, media and NGOs. In addition, information is exchanged internally in a company, between different companies and organisations, and through books, reports and the Internet. The issue of how chemical information is communicated in a textile supply chain has been addressed by Kogg (2009), who describes the greening process of a cotton textile supply chain at one company, and the work with upstream CSR (corporate social responsibility) including implementation and monitoring of restricted substances at another company. Massey *et al.* (2008) write about the need for information about toxic substances in articles and how the lack of an international system for the management of such information makes it more difficult for actors in the supply chain of, for instance, textiles to make informed decisions regarding chemicals. In a paper by Scruggs and Ortolano (2011), the chemical management strategies of 20 multinational consumer product companies with proactive approaches to chemicals management were investigated.

There is a need for more knowledge on how chemical risk information is handled, especially considering international supply chains. The aim of this chapter is to describe and evaluate the information flows regarding chemicals in global textile supply chains as illustrated by the case of Swedish textile retailers and their Chinese suppliers. The handling and management of chemical risk information by different actors in the textile supply chains were the objects of investigation and analysis.

4.1 Supply chains

A supply chain can be described as a system or a network of organisations, people, technology, activities and resources involved in moving a product or a service from supplier to customer (Nagurney 2006). Hence, supply chain management (SCM) relates to the management of multiple relationships along the supply chain (Lambert and Cooper 2000). When describing a supply chain, one important concept is the so-called 'focal company'. The focal company is generally in direct contact with the consumers and often designs the offered product or service and puts it on the market (Coyle *et al.* 2003; Seuring 2004; Gold *et al.* 2010). The focal company can set requirements for suppliers and sub-suppliers, and is thereby considered an important stakeholder in the supply chain (Pesonen 2001). In addition, it is common that the focal company is the first to face demands from other stakeholder groups, such as authorities, NGOs and the media. Starting from the focal company, a supply chain then includes all companies and organisations that the focal company interacts with, directly or indirectly, through its suppliers and customers (Lambert and Cooper 2000). This implies that supply chains are usually complex networks of suppliers and sub-suppliers and it has been suggested that the complexity of supply chains has increased following the trend of global purchasing (Teuscher *et al.* 2005). A schematic representation of the structure of a supply chain is given in Figure 4.1.

In the supply chain, information transfer is needed in order to link the different stages in the supply chain to each other and allow economic activities to be carried out. Traditionally, information has been viewed as moving upstream, from the focal company to its suppliers and further to sub-suppliers. The information is typically demand and sales data (Lambert and Cooper 2000). Seuring (2004) and Forman and Jørgensen (2004) write that supply chain management is often used in a way that focuses on demands directed at the suppliers and with the objective to bring goods to the customer. In reality, information flows are directed both up- and downstream. Examples of information directed downstream are prices, delivery dates, inventory availability and order status (Lambert and Cooper 2000). Other types of supply chain information seldom mentioned in literature are, for instance, information about the products' quality, appearance and function, probable risks

Figure 4.1 **An illustration of the complexity of a supply chain. Each of the ovals symbolises a company participating in the supply chain. In reality, the supply chains are usually more complex and extensive**
Source: inspired by Kogg 2009

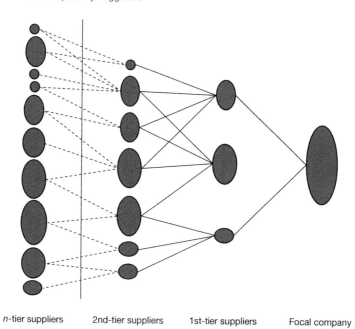

n-tier suppliers   2nd-tier suppliers   1st-tier suppliers   Focal company

with the product as well as social and ecological effects of the production processes. According to Gold *et al.* (2010), the current trend is that companies are more likely to include sustainability aspects in their supply chain management as a response to increasing environmental and ethical awareness. In order to increase the focal company's control and influence over the entire supply chain and decrease the environmental impact, active cooperation with suppliers and sub-suppliers has been indicated as important (Pesonen 2001).

4.2 Textile production

Textile production is a complex process, involving several steps (see Fig. 4.2). The raw fibres can be either natural (e.g. cotton and wool) or synthetic (e.g. polyester and nylon). The yarn is made during the spinning step before the cloth is formed by knitting or weaving. The wet treatment includes processes such as dyeing and printing of the cloth as well as processes intended to give the textile specific functions, such as crease resistance or dirt repellence (Ren 2000; European Commission

Figure 4.2 **Model of the textile supply chain, from fibre production to retailing**

Source: European Commission 2003; Lacasse and Baumann 2004

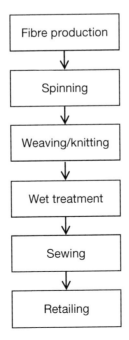

2003). Finally the sewing of the finished product takes place before the textile is transported to the retailers. Cotton cultivation and wet processing stand out as particularly chemical-intensive activities (Lacasse and Baumann 2004; Zhang 2009).

4.3 Different types of chemical risk information

Chemical risk information can be communicated in several ways and lack of information about chemicals has been highlighted as a major obstacle to efficient chemicals management (Commission of the European Communities 2001). For chemicals, safety data sheets (SDSs) are important carriers of risk information, which are supposed to contain relevant information about the substance in order to enable appropriate risk management measures. The content and appearance of SDSs are regulated within the European chemical legislation REACH (Registration, Evaluation, Authorisation and Restriction of Chemicals; European Commission 2006) as well as in the Globally Harmonized System (United Nations Institute for Training and Research 2008).

Communication of information related to chemical risks to consumers is mainly done through labelling. A label is a convenient way for consumers to see if one product is less likely to possess a hazard to human health or the environment than another product and is, for instance, based on more extensive chemical risk information (Blackburn 2009). There are several different labelling systems applicable to textiles. One of the most common labels is Oeko-Tex (International Association for Research and Testing in the Field of Textile Ecology 2009), a 'health' label indicating absence of particular substances in the finished textile. However, information about possible environmental impacts during production is not covered by the Oeko-Tex label. In contrast environmental labels often take the whole life-cycle into account, including all steps from fibre production to finished products. Some examples of environmental labels are the EU Ecolabel (European Commission 2011a), the Nordic Ecolabel (Nordic Ecolabelling 2011), Good Environmental Choice (Swedish Society for Nature Conservation 2011) and the Global Organic Textile Standard (International Working Group on Global Organic Textile Standard 2008).

4.4 Method

The study aimed to describe how companies along the supply chain handle flows of chemical risk information and thus it has been carried out as a case study (Meyer 2001; Yin 2003; Baxter and Jack 2008). The main method for data gathering has been semi-structured interviews (Gillham 2005) with Swedish textile retailers and Chinese textile producers (see Table 4.1 for details of the interviews). The

Table 4.1 **Overview of the respondents and the types of interview used for the study**

Actor	Type of interview	Approximate length of interview	How data was gathered
6 Swedish textile retailers (in total 8 respondents)	Semi-structured	1 hour	Recording
1 Swedish textile retailer	Email interview	N/A	In email
2 Chinese sewing factories	Semi-structured	1 hour	Recording
3 Chinese dyeing/printing factories	Semi-structured	1 hour	Recording

interviews were performed in 2008 and 2009. The Chinese producers were located in Guangdong and Shanghai, the first and fourth largest textile exporting regions in China (Li & Fung Research Centre 2007). For the interviews with Swedish retailers, companies of different size, selling either clothes or home textiles were chosen to get a variety of respondents. The interviewees at the retailing companies were at the time of the interviews all working with chemical or environmental issues in the companies. A majority of them were textile engineers, while a few had a degree in chemical engineering. Through two of the participating Swedish retailers, access to their Chinese suppliers was obtained. The first company (company A) is a Swedish clothes retailer, and their stores can be found in most Swedish shopping malls. They also have stores in a few other countries. Via company A, we gained access to one sewing factory, one printing factory and one dyeing factory in the Guangdong area. The second retailer (company B) is a large, multinational company, selling textiles as part of its assortment. Through company B, we gained access to one sewing factory and one combined dyeing and printing factory in the Shanghai area. At the Chinese factories, several representatives of the factories participated in each interview and in general at least the factory manager, the environmental manager and one administrator were present.

The interviews were recorded with an MP3-player and transcribed. The interviews with Swedish retailers were performed in Swedish and the interviews with Chinese producers in Mandarin; therefore, the quotes used in the text have been translated into English. The texts were analysed through content analysis (Mayring 2000), using inductive category development. The categories were based on the interview guides, including categories such as the type of information that was requested from up- and downstream actors, respectively. Some examples of other categories were the way in which specific actors in the supply chain are influenced by external actors, such as authorities setting up regulation and the media giving attention to certain issues.

Since some of the participating companies wanted to be anonymous, the names of all companies are excluded. One possible bias in the study might be introduced by the voluntary participation of the companies, leading to an inkling that companies that agreed to participate in the study may be more environmentally ambitious than the ones that declined to participate. Therefore, much of the results in this study can be seen as 'best case', but the limited number of participants was not seen as a problem since a majority of the Swedish retailers gave a uniform picture of how the information flows were functioning. However, the interviews with the Chinese suppliers only provide us with two examples of reality, and were probably some of the best examples of textile suppliers.

4.5 Results

The interviews showed two strategies for management of chemicals among the interviewed companies (as illustrated in Fig. 4.3). Most of the interviewed Swedish retailers, including company A's Chinese suppliers in the Guangdong province have the same strategy (strategy A). In contrast, one of the Swedish retailers (company B), including its Chinese suppliers in the Shanghai area, has a considerably different strategy (strategy B) for management of chemicals.

Figure 4.3 **Chemical-related information flows in the studied supply chains. The dotted lines indicate requirements for chemical use and training while the solid lines represent information feedback from textile and chemical producers. 'Greige cloth producers' includes all steps (such as fibre production, spinning and weaving) before dyeing and printing in the supply chains**

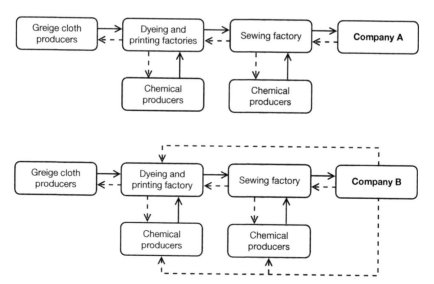

4.5.1 Strategy A

Most of the retailers included in the study have the same approach to managing chemical risks. They communicate their requirements regarding chemicals to their direct suppliers, often in the form of a list of restricted substances.

> This list of restricted chemicals is in the contract we make with the suppliers. They oblige themselves to follow the list. It is involved all the time when we make a business arrangement (respondent from Swedish retailer).

How strict and extensive the chemical requirements are varies somewhat between the different retailers and the list can be influenced by, for instance, the standards of Oeko-Tex and the EU Ecolabel. The most common case is that the list is limited to the chemical content of the final product, since that is what the retailer can control through laboratory tests. The tests are made in independent laboratories mainly in the producing countries and the retailers request the suppliers to send in samples of a specific textile for examination to one of the approved laboratories.

The case of Company A and its suppliers in the Guangdong province, China, can exemplify the strategies of these retailers. Normally, Company A communicates only with its direct suppliers, the sewing factories. In the company's code of conduct, a list of restricted substances is included, and when making a business agreement the sewing factories agree to follow the code of conduct. In addition, Company A arranges training and seminars with its direct suppliers to inform them about chemicals. Many of the respondents, representing Swedish retailers, arrange training with their direct suppliers, because they find it difficult to know whether the suppliers actually understand the reasons for having restrictions on some substances or if they only sign the list in order to be able to sell their products.

> It is important to communicate to make sure there is an understanding about the requirements (respondent from Swedish retailer).

At the direct supplier, the sewing factory, few chemicals are used and instead it has the task of redirecting requirements regarding chemicals to its suppliers, the dyeing and printing factories, since there is no direct communication between them and Company A.

> We only have contact with our direct customers [the sewing factories] (manager at dyeing factory).

The printing and dyeing factory follows the requirements given by Company A without reflecting further on them.

> All we need to do is to find the right chemicals to fulfil our customers' requirements. We don't need to change the chemical use ourselves (manager at printing factory).

The more distanced from Company A the supplier is, the less control there is over compliance since Company A only has direct contact with and control of its direct suppliers, while hazardous chemicals might be used early in the supply chain and then removed through washing before reaching the final supplier. The use of chemicals at the dyeing and printing factory in the supply chain of Company A is instead to a large extent influenced by the Oeko-Tex standard, and the factories buy chemicals that are approved according to Oeko-Tex. The chemical suppliers provide them with most of the information concerning Oeko-Tex. Since the chemicals are approved according to Oeko-Tex, the dyeing and printing factories do not find it necessary to request further chemical risk information such as SDSs. If they want a SDS for some chemical, they need to ask specifically for that from the suppliers, and if the chemical is bought via an agent, it may be a problem for them to obtain the SDS at all.

4.5.2 Strategy B

Company B, one of the interviewed Swedish retailers, has an unusual approach for management of chemicals. Like the other retailers in the study, it has a list of restricted chemicals and randomly checks compliance through laboratory tests. In addition, the company requires its suppliers to provide a list of all chemicals used for production as well as SDSs for these chemicals. The approach started as a measure to control the working environment at the suppliers and sub-suppliers, but has now become a way for the company to control and influence the suppliers' choice of chemicals to use in the manufacturing processes. If the suppliers cannot provide them with SDSs for all chemicals, Company B does not purchase any products from them.

> We give the suppliers clear signals that no SDS—no purchase (Chinese purchasing manager at Company B).

Company B requires its suppliers to have a written plan for procurement, storage and handling of chemicals. In practice, the suppliers need to communicate the demands further to the sub-suppliers. To avoid misunderstandings and information loss, company B now gives out its standard documents to both suppliers and sub-suppliers. Sometimes the company even communicates directly with the chemical producers. In addition, company B arranges training and seminars for its suppliers and sub-suppliers. If one supplier or sub-supplier is planning to make changes in the process, company B requires notification in advance and will decide whether the change is favourable or not.

> A large share of our work is how to communicate requirements, both how we communicate the requirements to our suppliers, and how the requirements are further communicated to the sub-suppliers (Swedish representative for Company B).

Initially, there was a problem with asking for SDSs for all chemicals since the dyeing and printing factory was not provided with them from its chemical suppliers.

However, after a while when the chemical suppliers were getting used to it, the flows of SDSs were functioning well. In addition, there are large differences in the quality and content of chemical risk information given by domestic Chinese chemical suppliers compared with the information given by multinational chemical suppliers:

> The information from big foreign companies is normative; it is formed in a systematic and scientific way. It can introduce the chemical risk in detail, and gives you the information about both the hazards and the way to keep these hazards away. Compared to the information given by foreign companies, the domestic producers normally provide very simple information; and are mainly about how to use the chemicals (engineer at dyeing and printing factory in supply chain of Company B).

4.5.3 Legislation

Regulations are important for influencing decision-making in the supply chain. Although Chinese regulations for management of hazardous chemicals exist (China's Academy of Safety Production 2005), the findings from the study show that implementation of this legislation is mainly concentrated on controlling wastewater discharge from industry. This has influenced the textile producers' selection of chemicals. Such legislation influences the producers to use chemicals that may leave lower concentrations in the wastewater. Most of the regulations concerning chemicals in China are less onerous than in the EU (Beyer 2006; Rooij 2006) and, according to the interviews, many of the Chinese textile suppliers consider EU standards to be hard to reach. The EU chemical legislation REACH (European Commission 2006) is given more attention by the European retailers than the Chinese producers since in practice the producers are not really affected by REACH. Instead REACH concerns chemical producers, particularly European chemical producers operating on the Chinese market. The retailers on the other hand have to be informed of the requirements in the legislation in order to set demands on their producers if necessary.

4.6 Discussion

The general impression is that information regarding chemical risks is only communicated to the next tier up- or downstream in the supply chain. One disadvantage with this way of working is that information might be lost or misunderstood between the different tiers in the supply chain and some of the retailers regard this as a problem:

> Since we do not own the factories, there is a problem for us to know what they use in the production. We do not have that information, and often our suppliers are only the sewing factories. They might have bought a textile from a sub-supplier. Since we do not have a business relation with

that sub-supplier, it is very difficult for us to get information from the wet processes where most of the chemicals are used... We would like to have a plan to follow this upstream, but we have not yet found the right way for this (representative from one Swedish retailer).

We set requirements on what is allowed in the final product, because that is what we can test for and follow up. We haven't yet come so far that we are able to control what is used during production (representative from another Swedish retailer).

These answers indicate that there is an ambition among some of the importing companies to change the way they receive information about chemicals used in the process, although they do not yet have the right tools and knowledge for implementation. According to Ganesan *et al.* (2009), retailers are increasingly working with managing their entire supply chains. This trend, with better control over and knowledge about the sub-suppliers, might in the long run lead to improved chemicals management in the supply chains. However, according to Scruggs and Ortolano (2011), only a few companies examine the chemical use in their supply chains thoroughly in order to obtain knowledge on all chemicals used in production. These companies do it on a voluntary basis in order to avoid or reduce hazardous chemicals in their products and supply chains.

As a measure to better control articles containing chemicals imported to the EU, it has been suggested that regulations for chemicals in articles (e.g. textiles) should be included in REACH (Rudén and Hansson 2010; Swedish Chemicals Agency 2011). Some interviewees from the retailing companies think that more information on which chemicals are used in the production process or a list of content on the final product would be beneficial. However, there are interviewees who do not think this would be favourable. 'I don't think complete declarations of contents on the products are the right way to go' (respondent from one Swedish retailer).

When comparing the strategies of the two supply chains included in this study, Company A and Company B, several differences can be observed. The most obvious difference is that Company A limits the contact with suppliers to the first tier level while Company B expands the communication to include sub-suppliers and chemical producers. According to Walton *et al.* (1998), this communication with second-tier suppliers is crucial for companies with high environmental ambitions. Another beneficial action for Company B is that it disseminates its standards throughout the whole supply chain, thereby avoiding standard violations due to misunderstandings and information loss. To check compliance with the requirements, Company A makes laboratory tests on random products while Company B practices a more integrated chemical risk management and requires its suppliers to communicate chemical use and SDSs. To test only the final product may be an indication that the focal company is only focusing on the end product, thus having little interest in the production process. The chemical risk management strategy used by Company B, also including companies further upstream in the supply chain, is in many ways favourable since it gives Company B a more transparent view of the suppliers and opens up possibilities for improvements in the use of chemicals. However, for the focal company to change the chemical management of the entire supply chain demands a lot of effort and may be costly and time consuming (Scruggs and Ortolano 2011). Therefore, it can be easier for a large company to make changes since it often has great leverage in the supply chain and the economic resources to work actively with chemical management. According to Ohashi *et al.* (2005), it is more probable that risk-related chemical information is lost in small- and medium-sized companies (SMEs) than in large companies. This would mean that the risk of information loss is larger in Company A's supply chain, in which most of the suppliers are SMEs, than in the supply chain of Company B, in which most of the suppliers are large companies. In addition, Company A is considerably smaller than Company B even though both companies are far larger than a SME according to the definition from the European Commission (2011b).[1]

For foreign retailers in China, training and education of their suppliers is important since China is still in the learning phase of environmental management and thus in need of deeper knowledge and understanding. It has also been suggested that the pressure from customers is important for companies to engage in better environmental management (Zhang *et al.* 2008). For retailers, it is important to narrow the understanding gaps. The sub-suppliers in Company B's supply chain think that the leverage of purchasing can be used to force the chemical producers to begin working with chemical information management. There is also a difference between Chinese and European chemical producers regarding the type and amount of chemical risk information. This is mainly due to weak local legislation. Between the chemical producers and the dyeing and printing factories, the chemical information is more focused on quality and performance of the product than on risks related to the chemicals.

4.7 Conclusions

The aim of this study was to describe and evaluate the flows of chemical risk information in a textile supply chain with a focus on Chinese producers and Swedish retailers.

It was common for Swedish retailers to communicate with Chinese suppliers in terms of a list of specific restricted substances that suppliers pledge to follow. The requirements on the lists are often limited to the chemical content of the final product because the retailers are more concerned about chemical risks related to the use phase. In addition, it is easier to control the content of chemicals in the final product through laboratory tests. In general, the chemical-related information is only communicated one step up or down the supply chain. One problem, related to the fact that focal companies do not communicate with the whole supply chain,

---

1 An SME is defined as a company with less than 250 employees and a turnover lower than €50 million (European Commission 2011b).

is the increasing risk for misunderstandings and misinterpretations. Textile supply chains are particularly vulnerable to these types of risk since sub-suppliers, not in direct contact with the retailers, use most of the chemicals in the production process. In order to support suppliers to better understand the requirements, retailers arrange training activities for those suppliers.

One of the retailers and its suppliers visited in the Shanghai area exhibits an unusual approach to chemicals management. The retailer's representatives have access to SDSs of all chemicals included in the production processes, and can trace their textile products all the way back to the cotton field. Most of the communication is between the retailer and the direct suppliers but, in addition, the retailer has contact with sub-suppliers and chemical producers. Different types of labelling programme are additional tools for importers and suppliers to communicate about chemicals. Labels such as Oeko-Tex are seen as valuable by the suppliers as instruments to increase the competitive power of Chinese textile products.

As a motivation for action, ambitious and effectively implemented laws and regulations have a crucial role. However, today, retailers often have more stringent requirements than local legislation demands regarding chemicals. To achieve a better management of chemicals throughout the supply chain, importers are recommended to expand their contact to more actors upstream in the supply chain.

References

Baxter, P., and S. Jack (2008) 'Qualitative Case Study Methodology: Study Design and Implementation for Novice Researchers', *The Qualitative Report* 13.4: 544-59.

Beyer, S. (2006) 'Environmental Law and Policy in the People's Republic of China', *Chinese Journal of International Law* 5.1: 185-211.

Blackburn, R.S. (2009) *Sustainable Textiles: Life Cycle and Environmental Impact* (Manchester: Woodhead Publishing).

Bruce, M., and L. Daly (2004) 'Lean or Agile: A Solution for Supply Chain Management in the Textiles and Clothing Industry?', *International Journal of Operations & Production Management* 24.2: 151-70.

China's Academy of Safety Production (2005) *Selection of Regulations about Hazard Chemicals* (Beijing: Chemical Industry Press, in Chinese).

Commission of the European Communities (2001) *White Paper: Strategy for a Future Chemicals Policy* (Brussels: Commission of the European Communities).

Coyle, J.J., E.J. Bardi and C.J. Langely, Jr (2003) *The Management of Business Logistics: A Supply Chain Perspective* (Mason, OH: South-Western, Thomson Learning, 7th edn).

European Commission (2003) *Integrated Pollution Prevention and Control: Reference Document on Best Available Techniques for the Textiles Industry* (Seville: European IPPC Bureau).

European Commission (2006) 'Regulation (EC) No 1907/2006 of the European Parliament and of the Council of 18 December 2006 concerning the Registration, Evaluation, Authorisation and Restriction of Chemicals (REACH), Establishing a European Chemicals Agency, amending Directive 1999/45/EC and repealing Council Regulation (EEC) No 793/93 and Commission Regulation (EC) No 1488/94 as well as Council Directive 76/769/EEC and Commission Directives 91/155/EEC, 93/67/EEC, 93/105/EC and 2000/21/EC', *The European Parliament and the Council of the European Union, Official Journal of the European Union* L396/1.

European Commission (2010) 'Textiles and Clothing Statistics', www.ec.europa.eu/enterprise/textile/statistics.htm, accessed 19 November 2010.

European Commission (2011a) 'EU Eclolabel', www.ec.europa.eu/environment/ecolabel/index_en.htm, accessed 12 October 2011.

European Commission (2011b) 'Small and Medium-Sized Enterprises (SMEs)', www.ec.europa.eu/enterprise/policies/sme/facts-figures-analysis/sme-definition/index_en.htm, accessed 2 January 2012.

Forman, M., and M.S. Jørgensen (2004) 'Organising Environmental Supply Chain Management. Experience From a Sector with Frequent Product Shifts and Complex Products Chains: The Case of the Danish Textile Sector', *Greener Management International* 45: 43-62.

Ganesan, S., M. George, S. Jap, R.W. Palmatier and B. Weitz (2009) 'Supply Chain Management and Retailer Performance: Emerging Trends, Issues, and Implications for Research and Practice', *Journal of Retailing* 85.1: 84-94.

Gillham, B. (2005) *Interviewing: The Range of Techniques* (Maidenhead, UK: McGraw-Hill Education).

Gold, S., S. Seuring and P. Beske (2010) 'Sustainable Supply Chain Management and Inter-Organizational Resources: A Literature Review', *Corporate Social Responsibility and Environmental Management* 17.4: 230-45.

International Association for Research and Testing in the Field of Textile Ecology (2009) *OEKO-TEX Standard 100, General and Special Conditions* (Zürich, Switzerland: International Association for Research and Testing in the Field of Textile Ecology).

International Working Group on Global Organic Textile Standard (2008) *Global Organic Textile Standard Version 2.0* (Pfullingen, Germany: International Working Group on Global Organic Textile Standard).

Kogg, B. (2009) *Responsibility in the Supply Chain* (Lund, Sweden: The International Institute for Industrial Environmental Economics, Lund University).

Lacasse, K., and W. Baumann (2004) *Textile Chemicals: Environmental Data and Facts* (Berlin: Springer-Verlag).

Lambert, D.M., and M.C. Cooper (2000) 'Issues in Supply Chain Management', *Industrial Marketing Management* 29: 65-83.

Li & Fung Research Centre (2007) 'Apparel Production and Cluster Development in China', *Industry Series* 10: 1-12.

Massey, R.I., J.G. Hutchins, M. Becker and J. Tickner (2008) *Toxic Substances in Articles: The Need for Information* (Copenhagen: Nordic Council of Ministers).

Mayring, P. (2000) 'Qualitative Content Analysis', *Forum Qualitative Sozialforschung/Forum: Qualitative Social Research* 1.2.

Meyer, C.B. (2001) 'A Case in Case Study Methodology', *Field Methods* 13.4: 329-52.

Nagurney, A. (2006) *Supply Chain Network Economics: Dynamics of Prices, Flows and Profits* (Cheltenham, UK: Edward Elgar Publishing).

Nordic Ecolabelling (2011) 'The Nordic Ecolabel', www.nordic-ecolabel.org/, accessed 12 October 2011.

Ohashi, T., K. Kasagi and T. Niihara (2005) 'Identification of Problems Associated with Exchanging Information across a Product Supply Chain for Chemicals Risk Management', paper presented at *Environmentally Conscious Design and Inverse Manufacturing, 2005. Eco Design 2005. Fourth International Symposium*, 12–14 December 2005.

Pesonen, H.-L. (2001) 'Environmental Management of Value Chains: Promoting Life-Cycle Thinking in Industrial Networks', *Greener Management International* 33: 45-58.

Ren, X. (2000) 'Development of Environmental Performance Indicators for Textile Process and Product', *Journal of Cleaner Production* 8.6: 473-81.

Rooij, B.v. (2006) 'Implementation of Chinese Environmental Law: Regular Enforcement and Political Campaigns', *Development and Change* 37.1: 57-74.

Rouette, H.-K. (2001) *Encyclopedia of Textile Finishing* (Berlin: Springer).

Rudén, C., and S.O. Hansson (2010) 'Registration, Evaluation, and Authorization of Chemicals (REACH) is but the First Step: How Far Will it Take Us? Six Further Steps to Improve the European Chemicals Legislation', *Environmental Health Perspectives* 118.1: 6-10.

Scruggs, C.E., and L. Ortolano (2011) 'Creating Safer Consumer Products: The Information Challenges Companies Face', *Environmental Science and Policy* 14.6: 605-14.

Seuring, S. (2004) 'Integrated Chain Management and Supply Chain Management Comparative Analysis and Illustrative Cases', *Journal of Cleaner Production* 12.8-10: 1,059-71.

Swedish Chemicals Agency (2011) *Action Plan for a Toxic-Free Everyday Environment English Summary of a Government Assignment* (Sundbyberg, Sweden: Swedish Chemicls Agency).

Swedish Society for Nature Conservation (2011) 'Good Environmental Choice', www.natur skyddsforeningen.se/bra-miljoval/in-english/about-bra-miljoval, accessed 12 October 2011.

Teuscher, P., B. Grüninger and N. Ferdinand (2005) 'Risk Management in Sustainable Supply Chain Management (SSCM): Lessons Learnt from the Case of GMO-Free Soybeans', *Corporate Social Responsibility and Environmental Management* 13: 1-10.

United Nations Institute for Training and Research (2008) *Understanding the Globally Harmonized System of Classification and Labelling of Chemicals (GHS)* (Geneva, Switzerland: Chemicals and Waste Management Programme).

Walton, S.V., R.B. Handfield and S.A. Melnyk (1998) 'The Green Supply Chain: Integrating Suppliers into Environmental Management Processes', *International Journal of Purchasing and Materials Management*, Spring 1998: 2-11.

Yin, R.K. (2003) *Case Study Research: Design and Methods* (Thousand Oaks, CA: Sage Publications).

Zhang, B., J. Bi, Z. Yuan, J. Ge, B. Liu and M. Bu (2008) 'Why Do Firms Engage in Environmental Management? An Empirical Study in China', *Journal of Cleaner Production* 16.10: 1036-45.

Zhang, Y. (2009) *Chemical Information in Two Textile Supply Chains: A Case Study of Producers in China* (Gothenburg, Sweden: Chalmers University of Technology).

Kristin Fransson has a background in chemical engineering and is now a PhD candidate in Environmental Systems Analysis. Her main research topic is chemical risk information and how it is communicated in the supply chains of consumer products.

Birgit Brunklaus is a senior researcher within the area of LCA-based methods, environmental management and organisation theory. She holds a research assistant position researching life-cycle management, which includes LCA method development and actors in supply chains. As a researcher she has been working with actors in the building and food industry.

Sverker Molander is a professor in Environmental Systems Analysis and has been working with information systems for impact assessment of chemicals. His background in environmental and systems sciences also includes development of environmental risk assessment methods and studies of risks related to emerging technologies, such as engineered nanoparticles.

Yuntao Zhang has a background in environmental science and has a Master's degree in Environmental Assessments and Measurements. The theme of his Master's degree work was 'Information flow in the textile supply chain'.

5

Innovation power of fashion focal companies and participation in sustainability activities in their supply network

Harrie W.M. van Bommel
Saxion University of Applied Sciences, the Netherlands

During recent decades, the fashion/clothing sector has become an extremely complex global supply network. Garment production is mainly located in Asia, while many consumers live in Europe and the United States. In addition, materials (fibres) are bought on the world market. At the same time sustainability has become an important topic in the sector. It seems that companies no longer wonder whether or not to manage social and environmental aspects in their supply network but rather how to do so.

Several organisations have developed competing labels (product-related), guidelines, codes of conduct and certification schemes (organisation-related) to improve the performance of social and environmental aspects in the supply network. Approaches differ greatly, from cooperation to standardisation and coordination (Forman and Sogaard Jorgensen 2004; Søndergård *et al.* 2004; Allwood *et al.* 2007; De Brito *et al.* 2008; Profas 2008).

However, present activities seem to be building on ad hoc decisions and it is hard to distinguish systematic patterns and rational strategies. We do not yet understand sufficiently how global supply chains develop and how sustainable development is integrated in them. The Investment Climate Department of the World Bank Group (World Bank 2003) also concluded that the existing system of implementing corporate social responsibility (CSR) in global supply chains may be reaching its limits in terms of its ability to deliver further sustainable improvements in social and environmental standards. Also the International Chamber of Commerce (2007) along with the Dutch Social and Economic Council (2008) have asked for more attention concerning the implementation of sustainability in supply networks.

This chapter reports on a study that addresses this issue in the fashion/clothing industry. Empirical research, based mainly on surveys and case studies, has up till now not succeeded in developing a strong theoretical basis. The frameworks found in the literature (for instance Sarkis 2003; Seuring and Müller 2008) are mainly descriptive, focusing on the pressures and incentives or the strategies and activities found in practice. Rarely do they address the question of why companies facing similar pressures and incentives choose different ambition levels, strategies and related activities. This process of strategy formulation and implementation is, therefore, mostly unexplored.

This chapter explores the empirical relationship between innovation characteristics of focal companies and the implementation strategy towards sustainability in their supply network. It starts by describing a conceptual framework that integrates innovation characteristics as important factors for analysing the different strategies found. Basically, this chapter reports on testing the propositions that were formulated on the basis of this framework in the fashion/clothing sector (Van Bommel 2011). This sector was selected because it is a well-known global industrial supply network, which faces a diverse set of sustainability aspects with many competing initiatives for improving these aspects. It, therefore, very well illustrates the complex relationship between the different aspects in the conceptual framework found in practice.

The structure of the chapter is as follows. After the presentation of the conceptual framework, the methodological approach of the survey is discussed. Next the 11 selected sustainability activities in the fashion/clothing sector are explained briefly. The results of the survey are presented and analysed, conclusions are drawn and recommendations for further research are formulated.

5.1 A new conceptual framework

Based on qualitative literature research in environmental, social/ethical and logistics/operations management journals a conceptual framework for analysing the implementation of sustainability in global industrial supply networks has been developed (Van Bommel 2011). Often external pressures are put forward as the main explanatory factors for sustainability strategies. Based on the assumption that the implementation of sustainability can be seen as a system innovation in our framework, the focus is not the external pressure but the innovation characteristics of the 'focal' company and the cooperative characteristics of its supply network. A 'focal' company is defined as a company that has the possibility to influence changes in its supply network.

The framework presented in Figure 5.1 distinguishes: pressures and incentives (**innovation pressure**); innovation characteristics of the 'focal' company and the cooperative characteristics of the supply network (**innovation power**); and the strategies, activities and performance (**innovation results**).

The pressures and incentives are represented by factors such as customer demands, response to stakeholders, competitive advantage, pressure groups and reputation loss. The relevance of these pressures and incentives will be closely related to the specific sector, product, service and the supply network. These factors are seen as context characteristics. Besides pressure from the market and consumers, pressure also comes from new government policies such as extended producer responsibility and integrated product policy (Scheer and Rubik 2006).

The capability to respond to this innovation pressure is supposed to be determined by the level of innovation power. This power is based on the innovation

Figure 5.1 **Implementation of sustainability in supply networks from an innovation perspective**

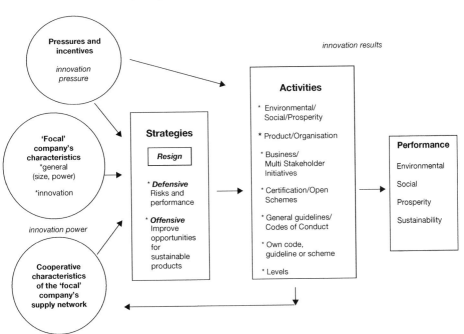

characteristics of the 'focal' company itself and the cooperative characteristics of the supply network (Omta 2002, 2004). By recognising the dominant innovation and cooperative characteristics, the selected strategy and related activities for the implementation of sustainability in the supply network might be better explained and understood.

The resulting activities can be divided into two categories: 'product' related and 'organisation' related. Well-known examples of a 'product'-related approach are the product labels concerning a specific sustainability (often environmental) aspect. 'Organisation'-related activities employ management systems to ensure that the specific sustainability aspects are managed properly in the organisation. Focal companies use these systems in their own organisation but will also increasingly demand the same activities from partners in their supply network.

The propositions based on the framework (Van Bommel 2011) state that a focal company with a low level of innovation power will participate in fewer and mainly defensive sustainability activities while focal companies with a high(er) level of innovation power will preferably participate in more proactive activities. The survey was performed to test this relationship between the level of innovation power in the focal company and the participation in sustainability activities in its supply network.

5.2 Methodology

The empirical research was carried out by an online survey among 91 fashion/clothing 'focal' companies in the Netherlands in April/May 2010. The survey was prepared and undertaken in cooperation with the Dutch trade association for fashion, interior design, carpets and textiles (MODINT 2010). The companies selected for the survey have participated in a survey conducted by MODINT before and can be seen as frontrunners on sustainability in the sector. They recognise sustainability as an important issue and participate in several competing sustainability activities. This is an important precondition for the research since companies need to be active in sustainability in order to investigate why their strategies differ. How the innovation characteristics of these 'focal' companies are related to the implementation strategies and activities found has never been looked at.

The survey contained four clusters of questions: 'general aspects'; 'influencing factors'; 'innovation power'; and 'sustainability activities'.

The questions concerning the **general aspects** were: turnover of the company in 2008; number of employees in the Netherlands; the location of the headquarters; and the business model (one out of seven) that characterises the company best. These models represent the different phases of the supply network—design, production, distribution and retail—as can be seen in Table 5.1.

Table 5.1 **Business models of fashion/clothing companies and the phases of the supply network**

Business model	Phase of the supply network			
	Design	Production	Distribution	Retail
Column-company				
Head-tail company				
Private label				
Brand				
Subcontractor				
Network company				
Retail company				

Only the column-company covers all four phases, including production, while it is assumed that control over the production phase is crucial for managing sustainability in the supply network.

The second cluster of questions asked to which extent 12 **factors influence** the attention paid to social and environmental aspects in the supply network. The five levels they could choose from were 'no influence' to 'very much influence' (score 1–5). The 12 factors selected were: 'personal motivation of management', 'reduction of costs', 'risk loss of reputation', 'pressure from NGOs', 'competition in the market', 'request from shareholders/owner', 'wanting to have a positive image', 'request/demand from partners in the supply network', 'demand from consumers', 'government by education and subsidies', 'government by agreements and covenants' and 'government by legislation'.

To measure the **innovation power** of the company (third cluster of questions) 30 statements representing six categories of innovation characteristics were used. The contact person was asked to give a score (on a five-point scale from 'fully agree' to 'fully disagree') for the extent to which the statement presented was applicable to the company as a whole. The six categories of innovation characteristics were: 'external orientation'; 'cooperation'; 'learning'; 'leadership'; 'autonomy'; and 'result driven' (Brooke 2006).

The fourth cluster of questions presented 11 **sustainability activities** (social and environmental) in the fashion/clothing sector. Measurement of strategies is hard because strategies are often not made explicit. Therefore it was determined to measure participation in activities and not strategies. Participation in sustainability activities will indeed reflect an often implicit strategy. Based on the results of a test of the questionnaire it was decided to include 11 activities. The respondent was asked if the organisation was familiar with the activity. If so, they were asked if they had joined the activity. When the answer was no, they were asked if they thought they might join this activity in the short term, in the near future or not at all. In the next section all 11 activities are explained briefly.

5.3 Selected sustainability activities in the supply networks of the fashion/clothing sector

The 11 sustainability activities that were selected for the survey can be categorised in four groups: the environmental/product-related group which includes four activities; the environmental/organisational group with two activities included; the social group with three activities; and the group 'others' which includes two activities.

The four environmental/product-related activities were GOTS (Global Organic Textile Standard), EKO, EU Ecolabel and Oeko-Tex. The label that is used to guarantee that cotton is produced organically (without pesticides and fertiliser) is **Organic Exchange**, certified by GOTS (2009). A Dutch initiative certifying the ecological conditions for the production of agricultural crops uses the **EKO logo**. It is well known for vegetables but also used for natural fibres in textiles (SKAL 2009). The **EU Ecolabel** was introduced by the European Union. The latest version of the ecological criteria for the award of the Community Ecolabel for textile products was published in 2009 (EU 2009). The criteria focus on the use of sustainable fibres, the durability and quality of the material and the restricted hazardous substances. The **Oeko-Tex Standard 100** is an international testing and certification system for textiles, limiting the use of certain chemicals. It was developed in 1992. The criteria used are developed based on the latest scientific findings concerning human ecological safety. At first the focus was mainly the safety (health) of the consumer using/wearing the textile/clothes. More recently and also indirectly the standard has included the environmental impacts of the life-cycle of textile materials and products (Oeko-Tex 2012).

Besides the environmental impact of the product/material itself, the level of environmental management in the organisations that are part of the supply network can also be looked at. Therefore two activities in the environmental/organisation group were included in the survey. They were the use of ISO 14001 and participation in recycling projects.

The international standard for **environmental management** (ISO 14001) can be introduced in the focal company's own organisation but also be demanded in the organisation of suppliers (Nawrocka *et al.* 2009). In the survey only this second element was included.

Besides the responsibility for the environmental aspects of the suppliers, 'focal' companies are increasingly feeling responsible for the environmental impacts at the end of the life-cycle of their products. Until recently, recycling of clothes was not a regular activity for 'focal' companies. Now recycling projects for fashion/clothes are being developed and the 'focal' companies are becoming involved.

The three selected activities concerning the social aspects of the supply network were SA8000, BSCI and FWF. The standard with the highest performance level on social aspects is the **SA8000** (Leipziger 2001; Stigzelius and Mark Herbert 2008). This certifiable standard is rarely adhered to in the fashion/clothing sector mainly because the high standard is difficult to meet and the costs for certification are high. Therefore, several other social initiatives, without certification, exist. The **Business Social Compliance Initiative** (BSCI 2009) is a business programme in Europe. The programme is not specific for the fashion or clothing sector, and without certification. In practice, many fashion and clothing companies join this initiative. It is an example of an 'open' scheme initiative. Participants promise to improve the social aspects and maintain transparent activities and results. Besides the certification scheme of SA8000 and the open business scheme of BSCI, several 'open' multi-stakeholder initiatives (MSIs) have been developed concerning the social aspects. Within these initiatives, the different stakeholders (for example the businesses, sector organisation, trade unions, consumer and human rights organisations) are represented, which creates public support. During the test of the questionnaire, several MSIs were included. After testing only the Dutch/European multi-stakeholder initiative **Fair Wear Foundation** (FWF 2009) remained in the survey because the others (from the UK and US) were hardly known.

Besides the nine environmental and social activities outlined above, two other activities were included in the survey. **Fairtrade** is a label used to show the consumer that an honest price has been paid to the producer. It is a well-known label for products such as coffee and bananas, but it is also being used for textiles, clothes and fashion. **Made-By** (Made-By 2008 and 2009) is a European non-profit organisation that assists fashion companies to improve social and environmental conditions in their supply network. Companies can become a Made-By partner brand and show that to the consumer with the Blue Button Label. With score-cards and a track and trace system they exchange information with other brands and the consumers.

5.4 Results

Forty-four out of 91 companies (48%) responded and 29 (31%) of them answered all questions. The answers given to the questions concerning the general aspects of the company are shown in Table 5.2.

Table 5.2 **Number of employees, owning the design and production phase by the respondents**

	Number of respondents (of 44)	**Number of respondents that answered all questions (of 29)**
Less than 50 employees*	28	22
Owning the design phase	37	25
Do *not* own the production phase	32	20

* Small and medium-sized enterprises (SMEs)

The results show that the respondents are mainly small- and medium-sized enterprises. The answers concerning the business models show that 85% of the respondents own the design phase and 75% of the respondents do *not* own the production phase. Owning the design phase means that they have the possibility to influence changes in the supply network (being a 'focal' company) but at the same time for controlling environmental and social aspects in the production phase they depend on others. This makes the sample a valid one for testing the proposition.

The answers given to the questions concerning the level of influence for the 12 influencing factors show that all factors are seen as being relevant by the respondents (the mean score for all factors is more than 3 on a scale of 1–5; N = 31). The differences found between the levels of influence given to the social versus the environmental activities was shown to be very small. No factor appeared to be *the* dominating external factor. This result supports the statement that the external pressure to pay attention to sustainability in supply networks is strong and is influenced by many different factors at the same time. The strong diffuse external pressure explains why focal companies act but they do not explain which strategy will be selected.

The variety of the scores given to the 30 statements in the questionnaire concerning the innovation characteristics of the focal company shows a clear differentiation between medium and high scores. Low scores were hardly found so the respondents appear to have medium to high innovation capacity/ power.

The differentiation in the scores enables us to test the proposition about the relationship between these levels and participation in sustainability activities. The aggregations of the scores and the results of the analysis are presented in the next section. The answers given to the questions concerning the 11 selected sustainability activities are shown in Table 5.3 (N = 29).

The number of respondents that said that the activity was known in the organisation is shown in black (first row). The number that actually joins the activity is shown in dark grey (second row) and the number that might join the activity in the short term or in the near future is shown in light grey (second row).

The results show that the 11 sustainability activities are all well-known (more then 10 out of 29 respondents) and also many respondents are participating in these activities (or planning to). These results confirm that the respondents are frontrunners in the sector. As previously stated, this was one of the reasons for selecting this group of companies within the sector. Yet, within this group of frontrunners there is still a relatively wide range of strategies found. This raises the question of why there is such a wide diversity in responses when the external context and external pressures are very similar. To investigate this, the hypothesis regarding the relationship with the innovation characteristics was tested. These analyses are presented in the next section.

Table 5.3 Acquaintance with, participation and possible participation in the near future in sustainability programmes and activities in the fashion/clothing sector (N = 29)

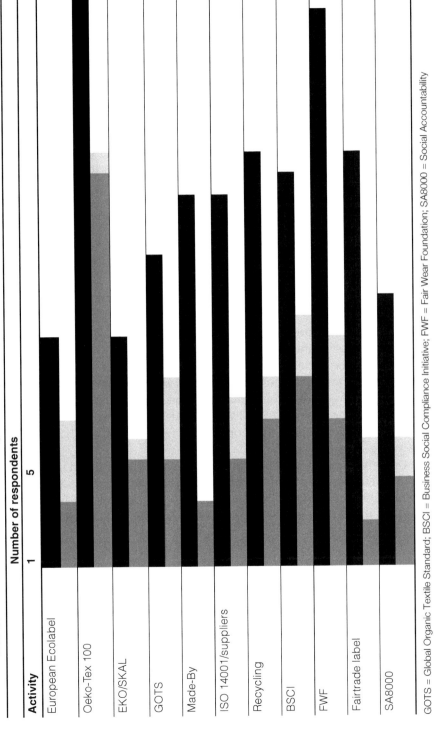

GOTS = Global Organic Textile Standard; BSCI = Business Social Compliance Initiative; FWF = Fair Wear Foundation; SA8000 = Social Accountability

5.5 Analysis

Before the scores of the innovation characteristics of the respondents could be related to the participation in sustainability activities, some recoding of the data took place. The scores of the *innovation* characteristics were summarised into a total innovation power score and the scores within each of the six categories were summarised to separate aggregated scores. This was done to make analysis of the results concerning the sustainability activities with the innovation characteristics possible at different levels.

To analyse the acquaintance of and participation in sustainability activities the answers were rescheduled in a five-point scale as follows for all 11 activities separately. The activity is:

1. Not known

2. Known but we don't participate

3. Known and we might participate

4. Known and we will participate in the short term

5. Known and we already participate

This new scale represents an increasing level of knowledge and participation in the specific sustainability activity.

To determine participation in groups of activities two 'total' scores have been developed: a total score for participation in 'social' activities; and a total score for participation in 'environmental' activities. The total score for social activities summarises the scores of BSCI, FWF and SA8000. The total score for environmental activities summarises the scores of EU Ecolabel, EKO, GOTS, ISO 14001 and recycling.

Oeko-Tex was excluded because this initiative is known and used by nearly all respondents and has been shown to be more specific on quality and consumer safety. Also the activities Made-By and Fairtrade were left out in the total scores because the participation was low and they could not be classified as being social or environmental.

Table 5.4 **Correlations between the scores of the innovation characteristics and the total score of participation in the social activities**

No.	Independent variable	Pearson's r
1	Statement 1 Extern	0.491**
2	Sum Extern	0.449*
3	Statement 5 Extern	0.425*
4	Sum Innov	0.387*

** Correlation is significant at the 0.01 level ($p < 0.01$); * Correlation is significant at the 0.05 level ($p < 0.05$)

Next, different analyses were carried out. The two total scores for sustainability activities have been related to the total innovation power levels (suminnov), the six scores for the separate categories (sumextern, sum... etc.) and to the individual scores of each innovation statement. This was done to determine the influence of these different innovation characteristics. Also all the activities (including those that were left out of the total scores developed) were related to the three levels of innovation scores. The most interesting results are summarised here.

Table 5.4 shows the significant correlations between the independent variables (scores of the innovation characteristics) and the total score of participation in the social activities in the supply network.

A significant relationship ($r = 0.387$, $p < 0.05$) between the level of innovation characteristics ('Sum Innov') and the total participation in social activities was found. This shows that focal companies with a higher innovation power are more acquainted with and join more social activities than companies with a lower innovation power.

The category 'external orientation' ('Sum Extern') was shown to have the strongest relationship with participation in social activities ($r = 0.449$, $p < 0.05$). Within the category 'external orientation' five statements were put forward. The relationship from the scores given to statements 1 ($r = 0.491$, $p < 0.01$) and 5 ($r = 0.425$, $p < 0.05$) are seen to have the most significant correlation with participation in social activities. Statement 1 concerns the insight the organisation has into recent developments and trends in the clothes and fashion sector. And statement 5 is about addressing sensitive topics in the sector by the organisation.

As mentioned above, the 'total' score for social activities contains three different activities. To analyse the relationship of these three social activities separately they were also related to the scores given to the innovation characteristics.

Table 5.5 shows the significant correlations between the independent variables (scores of the innovation characteristics) and the level of participation in the Business Social Compliance Initiative (BSCI).

Participation in the BSCI programme was observed to have the strongest significant correlation ($r = 0.414$, $p < 0.05$) with the sum of the innovation characteristics. The

Table 5.5 Correlations between the scores of the innovation characteristics and the level of participation in the Business Social Compliance Initiative

No.	Independent variable	Pearson's r
1	Sum Extern	0.513**
2	Statement 1 Extern	0.485**
3	Statement 5 Extern	0.485**
4	Sum Innov	0.414*

** Correlation is significant at the 0.01 level ($p < 0.01$); * Correlation is significant at the 0.05 level ($p < 0.05$)

FWF programme also showed a relationship which was not significant, while SA8000 did not show any relationship. Also, here the category 'external orientation' appeared to be the dominant category in the relationship with BSCI ($r = 0.513$, $p < 0.01$) and again the scores given to statements 1 ($r = 0.485$, $p < 0.01$) and 5 ($r = 0.485$, $p < 0.01$) are dominant in this category.

Remarkably enough, the results do not show a relationship between the total innovation score and participation in environmental activities.

From the six categories, 'external orientation' and 'result driven' show a small positive relationship with participation in environmental activities but this was not significant. Some of the other categories even show a negative (not significant) relationship.

The total score for environmental activities contains five environmental activities from which two are related to the organisation (ISO 14001 and recycling) and three to the product/material. Only the organisational environmental activities show a (not significant) relationship with the total score of innovation characteristics. And again the 'external orientation', as a category of the innovation characteristics, is shown to have the strongest relationship.

For the product/material -related environmental labels, the situation seems to be very different. GOTS does not show a relationship and the EU Ecolabel and also EKO-Skal even show a negative (not significant) relationship with the total score of innovation characteristics.

5.6 Conclusions

The results of the analysis show that the level of the innovation power of a focal company corresponds with the acquaintance with and the participation in social activities in their supply network. This conclusion supports the proposition developed in relation to the conceptual framework at least for the social activities. Why sustainability is an important aspect is very much influenced by the external pressure, but what to do, which social activities to join, is shown to be influenced by the capability of the organisation.

The most relevant innovation/power characteristics appear to be the insight the organisation has into recent developments and trends in the clothes and fashion sector and about daring to address sensitive topics in the sector.

The positive relationship found between the innovation characteristics and participation in social activities was not found for participation in environmental activities. The 'organisational' environmental activities do show some positive (but not significant) relationship while some 'product/material'-related environmental activities even show a negative relationship.

These conclusions show that decision-making for participation in environmental activities in the supply network is influenced by different factors from those involved in participation in social activities. And to be more specific: the choices made concerning the 'product/material'-related environmental activities show, again, a different relationship with internal factors.

5.7 Recommendations

Often it is assumed that external pressure leads to a corporate response. While the results of this survey do not disagree with this statement, external pressure by itself cannot account for the diversity in the responses by companies in similar circumstances. The results of the empirical survey support the proposition that the innovation characteristics of the focal company are related to the acquaintance with and participation in activities for improving social conditions in the supply network. The external orientation appears to be the most dominant factor in this relationship together with the nerve to address sensitive topics.

This insight is very useful for those who want to stimulate companies to become active on social and environmental aspects in their supply network. Pressure to put these aspects on the agenda is important but more attention should be paid to the capability of companies to react to this pressure. Putting pressure on companies that do not have the capability (innovation characteristics) to react might lead to a very defensive reaction.

The relationship found for social activities was not found for the 'product/material'-oriented environmental activities and only limited for the 'organisational' environmental activities. But why are these differences found between the social and the two categories of environmental activities? Is it because the organisational environmental activities use common approaches to those for the social activities, such as management systems and organisational audits, while the product/material-related activities have a stronger relationship with technical aspects and disciplines in the company and less with the organisational aspects? And why are the 'external orientation' and the 'courage to address sensitive topics' the dominating characteristics and how do they influence the decision-making process concerning participation in activities?

These questions call for more in-depth research. As part of an extended research programme, in 2012, in-depth case-studies will be conducted in 'focal' fashion/clothing companies in order to try to answer these questions.

References

Allwood, J.M., S.E. Lauresen, S.N. Russell, C. Rodiguez de Malvido and N.M.P. Bocken (2007) 'An Approach to Scenario Analysis of the Sustainability of an Industrial Sector Applied to Clothing and Textiles in the UK', *Journal of Cleaner Production* 16.12: 1,234-46.

Brooke Dobni, C. (2006) 'The Innovation Blueprint', *Business Horizons* 49: 329-39.

BSCI (2009) *Annual Report 2008* (Brussels, Belgium: Business Social Compliance Initiative).

De Brito, M.P., V. Carbone and C.M. Blanquart (2008) 'Towards a Sustainable Fashion Retail Supply Chain in Europe: Organisation and Performance', *International Journal of Production Economics* 114: 534-53.

EU (2009) 'Establishing the Ecological Criteria for the Award of the Community Ecolabel for Textile Products', Document number C (2009) 4595, *Official Journal of the European Union*, 29 July 2009.

Forman, M., and M. Sogaard Jorgensen (2004) 'Organizing Environmental Supply Chain Management; Experience from a Sector with Frequent Product Shifts and Complex Product Chains: The Case of the Danish Textile Sector', *Greener Management International* 45: 43-46.

FWF (2009) *Annual Report 2008* (Amsterdam: Fair Wear Foundation).

GOTS (Global Organic Textile Standard) (2009) *Licensing and Labelling Guide* (Stuttgart, Germany: International Working Group on Global Organic Textile Standard).

International Chamber of Commerce (2007) *ICC Guidance on Supply Chain Responsibility* (Paris: ICC).

Leipziger, D. (2001) *SA8000: The Definitive Guide* (Upper Saddle River, NJ: Pearson Education Limited).

Made-By (2008) *Benchmark for Social Standards* (Amsterdam: Made-By).

Made-By (2009) *Made-By Environmental Benchmark for Fibres* (Amsterdam: Made-By).

MODINT (2010) *Jaarbericht 2009* (Zeist, Netherlands: MODINT, in Dutch, summary available in English).

Nawrocka, D., T. Brorson and T. Lindhqvist (2009) 'ISO 14001 in Environmental Supply Chain Practices', *Journal of Cleaner Production* 17: 1435-43.

Oeko-Tex (2012) *General and Special Conditions of the Oeko-Tex Standard 100* (Zurich: OEKO-TEX).

Omta, S.W.F. (2002) 'Innovation in Chains and Networks', *Chain and Network Science* 2: 73-80.

Omta, S.W.F. (2004) 'Increasing the Innovative Potential in Chains and Networks', *Chain and Network Science* 4: 75-81.

Profas, C.G.G. (2008) *In Pursuit of Sustainable Supply Chains: Incentives and Barriers to Sustainable Supply Chain Management in Textile and Garment Supply Chains* (Master's thesis; Utrecht, The Netherlands: Department of Environmental Sciences and Innovation Studies, Utrecht University).

Sarkis, J. (2003) 'A Strategic Decision Framework for Green Supply Chain Management', *Journal of Cleaner Production* 11: 397-409.

Seuring, S., and M. Müller (2008) 'From a Literature Review to a Conceptual Framework for Sustainable Supply Chain Management', *Journal of Cleaner Production* 16: 1699-710.

Scheer, D., and F. Rubik (ed.) (2006) *Governance of Integrated Product Policy: In Search of Sustainable Production and Consumption* (Sheffield, UK: Greenleaf Publishing).

Skal (2009) *Facts and figures 2008* (Zwolle, The Netherlands: Skal Bio Controle).

Social and Economic Council (2008) *On Sustainable Globalization: A World to be Won* (SER Advisory Report; The Hague, The Netherlands: Social and Economic Council).

Søndergård, B., O.E. Hansen and J. Holm (2004) 'Ecological Modernisation and Institutional Transformations in the Danish Textile Industry', *Journal of Cleaner Production* 12: 337-52.

Stigzelius, I., and C. Mark-Herbert (2008) 'Tailoring Corporate Responsibility to Suppliers: Managing SA8000 in Indian Garment Manufacturing', *Scandinavian Journal of Management* 25: 46-56.

Van Bommel, H.W.M. (2011) 'A Conceptual Framework for Analyzing Sustainability Strategies in Industrial Supply Networks from an Innovation Perspective', *Journal of Cleaner Production* 19: 895-904.

World Bank (2003) *Strengthening Implementation of Corporate Social Responsibility in Global Supply Chains* (Washington, DC: World Bank).

Harrie W.M. van Bommel is a senior lecturer and researcher at Saxion University of Applied Sciences in the Netherlands. As an academic engineer in environmental science he has been specialising in sustainability and business. Besides teaching he is working on a PhD research project in cooperation with the University of Twente concerning the implementation of sustainability in global industrial supply networks in the fashion/clothing sector.

6

Sustainable colour forecasting

The benefits of creating a better colour trend forecasting system for consumers, the fashion industry and the environment

Tracy Diane Cassidy

University of Leeds, UK

Changes in fashion occur through combinations of design and marketing communications efforts directed by the industry and the timeliness of consumers' responses to such directives. The resulting changes in colour, style and decoration, or detail, are the ingredients of intended fashion trends that must resonate with the changes of attitudes, opinions, desires and needs of individuals, societies at large and their empirical environments at particular points in time (Sproles 1981: 118). Trends are linear in present time periods having either a long-term or a short-term existence or appeal; and cyclic in past and future time zones, though in subsequent lifetimes a trend will emulate the subtleties of the environmental and societal factors of those times resonating with the behaviours of that particular generation of consumers. Hence trends are viewed as an expression of the 'Zeitgeist', or the 'spirit of the times' (Yurchisin and Kim 2010: 1). Consumers are the vehicles that diffuse fashion trends through their acceptance and willingness to interact with them (Sproles 1981: 117). It is the volume of products, through mass production practices, and the mass communication of trends, through promotional efforts in retailing and the media, that the fashion industry relies on to promote mass consumption to ensure survival

(Sproles 1981: 117). However, in order for mass consumption to occur, trends need to be dynamic and appealing. Re-inventing the same trend with fresh appeal, creating 'follow-on' sales to complement the existing wardrobe for subsequent seasons, may be considered more challenging than introducing something viewed as being radically different, providing a new look for the next season to create 'new sales'; in which case existing product needs to appear out-dated and rendered obsolete, thus encouraging short-term trends rather than supporting long-term trends and consequently accelerating the rate of fashion change.

6.1 Planned obsolescence

Theoretically, for obsolescence to naturally occur from a consumer perspective, a product is required to be, or at least seen to be in a state of overuse. In other words the market has reached saturation and consumers are likely to become tired of the product's existence, and are therefore receptive to something new (Sproles 1981: 121). Industries respond to such situations by withdrawing and replacing the unwanted product with a new design. Sometimes products can become obsolete as a result of manufacturing problems such as materials or components no longer available or fit for purpose. However, it is more likely to be the decisions of consumers to render products obsolete through a change of taste, or opinion or attitude towards the product or its present condition, such as being worn or damaged. Frings (1996: 63) identified three main reasons for fashion change, all related to consumers, including changes in their lifestyles, psychological needs for change and to relieve boredom. However, changes of consumer taste, defined as 'prevailing opinion[s]' of appropriateness and attractiveness at a given time by Solomon and Rabolt (2004: 11), and the appeal of a product can be engineered to a degree by an industry. This practice, known as planned obsolescence, promotes feelings of dissatisfaction, encouraging consumers to think that they need something different (Yurchisin and Kim 2010: 62). Planned obsolescence is used as a business strategy in many industries. The process relies on a product being deemed obsolete on the grounds of being unfashionable or unusable and that this can be 'built into' the design. Anything deemed as fashion is 'by definition committed to built-in obsolescence'. Deliberately 'shortening [a product's] fashionable life' is at the heart of the strategy (*The Economist* 2009). In other words, purely because fashion changes over time, fashion-related items are expected to become unwanted and to be replaced with more desirable product; and it is the fashion-ability of the design that promotes obsolescence. Also intrinsic in this is that designers have the right to encourage the replacement of fashion products with further or more fashionable products. However, if the new design does not appeal to consumers for any reason, then the strategy can fail. Fashion flops of the late 1960s and early 1970s for instance are a good example of this (Diane and Cassidy 2005: 20).

Through the creation and promotion of trends, the fashion industry can exert power in generating regular sales of fashion product regardless of consumers' actual intentions to replace one existing product with another. Invariably, consumers are more likely to impulse purchase and only at a point when their storage space is too cramped will apparel items be selectively discarded to make room for the newly acquired garments. The obsolescence philosophy behind fashion trends, that is the deliberate shortening of the lifespan of fashion-related products to facilitate the continuation of sales, could be regarded as being one of the principal causes of current unsustainable fashion consumption, contributing to the many other sustainability issues inherent in the fashion and textiles industry's operations. Excessive consumption, or unsustainable consumption, can also be seen to be supported by the abundance of cheap merchandise both on the high street and online (Yurchisin and Kim 2010: 164).

6.2 Colour forecasting

The use of colour has long been a strategic design tool to drive the sales of fashion-related products (Brannon 2000: 117), and the decisions made to determine which seasonal colours to promote biannually, known as colour forecasting, are the forerunner of the entire trend forecasting process. This specialist industry sector is the driver of seasonal colour changes for a vast array of fashion-related products. The forecasting sector developed through a perceived need by manufacturers to produce merchandise that would create sales; and from the early to mid-20th century onwards the promotion of seasonal colours had become a powerful driving force for the fashion industry (Diane and Cassidy 2005: xii). Today colour is recognised as an important sales tool for other product types beyond apparel which includes fashion-related accessories such as shoes, handbags, scarves and costume jewellery, but also home products including wallpapers and paints, carpets and soft furnishings, tableware, towels and bed linen and even kitchen appliances. Further to this, colour is also important for the creation of sales for products as diverse as cosmetics and personal grooming items, stationery and cars. All such industries subscribe to the services of the colour forecasting sector to entice consumers to make purchases believing that the products are not only a necessity for them but are also in-keeping with the current fashion. Thus consumers are exposed to the seasonal colours or fashion colours beyond just the fashion sector which serves to further strengthen the consensus of the promoted colour stories or colour-ways and confirming them as being on-trend. A change made to this colour consensus on a seasonal basis then reinforces the planned obsolescence of a fashion trend.

6.3 The colour forecasting process explained

It has been said that the aim of trend forecasting is to predict, though others may say to predetermine, moods, behaviours and consumer buying habits at points ahead of the current time (Brannon 2000: 22-3). Colour forecasting is the precursor of the more generic trend prediction process where style and details are developed from the moods, themes, colours, keywords and descriptions that are all part of the initial colour forecasts. In essence, past trend predictions form an important part in the colour forecasting process as the forecasters are selling information that must be seen as a progression from that of previous seasons' forecasts otherwise subscribers would eventually question the value of the trend packages that they are purchasing. With past predictions in mind, forecasters then undertake research which invariably includes awareness and observations of the current climate, referring to the arts, film etc. as points of inspiration, keeping up to date with technological developments, not just in the textiles industry for example but all industries that will have an impact on consumer lifestyles. It is important for forecasters to have a good measure of consumer lifestyles in order to understand the kinds of goods and services that they are likely to purchase in the near future. However, because the colour forecast information is sold globally to an array of consumer product industries for innumerable target markets, the cues picked up from the environment and societies are generalised (Diane and Cassidy 2005: 27). Researching much earlier styling may also be included particularly if reflections of past decades or eras are an intended inclusion, such as the current and ongoing vintage trend. Brainstorming sessions may also be included during strategic stages of the data collection process (Linton 1994). Forecasters are also known to store unused data for future use. Such data stock will also be rummaged through as a part of this early stage of the process (Edelkoort 1999). After this initial data collection stage, selections are made to begin the building of colour stories. This stage is often more intuitive though does draw on experience and knowledge to make informed assessments of what colours are working well together in a fresh and exciting way. Forecasters with a good understanding of colour theories, colour mixing, colour psychology and emotional affects of colour, as well as a good colour sense and knowledge of what colours sell well for different product types, will have an added advantage in putting together colours with consumer appeal and creating aesthetically meaningful colour stories. A more controlled research process may then follow in order to either bring together more examples of the same colour or to bring in complementary colours to the scheme to make a more appealing collection (Diane and Cassidy 2005: 109).

The suggestion of other design elements such as texture and shape may also be made apparent through the colour stories (Linton 1994). Generally colour forecasts consist of a number of colour stories for each season, four or five is common. Each colour story will then consist of an agreed number of colours, usually around eight but may be as many as 12. The individual colour stories may be completely separate with no connections or an umbrella theme may be used to bring all of the divisions together in a unified whole to be marketed as such throughout the forecast package. It is believed that the seasonal colours of subsequent forecasts are developed in an evolutionary manner (Danger 1973: 480-82) though there would not appear to be any rigorous research evidence to date to substantiate this claim.

However, the colour stories themselves are usually developed around the four basic colour characteristics: bright colours; tonal colours with added grey; pastel colours or tints with added white; and dark colours or shades with added black. A palette of neutral colours may also be included as a colour story. Each palette for each colour story will generally include basic colours that sell well, known as staple colours (for example, black, white, navy and beige) and fashion colours, which are those determined to be the key trend colours for a given season (Brannon 2000: 126).

The most common tool used to develop the colour stories is the mood board. This may be an actual piece of mounting board cut to a particular size or it may be a designated space on a work surface or wall. If the data is to be made mobile then actual boards will be used and the visual representations and images etc. used to develop the colour story will eventually be permanently adhered to this board. An iterative process ensues as colours are added and taken away, working with one palette or colour story at a time or many stories simultaneously. All manner of visual representations will be used from sweet wrappers and gift wrap to ribbons and buttons, and other bits and bobs that consist of the colours that the forecaster is trying to express. Images are used to build the themes or moods for the colour stories. It is possible to work purely with colours first and then to determine the theme and support this with purposely sourced images, but more commonly the colours are pulled out of the images and other colour representatives to develop the palettes. The images will also be indicative of the essence of the environmental and social factors that the forecaster has honed in on during the initial research stage. Two examples of colour forecasting mood boards are shown in Figures 6.1 and 6.2.

Figure 6.1 **Mood board, theme: folk art**

Figure 6.2 **Mood board, theme: audacity**

6.4 The colour forecasting sector and colour marketing

The colour forecasting sector is made up of agencies operating at different levels, the majority being at a secondary level working with initial forecasts made by the few highly influential colour groups operating at the primary level. The key players at the primary level include the British Textile Colour Group and the Colour Association of the United States (CAUS). The colour groups are made up of individuals from the fashion and textiles sectors who attend biannual meetings in order to determine the colours for a given season approximately two years in advance. Each member delivers a presentation using a mood board that sets out their deliberations of the likely colours for that season. After each member has presented, around 25–30 in all, the group will draw out the commonalities from the colour stories presented to create a national colour card. This process is undertaken by colour groups in many of the major fashion cities around the globe. The national colour cards are then presented at the international colour meeting where the process is repeated. The resulting consensus this time is declared as being the international colour card and disseminated to the industry through trade fairs. The forecasters that form the secondary sector level will subscribe to this information and use this as the basis for their own forecasts to sell to fashion and textile companies and also to other consumer product industries. This reinforces the conviction of the key season's fashion colours to be marketed throughout the forecasting sector, the trade fairs and exhibitions and eventually to consumers through fashion media and consumer lifestyle magazines. The only aspect not taken into account thus far is the consumers' response to the colours now available to them to purchase. Buyers and merchandisers will also refer to forecast information to help them to make informed choices on which to develop their product ranges. They will invariably take into consideration previous sales data as this is a measure of their target market's consumer taste, at least theoretically. In reality sales data can only tell a story about purchases made at a given point in time in relation to what was made available to them to make purchase decisions from. Also very often it is the case that retailers play safe with colour by investing more heavily in the staple colours rather than in the fashion colours for the season. This practice occurs even though companies will invest in many forecast packages to make their own judgements on the consensus of colours being marketed to inform their buying. This suggests that retailers are not confident that the trend colours are indeed the preferred colours that their particular consumers are likely to purchase.

6.5 The sustainability issue of the colour forecasting process

The dilemma for retailers is then either to go with the forecasts and risk being left with unwanted stock because their consumers do not like the colour choices made available to them or to continue to play safe at the risk of losing sales because their product has not moved on from previous seasons, again being left with surplus stock. If the retailer gets it right it stands to increase its sales volume but at the expense of the environment by supporting even higher levels of excessive product consumption, which is one of the major contributing factors to an unsustainable fashion system; ultimately adding to the landfill problem. It can therefore be said that as a major driver of change and fashion consumption, the colour forecasting process not only contributes to unsustainable material consumption, fuelled by apparent consumer dissatisfaction (Fletcher 2008: 117), and disposal behavioural problems from a consumer perspective, but also contributes to the volume of unsold stock that retailers need to dispose of. While solutions to this excessive quantity of waste product are currently the subject of many research endeavours, and likewise progressive environmentally aware companies are also attempting to resolve such challenges, it would appear that the root of the problem is not being addressed. By making changes to the fashion system itself the amount of product waste will not be eliminated but could be better controlled, giving way to more opportunities to effectively recycle a more manageable amount of waste. What the industry and consumers need to accept is that the cost of product would need to be higher because quality and style would need to improve in order to slow the pace of fashion change; and the fashion system would need to adapt to meet the consumers' tastes in colour.

6.6 Colour, design and style rivalry

Peter Madden, CEO of Forum for the Future, reported on the need for 'a major shift in the fashion world' to address issues of sustainability including climate change that are exacerbated by cheap, throwaway clothing and the fast fashion business model (Forum for the Future 2010). The fast pace of fashion is currently supported by high productivity at low cost; in order to slow down the pace of fashion, a concept Fletcher (2008: 130) discussed as a sustainability solution for the industry, a method of lower productivity is required but not at the expense of profit otherwise the economy will suffer. Therefore products with lower volumes of sales will need to be more expensive to purchase and will be required to last longer. The challenge in this concept is not only quality and fitness for purpose, which is a lesser consideration when products are treated as disposable, but also that the products command designs that will satisfy consumers' aesthetic taste for longer periods of time.

Currently it is considered to be cost-effective for manufacturers to reproduce garment styles for a number of seasons with little or no adjustment to style, thus little or no changes are needed for the pattern cutting and assembly processes. This means that automated processes require no adjustments and operatives do not need to slow productivity to master the techniques required for a new style. This practice maintains a high production speed, increasing productivity which equates to lower cost product. The production method lends itself particularly well to basics such as T-shirts. To support this method of operating, in her delivery of the new colour trends to industry and public audiences, Li Edelkoort, from the colour consultancy agency Trend Union, sells the concept of consumers having a tendency to favour particularly comfortable garments and of being happy to purchase the same garment in different colours: hence, supporting the role colour plays in sales. However, as previously stated, consumers will only purchase products in the colours that are acceptable to them and regardless of whether products are purchased or remain as unwanted stock they still find their way to landfill. Fletcher (2008: 137) supports this concept stating that mass production is not only resource-hungry but also a rare reflection of consumer preferences; in addition throwaway products are 'less cherished and less personal' (Fletcher 2008: 159).

In 1947, fashion theorist Paul Gregory proposed that if a large number of retailers stocked similar fashion (as is the case today) the competitive rivalry of the retailers would create one of two scenarios. Either the retailers would become highly price competitive, creating price rivalry, or the quality of the product offering would be greatly improved, creating quality rivalry. Gregory argued that price rivalry was a condition that fashion product would not be subjected to. This assumption may have been based on the style rivalry prevailing at that time, which was most likely a result of how the fashion system operated then, with innovative designs predominantly from the couture designers that filtered down into mainstream fashion. It could be argued that couture designers, as innovative as their designs often were and still are, better respond to the desires of consumers than the majority of those who design for a company's particular target market. Also because garments are more expensive and more exclusive they become more highly prized, personal and cherished objects, which is the opposite of the values attached to disposable fashion. Gregory had recognised that style rivalry naturally stimulated sales without any pressure to improve the offering through marketing efforts or add on benefits. It would appear that today, over 60 years after Gregory's assessment of the fashion industry, style rivalry has indeed been replaced by price rivalry. While this may not be directly attributed to the colour forecasting or to the general trend-forecasting sectors, it is easy to see that the current system supports price rivalry through the promotion of generic themes and colour stories to all manner of industries globally on a seasonal basis, promoting planned obsolescence. The importance of style rivalry for fashion-related product industries should not be underestimated, it offers the potential for more product choice for consumers as well as better quality products; it can increase brand image and loyalty for retailers; bring about more creativity in design through materials and style which can also contribute to improved skills acquisition for a company's manufacturing operatives; and can ultimately provide a more manageable volume of waste product.

6.7 Marketing support for mass-produced fashion

Perhaps what Paul Gregory had not foreseen was the power that the media would have in supporting mass production practice, accelerating fashion change at a rate that could only happen if fashion product was cheap and thus retailers operated within a price rivalry system. Sproles (1981: 119) referred to mass production as the 'mass market theory of fashion': the combination of new style availability and the mass communication of information regarding these styles happening 'simultaneously to all socioeconomic classes' that enables fashion to diffuse 'horizontally' (trickle-across theory); and that 'real leadership of fashion comes from within an individual's own social class and peer groups'. In other words, fashion influence occurs 'informally between friends in similar social circles'. This would suggest that, while the marketing of indiscriminate trends may encourage retailers buy into the promoted trends to offer, what they believe to be, on-trend products, consumers are more likely to be directed by their own assessments of what fits in with their lifestyles and therefore their own tastes. King (1963 cited in Sproles 1981: 119-20) also agreed that mass production relies on the marketing strategies that promote the fashion change, but also noted consumers' choice to 'freely satisfy [their] personal tastes and needs rather than following the lead of' other influential people outside of their social groups; and that 'fashion innovators and opinion leaders' also exist within all social groups, thus influencing the horizontal flow of change.

Sproles also stated that if the *marketing system* continues to timely communicate new style en masse and if the new styles are affordable and readily available then the mass market theory can be determined as being a 'persuasive model of fashion leadership and diffusion' (Sproles 1981: 121). Therefore mass production can be seen to rely heavily on price rivalry, where the only benefit to consumers is cheap, readily available product, and the current forecasting system assists in the fast pace of fashion change through the promotion and planned obsolescence of seasonal trends. However, the low volume of sales on the high street tells the story of consumers not being enticed to purchase the resulting products, which if theorists such as Sproles and King are correct is because consumers are more likely to respond to their own lifestyle needs and tastes rather than manufactured trends. In addition to this Sproles stated that the mass marketing system supports 'merchandising, inventory, cash flow and store image, whereas the life of fashion spans years' (Sproles 1981: 122), denoting a naturally slower change to fashion than the current fashion system enforced by the industry.

6.8 An improved colour forecasting system

It could be considered that fashion forecasting coupled with price rivalry supported by marketing strategies has become more of a hindrance to the industry's growth as well as adding considerably to the problem of waste disposal management and its consequences on the environment. Such practice has led to the encouragement of high street sales without any improvements to the product offering, diversity or quality; and despite marketing efforts, such as market segmentation and target marketing strategies, consumers are either offered products that do not satisfy their tastes, which leaves retailers with unwanted stock to dispose of, or encouraged to quickly discard products to replace them with something else. Essentially, the forecasting sector does what it does and is unlikely to change. However, the way in which companies, retailers in particular, use colour forecast information can be changed by using a system that is more responsive to consumer tastes and that is capable of moving at a slower rate to benefit consumers, the economy and the environment.

A research survey was undertaken to evaluate the accuracy and effectiveness of the colour forecasting system which concluded that the current process was only around 51% effective in relation to consumer colour acceptance. Through the study it was envisaged that the inclusion of known consumer colour preference (or acceptance) data, which is intended to be specific to particular fashion-related products and markets, would replace the anticipation of consumer acceptance stage in the current process. This would enable companies to take control of their own forecasting process by translating the identification and analysis of trends, which may also include purchased inspirational forecast data, directly to the tastes of their core customer base. The proposed system model was tested using over a hundred industry personnel who were involved in using a colour forecasting process as a regular part of their job. Of the 111 respondents, 68.6% agreed that the current process should be improved, of which 58.3% were from the retail sector,

29.2% from the manufacturing sector and 27.3% from the forecasting sector. It is believed that higher levels of accuracy are desired by the retail sector as they are frequently left with unsold stock and consumer satisfaction is critical to building customer-brand loyalty. One respondent stated that it is possible to build an entire season's range purely based on knowledge of best sellers and not use forecast information. This adds weight to the argument that retailers would benefit more from offering products that better meet their target market's preferences than basing their ranges on predetermined forecasts. However it must also be recognised that using only previous sales data will only ever provide a limited colour palette. The survey respondents were also wary that the improved system would be based on a limited colour palette, suggesting that the same palette would be used season after season, which is not the case. Indeed the proposed improved system would allow for a much fuller gamut of colours than presently used in forecasts but would guarantee high levels of consumer appeal. In the first instance it was proposed that the system users would make colour selections, then test the colours with a sample of their target market to refine the season's palette. Many respondents recognised the timescale factor of this additional operation and the model was later refined. This more sophisticated model releases the user from the testing process by offering pre-designed colour palettes developed through a rigorous research study. Each palette offers an extensive choice for the forecaster-designer-buyer to make seasonal selections that reflect their target market's colour preferences specific to the product type. The palettes are based on contemporary colour mixing techniques which take colour bias into account to make better use of the three colour characteristics, hue, value and saturation, as discussed extensively and used in the works of Michael Wilcox (2009) and David Lloyd (2007).

Leatrice Eiseman, executive director of the Pantone Colour Institute, like many authors of colour, recognises colour as being a 'silent salesperson' (Eiseman 2000: 7) which makes a bold statement regarding the important role colour plays in product sales. To date however researchers studying colour in relation to sales and/or preferences have not moved beyond practices of testing a limited number of colours, which generally include one type of each of the hues, blue, red, yellow, brown, black and pink that was initiated by the likes of psychologist Eric Danger (1968, 1969); and the Luscher colour test developed by Dr Max Luscher who attempted to relate colour preferences to personality traits (Brannon 2000: 126). This has limited thinking when discussing the inclusion of colour palettes based on colour preferences into the colour forecasting process with industry personnel.

While often the terms warm and cool are used when discussing and describing colour, particularly among designers who tend to work with the psychological aspect of aesthetics (Eiseman 2000: 11), still few understand this aspect of colour in relation to colour preferences. Even though some colour experts and authors discuss colour under a small number of main palette types there is still little recognition of the importance of colour bias in colour preferences. One such colour author is Angela Wright; she pigeonholes colour into four types based on the four seasons possibly on the assumptions made by Max Luscher. The palettes are bright colours, tonal colours with added grey, pastels with added white, and shades with added black, known as winter, summer, spring and autumn palettes, respectively (Wright 1998: 38-44). Brannon (2000: 126) also discussed the seasonal colour palettes in relation to colour forecasting and colour preferences, relating cool undertones with winter and summer palettes, spring and summer as having warm undertones; winter and spring being bright colours and autumn and summer being muted or subdued; and winter and spring being intense, whereas summer and autumn are less intense. Such colour concepts in relation to colour preferences are still however under-developed and do not explain why one particular type of red will be a better seller than a slight variation of essentially the same colour. Perna (1987: 155) discussed the importance of reporting accurately on colour stating 'it is absolutely mandatory to be accurate about its value and intensity. It is not just blue—is it Bristol Blue, Cornflower, French, Royal, Azure, Blueberry or Ink?' It is clear that this is not just about the name given to the colour for marketing purposes but also highlights that each blue listed is subtly different. While the importance of being so precise in the colour distinction for forecasting and colour marketing is understood and rationalised, the same level of distinction is not currently applied to the preference of one type of, for instance, blue over another. This is essentially the difference between the proposed improved colour forecasting system and the current system; and between the research undertaken to validate this system and any other colour preference research study to date.

6.9 The benefits of the improved colour forecasting system

In this chapter the colour forecasting process and the forecasting sector has been outlined. The chapter has explained how the forecasters anticipate consumer colour acceptance and that the current process is used to create a consensus of colour on a seasonal basis in order to create changing colour trends to promote product sales. It makes clear that this specialist sector uses planned obsolescence strategies to enforce the perception of last season's colours being out-dated and the new season's colours being on-trend. However, the anticipation of consumers' acceptance and the promotion of the colour trends do not guarantee sales. This may be explained through the theories presented that suggest that consumer taste and lifestyle choices are influenced more by peers than by marketing efforts. The chapter clearly sets out how the current colour forecasting system supports the present unsustainable excessive product consumption, though this exists mainly through the price rivalry operations of the industry and fast-paced fashion changes. The rate of fashion change is currently driven by the forecasting sector in order to bring freshness to their biannual forecast packages. Without such change their customers (clients) would not be willing to subscribe to their services. However if consumers are not happy with the products made available to them they will not make purchases and retailers will be, and are, left with unsold stock that needs to be disposed of to make space for the next season's merchandise. In the latter sections the chapter highlights the benefits of style rivalry that would need to exist if the pace of fashion was reduced in order for the fashion industry to operate profitably. A further consideration is that not only would the environment benefit from a reduction in textile product waste but also people could benefit from the sense of value that they would bestow on themselves as worthy of better quality products, which would serve to enhance self-esteem and self-pride.

It could be stated that, even with a reduction in the annual volume of fashion product being sold and used owing to better quality goods in colours that are more appealing to consumers, products would still eventually be discarded and a waste management system is still required, albeit operating at a more manageable pace than the current system. The benefit of an improved colour forecasting system is that it would enable retailers to offer products that fit into colour palettes based on the coordination of colour biases. This would help consumers to better complement their wardrobes and would assist in the waste textile sorting process for recycling. On the basis of clothing being used for a longer period of time following an improvement in quality, it is more likely that waste product would eventually be broken down for recycling rather than ending in landfill and with a style rivalry strategy better quality products will result in better quality recycled products, which adds a further dimension to the rationale for improving the current colour forecasting system. However, implementing such a system would require investment from the retailers who would use it. At this moment in time this is fraught with difficulty as companies are likely to demand evidence of the benefits of the system through its successful application and in order to do this a number of retailers would be required to use it. This chicken and egg situation is also currently holding back the full development of the system from a research perspective; although one large UK retailer has currently expressed an interest, only time will tell if it will eventually invest in the final research stages to bring it to market. Failing this approach then a more innovative means of research development and testing will need to be realised in order to present the evidence that the industry would demand before fully appreciating the value of the new system to them, to society and to the environment.

References

Brannon, E.L. (2000) *Fashion Forecasting* (New York: Fairchilds Publishers Inc).

Danger, E.P. (1968) *Using Colour to Sell* (London: Gower Publishers).

Danger, E.P. (1969) *How to Use Color to Sell* (Boston, MA: Cahners Publishers).

Danger, E.P. (1973) 'Colour trends and consumer preferences', in G. Wills and D. Midgley (eds.), *Fashion Marketing* (London: George Allen & Unwin): 477-84.

Diane, T.D., and T. Cassidy (2005) *Colour Forecasting* (Oxford, UK: Blackwell Publishers).

Edelkoort, L. (1999) *The Theories behind Colour Forecasting*, presentation at the Briggait Centre, Glasgow, UK, 19 October 1999.

Eiseman, L. (2000) *Pantone Guide to Communicating with Color* (Sarasota, FL: Grafix Press Ltd).

Fletcher, K. (2008) *Sustainable Fashion and Textiles: Design Journeys* (London: Earthscan).

Forum for the Future (2010) *Fashion Futures 2025: Global Scenarios for a Sustainable Fashion Industry* (London: Forum for the Future, www.forumforthefuture.org/project/fashion-futures-2025/overview, accessed 22 September 2011).

Frings, G.S. (1996) *Fashion: From Concept to Consumer* (Upper Saddle River, NJ: Prentice-Hall, 5th edn).

Gregory, P.M. (1947) 'An Economic Interpretation of Women's Fashions', *Southern Economic Journal* 14.2 (October 1947): 148-62.

King, C.W. (1963) 'Fashion Adoption: A Rebuttal to the "Trickle Down" Theory', in S.A. Greyser (ed.), *Toward Scientific Marketing* (Chicago: American Marketing Association): 108-125.

Linton, H. (1994) *Colour Consulting: A Survey of International Colour Design* (New York: Van Nostrand Reinhold).

Lloyd, D. (2007) *The Colour Book* (Marlborough, UK: The Crowood Press).

Perna, R. (1987) *Fashion Forecasting* (New York: Fairchilds Publications Inc).

Solomon, M.R., and N.J. Rabolt (2004) *Consumer Behaviour in Fashion* (Upper Saddle River, NJ: Prentice Hall).

Sproles, G.B. (1981) 'Analysing Fashion Lifecycles: Principles and Perspectives', *The Journal of Marketing* 45.4 (Autumn 1981): 116-24.

The Economist (2009) 'Planned Obsolescence', The Economist, 23 March 2009, www.economist.com/node/13354332, accessed 22 September 2011.

Wilcox, M. (2009) *Blue and Yellow Don't Make Green* (Singapore: School of Colour Publishing/Imago Productions, 2nd edn).

Wright, A. (1998) *The Beginner's Guide to Colour Psychology* (London: Kyle Cathie).

Yurchisin, J., and K.P. Kim (2010) *Fashion and the Consumer* (Oxford, UK: Berg).

Tracy Diane Cassidy is a trained knitwear designer with experience of knitwear and bespoke bridal-wear design, manufacture and retail. She obtained her PhD through the investigation of colour forecasting and is the first author of the book *Colour Forecasting* published by Blackwell. Tracy holds a Lectureship in Fashion Marketing and continues to conduct research in fashion and textile design, trends and marketing.

7

Fashioning use
A polemic to provoke pro-environmental garment maintenance

Tullia Jack

The University of Melbourne, Australia

Clothing is implicated in many of the challenges facing sustainable consumption: materials are environmentally intensive; toxic chemicals are employed in manufacturing; product life is artificially short with correspondingly high material flows; and disposability results in masses of textile waste. The social need for clothing consumption stems from planned obsolescence; the very function of fashion fuels the excessive need for change, and the continual replacement of garments leads to a rising volume of textiles in landfill (Allwood *et al.* 2006; Caulfield 2009). Marketing plays a hand in this behaviour, utilising techniques that link products, such as clothes, to non-material needs (Berger 1972; Max-Neef 1992; Fletcher 2008). Consumption of fashion becomes a way to signal wealth, identity and social status. Wearing clothes is entrenched in modern life, yet implicated in many unsustainable social and environmental effects; similarly caring for clothes is implicated in unsustainable consumption of water, energy and chemicals (Fletcher 2008; Rigby 2010). This chapter addresses some of the environmental implications of laundering and explores ways that fashion designers are enabling pro-environmental maintenance through garment design.

Taking a whole systems perspective of clothing and fashion, there are five general stages that a garment goes through, each with a set of impacts: growing and material extraction; design and production; transport; use; and finally disposal (Hethorn and Ulasewicz 2008). Because a large portion of the ecological and economic costs are locked in at design phase (Hawken *et al.* 1999; Ryan 2008) any consideration of sustainable fashion should take into account all stages within production, including use, especially as, for the majority of clothes, the use phase bears the largest environmental strain (Rigby 2010: 4). The everyday practices of laundering—using machines, detergents, dryers and irons—consumes high volumes of water, energy and solvents (Rigby 2010: 1). Many garment life-cycle assessments (LCAs) confirm laundering as the most resource-intense stage in a garment's life (e.g. American Fiber Manufacturers Association 1993; Allwood *et al.* 2006). Of all the stages in the life of a garment, the most environmentally unsustainable is the use phase, yet this is often overlooked in sustainable fashion dialogue.

7.1 Use impact: Threat or opportunity?

The fact that the use phase bears the greatest environmental load may provide a reason for designers to resign responsibility; any advances in sustainable materials and production appear insignificant compared with the environmental impacts amassed by consumers. Pessimism breeds apathy. However, designers have considerable influence within the fashion system, and can enable pro-environmental behaviour in users, by embodying knowledge and behaviours within garments to enable ways of doing that are in harmony with sustainability. Using design strategies such as stain and odour resistance, and care labelling, designers can motivate users to wash less, saving critical environmental resources. Shaping laundry patterns towards sustainability can draw from the theory of social practices: the way that meaning and actions are formed and circulated within a community, and how ways of doing can be embodied in objects. People develop ideas and ways of doing in the context of fellow citizens, situational and cultural factors which form the foundation for behaviour (Spaargaren 2011). Practices emerge and circulate through society with associated objects (such as garments), skills and motivations (Reckwitz 2002). Motivations around cleanliness can be unravelled in order to facilitate social change in washing: 'If new patterns of laundering are to take hold, peoples' habits have to change' (Shove 2003: 139). Garment makers have a significant opportunity to address user habits and laundry patterns through design to change the way people expect to care for clothes, with the possibility of reducing inconspicuous consumption of water, energy and chemicals implicated in laundering.

Reducing the wash frequency of clothes has far-reaching benefits, with the potential to influence practices on a systems level. Using garment design as an intervention point communicates directly with a user at the point of action, with a determining stake in the way the garment will be used, and the resources consumed during maintenance. For example, a care label communicates directly with users as they prepare a load of washing. Intervening through objects leads to deeper engagement with ways of doing, reinforcing alternative expectations and practices to influence the amount of resources consumed: 'expectations and practices change, at different rates, in differing directions, with consequences for the consumption of environmentally critical resources like energy and water' (Shove 2003: 16). Fashion is not isolated from other everyday practices: there is potential for wider environmental gains. If sustainable practices can be integrated in laundry, they can also be amplified to other everyday practices. 'The environmental impacts of clothes laundry are complex and far-reaching. They have knock on effects on many different levels' (Rigby 2010: 6). Influencing garment maintenance addresses inconspicuous consumption embedded in laundry routines, with the potential to conserve resources in other everyday practices.

Providing washing information and creating mindfulness is effective for enabling pro-environmental behaviour, contributing to deeper satisfaction and engagement with lifestyle, and has been shown to have a positive effect on facilitating self-determination in consumers (Rosenberg 2004). However, engaging actors in mindfulness, and effectively communicating and changing motivations towards a mindful lifestyle, requires investment of time and energy. An efficient way of steering behaviour is to provide a path of least resistance (Fritz 1999). By considered design and communication strategies, garments can be used to create new default social practices that are more sustainable. If patterns of practice can be prompted through everyday objects, individual skills, behaviours and motivations gather momentum and advance towards pro-environmental everyday lives. The concern here is that without mindful engagement and understanding, 'green' habits have the potential to oscillate, or even provide the springboard for 'rebounding' unsustainable behaviour (Greening *et al.* 2000). Without addressing the plethora of implications of engaging people towards pro-environmental actions, fashion design that enables low washing is a valuable strategy with vast energy and water saving potential. Sometimes information can become overwhelming and even debilitating; oversaturated consumers may become fatigued and withdraw from active engagement. However, understanding the way clothes are used can spark creativity and lead to pro-environmental innovations in garment design. Some examples of designers and brands actively intervening in everyday practices to engender environmental outcomes will be explored, as the starting point towards a roadmap for fashion design to provoke pro-environmental garment use.

The role of garment design as a point of intervention to change social practices has been explored from different angles. The following examples have been categorised into two basic approaches. First, an object focus, examining garments that use existing wisdom and unrecognised ingenuity to engender low washing, and specifically developed clothing that intentionally causes users to consume fewer resources. Second, integrated efforts involving objects, in synergy with skills and motivations to create a concerted effort to engage pro-environmental laundry practices (Reckwitz 2002; Shove 2011). These approaches show that the physicality of objects and their inherent design features act as triggers to encourage pro-environmental behaviour most effectively when supported by efforts to provide users with know-how and meaning to consume fewer laundry resources.

7.2 Objects of knowledge: Aprons, bacteria and wine stains

Aprons have been used for centuries to protect a wearer's clothes. They have been used in domestic and industrial settings to prevent dirt from coming in contact with external clothes reducing the need for washing. Aprons are an effective way to prevent garments from getting dirty when a wearer is exposed to potentially dirty situations such as cooking or factory work. They require the participation of a wearer, who should recognise the potential of getting dirty, and responsively put on an apron.

Antibacterial fabric has been developed by many different textile technologists and is already available in the marketplace: for example antibacterial socks. Metabolising bacteria produce methane gas, so antibacterial translates as anti-odour. New Zealand's AgResearch has developed an antibacterial and anti-odour textile. The wool jersey fabric is designed to be used in a variety of garments from casual to evening. It claims to have permanent antibacterial and anti-odour properties, be machine washable and anti-leaching. Garments made using this fabric resist developing odours and need laundering less than traditional fabrics, if stains are avoided. Aside from chemicals needed to create antibacterial finishes, the concern is the development of resistant strains of bacteria, which can negatively impact the health industry where antibacterial textiles are imperative for sterile patient care. Additionally, while technical product innovations can influence the physicality of a clothing item, it is still up to the user to exploit low-washing qualities. This intervention's success is dependent on users to extend periods between washing.

Acknowledging perception as important in determining garment care, Lauren Montgomery Devenney's Wine Stain Dress questions attitudes to cleanliness (Fletcher 2008). The print of the fabric is inspired by wine stains, with expressive splashes of reds, browns and pinks. The complexity of the print is added to by any additional stains accrued by the wearer, increasing visual interest, connection and embodying memories. This approach capsizes cleanliness's connotations with high value. By engaging wearers in mindful wearing, Devenney encourages her community to question the need for cleanliness, enabling people to reconsider washing practices and save laundry resources.

7.3 Futured designers, integrated garments and involved wearers

Considering the way garments are used, MATERIALBYPRODUCT designer, Susan Dimasi, plans for her garments to develop a worn patina on the journey with their wearers. Her consideration extends past designing garments for ageing; Dimasi ensures that customers are prepared for the way garments will mature through personal communication during the acquisition process. With a background in historical garment maintenance for art galleries, Dimasi proposes that real value emerges from the individual way that garments wear. The MATERIALBYPRODUCT archives are worn frequently to give a sense of ways that garments map user experience. Archival images show the unique marks that appear with ageing, honouring old as beautiful. This aspirational imagery is also supported practically by thoughtful care labelling:

Figure 7.1 **MATERIALBYPRODUCT garments develop a worn patina over time; in this example the gold print has worn off the areas where abrasion occurs**

Culture: fabrics and prints are composed to evolve patina. Texta and liquid paper hand markings are designed to blur and fade. Soap and chalk marks will disappear with wear and wash. Ballchain inserted in seams will result in pulls in cloth. Fit is designed to be easy and never tight. Finish is hand-stitched and imperfect. Choose to preserve garment as new, or to evolve patina. Made in Australia in MBP work room.

Customers are also urged to maintain garments mindfully:

Refresh, hang in steam of shower. Spot clean, dab spot with mild detergent on clean cloth. Do not rub. Repeat until spot is removed. Handwashable, in cold water with mild detergent. Drip dry on hanger. Never wring. Drycleanable. Ask for a professional handwash service at a quality drycleaner. MBP recommends green dry cleaning.

Figure 7.2 **MATERIALBYPRODUCT care instructions**

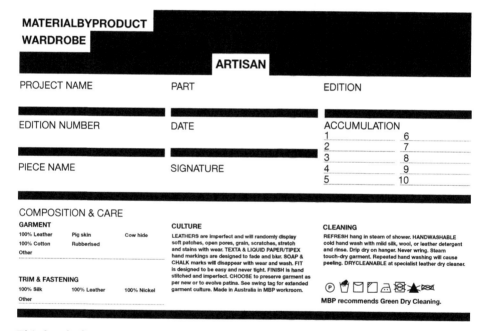

This level of customer engagement is made possible by the structure of MATERI-ALBYPRODUCT; garment price points are high, and customers' deep relationship with the label ensures receptiveness and responsiveness to information. Guiding user maintenance, and laundry resource consumption, is a luxury that is predominantly available to labels with strong client relationships.

British retailer Marks & Spencer use communication in a more accessible way to promote pro-environmental laundry practices: 70% of its garments' care labels carry the text 'Think Climate—Wash at 30°C'. Lowering washing temperature to 30°C saves around 40% of energy per wash, according to the Energy Saving Trust (Marks & Spencer 2012). To placate customer concerns that low washing temperatures do not clean as effectively, Marks & Spencer commissioned independent testing to ascertain minimum temperature requirements for effective washing. The findings from these tests were incorporated into its communication strategy: 'there's no significant reduction in performance for everyday loads, which guarantees a clean conscience'. More recently M&S added gels developed to wash at 15°C to its product offering. The Marks & Spencer tags provide a cost and time effective way to deliver pro-environmental skills and motivations, straight to the user in the moment of action.

Another initiative aimed at user behaviour is 'Drying for Freedom', an information movement that protests about the banning of clothes lines. Drying for Freedom incorporates a documentary film and webpage with information on drying clothes on the line, promoting the right of Americans to dry laundry outside. Drying laundry on the line is 'A simple single act which cuts carbon emissions and reduces energy bills'. Purely considering behaviour, without changing product, Drying for Freedom delivers information and motivations on positive everyday laundering action.

Emma Rigby is a designer researcher at London College of Fashion who is exploring why people wash clothes. Rigby investigates existing garments that require infrequent laundering, and creates new garments that respond to this knowledge. Collecting images and descriptions of existing garments from everyday people's wardrobes, Rigby created a taxonomy of design features that enable extended wearing between washes. She found that the least laundered garments incorporate a combination of design features, and was able to separate features into eight categories: odour resistance, fibre type, opening details, dark colour, required laundering method, use and function, positioning and fit and design. Using a combination of the design features Rigby created eight garments and is testing these in the wardrobes of everyday people in the United Kingdom. She hopes to discover more about the way garments designed intentionally for low wash, are actually washed. Throughout her research, Rigby's design approach looks at the physicality of garments and incorporates features to act as triggers encouraging pro-environmental behaviour.

Swedish denim company, Nudie, has had one of the greatest social impacts on denim washing practice. The company subscribes to practices of slow fashion and uses environmentally better materials and processes. Nudie's big contribution to sustainability, however, stems from its no-wash philosophy. Taking its sphere of influence beyond the product, it recommends a 'no-wash' period of six months when first breaking in a new pair of jeans. Beginning from an aesthetic imperative, customers are educated at point of purchase in not washing the jeans, utilising retail education infrastructure, and activating the system around the jeans to transfer washing skills to enable low washing, and coincidently pro-environmental practice.

One of the reasons Nudie has been so successful in recruiting wide populations to the practice of no-wash is the enabling cultural context it has established. Nudie has a cult status within the fashion industry: key figures, such as musicians and skaters, wear Nudie jeans. The coolth transferred to the brand is useful in creating acceptance of no-wash. The Nudie website has a gallery dedicated to displaying jeans that have not been washed, privileging worn jeans as objects of aspiration. Because of Nudie's credibility and cool factor, no-wash has grown into a global phenomenon and it is now commonplace, generating significant water, energy and chemical savings. Motivations, as well as skills and objects (Reckwitz 2002) provide the settings for practices, and Nudie brings the three areas together and success-fully engenders low washing behaviour across the international denim community, evidence that niche alternative practices can recruit a widespread population.

7.4 Ways forward

Many of the above examples use existing garments and create new knowl-edge systems around them. The more novel ones create new garments to elicit low washing; however the strategies with the furthest reaching social impact, MATERIALBYPRODUCT, Nudie and Marks & Spencer, use unmodified garments, with only the addition of new knowledge through swing tag or point of purchase education. In particular Nudie jeans now are not just 'Jeans', but 'Jeans that should not be washed'. It is important to develop garments that will provide wearers with a positive low-wash wearing experience, such as stain and odour resistance or fibre durability as explored by Emma Rigby, but communication and knowledge are of utmost importance in shaping laundry practice, and determining the resources consumed therein. Over the coming years, as energy and water become scarcer, fashion designers have the very real potential for a positive global impact by embedding low resource-consuming practices into garments and their users.

References

Allwood, J.M., S.E. Larson, C. Malvido de Rodrigues and N.M.P. Bocken (2006) *Well Dressed?* (Cambridge, UK: University of Cambridge Institute of Manufacturing): 84.
American Fiber Manufacturers Association (1993) *Resource and Environmental Profile Analysis of a Manufactured Apparel Product* (Prairie Village, KS: American Fiber Manu-facturers Association).
Berger, J. (1972) *Ways of Seeing: [v.1] Reproductions; [v.2] Nude or naked; [v.3] Possessions; [v.4] Language of advertising* (London: BBC Enterprises).
Caulfield, K. (2009) *Sources of Textile Waste in Australia* (Melbourne: Apical International Pty Ltd).
Fletcher, K. (2008) *Sustainable Fashion and Textiles: Design Journeys* (London: Earthscan).
Fritz, R. (1999) *The Path of Least Resistance for Managers: Designing Organizations to Succeed* (San Francisco: Berrett-Koehler).
Greening, L.A., D.L. Greene and C. Difiglio (2000) 'Energy Efficiency and Consumption: The Rebound Effect—A Survey', *Energy Policy* 28.6: 389-401.

Hawken, P., A.B. Lovins and H. Lovins (1999) *Natural Capitalism: Creating the Next Industrial Revolution* (Boston, MA: Little, Brown).

Hethorn, J., and C. Ulasewicz (eds.) (2008) *Sustainable Fashion: Why Now? A Conversation Exploring Issues, Practices, and Possibilities* (New York: Fairchild; Oxford, UK: Berg).

Marks & Spencer (2012) 'Plan A', www.plana.marksandspencer.com, accessed 10 January 2012.

Max-Neef, M.A. (1992) 'Development and Human Needs', in P. Ekins and M.A. Max-Neef (eds.), *Real-Life Economics: Understanding Wealth Creation* (London/New York: Routledge): 197-214.

Reckwitz, A. (2002) 'Toward a Theory of Social Practices: A Development in Culturalist Theorizing', *European Journal of Social Theory* 5.2: 243-63.

Rigby, E. (2010) *Clean by Design: Investigating the Relationship between Design, Consumer Behaviour and Laundry: A Social and Practical Study* (London: London Colledge of Fashion).

Rosenberg, E.L. (2004) 'Mindfulness and Consumerism', in T. Kasser and A.D. Kanner (eds.), *Psychology and Consumer Culture: The Struggle for a Good Life in a Materialistic World* (Washington, DC: American Psychological Association).

Ryan, C. (2008) 'Climate Change and Ecodesign', *Journal of Industrial Ecology* 12.2: 140-43.

Shove, E. (2003) *Comfort, Cleanliness and Convenience* (London: Berg).

Shove, E. (2011) 'Sustainable Practices: Beyond the ABC', paper presented at the *Sustainable Consumption Conference 2011*, Hamburg, 6–8 November 2011.

Spaargaren, G. (2011) 'Theories of Practices: Agency, Technology, and Culture Exploring the Relevance of Practice Theories for the Governance of Sustainable Consumption Practices in the New World-Order', *Global Environmental Change* 21.3: 813-22.

Tullia Jack is a student at the University of Melbourne, researching sustainable fashion under Professor Chris Ryan and Dr Janet McGaw. Her thesis uses social practice as a starting point to explore the way that people make sense and create culture around reducing resource consumption linked with cleanliness.

8

Fashion design education for sustainability practice
Reflections on undergraduate level teaching

Lynda Grose
California College of the Arts, USA

A recent internet poll by Cotton International asked readers to vote on the following question: 'Can the next generation of young fashion designers influence the sustainability of cotton growing?'[1] Results showed 50% voting 'yes', 33% responding 'no' and 17% stating 'not directly but they can help to influence those who can have such an impact'. Yet, 80% of the environmental cost of a product is set in the design stage. So why is there such a lack of faith in a designer's capability to influence ecological outcomes (including those in cotton cultivation) when their influence is so critical?

Perhaps this scepticism comes from the role of design being perceived as simply shaping material goods for sale, with the designer focused on the product, its materiality relevant to function, feel and style and its prominent positioning in the marketplace. Indeed, the entire fashion industry—jobs available to designers, the way collections are built, store layouts, the criteria for awards and, not least, undergraduate fashion education—is organised to support and reward the narrow role of fashion designer as a stylist.

---

1 www.cotton247.com/viewpoints/polls/ci/?polldate=2011-12-08, accessed 19 December 2011 [page no longer active].

Over the last 20 years sustainability efforts in fashion have been led mainly by the supply chain sector of the industry. Spurred in part by activists (in organic cotton, for example) linking through business to markets to 'pull' ecological advances faster than the 'push' of regulation or policy[2] and fuelled by landmark books such as Paul Hawken's *Ecology of Commerce*, this effort has seen companies aiming to achieve sustainability gains by re-calibrating existing systems of production. Sociocultural aspects are therefore not part of the critical thrust of this work (Gissen 2011), which emphasises technical solutions vs. social agendas and demand-side factors.

Yet, sustainability is not only about more and/or better technology but also about society 'reappraising its values in ways that re-define perceptions and accepted norms' (Farren Bradley *et al*. 2010). For the current fashion industry, and the consumer economy in which it operates, are human constructs founded on the belief that unlimited growth is possible and they are *utterly* dependent on degrading finite material resources and ecosystems to produce saleable goods to fuel that growth. The imperative, then, is to wean our industry off this dependency and to equip the next generation of designers with the ability to perceive the world in its infinite nature and to practise in it in fundamentally different ways—to forge new norms for practice.

This chapter notes the experience of developing an undergraduate Fashion Sustainability course at California College of the Arts. Providing examples of pedagogy, activities, projects and student work, it aims to illustrate the successes and the continued challenges in educating to enable critical and reflective sustainability practice.

8.1 Fashion design sustainability education at California College of the Arts (CCA)

Sustainable Fashion Design was first introduced at the undergraduate level at California College of the Arts in 1999, spearheaded by the chair of the fashion programme at that time. The six-hour studio elective was initially guided by methodologies informed by the instructor's practical experience as director of ESPRIT's *eco*llection, applying the Elmwood Institute's *Eco Audit Guide* (Capra *et al*. 1990) to that project, and consulting in the private and public sectors. The curriculum focused on raising awareness of fibre life-cycles and using identified impacts as starting points for design innovation. Cotton's cultivation and the global nature of commodity systems were also used as a means to understand systems thinking in a fashion industry context. Over the years, the sustainable fashion design curriculum has been developed with cumulative knowledge and response to the changing

---

2 W. Allen, farmer and founder of Sustainable Cotton Project (SCP), in conversation, Bakersfield, California, 1996.

cultural landscape, the growing interests of the student population, an increasingly robust body of sustainable design literature, the evolving ecological cognisance (and full-time presence) of instructors and shifts in the academic structure of the college itself. Fibre sourcing and processing impacts still form part of the seminar class, but the curriculum quickly moves to sociocultural considerations.

The Sustainable Fashion Design curriculum initiative, now required of all undergraduate fashion design students, comprises individual seminar and studio classes that are also linked across a broader interdisciplinary programme. Since students in all creative majors take humanities and science requirements as part of their art education at CCA, sustainable underpinnings are being seen throughout in courses dealing with ethics, environmental science, epistemology, critical studies, anthropology and cross-discipline classes with titles such as 'Economies of Desire' (Valero 2010), complementing and reinforcing the Sustainable Fashion Design education.

8.1.1 Sustainable Fashion Design Seminar

CCA's Sustainable Fashion Design Seminar is delivered in the fourth semester (sophomore level) as a 15-week series of 3-hour sessions. The class emphasises active, participatory and reflective learning.[3] The goals of this class are for students to understand the language of sustainability and the principles of deep ecology, develop research skills, become aware of the product life-cycle and to look critically at and reflect on the consumer culture in which we live and practise. The critical investigation fostered here forms an essential foundation for design and studio prototyping in the fifth semester and is a prerequisite for the Sustainable Fashion Design Studio class.

8.1.2 Sustainable Fashion Design Studio

Sustainable Fashion Design Studio is introduced in the fifth semester (junior level) as a 15-week series of 6-hour sessions. In this class the emphasis shifts from 'knowing to doing' (Flint 2010: 206), with weight given equally to process, outcome and reflection. Here, the purpose is to use the research from Sustainable Fashion Design Seminar on socio-ecological impacts as a method of inquiry to inform the design process itself; to offer students the opportunity to experience different approaches

---

3 The mechanisms for learning used in this class are both research based and experiential and include: class activities; primary and secondary research; assigned readings and written papers to help process and organise information; tools to capture data/information and make it understandable, accessible and practicable; class discussions to challenge conclusions and explore different perspectives and contexts; site visits to private companies and the thrift sector to view sustainability initiatives; questioning professionals to test student's confidence in their research skills; de-briefings and reflection; cotton farm tours, where students directly experience the landscape of industrial agriculture; and visiting lecturers.

to creative making with sustainability as the core directive; and to allow a new aesthetic, reflecting the values of sustainability, to emerge. Rigorous interdisciplinary research and discursive application to design are a constant, but students are free to develop their own areas of interest, so the prototype outcomes for all projects are inevitably diverse. Class critiques test the rigour of research, discursive justification, the craftsmanship of prototype execution, and include reflection on the different sociocultural norms the prototypes present.

8.2 Sustainable fashion design pedagogy

The following section outlines three pedagogical approaches that have formed the basis for and/or influenced the Sustainable Fashion Design curriculum at CCA. These classes do not aim to provide prescriptive answers or solutions to socio-ecological issues, but to concern the students with the global and eco-ethical challenges that they will inevitably face as they mature into leadership positions in 21st century fashion practice.

8.3 Seminar examples

8.3.1 Ecology of a garment exercise (approx. 1 hour duration)

The instructor arranges ecological impact categories tracked internationally by scientists (global warming, carcinogens, water eutrophication, habitat destruction, ozone depletion, etc.) around an image of a fashion product and invites the class to note where in the product's life-cycle impacts in each of these categories might occur. This is an active and participatory exercise and quickly reveals the students' intuitive knowledge of contemporary ecological and social issues. Once a number of points have been captured, the tutor uses them as a means to invite deeper discussion.

During one such session a student offered 'car parks and shopping malls' as major contributors to habitat destruction. This point provided an opportunity to discuss how economic health is measured (new construction being one such indicator). Yet announcements on the positive economic gain of new construction are never coupled with the ecologically detrimental impacts of habitat destruction even though the two are inextricably linked. In this particular class discussion, Donella Meadows' reference to the work of F. Kofman on how language influences perception brought cross-discipline and cultural relevance to the discussion.[4]

---

4 F. Kofman cited in Meadows 2008: 'Language act(s) as (a) filter…through which we perceive our world… A society (or industry) that talks incessantly about "productivity" but

In this way, through their own observations, students start to recognise the links between nature and human activity. They become aware of how cultural behaviour is directed by invisible structures and systems, which can encourage or stifle different ways of thinking, and how language reinforces cultural norms. And they begin to imagine how designers might use both visual and written language to help people perceive the world they live in differently. Field trips taken later in the semester see students referring back to these exercises and the language of ecology as touchstones to critically assess the values behind the terms used to market sustainability. Active observations, theoretical readings and practical application are thus fused into each class project or activity.

8.3.2 *The Story of Stuff* and Local Wisdom
(approx. 2 hours duration)[5]

In this exercise students watch the 12-minute movie, *The Story of Stuff*, an animation linking the depletion of natural resources and social injustice to manufacturing, commerce and the consumer economy. But the class views the movie only after participating in an exercise patterned on the Local Wisdom project in which each student presents a garment they have kept for a long time and tells the class why it is significant to them. As students share their clothing stories, the class becomes aware of the sociocultural meaning of things in general, and the power of clothing in particular to communicate and hold ideas about status, memory, accomplishment, a right of passage and so on…a process which inevitably draws on the ethnic, economic diversity and political background of the students, to enrich the class experience.[6]

This session concludes with critical reflection on *The Story of Stuff*, noting how fashion is depicted in the movie as the main perpetrator of short-term trends fuelling consumption, while the positive and often uniting sociocultural aspects of clothing are completely neglected. In this way, students begin to recognise the emergent role of design in leveraging (rather than ridiculing) the relationships people have with clothing to enable a shift in cultural behaviour. And perhaps even

---

that hardly understands (or) uses the word "resilience" is going to become productive and not resilient. A society (or industry) that doesn't understand or use the term "carrying capacity" will exceed its carrying capacity'.

5 www.storyofstuff.com/, www.localwisdom.info, accessed 21 September 2012.

6 During one such session, a Taiwanese-born student presented her mother's designer-label garment, explaining that her mother was the first in her family to pursue a professional career and break free of sustenance farming in mainland China—a decision that resulted in her being shunned. For the mother, designer clothing represented accomplishment and courage, and in a sense vindicated the decision she had made. As a whole, the reflective discussion in this project arcs across a range of sociocultural topics (in the above case, contemporary perceptions of designer labels, women's rights, the social ramifications of mass migrations from rural to urban areas in China) and builds a collective sense of empathy in the class.

more importantly, they start to identify and resist simplistic, idealistic and/or polarising views from both sides of the political spectrum of sustainability and to cultivate their own neutral path.

8.4 Sustainable Fashion Design Studio curricular examples

8.4.1 Design and making as tools for inquiry and reflection

The main pedagogical approach in the Sustainable Fashion Design Studio is to provide and mirror the sustainable education ethos of: 'consciousness, structure and agency' (Goldberg 2009). By enabling students to form an interactive relationship with ecological issues as agents in their own craft, and reflecting on the outcome, they become engaged and active, the logic of current fashion practice becomes apparent (**consciousness**) and, as it does, it can be critically investigated through a number of lenses (**structure**). As idealism is tempered, students realise that ideas for sustainability are not fixed, but emergent and they begin to develop a grounded perspective regarding their own potential as fashion practitioners in furthering change (**agency**). The following project illustrates an example of this process.

8.4.1.1 Community Repair: Strategic social skill mobilisation for sustainable fashion (Von Busch 2011)

This project assigns students to conduct a repair or collaborative making project with a stranger over a 4-week period, the stipulation being to provide a reciprocal act or exchange, as in a gift culture. The deliverable and process are left open to allow a variety of approaches and outcomes by each of the student groups.

In one case, the student group partnered with the local non-profit, Turning Heads,[7] an organisation fostering empowerment for at-risk teenage girls by developing sewing and entrepreneurial skills. Turning Heads participants were invited to co-develop a tailored jacket and the students reciprocated by providing embroidery and printing workshops and exhibiting the final garment in one of CCA's gallery spaces. This iteration of process-based teaching/learning saw students 'letting go' of their creative control to accommodate the needs of the makers, while ensuring the product was delivered on time and to a critically recognisable quality. Long-term planning, logistics, communication and collaborative skills were brought to bear on their design process to create an experience altogether more complex and interrelational than typical undergraduate design, which privileges solitude and personal expression; or the industrial fashion design process, which is generally reduced to a prescribed proto and spec sheet for duplication overseas.

---

7 www.turningheads.org, accessed 21 September 2012.

In the project's second reciprocal phase the students were again guided by the goals and needs of the makers—what new skills *they* would next like to explore and develop—while simultaneously negotiating how the outcomes from addressing these needs might be formed into a whole collection. The critical thrust of the design process was thus informed by the well-being of the maker-collaborators as much as traditional fabric selection, style and silhouette considerations. Students experienced directly how design principles or intent are redirected when social values are integral and, through both process and product execution, how the resulting aesthetic is also 'nudged', as it is allowed to express the 'common-wealth' of the maker-collaborators—an 'aesthetic(s) of the common(s)' (Valero 2010).

Besides these detailed insights, the project also triggered reflection more broadly on the lack of 'social currency' in our culture (the non-CCA partners, for example, felt their skills inadequate to the task, and were initially suspicious and reluctant to participate in the project and students were also aware of their own resistance to forging new relationships) and on the inherently antisocial nature of the current fashion sector, which positions each practitioner in a linear and segmented supply chain, divorced from each other by technology, distance and specialised job description. And yet with all this physical and social fracture, the complexities of sustainability demand that designers form multidisciplinary collaborations—with green chemists, farmers, environmental and social scientists, economists…and more—to create synergies and optimise new ideas for sustainability.

Thus, students who were initially confused about the sustainability scope of the project came to understand that social and ecological sustainability are interdependent. On the practical side, they built valuable social and management skills for practice—adaptability, listening, negotiating mutually beneficial outcomes, collaboration and mentoring—and developed resources for continued collaboration. On a more personal level, they experienced empathy, trust and companionship from making work that contributes to community. Learnings were multi-dimensional and both process and outcome based—realised and delivered through critical design *and* making.

8.5 Science embedded in Sustainable Fashion Design Studio

Undergraduate design education generally aims to ensure that students will be able to practise with a working knowledge defined by their respective professions, and is delivered through sequentially required classes in each creative major. CCA's curriculum also fosters inter-disciplinarity, facilitated in part by a menu of subjects in the humanities and sciences, which are provided across all majors. These classes provide a rich context and value-based foundation for design for sustainability. But since they are taught separately, these courses compete with major studio classes for the prioritised attention of the students and the content may not be understood as relevant to practice unless students seek to make the cognitive links for themselves. To better support integrative learning, a number of informal pilots have been launched across the college. These lateral learning routes offer much promise, for they blur the boundaries between disciplines, foster new collaborations between faculty and actively exemplify the new relationships that sustainable fashion design education is aiming to instil into practice.

One such pilot is 'Science at CCA', which is spearheaded by the division of Humanities and Sciences. The goal of this initiative is to support 'interdisciplinarity pedagogy' and to implement scientific instruction into the studio curricula. It requires scientists to be 'embedded' in studio classes and to assist students in conducting rigorous research and fact-based, cognitive approaches to inform their creative projects. While a common theme is assigned each semester (water was the theme for fall 2010 and 2011: 'Waterworks'), the curricular structure and product outcomes are left flexible to allow instructors to organise a 15-week class around the theme or to apply it to a single project in the existing curriculum. The semester concludes with student work from all participating disciplines being exhibited together.

The Fashion Design Waterworks project invited three scientists into the studio classroom: CCA's Assistant Professor of Geology, an agricultural crop water specialist and the Director of Global Environmental Site Compliance for Levi Strauss and Co. Scientific inquiry therefore spanned natural water cycles, long-term trends for fresh water, fibre life-cycle impacts and how 'peak water' might affect long-term business strategies.

Student responses ranged from practical to experimental and reflective. Some applied life-cycle data to develop garments aiming to influence social norms around cleanliness and to reduce water use in home laundering; others responded to long-term trends in fresh water availability and experimented with textile finishing effects that are enhanced rather than degraded in saltwater conditions; another project documented the historical significance of salt to human well-being, as a means to reflect on shifting sociocultural beliefs and to gain insight into the contemporary perceptions that salt is 'bad'; while another team noted the limitations of a company reducing the water footprint of one product while expanding business volume overall. By presenting an adaptable garment which explored how the wearer's need to feel refreshed might be satisfied in other ways besides making an additional purchase, students suggested a redesign of the business model to reduce the absolute water footprint of the company. As a group then, students were able to experience and witness the multiple approaches to sustainability and to challenge a variety of social and industrial norms.

'Embedding' scientists directly into the studio enables students to experience science as a method of inquiry to inform practice much more quickly than might be achieved in a straight science course outside the creative discipline. Students were able to link human activity to natural systems, develop a comfort for working alongside scientists as peers and felt bolstered in delivering quantitative research with scientific rigour; and they experienced how their own skills complement the methods of science—linking data to wearer behaviours and giving visual form to desirable new ways of living within nature's limits.

8.6 The field as an extension of the fashion design studio

A now well-established college-wide initiative, which also aims to facilitate cross-discipline collaboration is ENGAGE at CCA. Coordinated by the Center for Art and Public Life and activated across academic programmes, ENGAGE serves as a hub, connecting interested faculty and students to community partners and relevant outside experts. Here, the field is seen as an extension of the studio as students are placed at the centre of project-based learning with a focus on real life experience in community engagement.

One of the Fashion Design ENGAGE initiatives partners with Bridging Cultures Through Design outside expert Mimi Robinson, who takes students to Guatemala to work with indigenous communities to help support micro-enterprise opportunities. Here comprehension is facilitated through practical, experiential and reflective means. For students learn first hand the capabilities of artisan groups and how to negotiate the opportunities and barriers to local and regional markets. But, perhaps more importantly, when working alongside and being taught by indigenous women how to weave on a back strap loom, students literally 'feel' the speed and rhythm of the 'technology', its scale and portability; they become intimately familiar with the materials and symbolism woven into the textiles and even the width of the fabric—all of which have co-evolved in relationship to place and culture. It is through this first-hand experience that students more easily grasp issues of speed, scale, globalisation and anonymity in the current fashion system.

Critical understanding of consumerism and social justice continues when, on return to the US, the material excess and social degradation (sometimes referred to as 'culture shock') is simply…apparent. For this class, students might be guided to writings by Chip Morris, Wendell Berry or Paola Gianturco, in which they find their own experiences and insights echoed and build confidence in their abilities to make discerning ethical choices in their own work.

The effectiveness of this type of pedagogy is observed by a number of education practitioners. Leerberg, Riisberg and Boutrup, of Kolding School of Design, Denmark, for example note that 'designers are…better…learning about sustainability issues in bodily ways than through abstract models…(and) understand intellectual problems through acting and creating' (Leerberg *et al.* 2010: 113).

8.7 Outcomes

After teaching Sustainable Fashion Design at California College of the Arts for more than 10 years, we have observed multiple dynamics that are both affected by and influence the effectiveness of the classes. These outcomes are challenging to anticipate and track, for they are generative and occur inside the college, inside the classroom and outside in the community/industry at large in unpredictable ways.

The programme began as a single elective class taught by a part-time instructor and has grown into multiple seminar and studio classes with a full-time instructor presence. The broader college governance responsibilities of full-time faculty has opened awareness of and access to faculty resources in other divisions of the college and has fostered cross-discipline links to enrich both the learning and the teaching experience.

In students specifically, positive learning outcomes are recognised in their ability to assemble disparate information and to provide discursive argument for relevant sustainable design strategies—'a well crafted concept'. In practice positive outcomes are recognised as a student's ability to make sense of the world and match what they do in that world with the values they hold. This act of taking agency or, as Leerberg *et al.* (2010) call it, 'taking a stance as a designer' is guided by the same discursive process from the classroom—but applied at a larger scale.

To the detail of student learning, we see that sustainability often provides purpose, which spurs students to bring their design work to a higher level, and this inevitably enhances their work in other studio classes. As one student notes:

> I realized that I could be challenged to a completely new level… To discover that fashion can be used as a tool for change empowered me and I enjoyed pushing against…conventional thoughts or methods. The class shaped my thinking…and gave me purpose.

Not all undergraduate students fully grasp the complexities of sustainability in the classroom, and not all who do, go on to sustainability practice. Yet we see that as the students' (and society's) understanding of sustainability deepens and broadens beyond materiality and processing considerations, so the directions and opportunities for sustainability practice also open up. The majority of students graduating from the CCA fashion programme are hired into the conventional fashion industry, yet we notice students have developed 'critical skills to reassess their role as fashion designers, and…to shape new paths'. These patterns of activity range from modest to ambitious and are found operating within, independent from or linking to the mainstream fashion sector. Over time, we expect this activity to diversify, and to arc further across disciplines and sectors of the economy, as each generation of graduates builds on and expands their 'ecologies'[8] of critical design practice.

8.8 Sustainable fashion design practice

8.8.1 Practicality

CCA fashion alumni are pursuing sustainability not as an ideology, but in very practical ways. They understand the fashion system and navigate within it, around it

---

8 O. Von Busch, in conversation, Green Gulch Zen Center, Muir Beach, California, December 2011.

and outside it to create their own 'niches'. Some students work for several years in conventional positions before finding, requesting and attaining a promotion into a sustainability role. Other graduates are very clear that they prefer to practise outside the commodity fashion sector and have created hybrid professions piecing together part-time work to ensure a solid financial base from which they can pursue crafting products for sale through local renegade craft and internet platforms.

8.8.2 Experimentation

Inter-disciplinary education provides graduates with the ability to work in a variety of capacities, and to explore creative endeavours beyond the product. An alumna who graduated in 2008, for example, applied her skills to directing a documentary film on working in a large Indian textile mill, has developed a design mentorship programme on sustainable textile practices for international students and is planning a professional workshop on industrial textile waste reduction.

8.8.3 Adaptability and flexibility

We see students demonstrating confidence to craft professional paths to meet their values. One alumna who graduated in 2003, for example, developed her own line of 'slow fashion' sweaters, led workshops teaching craft skills, and now fashions bespoke, locally produced menswear—each position better enabling her to practise her 'point of view' about fashion and sustainability.

8.8.4 Entrepreneurship

Despite the difficult economic landscape (and perhaps *because* of it), an increasing number of graduates are interested in starting their own businesses. These students are often prompted by an experienced clash of values. One witnessed the seasonal waste generated by fabric sample headers and decided to use these as a resource for a refined line of clothing, which she now sells through regional boutiques and e-commerce.[9] For another, witnessing the sheer volume of merchandise moving through the commodity fashion system prompted her to launch a line of locally made zero waste clothing, supported by the recently established San Francisco Fashion Incubator (SFFI).[10] Another who graduated in 2006, established a micro-enterprise initiative in Ghana, working with traditional textiles and local women to produce garments sold in the local market.

8.8.5 Agency

These examples represent a very short list of CCA alumni activities in sustainable fashion design practice. But what is already telling is their self-made or self-initiated

9 Piece × Piece, www.pxp-sf.com/collection.php, accessed 21 September 2012.
10 www.fashionincubatorsf.org/index.html, accessed 21 September 2012.

nature—where students had the consciousness, confidence and ability to take action. Says one graduate: 'I made my own position over and over again'.

8.8.6 Critical thinking

We witness students asking 'deeper questions about the nature of business' (Capra 2011). As one graduate observed while working with smallholder cotton farmers: 'Fair Trade may ensure that extra money goes to the farmers, but it doesn't necessarily go to the farm workers'. Identifying a gap between intent and practice she has since joined the board of a non-profit organisation to help map and meet the needs of cotton farm workers and notes: 'The needs may or may not be quantified in economic terms, especially in rural areas, where money isn't necessarily the desired means of exchange', indicating a sensitivity to place and culture and a readiness to let go of Western constructs and perceptions of what is 'better' or 'best'.

8.9 Continued challenges

One of the greatest challenges for the college, the programmes and instructors alike, is the cost of education in the US and the loan debt borne by students, which creates the very real pressure to find employment immediately on graduation. This in turn creates inevitable tension between training to support what is (an unsustainable industry) vs. envisioning and testing what can be (creating a new industry). Though CCA's founding principles, its mission and culture (craft-based/non-profit) and small size (1,800 students total) support values-based learning, still the internal culture and wider societal realities are always in precarious balance.

The bias towards sustainability as a concern of materiality and processing is still so prevalent in the fashion industry, that the holistic thinking activated in CCA students can be effectively dis-abled in practice. Most design positions, even at the most progressive companies, still largely focus on garment styling. Though this is slowly changing, we find that the integrative capabilities of new graduates are generally under-recognised and under-used.

8.9.1 Internal

The administrative structures of the college—payment systems, unit allocation to teaching lines and to classes—do not readily support cross-subject, cross-division and cross-faculty collaboration and are slow/unwieldy to transition. Nonetheless, informal, faculty-led, cross-discipline collaborations are forming new social ecologies that co-exist alongside, in between and inside the old structures and may eventually make them redundant.

Many of the artefacts developed in fashion for sustainability studio classes have the potential to be living labs, tested on wearers and documented by ethnographic researchers for the lifestyle changes and new business 'post-growth' models they might inspire. We see this potential to 'transcend the boundaries of academic research, professional knowledge and commercial production' (Farren Bradley *et al.* 2010: 265), exciting to consider. However, as an undergraduate course, we lack the means to pursue this more lengthy investigation, though it's clear it would add new knowledge to the international discourse on fashion and sustainability.

8.10 Conclusions

This chapter looked reflectively and critically at the undergraduate fashion design for sustainability classes that have been taught at California College of the Arts since 1999. It laid out examples of pedagogy and student projects illustrating how the classes provide *consciousness, structure and agency* for sustainability practice. It also referenced a number of college-wide initiatives that provide alternative peda-gogical approaches complementing the fashion for sustainability learning as well as some patterns of practice that are opening up as graduates find their own ways to engage in sustainability as practice.

These accomplishments are modest, yet we are starting to see CCA fashion alumni negotiating (and in so doing challenging) long-established professional norms. And as these young designers become exposed to much broader influences than can be afforded through the simple lens of business and the market, this will inevitably re-inform fashion design practice—and education for practice.

CCA's fashion faculty are now actively requesting development for sustainabil-ity education for themselves. This presents great opportunity and potential for the programme as a whole, for the instructors' own professional expertise, skills and perspective—in patternmaking, design, textiles, elements of business, fashion history—will be brought to bear on sustainability principles and vice versa, and this will generatively integrate sustainability across the entire fashion design cur-riculum in ways we cannot imagine in advance. This active interest, combined with new professional norms and new pedagogical norms being opened up by alumni and faculty, respectively, is slowly starting to generate a process that David Orr calls 'a continuous recreation or co-evolution, where both education and society are engaged in a relationship of mutual transformation' (Orr 2001: 9).

Though this is encouraging, it's worth noting that those graduates who have been the most ambitious in forging the new forms of practice, have also felt the most isolated in their efforts. Says the graduate who is now researching measures of well-being for cotton farm workers in developing countries: 'I went from a very safe place of exploration…to a very lonely and scary place…of practice and execu-tion. My ideas were met with a lot of scepticism and blank stares…it's a constant push and pull'.

For us, these expressed sentiments further underscore the importance of teach-ing not only *about* sustainability and the impacts of the fashion sector, but also instilling skills, which enable students to pursue fashion design *as* sustainable practice. They also acknowledge the deep work still required to enable society (and design educators) to reappraise values, and to redefine perceptions about the role of design and fashion designers. In the meantime, to Cotton International's poll, we would answer, 'Yes the next generation(s) of young fashion designers can influence the sustainability of cotton growing. Indeed they already are'.

Bibliography

Capra, F. (2011) 'In Conversation', *Fashion Sustainability Summer Workshop Series*, San Francisco, 4–6 August 2011.

Capra, F., E. Callenbach and S. Marburg (1990) *The Elmwood Guide to Eco Auditing and Ecologically Conscious Management* (Berkeley, CA: The Elmwood Institute).

Farren Bradley, J., S. Sayce and A. Lewis (2010) 'Sustainability and Built Environment Professionals: A Shifting Paradigm', in P. Jones, D. Selby and S. Sterling (eds.), *Sustainability Education: Perspectives and Practice across Higher Education* (London: Earthscan): 257-72.

Flint, D. (2010) 'Developing Critical Faculties: Environmental Sustainability in Media, Communications and Cultural Studies in Higher Education', in P. Jones, D. Selby and S. Sterling (eds.), *Sustainability Education: Perspectives and Practice across Higher Education* (London: Earthscan): 201-17.

Gissen, D. (2011) 'APE', in L. Tindler and B. Blostein (eds.), *Design Ecologies* (New York: Princeton Architectural Press): 63-75.

Goldberg, M. (2009) 'Social Conscience', in A. Tibbe (ed.), *Sustainability Literacy, Skills for a Changing World* (Dartington, UK: Green Books), as cited by D. Flint, 'Developing Critical Faculties' in P. Jones, D. Selby and S. Sterling (eds.), *Sustainability Education: Perspectives and Practice across Higher Education* (London: Earthscan): 206.

Leerberg, M., V. Riisberg and J. Boutrup (2010) 'Design Responsibility and Design as Reflective Practice: An Educational Challenge', *Sustainable Development* 18: 306-17 (www.//onlinelibrary.wiley.com/doi/10.1002/sd.v18:5/issuetoc, accessed 20 September 2012).

Meadows, D.H. (2008) *Thinking in Systems: Primer* (White River Junction, VT: Chelsea Green Publishing): 174.

Orr, D. (2001) 'Foreword', in S. Sterling (ed.), *Sustainable Education: Revisioning Learning and Change* (Totnes, UK: Green Books): 9.

Valero, I. (2010) 'Aesthetic(s) of the Common(s)' and the 'Economies of Desire', Ignacio Valero, 'EcoDomics: Beyond Palm Trees, Orangeries and the Ecology of Illusions', in Natasha Wheat (curator) and Susan Magrish Cline (designer), *Here/Not There* (Chicago: Museum of Contemporary Art Chicago): 22-33.

Von Busch, O. (2011) 'Community Repair', www.kulturservern.se/wronsov/selfpassage/CoRep/CoRep.htm, accessed 6 January 2012.

Lynda Grose is a designer, consultant and assistant professor at California College of the Arts. She cofounded ESPRIT's ecollection line, the first ecologically responsible clothing line developed by a major corporation. Lynda now advises across private and non-profit sectors to further sustainability in the fashion and textile industry and recently co-authored the book, *Fashion and Sustainability: Design for Change* (Laurence King Publishing, 2012).

9

Upcycling fashion for mass production

Tracy Diane Cassidy
University of Leeds, UK

Sara Li-Chou Han
Manchester Metropolitan University, UK

In the UK more than 2 million tonnes of clothing and textiles are purchased each year of which around only one-eighth will be recycled. It was reported that the British clothing and textiles sector alone creates a staggering 3.1 million tonnes of CO_2, some 2 million tonnes of wastage plus an additional 70 million tonnes of wastewater per annum, with 1.5 million tonnes of textile waste ending up in landfill (Minney 2011: 162). Waste and surplus materials from the textiles and garment manufacturing industries and unsold stock from the fashion retail sector, contribute to the landfill problem (Waste Online 2010). While attempts are made by companies to redistribute unwanted clothing from the UK and other developed countries to developing countries, mainly through charity organisations, landfill is still a prime site for much of the textile waste. However, a large majority of the clothes discarded are still wearable and often in very good condition (Farrant *et al.* 2010: 726). Wayne Hemmingway, designer and co-founder of Vintage Festival, a three day event at Southside, London (UK), where vintage clothing and accessories and other personal and homeware products are resold, regards the solution to the problem of textile waste as lying in the attitude towards fashion as being in constant change, whereby if the goal of fashion was to be fun and non-competitive then fashion consumption could be very different and its subsequent waste more manageable (Minney 2011: 51). Fletcher also pinpointed the necessity for the industry as a whole to 'rethink the role and value of fashion product' (Fletcher 2008: 108). This chapter explores the relatively newly coined 'upcycling' process as a viable recycling method for re-using what would otherwise be textile waste; and compares the upcycling process with a typical fashion production process model. The barriers to be overcome by the fashion industry are identified should an upcycling process be adopted for mass fashion production, which has already been earmarked as an 'emerging industry' (Williams 2011). The chapter concludes with some solution suggestions.

9.1 Textile waste and the textile sector

It has been reported that textile-related industries and consumer textile waste equates to nearly 40 kg per person per annum in the UK alone, and that merely a quarter of this waste is recycled. The remaining waste, which is in the region of 30 kg per person per annum, goes to landfill. The consequences to the environment include the production of methane gases and toxic leachate that pollute the air and groundwater supplies, respectively (Cupit 1996: 21, cited in Fletcher 2008). Fletcher concurs, declaring that much of the waste that finds its way to landfill is a consequence of mass-produced goods and the excessive consumption habits and behaviours of individuals (Fletcher 2008: 137). Walker suggests that fashion by its very nature is suggestive of transience, destined for a short lifespan and totally the opposite of the prolonged existence that products require to be deemed as sustainable (Walker 2007: 71). Upcycling advocate and founder of the upcycling fashion company From Somewhere (established 1997), Orsola de Castro, blames the fast fashion system that makes 'ultra-cheap' clothing available to the mass market for over-consumption behaviour, with the resulting textile waste; plus the over-production of fabrics in the manufacturing sector, the amount of 'unworn, partially finished and finished' but damaged products that never reach the retail sector and over-stocking retail stores are all contributing factors (Williams 2011).

However, putting the size and importance of the textiles industry into perspective, it has been reported that the sector has a workforce of around 340,000 employed in no less than 70,000 companies that are mostly small to medium enterprises (SMEs) in the UK. According to EU law, SME is defined as follows: a small company has less than 50 employees and a turnover of less than €10 million; a medium-sized company has less than 250 employees and a turnover of less than €50 million; and a micro-enterprise has less than 10 employees and a turnover of less than €2 million.[1] The apparel sector alone employs around 105,000 people in around 26,000 businesses of which almost 80% are sole trading companies. It is estimated that the apparel industry contributes around £4.1 billion to the UK economy and the

---

1 European Commission: www.ec.europa.eu/enterprise/policies/sme/facts-figures-analysis/sme-definition/index_en.htm, accessed 14 March 2011.

entire textile sector contributes some £10 billion. The fashion and textile sector is an equal opportunities sector; approximately 57% of the workforce are male and 43% female. It also has a reputable track record for re-training adults looking for career changes (Skillset Textiles 2010). As Walker concurs, it is equally important to 'embrace economic viability, social well-being and environmental gains' (Walker 2007: 75). Hence, the issue under consideration in this chapter is not merely how to tackle the ongoing problem of waste textile but to address the issue in a manner that will not compromise employment and business opportunities for local and national economies. Owing to the inherent labour intensity (Fletcher 2008: 101) and high level of skills acquisition of designers required by the upcycling process, it is considered that this process can meet the objectives of the chapter, though there are a number of challenges to contend with that will be highlighted and discussed along the way.

9.2 Managing waste through recycling

Recycling textiles is not a new practice. During the Industrial Revolution in the 1700s and 1800s a lucrative sector developed around Batley, West Yorkshire (UK), it would appear that even at this time entrepreneurs foresaw the economic benefits of reducing unwanted garments back to fibre and yarn to re-use, if not also the environmental benefits. Today Oxfam's recycling plant Wastesaver handles around 100 tonnes of unsold and unwearable garments per week. The plant is located in Huddersfield, also in West Yorkshire, keeping the roots of this sector alive and possibly of greater importance now than then (Waste Online 2010).

Two fundamental sources of textile waste have been identified, post-consumer waste and post-industrial waste, otherwise known as pre-consumer waste (Potts 2011). What to do with pre-consumer waste has been an issue for the industry for many years. For the retail sector pre-consumer waste includes unsold and damaged stock. This problem had evidently escalated to such an extent that fashion company H&M had been accused of damaging, bagging up and dumping surplus stock outside their own outlet in Manhattan, New York (Dwyer 2010). Since this claim H&M and other companies such as Marks & Spencer direct unsold and damaged clothing to charities such as Oxfam and to the Newlife Foundation for Disabled Children. For the manufacturing sector fabric cut-offs and end of roll fabric constitute waste. End of roll fabric in particular is problematic as many brands will order far more fabric than required in order to replenish stocks in the event of particular lines being more popular than expected. Within the textile mills there is a large amount of fabric waste at the onset of the printing process. It is commonplace for around 30 metres of fabric to be discarded at this stage to align the pattern; this is known as feeder cloth. The director of the company Ocean Lanka in Sri Lanka stated that around 8% of fabric is wasted in the weaving process as its 'behaviour can not be easily predicted' (Williams 2011).

Depending on the individual, post-consumer waste may be taken to clothes banks provided by charity organisations which are located at local recycling sites, supermarket and council car parks, etc.; taken directly to charity shops; donated to local jumble sales organised for instance by churches and schools; or put out with domestic rubbish heading directly to landfill (Waste Online 2010). With the current vogue for vintage and retro fashion in the UK, USA and much of Europe and the popularity of online auction sites, older garments, particularly branded goods, are being sold to be worn or collected in their original state. The resale of clothing has escalated in recent years through online auctions such as eBay and **fashion swap websites** such as Swap Style.[2] This type of re-use recycling is most beneficial to the environment requiring the least resources, mostly only for transportation (Fletcher 2008: 100). Some products may be repaired or reconditioned to make them useable requiring new components, such as a zip or button, or patches of new or recycled fabrics; this type of recycling offers job and business opportunities (Fletcher 2008: 100). Such practice was commonplace in most countries and in the UK well into the 1970s, particularly by older generations who grew up during times of austerity. The availability of cheap clothing of more recent decades has been recognised as one of the prime reasons for this type of recycling practice to lose favour with the general public (Fletcher 2008: 101). However, the more recent craft revival in the UK, and much of Europe and the USA, has encouraged individuals to adopt this once considered 'make do and mend' practice for new enterprise opportunities, in particular women returning to work following a career break, those made redundant and retirees. While many operate as hobby traders, some have developed into more bona fide companies such as the charity organisation TRAID Remade that supplies chain stores such as TopMan and the London-based company Junky Styling[3] (Fletcher 2008: 103). TRAID (Textile Recycling & Aid for International Development) is further discussed in Section 9.3, Upcycling. Fletcher (2008: 100) also professed that this process 'brings significant environmental savings' only using energy to 'collect, sort and resell' and is therefore 10 to 20 times less resource-hungry than producing brand new items.

Other types of recycling require energy-intensive processes in order to break down the products for re-use, such as back to yarn to be remade into garments (Fletcher 2008: 98); while more energy intense than re-using or repairing garments, this method still requires fewer resources than manufacturing with virgin materials. While the benefits to the environment cannot be underestimated, recycled goods have acquired the misfortune of a low quality perception from consumers because of the past practice of companies using recycled materials to deliberately produce such lower grade products, now referred to as down-cycling (Fletcher 2008: 100). Unwearable garments are destined for the flocking industry to be shredded for non-fashion goods such as furniture padding and roofing felts (Waste Online 2010); and some offcuts are pulped to recycle into low-grade products such as

---

2 www.swapstyle.com, accessed 21 September 2012.
3 www.junkystyling.co.uk, accessed 21 September 2012.

mops and mats (Williams 2011). Woollen garments are sold to specialist companies that recycle them into new yarns and fabrics, and cottons and silks are sorted into grades to be recycled mostly into wiping cloths and industrial applications, while some are recycled into paper-based products. Sorting and grading is undertaken by skilled workers (Waste Online 2010).

Figure 9.1 shows, simplistically, the direction that most of the textile waste takes. It is not claimed to be a totally inclusive representation of the real world, nor does it attempt to demonstrate the amount of waste that moves around. The figure does however demonstrate the ideal where products continue to be used rather than being directed to the dead-end landfill that appears in bold. The diagram also shows that currently the recycling of fashion product continuing as fashion product happens at the top (consumer) end mostly through the efforts of individuals, communities and society rather than at an industrial level where the majority of recycling becomes part of a 'down-cycling' process losing quality and value. While it cannot be argued that the down-cycled products, such as roof felting and furniture fillings, are not viable and sustainable products in their own right, the fashion

Figure 9.1 **Waste sources and current recycling routes**

Source: an interpretation of the literature developed by T.D. Cassidy

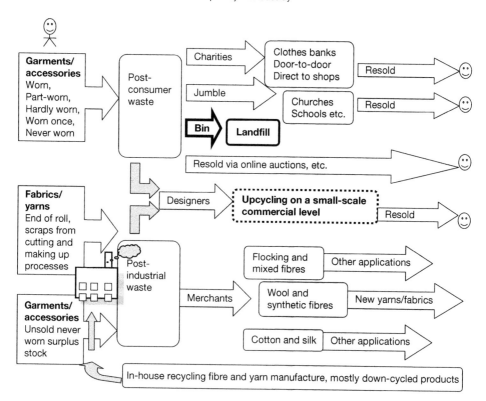

industry is still not taking full advantage of the potential of employing an upcycling process that relies less on virgin raw materials. The upcycling concept shown with a bold broken line in the diagram is currently employed by very few entrepreneurial designers selling on a very small scale. Also it should be stressed that, currently, clothes banks such as those provided by Recyclatex run by the Textile Recycling Association to local councils and charities, are reported to be operating only at around 25% of their full capacity (Waste Online 2010).

9.3 Upcycling

The term 'upcycling' was probably first used by William McDonough and Michael Braungart (2002: 56-57) when they discussed the recycling process as 'down-cycling' because of the lower grade products that often result. They suggested that a process should exist where the resulting products were at least of equal value or preferably of a higher value than the original goods and components and referred to this as upcycling. Upcycling is a different type of recycling method making use of the materials and components of discarded goods to transform them through clever design and skilled craftsmanship into new, high-value products. Often the products directly reference their original form and make use of these features as witty, postmodern design features, adding to the desirability of the finished article. While reporting for the German international broadcaster, Deutsche Welle, Potts (2011) referred to the upcycled designs that London fashion designers at the high-end of the market are producing as being 'commercially and aesthetically more valuable'. Nor is this a new concept; during the Second World War women frequently recycled clothing largely because of rationing, so much so that this practice was dubbed 'make do and mend'. During the 1940s this culture and practice was very well supported by the Women's Institute,[4] a largely voluntary organisation, where ideas for remaking garments and other recycling tips were shared (Craddick-Adams 2005). Upcycling is also beginning to be embraced in the highly influential celebrity arena. At the 2011 Oscars, film producer Livia (Giuggioli) Firth accompanied her husband Colin Firth wearing an upcycled dress created by Orsola de Castro who used pre-consumer waste: high-end Italian end-of-roll fabric with discarded offcuts of silk and organza (Marsden 2010). Miriam Clegg, the wife of the UK's Deputy Prime Minister Nick Clegg, has also been reported to be a supporter of wearing upcycled fashion (Williams 2011).

Upcycling is considered to be more beneficial than recycling as the process uses less energy and is not dependent on virgin resources. Waste Online (2010) agrees that re-using textiles reduces landfill space and pressures on resources required for virgin raw materials. Upcycling can offer an alternative, turning end-of-life

4 www.thewi.org.uk, accessed 24 September 2012.

garments and textile waste into fashionable products with a high retail value and assisting the industry to develop more sustainable production methods. It has been suggested that upcycling is not merely a solution to the textile waste issue but should be considered as a new way of 'thinking about and working with' a resource abundantly available 'in our communities'—a method of 're-imaging our waste' (Digital Universe 2011). To date, a small number of independent companies have succeeded in operating within a niche market over a number of years taking upcycled fashion product to market using small-scale business models, though most sell only within the close locality of the business.

Other examples include TRAID (Textile Recycling & Aid for International Development), Worn Again and retail giant Tesco. TRAID is a charity organisation that uses profits from upcycled fashion to benefit social and environmental projects on a global scale; typical recycling includes making bags from suits and dresses. The organisation's Communications Manager, Leigh McAlea, stated her belief that the most likely motivation for purchasing, wearing and using upcycled products is the desire for individuality, which may be perceived as a reaction to the homogeneity of mass-produced fashions on the high street, resulting in 'everyone looking the same', affirming that upcycled products are distinctively 'unique and ethical' (Potts 2011). TRAID declares its recycling process as one of collecting via its own clothes banks, transporting to a plant for sorting by hand and reselling products that are in good condition in one of its 10 shops trading under the TRAID brand name in the London location. TRAID markets its goods as being high-quality, second-hand, vintage and designer clothing and accessories using its own TRAIDremade label. Products are also available online.[5] Their products are 'one-off, sustainably remade by hand in Brighton [UK]' and are said to reflect current fashion trends, while being inspired by the characteristics of the fabrics and trims they happen to be working with.[6] Worn Again celebrates being voted number one eco-brand by *The Independent* newspaper on its website.[7] The company assists large organisations to re-use waste materials using an upcycling process. The materials may not have begun life as fashion products, for instance old uniforms and decommissioned hot air balloons have been successfully upcycled into new fashion bags and accessories (Potts 2011). Mainstream retailer Tesco has also declared an interest in upcycling, supporting the creation of collections made from the pre-consumer waste from its own end-of-line seasonal ranges. Tesco's collaboration with the upcycling company From Somewhere has resulted in the production of six pieces under the Florence & Fred label (Carter 2010). Orsola de Castro of From Somewhere has been reported to be the first to operate an upcycling enterprise on an industrial scale (Williams 2011).

Creating products using upcycling methods poses challenges to the mass production sector. Tesco's executive, Alan Wragg, commented on the difficultly experienced

---

5 www.traidremade.com, accessed 24 September 2012.
6 www.traid.org.uk, accessed 24 September 2012.
7 www.wornagain.co.uk, accessed 24 September 2012.

with balancing an upcycling process for mass production and 'maintaining healthy sales figures', as the process is basically one of 'bespoke, hand-crafted, individual pieces', and believes that a considerable 'revolution' would be required to make sufficient changes to the traditional manufacturing system. While Tesco plans to be a 'market leader in sustainable fashion', it has recognised that the costs incurred by the upcycling process need to be reduced dramatically in order to make the process a commercially viable one (Potts 2011). While large companies profess the need for volume (Potts 2011), evidence of unsold stock, even after numerous sales on the high street, would suggest that supply is currently far exceeding demand anyway. Carter (2010) reported on the fact that some top-end design companies are incinerating unsold stock as a brand protection strategy, which adds weight to the argument of over-production but also sends out a somewhat immoral message of an anti-upcycling ethos among some fashion companies as they would rather destroy perfectly good products than sell them cheaply, where they may then be upcycled. De Castro has also pointed to the fact that logos are a massive obstacle for upcyclers, as any reference to a brand cannot lawfully be used. Further to this, many companies enforce a 'non-repurposed' proviso on fabrics so that they cannot be used other than for the original purpose for at least six months after the season for which they were purchased. Some companies go a stage further making it necessary for surplus fabrics to be destroyed (Carter 2010). A further complication for mass upcycling includes the lack of flexibility in pattern and product consistency that the industry has imposed on itself (Carter 2010).

Cyndi Rhoades, Chief Executive of Worn Again, commented on the challenge of the industry relying on rolls of fabric that helps to standardise production, whereas upcycling uses 'random pieces of fabric of different sizes and shapes' (Potts 2011). Perhaps the most challenging aspect is the slowing down of the entire system, the opposite to the current quick response culture and fast fashion operations of today's industry, particularly for the textile sector, as fabric pieces are readily available. Overall longer lead-times would be necessary to change the balance of supply and demand (Digital Universe 2011), which, as previously pointed out, may not necessarily be a negative consequence. On the plus side the slowing down of fashion is considered to add value to the products for the wearer and encourages individuals to keep the product for longer before discarding. This has obvious challenges in terms of design to link strongly with consumers' taste in style and colour and their lifestyles, plus other design features of the products (Fletcher 2008: 73). Upcycling also supports the sourcing of local materials and components, using local workers and operating short production runs (Walker 2007: 76), reducing transportation costs and other benefits such as reducing air pollution, road congestion and the need for packaging (Fletcher 2008: 81). The challenge also remains to create a 'sustainable production line' (Potts 2011) because, while small volumes of upcycling are better than none at all, as de Castro stated, realistically to have significant impact upcycling needs to happen in high volume. De Castro also stated that, at this stage, upcycling is a 'marketing exercise' and it will take the industry a long time to change (Carter 2010). It is hoped that the comparison of the processes discussed in the following sections will go some way in encouraging such change to happen in the short term.

9.4 Upcycling process

Worn Again makes its upcycling process available to the general public on its website adapted in Figure 9.2.[8] It declares the materials, deconstruction and cleaning stages as additional to the mass production process. However in reality it is the sourcing of materials that is different.

Fletcher (2008: 98) discussed the reclamation process which has been adapted as a visual representation in Figure 9.3.

Figure 9.2 **Upcycling process used by Worn Again**
Source: adapted from the original

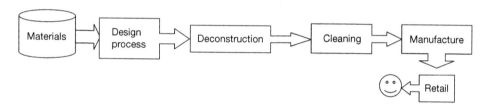

Figure 9.3 **Fletcher's reclamation process**
Source: as interpreted from the text (Fletcher 2008: 98)

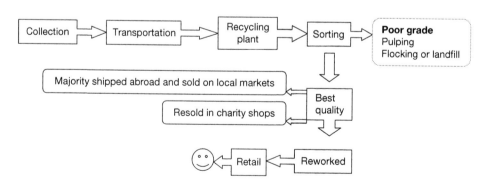

8   www.wornagain.co.uk/pages/the-process, accessed 24 September 2012.

In addition we give our example of a typical upcycling process to produce one-off garments using denim, shown in Figure 9.4. Denim can be viewed as being an ideal fabric both for upcycled garments and garments made using virgin materials because of its hard-wearing qualities and a general acceptance and practice of wearing garments many more times before laundering than garments made of other fabrics (Fletcher 2008: 172). In the first instance unsold and unwanted denim garments are sourced from charity shops, clothes swaps and donations from family, friends, etc. Most are bought from charity shops for around £5.00 per sack. Garments are sorted into those that can be quickly and easily altered in some way to refresh the garment, for example some denim jeans lend themselves well to simply cutting off the legs to create hot pants (shorts), and with minimum unpicking to make miniskirts. Such garments currently retail for around £15 to £20 and take approximately 20 to 30 minutes to make. Other garments are selected for unpicking to re-use the fabric pieces.

Garments are unpicked by hand using an unpicking tool, embroidery scissors and dressmaking shears. Over-lock stitching is unpicked first using embroidery scissors. It takes approximately 30 to 60 minutes to completely unpick one pair of jeans. Sewing threads must also be removed from the fabric pieces. A second sorting stage is then undertaken to bring together similar constituent pieces ready to be re-used. Jeans usually consist of two front leg pieces with pockets and studs, two back leg pieces usually with patch pockets, a waist band with a stud button and two back yoke pieces. There is normally around three square metres of fabric made

Figure 9.4 **Upcycling process used for commercial purposes, from the sourcing stage to the design process**

Source: photos by Sara Li-Chou Han

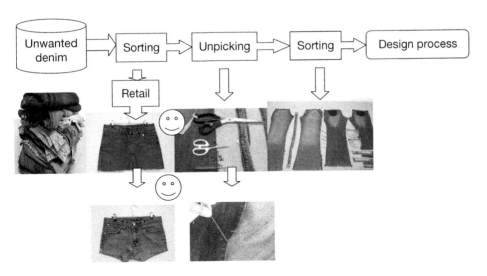

available for re-use. This concludes the deconstruction process. The next process is the designing of the new product; the mannequin is an invaluable tool for this process, particularly if conventional pattern pieces are not used. The design process used to create a small range of one-off designs is shown in Figure 9.5.

Selected pieces of fabric are draped on the stand to create unique garments. Owing to the inconsistency of the source materials no two garments are ever the

Figure 9.5 **Designing on the stand**

Source: photos by Sara Li-Chou Han

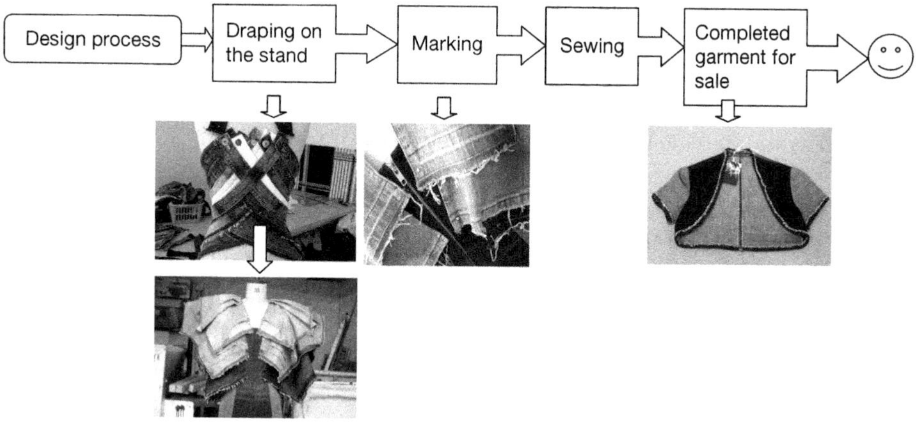

Figure 9.6 **Designing using a paper pattern**

Source: photos by Sara Li-Chou Han

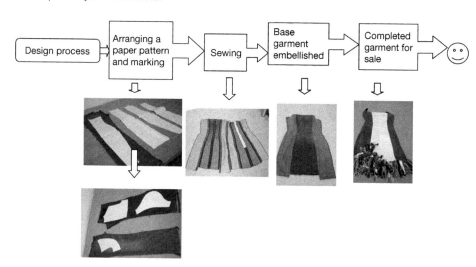

same. Different arrangements are photographed until the most desirable shapes are realised. The location of each piece is marked in relation to the other pieces prior to sewing them in place. Garments can also be made using a paper pattern mimicking the traditional dressmaking practice and flat pattern cutting principles used in the clothing industry. The leg sections of denim jeans lend themselves well to this method. The new pattern pieces are sewn together, often forming a base to be embellished with further unpicked or shredded pieces. The waste fabric that results from the cutting stage can be used during the embellishment stage. This process is shown in Figure 9.6.

A minidress such as the one shown as the final garment in Figure 9.6 takes approximately four hours to unpick, re-cut, sew and embellish and would normally sell between £60 and £150, depending on the extent of the embellishment. Shrugs, shown as the completed garment in Figure 9.5 make good use of smaller fabric pieces. Trims, bindings and cord fastenings are also recycled from the materials.

9.5 Mass production design and manufacturing process

Burke (2008) discusses a process of sourcing, where trade fairs, shows and exhibitions are given as the principal destinations for sourcing materials, followed by designing and manufacturing as the main areas of consideration when set-ting up a fashion enterprise. Although she is not explicit about the size of such an enterprise, it can be surmised that she is referring to a small sized company, which may even be a micro-sized enterprise according to the definition by the European Commission earlier in the chapter. Burke then proposes eight stages for the design and production cycle (2008: 109) which is to be repeated at least twice per year in line with the spring/summer and autumn/winter seasons, or more than twice if working with a fast fashion business model. The eight stages, or steps, are shown in Figure 9.7.

Figure 9.7 **Burke's design and manufacturing process**
Source: as interpreted from the text (Burke 2008)

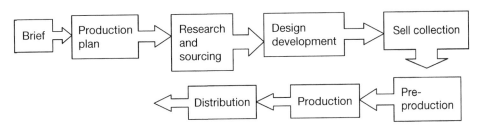

First of all the brief describes what is to be achieved (Burke 2008: 111); it inspires the designer and sets aims, objectives and constraints and guides the research and design processes (Seivewright 2007: 12). This is followed by a process where design and manufacturing is planned in relation to the fashion calendar in order to produce a critical path that will ensure that the product is delivered to the retail sector at the correct time. The next stage involves researching the market and trend information (Burke 2008: 111). Fabrics and trims are sourced and selected, and experts may also be sought to make up samples unless this is to be done in-house. Burke states that sourcing can stimulate design ideas. The market research and trend information is then worked into design ideas. Historical influences, cultural influences, such as art, literature and music and contemporary trends are all used as research resources (Seivewright 2007: 28-32). Designs may be hand drawn or a computer with a specialist CAD programme is used (Burke 2008: 116). Colour is often said to be a designer's starting point for a collection (Seivewright 2007: 23) and inspirations for texture lead to fabric suggestions and surface design (Seivewright 2007: 24). When designs have been selected then technical drawings are produced for the specification sheets that are used to record the technical information required to produce each garment. The first patterns are drafted and first samples produced. The costs are then determined and the collection is finalised in line with the available budget (Burke 2008: 116). Before the range goes into production the collection is sold to buyers in the retail sector, unless the company also retails (Burke 2008: 118). A pre-production stage then takes place which involves dealing with paperwork as orders are received. Fabric and trim orders must be confirmed with delivery dates and quantities to meet the critical path and labels, tags and packaging orders must also be confirmed. Pattern grading can now take place and then lay planning (Burke 2008: 118). The production stage then follows and finally the goods are packed and distributed for retail (Burke 2008: 120).

McKelvey and Munslow's (2003: 3) design process has been adapted and shown in Figure 9.8. The design process includes working with colour, silhouette, proportion, fabric, print, pattern, texture, sampling and the construction stage.

Figure 9.8 **McKelvey and Munslow's design process**

Source: as interpreted from the text (McKelvey and Munslow 2003)

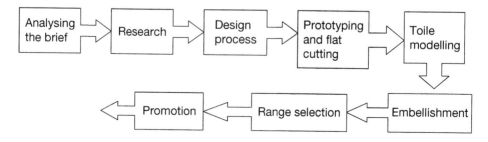

9.6 Challenges to be overcome

From the discussions in this chapter, for mass upcycled fashion production to be a viable option, a number of challenges are presented. These basically come under the guise of managing the labour-intensity and operating cost of the process itself, and in changing the way consumers and the industry perceive and interact with fashion. However, even before an upcycling process can be engaged with, large quantities of textile waste must be made readily available for the larger manufacturers. Currently such resources are more apt for the small, designer-led enterprises, as shown in Figure 9.1, as there is a lack of consistency in the fabric types, colours and so on that beckon one-off upcycled products as an end result. Large sections of waste fabrics and offcuts would better serve the industry, which would also reserve much of the post-consumer waste for small enterprises that can better manage a small-scale process. Larger companies would benefit from specialist deconstruction plants to collect, sort, grade and clean fabrics and thus absorb some of the additional costs. Fabrics could then be quickly sourced by type and colour etc. and reclaimed components such as fastenings could be purchased in bulk. This would also benefit small enterprises that are seeking a large selection under one roof and prepared to supplement their charity shop and other specialist finds. It is envisaged that this type of plant would be a more feasible option for large manufacturers rather than undertaking the deconstruction and cleaning processes in-house. As the textile industry would suffer from a reduction in virgin fabric production, it would seem sensible for this sector to diversify into the deconstruction sector. As a skilled workforce would be needed, this may be the catalyst that is needed to inject a renewed need and interest in textile-related higher education provision. Fletcher's reclamation process shown in Figure 9.3 provides a good business model for such a deconstruction sector.

Using solely recycled fabrics and components would not be a sustainable practice, as eventually a supply of garments made initially from virgin resources would be needed at some point to replenish the recycling system. Therefore it is suggested that larger manufacturers adopt a two-tier production system, as shown in Figure 9.9, which is offered as a simplistic business model. Perhaps one of the most challenging production processes to adapt for mass upcycling is the cutting process. Most large manufacturers use spreading machines and bulk cutters; using smaller pieces of haphazardly shaped fabric would require new technologies or modified processes to be developed. This would require capital outlay in the first instance but should reduce costs in the long term. An alternative may be to bond the fabric pieces to a dissolvable non-woven material such as those used for embroidery; this would enable current lay planning and laser cutting processes to remain relatively unchanged. Also the manner in which the sewing room operates would need to be adapted to allow more flexibility and would require a multi-skilled workforce. The resurrection of the concept of team systems, or modular manufacturing, where operatives perform more than one operation would offer a more flexible approach

Figure 9.9 **A mass upcycling process suggested for the fashion industry**

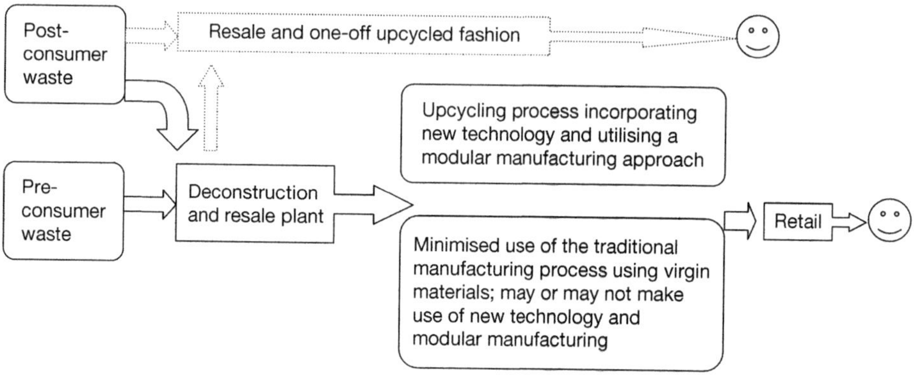

(Carr and Latham 1994: 245); even though this method of operating has never really found favour with the industry to date, some may think this change to be the ultimate challenge. It is also likely that designers/product developers would need to be situated within this manufacturing hub to design products in accordance with the materials available. It is also envisaged that designers would be more involved in the sourcing and purchasing of fabrics.

After all of this, the challenge to re-educate the public and the industry to adopt a new attitude towards fashion, one of individuality and added value in order to help prolong trends and the wearability of garments, thus slowing down the pace of fashion change, may be the least problematic. Media could do much to assist here; after all it is the marketing of fast-paced trends that has helped to bring us to the point we are currently at regarding excessive fashion consumption and waste. The issues highlighted in this concluding section of the chapter are still subject to rigorous research in order to bring the concept into the real world.

References

Burke, S. (2008) *Fashion Entrepreneur: Starting Your Own Fashion Business* (London: Burke Publishing).

Carr, H., and B. Latham (1994) *The Technology of Clothing Manufacture* (Oxford, UK: Blackwell Publishers, 2nd edn).

Carter, K. (2010) 'Ethical Fashion: Tesco Launches Recycled Clothing Collection', 2 March 2010, www.guardian.co.uk/lifeandstyle/green-living-blog/2010/mar/02/tesco-ethical-fashion-range, accessed 11 January 2011.

Craddick-Adams, P. (2005) 'BBC History Trails: Wars and Conflict: The Home Front in World War One', 14 March 2005, www.bbc.co.uk/history/trail/wars_conflict/home_front/the_home_front_01.shtml, accessed 12 January 2012.

Cupit, M.J. (1996) Opportunities and Barriers to Textile Recycling (Abingdon, UK: AEA Technology).

Digital Universe (2011) 'Upcycling: Re-imagining Our Waste', www.digitaluniverse.net/upcycling, accessed 11 January 2012.

Dwyer, J. (2010) 'A Clothing Clearance Where More Than Just the Prices Have Been Slashed', 5 January 2010, www.nytimes.com/2010/01/06/nyregion/06about.html, accessed 11 January 2012.

Farrant, L., S.I. Olsen and A. Wangel (2010) 'Environmental Benefits from Reusing Clothes', *International Journal of Life Cycle* 15: 726-36.

Fletcher, K. (2008) *Sustainable Fashion and Textiles: Design Journeys* (London: Earthscan).

McDonough, W., and M. Braungart (2002) *Cradle to Cradle: Remaking the Way We Make Things* (New York: North Point Press).

McKelvey, K., and J. Munslow (2003) *Fashion Design Process, Innovation and Practice* (Oxford, UK: Blackwell Publishers).

Marsden, J. (2010) 'Eco-fashion Takes Over the High Street', 10 March 2010, www.metro.co.uk/lifestyle/816875-eco-fashion-takes-over-the-high-street, accessed 11 January 2012.

Minney, S. (2011) *Naked Fashion: The New Sustainable Fashion Revolution* (Oxford, UK: New Internationalist Publications).

Potts, N.M. (2011) 'Upcycling Meets the Street of London', 14 February 2011, www.dw-world.de/dw/article/0,,6433913,00.html, accessed 11 January 2012.

Seivewright, S. (2007) *Research & Design* (Lausanne, Switzerland: Ava Publishing).

Skillset Textiles (2010) 'UK Government: Skillset Sector Skills Council', www.readingroom.lsc.gov.uk/sfa/cas/cas-skillsettextilesv2may2010.pdf, accessed 5 January 2012.

Walker, S. (2007) *Sustainable by Design: Explorations in Theory and Practice* (London: Earthscan).

Waste Online (2010) 'Textile Recycling Information Sheet', www.dl.dropbox.com/u/21130258/resources/InformationSheets/Textiles.htm, accessed 2 June 2010.

Williams, S. (2011) 'Sri Lanka Upcycling Factory Makes Waves in the Fashion Industry', The Telegraph, 16 January 2011, www.fashion.telegraph.co.uk/news-features/TMG8254833/Sri-Lankan-upcycling-factory-makes-waves-in-the-fashion-industry.html, accessed 11 January 2012.

Tracy Diane Cassidy is a trained knitwear designer with experience of knitwear and bespoke bridal-wear design, manufacture and retail. She obtained her PhD through the investigation of colour forecasting and is the first author of the book *Colour Forecasting* published by Blackwell. Tracy holds a Lectureship in Fashion Marketing and continues to conduct research in fashion and textile design, trends and marketing.

Sara Li-Chou Han currently works as a freelance designer-maker, creating upcycled fashion products to be shown off-schedule at London Fashion Week. She has worked in freelance fashion styling and PR, and is currently studying for an MSc by Research at Manchester Metropolitan University, focusing on design for upcycling. She also teaches workshops in recycled and sustainable fashion practices.

10

Creating new from that which is discarded

The collaborative San Francisco Tablecloth Repurposing Project

Connie Ulasewicz and Gail Baugh
San Francisco State University, USA

In San Francisco, as in most municipalities, there is no regular collection system for pre-sorted, discarded textiles at the consumer or industry level as exists for paper products, plastic materials, glass and canned goods. Historically, textile products did not have the same resale value as aluminium cans, glass bottles and newspapers, and were not part of the initial solid waste recycling programmes of the 1980s (Domina and Koch 1997: 96). A complex textile recycling industry does exist (Hawley 2008: 213), consisting of large quantities of consumer and business textile products, termed post-consumer waste (Domina and Koch 1997: 101), discarded to landfill, or donated to local and national charities and non-profit organisations. These organisations market and sell the products to consumers; any products not sold through their retail channels are sold off to rag sorters and brokers, or discarded to landfill. In the US an estimated 60% of the product purchased from the non-profit organisations by the recyclers is exported (SMART 2012) for sale in developing countries, for example to Kenya in Africa or Bolivia in South America. As these countries develop, the desire and need for these used textile products diminishes, replaced with the desire for new products (Hawley 2008: 229). In 2009, discarded textile products were estimated at 12.7 million tons, or 5.2% of all municipal solid waste collected by garbage services in the United States (USEPA 2009). Less than 15% of all textile waste placed in the garbage was recovered (re-used or exported) (USEPA 2009); the remaining 85% goes to landfill (SMART 2012). For every ton of textile products diverted from landfill and re-used, an estimated 20 tons of CO_2 is saved (Hunt 2011: 14).

While there is much documentation regarding the textile waste generated by consumers, the documentation of textile waste created by the hospitality and tourism industries is lacking. More than 16 million people visited the city of San Francisco in 2011, spending $8.5 billion, with business and leisure travel on the rise (Finz 2012: D 1). In these industries textiles are replenished for bedding, drapery, furniture and carpets because of excess use or updated design concepts. Restaurants and banquet tables require clean tablecloths and napkins for each sitting of customers, creating textile waste when stains, holes and other damages are created from continual use. As landfill space becomes scarce, the City and County of San Francisco has pledged to reduce solid waste deposited into landfills to zero by 2020 (City and County of San Francisco 2002). New models must be considered that explore methods to extend the life of discarded hospitality industry textile products, diverting them from the traditional textile recycling industry and landfill.

This case study investigates a collaborative effort in the city of San Francisco among government, business and a local trade organisation for the purpose of converting textile waste into a manufacturing resource. The ultimate goal of the study is to understand what usable discarded textiles from the waste stream of the hospitality industry can be diverted as a consistent supply for repurposing into new products. An additional component of this study is the heightened consumer interest and demand in purchasing products with a perceived environmental impact that correlates with its true impact (Chen and Burns 2006). In this chapter, the term 'repurpose(d)' is used to define the collecting and sorting of discarded materials as the resource for new products designed and manufactured in the location of discard. As the rise and influence of LOHAS (lifestyle of health and sustainability) consumers grow, so will the demand for and growth of repurposed products (Blossom 2011).

10.1 Synopsis of two textile supply chains

Exploring methods to reduce dependence on new or primary fibre and textile product supply chains and shift to usage of the discarded or secondary fibre and textile product supply chain is paramount. The international non-profit trade association, the Secondary Materials and Recycled Textiles Association or SMART, has as a goal, 'to promote the interdependence of all industry segments…as they use and convert recycled secondary materials from used clothing, commercial laundries' (SMART 2012). Its ultimate goal is to divert these products from ending up in landfill and further to explore how to extend the textile product life-cycle.

The Sustainable Apparel Coalition, founded in 2011 and representative of global apparel and footwear companies, created as one of their desired outcomes to, 'develop effective uses for textile waste, creating a second life for materials' (Sustainable Apparel Coalition 2012).

10.1.1 Primary fibre/textile supply chain

The textile, clothing and sewn products industry was built on the model of a one-way, cradle to grave system (McDonough and Braungart 2002) with resources grown or manufactured for singular use followed by disposal (see Fig. 10.1). This linear model is due in part to product innovations marketed to and supported by changing consumer demands, requiring the continual availability of new goods in the marketplace (Guide *et al.* 2008). Designers and manufacturers create products based on the false premise that production of new yardage from virgin fibre will be continuously available. In 2010 and 2011, product sourcing managers faced the reality of cotton fibre in short supply with prices rising, while escalating oil prices were putting pressure on the cost of polyester fibre (D'Altorio 2010). Fibre supply became a finite quantity, instead of increasing, to meet the growing demand for textiles and textile products. Retailers' strategies to expand their businesses depended on access to plentiful, well-priced fibre and textile products. The 2010/2011 fibre shortages and price escalations proved it to be difficult to maintain expected profit margins for global retailers and support the challenges of the traditional primary fibre/textile supply chain.

10.1.2 Secondary fibre/textile supply chain

As the traditional fibre/textile supply chain has its own life-cycle, so, too, does the secondary fibre/textile supply chain. Supported by Japanese fibre innovations, developing textile waste removal efforts and the emerging interest from particular consumer market segments seeking products made from recycled or repurposed materials, a secondary supply chain of discarded textile products collected for re-use has emerged (Owen 2011). This supply of textile products is a complex mix of blended fibres, combined fabrics, specialised fabric finishes and intricately sewn products. These discarded textiles were originally designed or produced using the primary fibre/textile supply chain without re-use in mind. The evaluation of discarded textile products for manufacturing new products provides a new secondary supply chain resource.

Figure 10.1 **Cradle to grave fibre/textile production and consumption model**

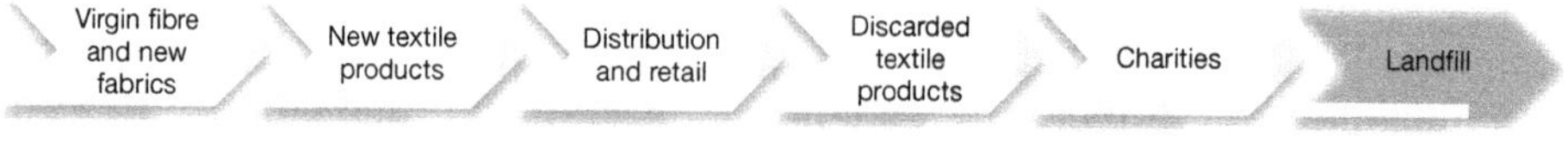

Industry efforts to date concentrate on temporary diversion of textile waste, such as reselling the same product as in the traditional textile recycling industry, or repurposing into a new product. An example of repurposing would be Martex Fiber (Martex Fiber Southern Corp 2011), a global importer and exporter of textile waste, which offers waste removal services for fibre, fabric and product manufacturers for the purpose of new yarn and fabric production (Bloomberg Business Week 2012). A new West Virginia, US, apparel manufacturer, SustainU, makes clothing from 100% recycled materials for its knitted tops sold to colleges and universities (Laporte 2012). Technological advances in fibre and yarn manufacturing, utilising existing fibre and fabrics for new fibre manufacturing, now make it possible to conserve fibre resources for new production.

Teijin Fibers, a Japan-based fibre mill, has invented a procedure to chemically recycle (depolymerise and repolymerise) existing polyester fibre products into new, high-quality polyester fibre (Eco Circle 2008). The process uses fewer chemicals, produces lower emissions and uses less energy than virgin polyester fibre manufacturing. Toray Fiber, another Japan-based fibre mill has also developed similar fibre recycling in nylon and polyester fibres (Toray 2011). Teijin Fibers and Toray Fiber collect only their own textile products for producing new fibre. They contract with their customers, such as Patagonia or Nike, to collect their post-consumer products, shipping them back to the fibre mill for chemical recycling into new fibre, manufacturing into new products and purchase by Patagonia or Nike (Eco Circle 2008).

Manufacturing previously used fabric into new products provides an opportunity to keep fabric out of the waste stream and remain in a new secondary fibre/textile supply chain, a cradle-to-cradle model (McDonough and Braungart 2002). The collection of discarded textile products for manufacturing of category specific new products provides the spark to invent new manufacturing models and perhaps a new industry. The intent of this study is an exploration of a new collection, sorting and manufacturing system for the repurposing of hospitality and tourism textile waste.

10.2 San Francisco's 'zero waste' by 2020

The City and County of San Francisco (2002) has pledged to reduce solid waste deposited into landfills to zero by 2020. San Francisco had achieved 72+% total solid waste diversion by 2009, the highest large city waste diversion programme in the United States (Green 2009). However, 3.8% of solid waste collected annually in San Francisco is textile waste that goes to landfill (E.S. Associates 2006). To date, there has been no focus by either the SF Department of the Environment or the city-contracted waste collection agency, Recology, to study the issue of textile waste.[1] San

1 Personal interviews with Jack Macy, San Francisco Department of the Environment, and Bob Besso, District Waste Management Director, Recology, 15 November 2009.

Francisco Department of the Environment advises consumers to send unwanted clothing to various non-profit or for-profit used clothing retailers (Eco-findeRRR 2012), yet lacks alternative options that will remove discarded textiles from the landfill. San Francisco cannot fulfill its zero waste pledge unless it addresses textile waste.

10.2.1 Collaborative working model

San Francisco is one of the top global destinations for tourism and conventions, both industries using and creating categories of wasted materials discarded to landfill. The San Francisco Department of the Environment (SFDOE) identified for potential diversion a large category of textiles used daily by the tourism and convention industries: tablecloths. Industrial tablecloths are sheets of flat, woven fabric, in standardised round, square and rectangular sizes manufactured in singular or blended fibre combinations of cotton and polyester. Polyester, when discarded to landfill, creates environmental problems through the slow degradation and waste of a polymer derived from non-renewable petroleum resources (Zou *et al.* 2011: 769). Hilary Near of the SFDOE reached out to the San Francisco/Bay Area sewn products trade association, PeopleWearSF, to explore potential methods to divert and re-use this textile tablecloth waste. PeopleWearSF (PWSF) is a collaborative network of industry professionals whose mission is to use their knowledge and skills in designing, manufacturing and marketing products that have a positive impact on the planet, people and the local economy. The organisation accepted the challenge and opportunity to investigate how this discarded textile waste could create a secondary supply chain for the sewn products industry.

10.3 Premise of the case study

In 2011, a core group of PWSF board members launched the San Francisco Tablecloth Repurposing Project. Their challenge was to collaboratively work with the City of San Francisco and the Hotel Council of San Francisco to develop a plan for repurposing discarded hotel linens while supporting the citywide goal of zero waste by 2020 (City and County of San Francisco 2002), and locally manufacturing a new product for consumer purchase.

10.3.1 San Francisco hotel industry waste management

The Hotel Council of San Francisco is a non-profit organisation representing all segments of the San Francisco lodging industry. One of its philanthropic missions is to divert usable discarded materials (including sheets and towels), both new and partly used amenities (including shampoo, soaps, tissues, toothpaste and other toiletry items), furniture and kitchen equipment from landfill and into the hands of community-based charitable organisations (Hotel Council of San Francisco 2012). To reach these organisations, the Hotel Council works through the San Francisco Hotel/Non-Profit Collaborative. Jo Licata, Community Projects Manager, Hilton San Francisco Union Square, is a founding member of the San Francisco Hotel/ Non-Profit Collaborative. Under her leadership, the Collaborative works with the Hotel Council to focus donations where they can best be utilised. Over 4,500 kg of materials per month, including soaps, shampoo and toothpaste, are donated to the Collaborative for distribution (Hotel Council of San Francisco 2012). Discarded tablecloths are not a requested item for this method of diversion, making them a perfect source of waste stream diversion for repurposing.

10.3.2 Quantity of tablecloths

Data obtained from three multinational San Francisco hotels (each with over 500 guest rooms) revealed that on average 15–100 tablecloths, of varying sizes, are discarded each month. The supplier of tablecloths to restaurants discards up to 5,000 tablecloths (2 tons) per month.[2] The criterion for tablecloth discard is consistent: permanent stains, holes, tears or other damages. The expected lifespan of the tablecloths ranges from 2 to 5 years depending on the type of use, fibre content, construction and finishes that affect the soil release and general appearance of the products. Some of the discards are re-used as rags for cleaning and others are discarded to landfill.

10.3.3 Tablecloth characteristics

The tablecloths are 100% polyester or a blend of 50% polyester and 50% cotton fibre content, utilising several weaves (balanced plain, oxford or sateen), all approximately 8 oz/sq yd (300 g/m^2), some treated with a stain-resistant finish. Tablecloth fabrics are laundered frequently, often after a single use, and are manufactured with a polyester fibre content to enhance washing, drying, pressing and cost efficiencies, not possible using 100% cotton fibre content. Sizes range from 152 to 335 cm round, 114 to 229 cm square, and 152 × 229 cm to 229 × 396 cm oblong or oval, mostly with rolled hems (Fig. 10.2).

10.4 Creating a new manufacturing and consumption model

With the identification of the discarded tablecloths as the material for transformation, an investigation into their properties ensued. Basic manufacturing

---

2 Personal interview with Hilary Near, SF Department of the Environment, 9 February 2010.

Figure 10.2 **Discarded tablecloths**

questions as to the consistency of fibre content, size, colour and quantity needed to be clarified to transition the old and make new. Two manufacturing models were reviewed for potential usage with this textile waste. The existing remanu-facturing model of recuperating particular components or parts of products and reprocessing or renewing for reassembly (Pialot *et al.* 2012) was not chosen, as the reason for discarding the tablecloths was because of stains or holes that could not be renewed. As the tablecloths were not being disassembled, processed and sold, a traditional recycling model was also deemed inappropriate (Beamon 1999). The profitability of repurposing these goods ultimately depended on the quality and quantity of this product and the product for which it would be repurposed (Attasu *et al.* 2008). The question of what products consumers require, their demand for 'environmental stewardship', and their willingness to pay for such a product (Rodie 2010), were an integral component of potential product review and consideration.

10.4.1 Product design using discarded tablecloths

The parameters of product design required attention to the limitations of the tablecloths including variations in tablecloth size, fibre content, fabric colour and irregular positioning of stains or holes. A major qualification for design was a product where the 'used' nature of the materials created new value through the transformation into something new (Norris 2010). Consideration was given to a product that could be sold in and promoted by a San Francisco Hotel gift shop, further supporting the Hotel Council mission of environmental stewardship. Product consideration was also supported by San Francisco's recent ban on the use of plastic bags at grocery stores (Sabatini 2012), supporting the investigation into the production of re-usable bags. Market research highlighted a multitude of shopping bags promoting varying details of sustainable materials positioned for the LOHAS consumer (Howard 2007). Bringing re-usable bags to grocery or other stores is a practice that has tripled in the past six years (LOHAS 2010), supporting the usage and consumer acceptance of this product category. A collaborative decision was made to prototype several bag silhouettes manufactured from the secondary supply chain of discarded hotel tablecloths.

The PWSF team worked with local patternmakers and sample makers, developing prototypes and ultimately deciding on three styles of basic shopping bags, each with an external pocket. The external pocket was designed as a place for digitally printing a customer name, logo or other personalised graphics to brand the bags, creating a unique motivation for purchase and a 'desire-by-association' for the consumer (Arieff 2011). Intrinsically there is a social value (LOHAS 2010) in using these repurposed bags, a representative product of a lifestyle that supports waste reduction and the local manufacturing industry.

Decisions on graphic images included the typeset words 'Made in San Francisco from locally discarded tablecloths', or 'My first life was as a tablecloth'. After careful review, a decision was made to design a recognisable logo that communicated the geographic location (Remade in San Francisco) of manufacture. Other logos and images for inclusion would be determined by and representative of the organisation purchasing or promoting the bags: hotel names, company names or conference names.

10.5 Production realities of a secondary supply chain

The reality of production planning from a secondary fibre/textile supply chain differs extensively from a primary fibre/textile supply chain. Because of the continuous cycle of using, laundering and pressing, variation in fibre content and design, these polyester or polyester/cotton blend tablecloths are available for repurposing in varying quantities at various times over their lifespan. As the tablecloths are laundered an indeterminate number of times, the label bearing the fibre content and quantity is often faded and illegible, a lack of information worth noting, but one that does not impinge on their re-use into bags where the fibre content is currently not a Federal Trade Commission (FTC) requirement (Federal Trade Commission 2010).

While the San Francisco Hotel/Non Profit Collaborative embraced the concept of repurposing tablecloths, they lacked a monitoring system for documenting where and when, during the process of using to cleaning, the decision for discard was made. It appears that some hotels make this determination when the tablecloth is inspected during the cleaning process, while others when the tablecloth is spread on the table for use. At no time is there a separation by size, colour or damage. This project brings to light the need for a systemic approach to sorting discarded tablecloths by size and colour, while documenting the quantity and quality of damages; an inventory before entry into the new secondary supply chain is mandatory.

10.5.1 Manufacturing process: Digital printing

Digital printing techniques provide flexibility in image design, minimising energy use, wastewater and use of dye. The digital printing process does not use colour separation (no screens required), and the use of disperse dye in the heat transfer process means the printed images are colourfast, particularly important for the tablecloths with a polyester fibre content in excess of 50% (Cohen and Johnson 2010). Digitally printing the image on the tablecloth, using an inkjet large-format printer, allows for more complex images than traditional screen printing and additionally creates opportunities for customisation in small print quantities. Creating a digital file, rather than burning colour-separated screens, insures less waste generated and more efficient printing on the fabric and economic use of the fabric printed (Seiren 2012).

For this project a pocket piece was not cut before printing; rather the graphics were printed on the tablecloth and then cut. The width of the tablecloth determined the placement of the pockets that were first plotted out on the computer screen, with 20–30 pockets fitting on each cloth. The digitised pocket graphics were digitally printed, using disperse dyes, onto 122-cm heat transfer paper before being transferred on to a tablecloth. Several prototypes of pockets were required because of the lack of knowledge of fibre content and variations in weave structure and

Figure 10.3 **Digital printing process**

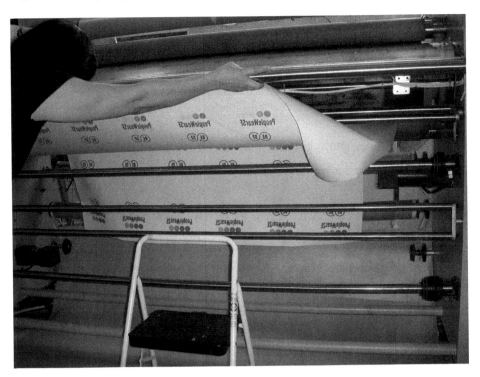

hand, depending on how frequently the tablecloth was laundered and pressed. The quality of the heat-transferred images depended on a perfect calibration of three variables of temperature, pressure and speed requirements for transferring the graphic design from the paper to the fabric (Fig. 10.3). The fibre content, possible finishing and density of the tablecloth weave influenced the image quality. The person assisting with the printing required confidence building and retraining regarding the acceptability and desirability of printing on small stains, flaws or holes. For final production, six tablecloths were printed and moved on to the cutting stage.

10.5.2 Manufacturing process: Cutting and sewing

The manufacturing process traditionally begins with an approved prototype and final product spec sheet ensuring that all products produced are the same, meeting the approved standards. Using fabrics from the secondary supply chain, it was challenging to create an approved prototype and spec sheet because of the colour, stain and other damage variations of the approved, upcycled piece goods. The anticipation was that the final products would actually be individualised and enhanced by the use of damage variations, and product value would be increased by their usage. A spec sheet highlighting this information was created.

The cutting process for this secondary textile supply chain was slow as the width and length of each tablecloth varied, and all hemmed edges of the repurposed tablecloths required removal. The efficiency of continual stacking of fabric layers was not possible; multiple or single layer cutting was performed. The cutters required retraining to understand that flaws, small holes and stains were usable yardage and the bundling together of different shades of fabrics was permissible. The sewing process was quite similar to that of goods from the primary textile supply chain, with a retraining that varying shades of fabric, binding and pocket pieces

Figure 10.4 **Large shopping bag manufactured from repurposed tablecloths**

were permissible to sew together. The latitude and acceptance of slight colour shading and fabric weave variations was great.

After 6 months of design development, a collaborative decision was made to produce a small production lot of bags for initial marketing and sales response. Forty-eight pieces of each of three bag styles (Figs. 10.4–10.6) were manufactured at a local sewing factory, totalling 144 finished bags. Twenty-five of the initial 140 discarded tablecloths were repurposed throughout the initial sample making phase and manufacturing process.

Figure 10.5 **Computer bag manufactured from repurposed tablecloths**

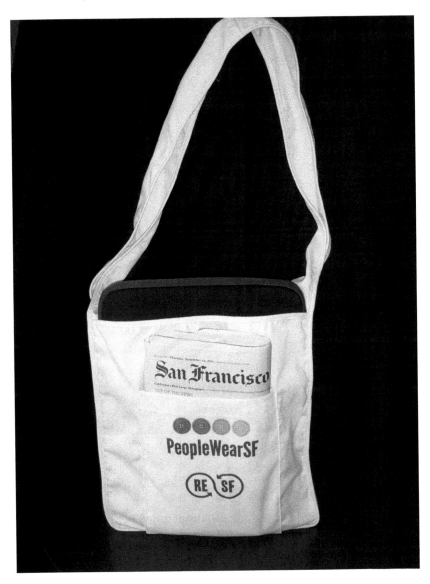

Figure 10.6 **Small shopping bag manufactured from repurposed tablecloths**

10.5.3 Product distribution

The project required more time than initially planned because of a number of factors: re-sorting collected tablecloths for fibre content, size and colour, and sewing factory scheduling. Hence, it is too early for solid product distribution information.

What is evident from the initial responses by those individuals involved in the manufacturing process is that the pocket branding idea is easy to understand and the repurposing of tablecloths from San Francisco is a favourable idea. The Tablecloth Repurposing Project was previewed to a group of over 50 garment industry professionals at a PeopleWear SF general meeting with the following response: seven bags were purchased, one client asked to sell them in his sewing supply shop, and another in her patternmaking studio. The bags are also under review by major clients of the San Francisco Hotel industry for use as totes for conventions in San Francisco.

10.6 Discussion and conclusions

This case study was undertaken to contextualise how usable discarded textiles from the waste stream of the San Francisco hospitality industry could be diverted and become a consistent supply for repurposing into new product. Traditionally, products are designed, produced and purchased with the understanding or assumption of eventually being discarded, so that new products can be consumed. The hospitality industry always requires clean table service, inspecting tablecloths during the laundering process or when preparing for an event, using criteria that when tablecloths are damaged, they are discarded without repair and replaced with new cloths. As noted by the San Francisco Department of the Environment (SFDOE), tablecloths are discarded with small imperfections; holes and stains are not acceptable for meeting the restaurants' or hospitality industry's standards. To organise a supply of textile products, such as the tablecloths, intended as the resource for new manufactured product such as the shopping bags, required a rethinking of the textile product supply chain. The new model considered how products are designed, manufactured, distributed and collected for sorting as repurposed materials for newly designed and manufactured products, on a more continual or directed basis.

To provide manufacturing efficiency, the carefully orchestrated collection and sorting by product size, fibre content, colour and quality according to design concept is important to creating effective production models utilising existing textile products. For the San Francisco Tablecloth Repurposing Project to be viable, the current tablecloth discarding process must be revamped and elevated in importance, as the tablecloths have a value as repurposed material, rather than landfill material. The need to facilitate textile sorting is gaining momentum as a global awareness of the importance of re-use of post-consumer textiles increases (Deschamps 2012).

The first step in creating this secondary supply source of existing textile products requires a collaboration of government agencies (such as the SF Department of the Environment, in partnership with its contracted waste collector, Recology) to identify potential sources of usable textile waste, experienced textile product designers and merchandisers to develop the new products, and a factory with a flexible manufacturing plant to accommodate a variety of experiments in production. The second step is to organise a consistent supply of identified discarded textile products to scale up the manufacturing model to large volume. The third step is to train the factory management to learn how to cut and sew from a different type of fabric source that is not new fabric yardage. The implementation of these three steps will lead to a systemic beginning for the secondary fibre/textile supply chain.

10.7 Opportunities

New industry can be established, founded on the opportunity to effectively learn how to use large amounts of discarded textile products, employing a trained workforce that collects, sorts by design, transports, cuts, sews, distributes and markets new products that would otherwise lie dormant in a landfill (Fig. 10.7). This new industry has an added benefit in that it addresses the market demand for living lightly on the Earth, reducing the consumption of not-so-easily-renewable resources, and giving new life to discarded products.

Figure 10.7 **Secondary fibre/textile supply chain model for design, manufacturing and retail of new product**

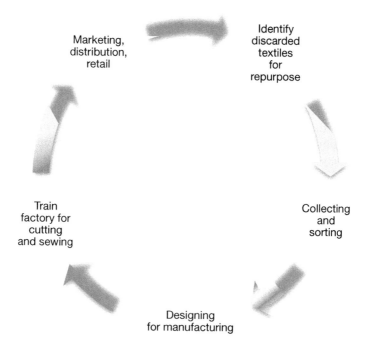

Further, there is an inherent need to consciously define and disseminate industry terms and definitions in a manner and method that embraces their importance and ends the confusion for the consumer over the environmental claims being stated about products (Niinimaki and Hassi 2011). As designers, manufacturers, marketers and retailers use the same terminology, or 'environmental product declarations' (EPDs) to communicate to consumers the true value of the products they purchase, confusion will dissipate (Anderson and Tukker 2006). The goal is to change the traditional linear pattern that consumers go through in consuming products: acquisition, usage and disposition (Shim 1995: 39). It is the combination of the historical, social and environmental components of the new products made from repurposed materials that will create value for customers. As the numbers of LOHAS consumers grow, because products are clearly labelled and branded with consistent definitions of the secondary supply chain, the market value of the products they purchase will rise (Howard 2007: 58). This repurposed tablecloth to shopping bag product is timely, for consumers have an interest in what they consider sustainable, and they make more product purchase decisions based on environmental impact (cKinetics 2010).

What once was non-valued waste, these discarded tablecloths have become a value-added product for repurposing. As this study has shown, new secondary textile supply chains can be realised when business and community organisations collaborate to support innovative strategies. With the promotion of the productive use of textile waste as its mission, the findings from this study are transferable to other locations. The San Francisco Tablecloth Repurposing Project is now in progress, reaching the initial goal of supporting the citywide goal of zero waste by 2020. Sincere congratulations to all who have contributed time, energy, frustration and product to this project. We have only just begun!

References

Anderson, M.M., and A. Tucker (2006) 'Perspectives on Radical Changes to Sustainable Consumption and Production (SCP)', *Workshop of the Sustainable Consumption Research Exchange (SCORE!) Network*, Copenhagen, Denmark.

Arieff, A. (2011) 'The Future of Manufacturing is Local', *New York Times*, 27 March 2011, www.opinionator.blogs.nytimes.com/2011/03/27/the-future-of-manufacturing-is-local, accessed 24 September 2011.

Atasu, A., M. Sarvary and L.N. Van Wassenhove (2008) 'Remanufacturing as a Marketing Strategy', *Management Science* 54.10: 1,731-46.

Beamon, B.M. (1999) 'Designing the Green Supply Chain', *Logistics Information Management* 9.2: 332-42.

Bloomberg Businessweek (2012) 'Martex Fiber Southern Corp', www.investing.business week.com/research/stocks/private/snapshot.asp?privcapId=52391962, accessed 25 January 2012.

Blossom, E. (2011) *Material Change: Design Thinking and the Social Entrepreneurial Movement* (New York: Metropolis Books).

Chen, H.L., and L.D. Burns (2006) 'Environmental Analysis of Textile Products', *Clothing and Textile Research Journal* 24: 248-60.

cKinetics (2010) 'Exporting Textiles: March to Sustainability', www.ckinetics.com/MarchTo Sustainability2010, accessed 1 June 2011.

Cohen, A.C., and I. Johnson (2010) *Textile Science* (New York: Fairchild Books): 179.

D'Altorio, T. (2010) 'As Cotton Prices Increase… the Clothing Industry Faces a Dilemma', Investment U Research, 2 August 2010, www.investmntu.com/2010/August/cotton-price-increase.html, accessed 27 January 2012.

Deschamps, M.J. (3 April 2012) 'Just-Style Management Briefing: Sustainable Solutions to Boost Textile Recycling', www.just-style.com/management-briefing/sustainable-solutions-to-boost-textile-recycling_id113956.aspx, accessed 9 April 2012.

Domina, T., and K. Koch (1997) 'The Textile Waste Lifecycle', *Clothing and Textile Research Journal* 15.2: 96-102.

Eco-findeRRR (2012) 'San Francisco Green Business Checklist', www.sfenvironment.org/downloads/library/public_hearing_notice_and_all_checklists.pdf, accessed 5 April 2012.

Eco Circle® (2008) 'The Meaning of "Recycling" is Changing', www.teijinfiber.com/english/products/specifics/eco-circle.html, accessed 10 November 2011.

E.S. Associates (2006) *Waste Characterization Study* (San Francisco: San Francisco Department of the Environment, City and County of San Francisco).

Federal Trade Commission (2010) 'Writing a Care Label', www.ftc.gov/bcp/edu/pubs/business/textile/bus50.shtm, accessed 15 March 2012.

Finz, S. (2012) 'Tourism Bouncing Back With Economy', *San Francisco Chronicle*, 27 March 2012: D1 & D5.

Green, E. (2009) 'L.A. trails SF in composting', *Los Angeles Times*, 7 November 2009.

Guide, V.D.R., R.H. Teunter and L.N. Van Wassenhove (2008) 'Matching Demand and Supply to Maximize Profits from Remanufacturing', *Manufacturing and Service Operations Management* 5.4: 303-16.

Hawley, J. (2008) 'Economic Impact of Textile and Clothing Recycling', in C. Ulasewicz and J. Hethorn (eds.), *Sustainable Fashion Why Now* (New York: Fairchild Press): 207-32.

Hotel Council of San Francisco (2012) 'Community', www.hotelcouncilsf.org/content/community.asp, accessed 29 January 2012.

Howard, B. (2007) 'LOHAS Consumers are Taking the World by Storm', *Total Health* 29.3: 58.

Hunt, L. (2011) 'Charities Suffer as Criminal Gangs Target Lucrative Clothing Recycling Sector', *Ecologist* 40.21 (March 2011): 14-16.

Laporte, N. (2012) 'Hiring the Blind, While Making a Green Statement', *New York Times*, 24 March 2012, www.nytimes.com/2012/03/25/business/sustainu-an-apparel-maker-turns-to-blind-workers.html, accessed 25 March, 2012.

LOHAS (Lifestyle of Health and Sustainability) (2010) 'Consumers & Individual Action in the LOHAS Space: A Global Perspective', www.lohas.com/consumers-individual-action-lohas-space-global-perspective, accessed 5 August 2011.

Martex Fiber Southern Corp (MFSC) (2011) 'Martex: 'Your Waste is Our Raw Material', *Apparel* 53.3: 38.

McDonough, W., and M. Braungart (2002) *Cradle to Cradle* (New York: North Point Press).

Niinimaki, K., and L. Hassi (2011) 'Emerging Design Strategies in Sustainable Production and Consumption of Textiles and Clothing', *Journal of Cleaner Production* 19.16 (November 2011): 1876-83.

Norris, L. (2010) *Recycling Indian Clothing: Global Contexts of Reuse and Value* (Bloomington, IN: Indiana University Press).

Owen, K. (2011) 'As the Holidays Approach, Re-Gift Old Clothes by Recycling Instead of Discarding', SMART: Secondary Materials and Recycled Textiles Association, www.smartasn.org/news/pr_113011.cfm, accessed 20 December 2011.

Pialot, O., D. Millet and N. Tchertchian (2012) 'How to Explore Scenarios of Multiple Upgrade Cycles for Sustainable Product Innovation: The "Upgrade Cycle Explorer" Tool', *Journal of Cleaner Products* 22.1 (February 2012): 19-31.

City and County of San Francisco (2002) 'Resolution #679-02: San Francisco Board of Supervisors-File 021468', 11 October 2002, www.sfbos.org/ftp/uploadedfiles/bdsupvrs/resolutions02/r0679-02.pdf, accessed 30 September 2012.

Rodie, J.B. (2010) 'From Waste to Worth', *Textile World* 160.6: 23.

Sabatini, J. (2012) 'San Francisco Shoppers Can Add Bag Fee to Bills', *The Examiner*, www.sfexaminer.com/blogs/under-dome/2012/02/san-francisco-shoppers-can-add-bag-fee-bills, accessed 19 March 2012.

Seiren Co. Ltd. (2012) 'What's Viscotecs?' www.viscotecs.com/english/about, accessed 30 March 2012.

Shim, S. (1995) 'Environmentalism and Consumer's Clothing Disposal Patterns: An Exploratory Study', *Clothing and Textile Research Journal* 13.1: 38-48.

SMART (Secondary Materials and Recycled Textile Association) (2012) 'Donate Recycle Don't Throw Away', www.smartasn.org, accessed 20 January 2012.

Sustainable Apparel Coalition (2012) 'Waste', www.apparelcoalition.org/desired-outcomes, accessed 1 October 2012.

Toray, (2011) 'Toray Draws Up Strategy to Expand Fibers and Textiles Recycling Business', www.toray.com/news/fiber/nr111021.html, accessed 27 January 2012.

USEPA (United States Environmental Protection Agency) (2009) 'Municipal Solid Waste in the United States: 2009 Facts and Figures', p. 57, www.epa.gov/wastes/nonhaz/municipal/pubs/msw2009rpt.pdf, accessed 10 November 2010.

Zou, Y., N. Reddy and Y. Yang (2011) 'Reusing Polyester/Cotton Blend Fabrics for Composites', *Composites Part B: Engineering* 42.4 (June 2011): 763-70.

Connie Ulasewicz has over 25 years of garment industry experience managing production, merchandising and sales, and is the co-author of *Made In America: The Handbook for Sewn Products Manufacturing* and *Sustainable Fashion: Why Now?* An Associate Professor of Apparel Design and Merchandising, her research focuses on community-based sustainable practices.

Gail Baugh is an experienced fashion industry professional with over 30 years' senior management retailing, sourcing, designing and manufacturing experience at Macys and NI-Teijin Shoji (USA), Inc. Author of *The Designer's Textile Directory*, she teaches sustainable practices as a lecturer for textiles, merchandising and international business for the fashion industry.

Part II
Marketing, brands and regulatory aspects in the textile and fashion industry

11

Sustainable consumption and production patterns in the clothing sector
Is green the new black?

Ines Weller
University of Bremen, Germany

Is green the new black? Some evidence suggests so. The fashion industry today has become increasingly concerned with ecological and social problems in the textile chain. For example, many global fashion companies and manufacturers/retailers of popular labels, such as C&A, H&M and Zara, include some ecological clothing in their clothing lines. According to the Textile Exchange *2010 Global Market Report on Sustainable Textiles*, the retailers named above were even among the top ten using organic cotton (Textile Exchange 2010b). Furthermore, an increasing number of fashion designers and manufacturers of new labels are paying attention to trends in eco-fashion. This is further suggested by an increase in the number of suppliers entering the market in recent years with explicitly social-ecological profiles (Brodde 2009; Kloos 2009). Another indicator is the recent yearly market growth rate for organic cotton: 20% between 2008 and 2009, and 15% between 2009 and 2010 (Textile Exchange 2010a). In the media, debates about eco-fashion have also clearly become more prominent.

On the other hand, there are some arguments opposing the assumption that green is the new black. For example, ecological clothing maintains a low market share; despite the high growth rate of organic cotton, it still accounts for only 1.1% of total cotton production (Textile Exchange 2010a). Clothing made from organic cotton has considerably less relevance than the organic food industry (with a European market share well under 5%); the demand for organic food products is ten times greater than the demand for organic cotton (Willer and Kilcher 2009). A further problem relates to structural deficits in eco-fashion, especially in Germany and Austria, where eco-fashions are mainly sold online or by mail order; such fashions only have a slight presence in conventional textile outlets (Lorek and Lucas 2003; Knieli *et al.* 2007; Ahlert and Rohlfing 2010). A German study conducted in 2003 concluded,

> The majority of eco-textiles (80 to 90 percent) are bought via mail-order trade. In the textile market the relation between stores selling clothing and mail-order trade is that mail-order traders have less than a 10 percent market share, which turns it into a niche market itself. So eco-textiles are a niche market in a niche market (Lorek and Lucas 2003: 28).

The German company, hessnatur, which promotes itself as a market leader in the organic clothing sector, also sells its popular eco-fashions predominantly by mail order (hessnatur 2012).

It seems unlikely, therefore, that 'green' clothing will be viewed anytime soon as similar in importance to the colour black. For the further development of sustainable consumption and production patterns in the clothing sector, the relationship between ecology and fashion must be examined as an important factor. In this context, the extent to which ecological and fashion requirements in clothing can be combined represents an important question.

The background for this chapter is a research project investigating the interrelationship of fashion and ecology, and its perception by various actors in Germany.[1] The colour black in women's clothing was a focal point of the project because of its general pre-eminence in fashion over other colours (Mendes 1999). Black clothing achieves sustained high levels of demand. On the other hand, black colouring in clothing can be associated with particular ecological problems; it is extremely resource-intensive compared with other colours because more colouring agents, additives and wastewater are required for production. Furthermore, some health and ecological risks are associated with certain colouring agents used to produce a black colour, such as sulphur dyes (Christie 2001). The resulting hypothesis is that, by exploring the colour black in clothing lines, interrelationships between fashion and ecology can be identified easily.

11.1 Ecological clothing in Germany

Ecological clothing appeared on the German market at the end of the 1970s. A major corporate pioneer was hessnatur, founded in 1976. At that time, ecological

---

1 The context of this chapter is the research project, 'Sustainable consumption and the interrelationship of cultural and ecological-technological factors: the example of women's black clothing', funded by the German Research Foundation. The project was developed by and is being conducted in cooperation with Professor Dr Christine Eifler.

clothing was understood as natural clothing manufactured using ecologically produced natural fibres, such as cotton or wool. In the manufacturing process, the use of textile chemicals that were either damaging to the environment or to a person's health were to be avoided and/or reduced. Reports and debates on the possible health dangers of clothing in Germany in the 1980s created a focus on the health risks caused by textile chemicals, such as formaldehyde compounds or azo dyes (Weller 2000).

Ecological clothing, therefore, provided German consumers with some perceived protection against pollutants used in conventionally manufactured clothing. At the end of the 1980s and the beginning of the 1990s, many smaller clothing manufacturers followed the example of the eco-pioneer hessnatur and specialised in sales of ecologically and environmentally friendly clothing. Larger textile companies, such as the Steilmann-Group, also developed eco-collections, resulting in a significant increase in the turnover of ecological clothing. Unfortunately, its appeal was short-lived, dropping off considerably by the end of the 1990s (Rohlfing 2010). Many smaller providers of ecological clothing quickly went out of business because of the extremely low demand for their products. In its introductory stage, ecological clothing was characterised by a design that was oriented around natural materials and colours (Weller 2000; Rohlfing 2010).

At this time in Germany, wearers of ecological clothing were regarded as unfashionable 'wide eyed muesli freaks in baggy, self-knitted outfits' (Schneidewind *et al.* 2003). This image went hand-in-hand with a decision to generally avoid use of the colour black in ecological collections, except for naturally coloured black wool. Natural textile suppliers maintained the point of view that the colouring agents available at the time to produce the colour black could not meet ecological and health-related requirements.

Since 2000, a continuing upward trend in ecological fashion has been observed. More suppliers of ecological and fairtrade clothing have appeared in the German (and international) clothing markets. Simultaneously, global textile companies are paying more attention to ecological and/or social concerns. One characteristic aspect of these developments is the collective effort that has been demonstrated to design fashionable ecological clothing and move away from an unfashionable eco-image.

11.2 Environmental and social hot spots in the textile chain

Since the 1990s, problems in the various stages of the life-cycle of textiles have been identified as central *ecological* weak points of the global textile economy (Enquête-Kommission 'Schutz des Menschen und der Umwelt' 1994; Schönberger and Schäfer 2003; Weller 2004; Steinberger *et al.* 2009), as shown in Table 11.1.

Table 11.1 **Environmental and social hot spots in the textile chain**

Source: Authors' own compilation

Natural fibre production	Use of pesticides in cotton cultivation Water consumption during cotton production
Synthetic fibre production	Use of non-renewable resources
Textile finishing	Amount and variety of textile chemicals Freshwater consumption and wastewater loads
Use phase	Energy consumption during care of textiles Short lifespan of clothing
Waste phase	Amount of used clothing Low rates of recycling and recovery

A major *social* problem in the textile chain is categorised as working conditions. Specific problematic issues include low wages, excessive working hours, temporary work contracts, sexual discrimination and to some extent unprotected informal work from home. Such conditions occur, though not exclusively, in Eastern Asia and Eastern Europe (CCC 2009). Further, textile workers and local residents are subjected to health risks and hazards by textile companies whose work safety and environmental protection measures are inadequate (Greenpeace International 2011).

11.3 Sustainable consumption and production patterns in the clothing industry

Sustainable development has been defined in many different ways, but a widely adopted definition has been provided in the Brundtland Report. According to this, sustainable development is 'development which meets the needs of the present without compromising the ability of future generations to meet their own needs' (WCED 1987: 43). Sustainable development is hereby characterised as a normative concept with intergenerational and intragenerational justice as core elements. The key objective of sustainable development is to preserve the reproductive capacity of nature and society for future generations. Given the global growth rates, the increasing use of natural resources and associated environmental problems necessitate fundamental changes in non-sustainable production and consumption patterns (Worldwatch Institute 2004; Lebel *et al.* 2010). This means that consumption and production patterns must be implemented to 'respond to basic needs and bring a better quality of life, while minimizing the use of natural resources, toxic materials and emissions of waste and pollutants over the lifecycle, so as not to jeopardize the needs of future generations' (Ofstad 1994 cited in Jackson 2006: 5). To achieve these general objectives of sustainable consumption, ecological, social and economic requirements need to be identified for different areas of consumption, including food and clothing.

Three approaches regarding the options of *consumers* have been distinguished in the research for sustainable consumption. They include: consumption of resource-efficient and environmentally sound products ('consuming differently'), consumption of fairtrade products ('consuming responsibly') and reduced consumption ('consuming less') (Jackson and Michaelis 2003; Weller 2008). Sustainable consumption of clothing, therefore, refers to purchasing and consuming ecological and fairtrade clothing. In addition, resource-efficient use of clothing and the level of consumption also are important variables. The focus in the following is on 'consuming differently', or purchasing ecological clothing.

Textile *production* is regulated by requirements to minimise resource consumption and harmful effects on the environment/climate in production processes. An end product should also meet the requirements for sustainable consumption. Subsequently, textile manufacturers offer a wide range of ecological clothing. However, there are significant differences as to which ecological problems are addressed and the extent of intended ecological improvements. The material basis of ecological clothing is currently either organic cotton or recyclates, especially from PET drinking bottles. Both ecological innovations address ecological problems in the textile chain; for example, switching to organic cotton ensures that pesticides, herbicides and insecticides are avoided while consumption of resources is reduced. Using recyclates reduces the consumption of non-renewable resources. Both materials show a high potential for benefiting the environment, but an extremely low market share is predictive that the potential will never be fully reached (Weller and Walter 2010).

Assessing the extent to which the environmental problems associated with textile finishing as another ecological hot spot are being addressed by manufacturers is a challenging task. A wide range of ecological improvements can be observed, however. They include energy- and water-saving technologies, limitations on or avoidance of ecologically problematic textile chemicals, and development of new dyeing technologies (Weller and Walter 2010). Each improvement, however, focuses on an isolated problem. A contemporary strategy that is geared towards reducing problem substances used in textile finishing globally is the 'detox campaign' initiated by Greenpeace; several textile companies currently participate. The goal is to comprehensively reduce the use of toxic textile chemicals by revising industry regulations and substituting safer chemicals for toxic ones (Greenpeace International 2011).

Consumers interested in ecological clothing can find certain information about ecological improvements on eco-labels.[2] For example, eco-labels provide information on the use of organic cotton, limits on harmful substances in the end product, and the non-use of dangerous textile chemicals. Large numbers and the varied content of eco-labels within the clothing industry, however, may create confusion,

---

2 VERBRAUCHER INITIATIVE, 'Label online', www.label-online.de, accessed 23 January 2012.

rather than clarity, among consumers. A reputable eco-label for widely comparative and comprehensively improved ecological clothing is the Global Organic Textile Standard (GOTS). Clothing manufactured under this label is typically produced from natural material. This standard applies to all stages of textile production and addresses ecological and social criteria in the production process as well as the product itself. Since 2000, the number of small manufacturers and labels with social-ecological profiles has increased, indicating that their business objectives include fulfilment of GOTS criteria (Kloos 2009).

To achieve substantial ecological improvements within the clothing industry, there must be a clear increase in the demand for eco-fashions. Attention, therefore, must be given to consumers and to fulfilling their expectations. In this context, anticipation surrounds an increasing demand from a specific market segment, known as 'Lifestyles of Health and Sustainability' (LOHAS). LOHAS consumers are expected to consider ecological, social and health-related requirements when making purchasing decisions. They are regarded as a customer group with above-average incomes and a high percentage of women. They consume under the motto, 'shopping for a better world and an improved well-being' (Kirig and Wenzel 2009). There are two main reasons for the eco-fashion industry's interest in this group. First, consumers attracted to this market represent a rapidly growing target group.[3] Second, LOHAS members appear to be interested in ecological and fair clothing, but they also expect eco-fashions to reflect good taste in fashion while fulfilling ecological requirements (Kirig and Wenzel 2009).

11.4 Relationships between fashion and ecology: A German case study

In order to investigate how perceptions of the relationship between fashion and ecology have developed and changed over the last 30 years, I focused my analysis on environmental actors. Specifically, a document analysis of the magazine *ÖKO-TEST* was conducted. This consumer magazine was introduced in 1985, with the aim to inform consumers about ecological and health aspects of products used in daily life. It is published monthly and provides current ecological and health-related information.

The document analysis consisted of two stages; the first stage was a quantitative analysis of articles on clothing in general, and articles about black clothing, specifically. Second, a qualitative analysis of articles about clothing was carried out to identify references to the environment, health and culture/fashion. In this context, statements about the relationship between fashion and ecology were analysed. The

3 www.lohas.com, accessed October 2012.

Table 11.2 **Proportion of articles relating to the colour black compared with all articles on textile products**

Year	Proportion (%)	Year	Proportion (%)	Year	Proportion (%)
1985	0	1994	0	2003	9.9
1986	0	1995	12.5	2004	21.9
1987	0	1996	33.3	2005	11.8
1988	0	1997	0	2006	10.0
1989	0	1998	66.6	2007	8.7
1990	0	1999	16.7	2008	4.1
1991	0	2000	16.7	2009	11.1
1992	12.5	2001	30.8		
1993	20.0	2002	8.3	Ø1992-2009	16.3

analysis was conducted for articles published between March 1985 and December 2009.

The following results of the document analysis include the quantitative development of articles published since 1985 that specifically address either black clothing or changes in the perception of the relationship between fashion and ecology. Table 11.2 shows the proportion of articles about the colour black compared with all articles on textile products.

Table 11.2 shows that black clothing was initially not a topic covered in *ÖKO-TEST*. In fact, there were no articles on black clothing between 1985 and 1992, the time period during which ecological clothing lines were not offering fashions characterised by the colour black. The absence of black provides insight into the relationship between fashion and ecology in the early beginnings of the natural textile industry. However, lack of interest in black fashions did not last long and, in 1992, a discussion on black clothing appeared in *ÖKO-TEST*. Since that time, the ecological, health and fashion aspects associated with the colour black have been frequently discussed in articles on textiles.

The qualitative analysis of statements about the relationship between fashion and ecology revealed that perceptions regarding this relationship clearly changed between 1985 and 2009. Three distinct viewpoints emerged during this time period; they are described below.

11.4.1 Ecological requirements determine natural fashion; fashion and ecology are incompatible

Initially, articles in *ÖKO-TEST* prioritised ecological requirements over fashion and promoted purchase of natural textiles and fashions. According to the articles, ecology ruled the relationship between fashion and ecology. Fashion was considered of secondary importance. This viewpoint was expressed most notably between 1985 and 1992. Manufacturers of natural textiles had 'problems...with the term fashion. For fashion you need colour...and coloured clothing is no longer considered...natural' (Moeller 1990: 74).[4] A basic assumption in discussions on clothing was that ecology and fashion were not compatible: 'Conventional fashion has negative environmental impacts; natural fashion is...not feasible' (N.N. 1992: 89).

This viewpoint emphasised the differences between ecology and conventional fashion by promoting, for example, the durability and comfort of natural textiles. A feature of the 'more consistent natural fashion' was its 'timeless beauty in colour and shape' (Sabersky 1992: 70). Ecological requirements were of prime importance for natural fashion. Fashion requirements were subordinate.

11.4.2 Fashion and ecology are equally important for natural fashion

After the early years of eco-fashion, statements on fashion and ecology changed noticeably. Aesthetic fashion became an important consideration for natural fashion design, and this viewpoint and related discussions appeared in *ÖKO-TEST* between 1993 and 2000. It was noted that natural fashion was 'for the first time moving away from the images of wide-eyed muesli-freaks in self-knit outfits' (Sabersky 1993: 15). Natural fashion was more oriented to conventional fashion and its trends: 'Apart from wearing comfort and durability...the fashion aspect has become more and more important for producers of natural textiles' (Schumacher 2000: 119). At the same time, it was stressed that 'the new natural fashion follows international trends but does not follow every fashion poppycock' (Sabersky 2002: 44).

In contrast to articles written before 1993, discussions advocated that natural fashion follow conventional trends. It became important that 'Natural fashion does not look like natural fashion' (Sabersky 1994: 29). Natural fashion was only to be distinguishable from conventional fashion by its ecological qualities. This change in perspective occurred because supply was not meeting demand for the natural fashion industry; 'unfortunately, the eco collections are still left hanging in the shops' (Sabersky 1999: 61).

11.4.3 Ecology is an incidental additional benefit of (natural) fashion

Since 2000, further changes have been noticed in the way *ÖKO-TEST* presents the relationship between fashion and ecology. For example, explicit statements that distinguish natural fashion from conventional fashion on the basis of ecology are

---

4 Direct quotes have been translated into English.

seldom made. The few remarks that have appeared about natural fashion have described the relationship between fashion and ecology as highly compatible: for example, 'eco-fashion can be wonderful and extremely stylish...' (N.N. 2008: 120). Strict distinctions between conventional and natural fashion no longer exist, and the connections between clothing and natural textiles are referred to in casual terms.

Another observation is *ÖKO-TEST*'s description of an evolving closer relationship between fashion and ecology. Casual reports about the natural fashion industry and current fashion trends have been published along with reports about steps taken by conventional fashion manufacturers to integrate ecological requirements into their collections. One such report included the commentary that 'green awareness is also currently sweeping through the world of fashion' (N.N. 2009: 150). Overall, recent articles indicate that fashion and ecology are no longer considered incompatible and distinctions between conventional and natural fashion are rarely made.

11.5 Discussion of results

Perceptions and discussions in the German consumer magazine *ÖKO-TEST* about the relationship between fashion and ecology changed dramatically between 1985 and 2009. Initially, stark contrasts were made between eco-fashion, for which ecological requirements were of prime importance, and conventional fashion, which was oriented towards trends. Today, fashion and ecology are viewed as compatible, rather than contradictory. The results indicate that the early days of German eco-fashion were characterised by fashion shortfalls arising from the design and production of natural textiles according to ecological criteria. Insufficient attention to fashion was reflected by the absence of the colour black in natural fashions. The natural clothing industry avoided the colour for ecological and health reasons initially, although black was a very important colour for clothing in the 1980s. In conclusion, the findings suggest that this initial disregard for conventions in fashion and the colour black contributed to the Germans' image of eco-fashion as anti-modern.

Modern eco-fashions fulfil fashion requirements, and offerings for ecological clothing that is also fashionable are more visible. However, it seems that the anti-modern image is still prevalent. It is even found among members of the consumer group LOHAS, who are especially interested in sustainable and healthy products. A recent Austrian study reported that LOHAS consumers consider ecological clothing 'still as unfashionable, alternative, boring or extremely colourful clothing lines as before' (Mert 2010).

The results of this study underscore the thesis that the early market entry of natural clothing and communications about the first eco-collections have led to a collective knowledge base about their fashion shortfalls in Germany. This knowledge still influences the perception of ecological clothing and the hesitant demand for eco-fashion (Lorek and Lucas 2003; Ahlert and Rohlfing 2010). The finding raises the question whether the collective knowledge about the fashion deficits of natural fashion is uniquely important for Germany or if it can be valuable to other countries. The lack of change in the collective knowledge about eco-fashion is exacerbated by the fact that eco-fashion is still not present in retail markets (textile retail outlets, clothing lines by international top designers and global mass-markets) to the extent that the colour black is represented. Increasing eco-fashion's visibility in this context would be an important consideration if green was indeed to become the new black.

References

Ahlert, D., and M. Rohlfing (2010) *Ökologische Bekleidung aus Kunden- und Anbietersicht. Status quo und Konsequenzen* (Köln: BTE-Fachdokumentation).

Brodde, K. (2009) 'Grüne Liste', www.kirstenbrodde.de/wp-content/uploads/2009/05/gruneliste1.pdf, accessed 12 April 2012.

WCED (World Commission on Environment and Development) (1987) *Our Common Future* (Oxford, UK: Oxford University Press).

Christie, R.M. (2001) *Colour Chemistry* (Cambridge, UK: Royal Society of Chemistry, Great Britain).

CCC (Clean Clothes Campaign) (2009) 'Let's Clean Up Fashion 2009: The State of Pay behind the UK High Street', www.labourbehindthelabel.org/images/pdf/letscleanupfashion2009.pdf, accessed 13 January 2012.

Enquête-Kommission 'Schutz des Menschen und der Umwelt' des Deutschen Bundestages (Hrsg.) (1994) *Die Industriegesellschaft gestalten: Perspektiven für einen nachhaltigen Umgang mit Stoff- und Materialströmen* (Bonn).

Greenpeace International (2011) 'Dirty Laundry 2: Hung Out to Dry. Unravelling the Toxic Trail from Pipes to Products', www.greenpeace.org/international/Global/international/publications/toxics/Water%202011/dirty-laundry-report-2.pdf, accessed 12 January 2012.

hessnatur (2012) 'Zahlen und Fakten: Butzbach', www.hessnatur.info/de/fakten/zahlen-und-fakten.html, accessed 2 April 2012.

Jackson, T. (ed.) (2006) *The Earthscan Reader in Sustainable Consumption* (London: Earthscan).

Jackson, T., and L. Michaelis (2003) *Policies for Sustainable Consumption: A Report to the Sustainable Development Commission* (London: Sustainable Development Commission).

Kirig, A., and E. Wenzel (2009) *LOHAS: Bewusst grün – alles über die neuen Lebenswelten* (München: Redline Verlag).

Kloos, D. (2009) 'Sozial-ökologische Mode auf dem Prüfstand: Überblick und Analyse', www.suedwind-institut.de/fileadmin/fuerSuedwind/Publikationen/2009/2009-3_Sozial-Oekologische_Mode_Langfassung.pdf, accessed 12 April 2012.

Knieli, M., S. Katzmann, E. Tangl and R. Hasslinger (2007) *Ökotextilien – aus der Nische zum Trendprodukt!* (Berichte aus Energie- und Umweltforschung 32/2007; Wien, Austria: Bundesministerium für Verkehr, Innovation und Technologien).

Lebel, L., R. Daniel and S. Lorek (eds.) (2010) *Sustainable Production Consumption Systems: Knowledge, Engagement and Practice* (Springer: Dordrecht).

Lorek, S., and R. Lucas (2003) *Towards Sustainable Marketing Strategies: A Case Study on Eco-textiles and Green Power* (Wuppertal, Germany: Wuppertal Institute).

Mendes, V. (1999) *Dressed in Black* (London: V&A Publications).

Mert, W. (2010) *Nachhaltige Trendsetter: LOHAS auf dem Weg in eine zukunftsfähige Gesellschaft* (Berichte aus der Energie- und Umweltforschung; Wien, Austria: Bundesministerium für Verkehr, Innovation und Technologien, www.fabrikderzukunft.at/fdz_pdf/endbericht_1039_nh_trendsetter.pdf, accessed 24 January 2012).

Moeller, E. (1990) 'Natürlich umgarnen', *ÖKO-TEST-Magazin* 12: 71-74.

N.N. (1992) 'Interview: Das ist mein Stil', *ÖKO-TEST-Magazin* 5: 82-89.

N.N. (2008) 'Schick und ökologisch korrekt', *ÖKO-TEST-Magazin* 2: 120.

N.N. (2009) 'Saubere Sachen statt dreckiger Mode', *ÖKO-TEST-Magazin* 3: 150.

Rohlfing, M. (2010) Ökologische Bekleidung. Eine Multiagentensimulation der zukünftigen Marktentwicklung (Wiesbaden: Gabler Verlag l Springer Fachmedien).

Sabersky, A. (1992) 'Mehr als ein Trend', *ÖKO-TEST-Magazin* 5: 68-77.

Sabersky, A. (1993) 'Stoff ohne Ende', *ÖKO-TEST-Magazin* 5: 10-17.

Sabersky, A. (1994) 'Maschen groß in Mode', *ÖKO-TEST-Magazin* 9: 28-39.

Sabersky, A. (1999) 'Naturmode: Frech, figurbetont und farbenfroh', *ÖKO-TEST-Magazin* 3: 54-61.

Sabersky, A. (2002) 'Modetrends Sommer 2002: Comeback der Baumwolle', *ÖKO-TEST-Magazin* 4: 44-47.

Schneidewind, U., M. Goldbach, D. Fischer and S. Seuring (eds.) (2003) *Symbole und Substanzen: Perspektiven eines interpretativen Stoffstrommanagements* (Marburg, Germany: Metropolis Verlag).

Schönberger, H., and T. Schäfer (2003) *Beste verfügbare Techniken in Anlagen der Textilindustrie* (UBA-Texte 13/03; Berlin: UBA).

Schumacher, B. (2000) 'Ökologischer Versandhandel: Bestellen find ich gut', *ÖKO-TEST-Magazin* 3: 119-27.

Steinberger, J.K., D. Frio, O. Jolliet and S. Erkman (2009) 'A Spatially Explicit Life Cycle Inventory of the Global Textile Chain', *International Journal of Life Cycle Assessment* 14 (March 2009): 443-55.

Textile Exchange (2010a) '2010 Farm & Fiber Report: Executive Summary', www.textile exchange.org/sites/default/files/te_pdfs/Farm%20%26%20Fibre%20Report%202010%20Final%20%28EXEC%20SUMMARY%29%20100111%20-Small.pdf, accessed 12 April 2012.

Textile Exchange (2010b) '2010 Global Market Report on Sustainable Textiles', www.textile exchange.org/sites/default/files/te_pdfs/2010%20Global%20Market%20Report%20on%20Sustainable%20Textiles-Executive%20Summary.pdf, accessed 12 April 2012.

Weller, I. (2000) *Stand und Perspektiven ökologischer Innovationen im Textilbereich* (ISOE-DiskussionsPapier DP 15; Frankfurt am Main, Germany: ISOE).

Weller, I. (2004) *Nachhaltigkeit und Gender: Neue Perspektiven für die Gestaltung und Nutzung von Produkten* (München: Oekom Verlag).

Weller, I. (2008) 'Konsum im Wandel in Richtung Nachhaltigkeit? Forschungsstand und Perspektiven', in H. Lange (ed.), *Nachhaltigkeit als radikaler Wandel. Die Quadratur des Kreises?* (Wiesbaden, Germany: VS Verlag für Sozialwissenschaften): 43-70.

Weller, I., and S. Walter (2010) 'Ecology & Fashion: Development Lines and Prospects', *2nd Global Conference: Fashion—Exploring Critical Issues*, Oxford, UK, 23–26 September 2010 (www.inter-disciplinary.net/wp-content/uploads/2010/08/sabwalterpaper.pdf, accessed 27 January 2012).

Willer, H., and L. Kilcher (eds.) (2009) 'The World of Organic Agriculture: Statistics & Emerging Trends 2009', www.orgprints.org/15575/3/willer-kilcher-2009-1-26.pdf, accessed 20 January 2012.

Worldwatch Institute (ed.) (2004) *State of the World 2004. Special Focus: The Consumer Society* (New York: W.W. Norton & Co).

Ines Weller is a professor at the University of Bremen (Germany), Research Center for Sustainability Studies (artec) and at the Center for Gender Studies. Her post-doctoral studies ('Habilitation') are in the area of environmental planning, especially sustainable product design. Ines holds a PhD in the teaching of chemistry and a diploma in chemistry. Her research and teaching interests are social-ecological research, sustainable production and consumption patterns, gender, environment and sustainability.

12

Redefining 'Made in Australia'
A 'fair go' for people and planet

Cameron Neil
Net Balance, Australia

Eloise Bishop
Ethical Clothing, Australia

Kirsten Simpson
Net Balance, Australia

The Australian textile, clothing and footwear (TCF) manufacturing industries have endured a difficult three decades, undergoing significant restructuring as a result of opening up the local TCF industry to foreign competition and working to maintain local and global market relevance (Diviney and Lillywhite 2007). With growing concern worldwide over the negative social and environmental impacts of the global fashion industry, there is an opportunity for Australia to pursue ethical and sustainable production as a competitive advantage both at home and abroad. Recent success of Ethical Clothing Australia, a domestic innovation to tackle unfair labour practices in local textile, clothing and footwear manufacturing, provides a case example of the possibilities for the sector as a whole to reposition and reinvent itself.

In this chapter, the authors briefly discuss the state of the Australian fashion industry, the local and global context of ethical and sustainable fashion, and introduce Ethical Clothing Australia. A case is made for redefining 'Made in Australia' to be characterised by innovation in ethical and sustainable production of textiles, clothing and footwear. The authors believe this may provide the sector with a competitive advantage and assist it to grow domestic market share, find more success in export markets, and become a thriving manufacturing sector.

12.1 Introducing the Australian textile, clothing and footwear industries: Three decades of struggle

The Australian textile, clothing and footwear (TCF) sector has been subject to substantial structural change and decline over the past few decades (Parliament of Australia 2012). This change has been brought about by a number of shifts in Australian Government policy, increased accessibility of consumers to international goods and the impacts that globalisation has had on the Australian marketplace more broadly.

One of the key drivers in the decline of the sector was the Australian Government's decision to liberalise textile and clothing trade policies in the late 1980s and early 1990s, in particular the reduction of import tariffs on TCF products (Weller 2007a). Implementation of these policies opened up the Australian TCF sector to imported goods and international markets. While this policy change was in alignment with the World Trade Organisation's global objectives for trade liberalisation (WTO 2007a) in the industry, a number of factors unique to the Australian context have subsequently impacted on the economic viability of the sector. These factors include the reduction of industry-wide government subsidies in preference to other local manufacturing industries (WTO 2007b), implementation of this policy much earlier than in other international markets allowing the flood of comparatively cheaper overseas goods into Australia, and the high cost of manufacturing onshore due to Australian labour standards and laws (Weller 2007a). It is thought that, combined, these factors have steadily resulted in a loss of competitive advantage across the sector.

Part of the decline can also be attributed to the increased choice available to consumers, cheaper product options made offshore and international brands. We now live in a world where consumers have access to internationally produced goods in-store and over the Internet (Access Economics 2010), in most cases allowing them to completely bypass Australian fashion manufacturers and suppliers. Most recently, major international retailers have also entered the Australian market, such as Zara and Top Shop. This increased access to international goods has further affected the economic viability of the local industry as consumer dollars are increasingly being spent offshore.

After 30 years of decline it is imperative for the TCF sector to look at how it will not only survive the next 30 years, but grow and thrive in a global market place (Green 2008). This has the potential to involve increasing market share within Australia and carving a niche in global markets. Redefining the made-in-Australia proposition and changing consumer perceptions in the context of growing concern with ethical and sustainable production of fashion, may be one angle that fuels innovation and growth in the Australian TCF sector.

12.2 The rise of sustainable and ethical fashion

The struggle of the Australian TCF sector over the last three decades has coincided with a slow, yet steady, rise in ethical and sustainable fashion. As discussed in Sass Brown's book, *Eco Fashion*, one of the strongest trends in fashion globally is the production of desirable and well-designed apparel and accessories with a conscience (Brown 2010). This rise can be attributed to acute concerns over the social and environmental impact of fashion production and consumption (see for example Draper *et al.* 2007). Many of these concerns relate to the effects that globalisation has had on the fashion industry. Increasing competition for market share, and the dominance of high-volume, low-margin business models have resulted in many negative impacts. Labour rights have been squeezed on cotton farms and in factories, human health has been compromised through use of toxic chemicals in fabrics and textiles, there has been a substantial increase in waste and pollution along the supply chain and large amounts of fashion waste now ends up in landfill (Draper *et al.* 2007).

The length and complexity of TCF supply chains has made it difficult for business, governments and NGOs to tackle the ethical and sustainability impacts of production and consumption. A great deal of effort has been put into tackling these impacts through the development of policy instruments and voluntary schemes. Unfortunately, these efforts generally address only one or two issues (e.g. non-toxic chemicals, labour rights) in one part of the supply chain and often only in one consuming or producing country (Golden 2010). This limiting of scale and fragmentation of stakeholder effort often leads to confusion for consumers (Golden 2010). They are left wondering what ethical and sustainable fashion is and what choices they should be making to reduce the negative impacts of their fashion consumption.

Despite the challenges and difficulties, the call for more ethical and sustainable fashion from governments, consumers and businesses has continued to grow. In recent years, innovations in eco-labelling (e.g. GOTS,[1] Fairtrade,[2] Oeko-Tex,[3] Eco

---

1 Global Organic Textile Standard, www.global-standard.org, accessed 25 September 2012.
2 Fairtrade certification of cotton globally (www.fairtrade.net/cotton.html) and Fairtrade certified garments in the USA (www.fairtradeusa.org/products-partners/apparel-linens), websites accessed 26 September 2012.
3 Oeko-Tex provides a number of certifications addressing the use of harmful chemicals in supply chains (www.oeko-tex.com, accessed 26 September 2012).

Index[4]), high profile business platforms (e.g. the Sustainable Apparel Coalition,[5] the Global Social Compliance Program[6]), and retailer approaches to ethical and sustainable fashion (e.g. Marks & Spencer's Plan A[7]) have emerged. These innovations provide opportunities to consolidate efforts across TCF supply chain issues and to increase the scale of their impact. They also provide an opportunity to engage the fashion industry and their customers in creating and consuming ethical and sustainable fashion.

12.3 An Australian ethical fashion innovation: Ethical Clothing Australia

Industry research and evidence from trade unions undertaking compliance checks of the TCF supply chains have found ongoing non-compliance with legal requirements in the sector (Textile, Clothing and Footwear Union of Australia 2012). This is largely because the industry, particularly since import tariffs were cut, has moved towards a model of outsourced labour in an effort to remain competitive in the face of increased imports. A large proportion of the industry also operates informally and on a cash basis. Under this outsourcing approach many workers are effectively 'out of sight', working from home. Such practices allow non-compliant businesses to undercut other businesses that provide legal rates of pay and entitlements.

This drive to be competitive has seen much of the TCF manufacturing in Australia move away from factory-based workers towards homeworkers. The Textile Clothing and Footwear Union of Australia has found that TCF homeworkers may work 12 hour days, six or seven days a week and it is not uncommon to find homeworkers in Australia receiving less than half the award wage (Australian Senate 2012). This can be as little as six dollars per hour. While their prevalence has diminished in recent years, factory-based workers are not immune to exploitation and poor working conditions. This can include underpayment, an unsafe workplace and a lack of basic entitlements such as superannuation and WorkCover insurance.

---

4 Eco Index is currently in beta (www.ecoindexbeta.org, accessed 25 September 2012) but is being supported by the Sustainable Apparel Coalition to move it from outdoor clothing only to cover all apparel.
5 The Sustainable Apparel Coalition (www.apparelcoalition.org, accessed 26 September 2012) brings together leading apparel manufacturers, brands, retailers and other stakeholders to tackle social and environmental impacts of apparel production and consumption.
6 The Global Social Compliance Program (www.gscpnet.com, accessed 26 September 2012) is a business-driven programme for the continuous improvement of working and environmental conditions in global supply chains.
7 www.plana.marksandspencer.com, accessed 26 September 2012.

The Australian Government has committed to providing a safety net for all Australian workers through its national Fair Work policy framework (Department of Education, Employment and Workplace Relations 2009). Recently the Commonwealth Government amended legislation relating to the TCF sector to address some deficiencies in law including the coverage of outworkers, the recovery of unpaid wages and the right of entry to investigate workplaces (Parliament of Australia 2012).

In response to ongoing concerns about the exploitation of homeworkers in the 1990s, TCF employer representatives and Textile Clothing and Footwear Union of Australia (TCFUA) agreed to develop a code of practice for workers in the TCF sector. As a result the Homeworkers Code of Practice (Australian Competition and Consumer Commission 2011) was launched in 1996. The 'No Sweat Shop' label trademark (as ECA was then known) was subsequently launched in 2001. In May 2008, funding from the Commonwealth Government was received to further develop and promote the code and the label. In collaboration with employer and union representatives, the 'No Sweat Shop' label was transitioned to the 'Ethical Clothing Australia' label in 2010.[8]

The Ethical Clothing Australia (ECA) label is a unique initiative that is gaining strong support from the local Australian TCF industry. ECA aims to address exploitation of workers in the local TCF sector, and also helps consumers make an informed choice for ethical shopping. The programme that sits behind the ECA label assists the industry to ensure that the Australian workers making their products receive fair wages and decent working conditions. It does this through an accreditation and labelling system.

The accreditation system is underpinned by thorough compliance checks performed by the trade union, rather than a company appointed auditor, as well as industry education campaigns. The TCFUA has undertaken approximately 1,400 compliance checks covering more than 500 suppliers. As a result, since government funding of the ECA began in 2008 more than 6,000 homeworkers have been provided with advice or assistance through the ECA programme.[9]

Transparency in supply chains is critical in monitoring ethical compliance and the ECA programme promotes trust in the accreditation system, to both industry and consumers, by mapping and monitoring performance among businesses' suppliers. Australian garment supply chains are often complex and businesses lose track of where their products are manufactured. For example, a business which is now accredited with ECA originally thought it had 72 supply chain participants. Through undergoing the ECA supply chain mapping process it was uncovered that it actually had 320 participants.

Once compliant, accredited brands are then given the opportunity to sign a licence agreement which enables them to display the ECA trademark on their Australian-made products. This trademark provides consumers and buyers with a way to identify and support ethical, Australian-made products. At the time of writing there are currently more than 70 successfully accredited Australian manufacturers.

8 www.ethicalclothingaustralia.org.au, accessed 25 September 2012.
9 *Ibid.*

An expanded and more targeted promotional strategy has enhanced ECA brand recognition in the Australian TCF industry. This has resulted in an increase in the uptake of the ECA programme. Some of Australia's best known fashion designers have joined the programme, including Collette Dinnigan,[10] Lisa Ho[11] and Ginger & Smart,[12] as well as Cue,[13] one of the country's largest manufacturers of women's clothing, and iconic swimwear label, Jets.[14] In additional to fashion brands, other ECA accredited businesses include manufacturers of corporate wear, school uniforms, sportswear, work wear, maternity and infant wear, swimwear and footwear.[15]

The broad range of ECA accredited businesses has been driven by the Commonwealth Government's support of the accreditation programme and promotion throughout the TCF industry. In addition, Australian businesses tendering for clothing and footwear procurement contracts with Commonwealth Government entities must either be accredited or seeking accreditation with ECA. Likewise, this also applies to TCF businesses applying for certain government grant programmes, such as the Textile Clothing and Footwear Strategic Capability Program (AusIndustry 2012).

With major TCF brands and retailers increasingly supporting the labelling system (doubling the number of accreditations in 2011),[16] ECA launched its first consumer awareness campaign in October 2011. The 'Meet Your Maker' campaign was aimed at educating consumers about the importance of ethical manufacturing in the Australian TCF industry. It also aimed to assist consumers with making informed and ethical shopping choices.

The 'Meet Your Maker' campaign is built on the consumer's desire to know more about the people behind the products (i.e. clothing) they buy, in a particular the makers. The campaign uses a similar approach to Fairtrade's model of promoting their farmers and growers. A website (www.meetyourmaker.org.au) was created that provides information on the makers behind particular brands. Consumers are encouraged to use their smart phone to scan a QR code on the swing tags on products of participating brands, which takes them to the website where they can post a comment. The website is also linked to the website of accredited businesses who participated in the campaign.

While ECA's current charter is to assist businesses to map and monitor supply chains, to enable the workers making their products to receive fair wages and decent conditions, this scope has the potential to be expanded in the future. In April 2011 ECA was commissioned by the TCF Innovation Council to undertake a survey to assess the feasibility of establishing a new voluntary Ethical Quality Mark

---

10 www.collettedinnigan.com, accessed 25 September 2012.
11 www.lisaho.com, accessed 25 September 2012.
12 www.gingerandsmart.com, accessed 25 September 2012.
13 www.cue.cc, accessed 25 September 2012.
14 www.jets.com.au, accessed 25 September 2012.
15 www.ethicalclothingaustralia.org.au
16 *Ibid.*

(EQM) for Australia.[17] The survey first asked respondents to consider a range of environmental factors and how relevant they were to the TCF industry. Second, it asked for information on preferred form of the EQM. The findings and recommendations of this study are, at the time of writing, being considered by the TCF Innovation Council.

12.4 Redefining 'Made in Australia'

The creation of the ECA programme and label may provide a model for how the Australian TCF industry could redefine 'Made in Australia'. ECA is a unique formulation as a business–union partnership, which is supported by the Commonwealth Government (Department of Education, Employment and Workplace Relations 2011). Participation in the programme has grown substantially with Australian manufacturers and retailers since inception. This is an indication that the ECA has developed a model in which the industry sees current and future value.

International and Australian research suggests there is a growing market for ethical products. Research conducted by marketing strategists, The Mobium Group, found the market for sustainable products to be growing by 20% annually. The ethical and sustainable products industry in Australia was worth $AUS19 billion in 2009 and was estimated to grow to a value of $27 billion by 2011 (Mobium Group 2007–2010). It is likely that rising awareness and these growth trends will help to further increase the trend towards ethical and sustainable product development in the future.

Given the current challenges of international competitiveness, Australian fashion businesses need to reposition themselves. The increase in consumer trends towards more sustainable production and consumption of consumer goods may provide the industry with an exciting opportunity. Repositioning the Australian fashion industry as a 'home of ethical and sustainable manufacturing' may capture a market segment of sufficient size at home and abroad.

Could innovation in textiles, a reputation for quality apparel, fashion that is made without labour exploitation and negative environmental impacts, a reduction in environmental impacts from consumer use and disposal through pioneering design principles, be a pathway to a thriving Australian TCF sector?

12.4.1 The challenge of becoming 'ethical and green'

While this opportunity for an 'ethical and green' fashion industry may exist, the Australian TCF sector faces a number of challenges which directly influence their ability to implement ethical and sustainable practices into their sourcing, manufacturing and production processes.

17 *Ibid.*

As the industry is now truly global, the Australian TCF sector will continue to face pressure from comparatively lower priced overseas imports (Weller 2007a). At present these pricing pressures are further intensified by the current high value of the Australian dollar which renders imported goods cheaper than those manufactured locally (Australian Government Department of Foreign Affairs and Trade 2011). It is anticipated that a collapse of local consumer spending, as a result of slowing economic conditions in Australia, could also impact on the ability of the sector to maintain profit margins. These cost and pricing pressures directly impact on the sector's ability and will to invest in ethical and sustainability related programmes. Further innovation in business models that diverge away from those based on high volume, low margin is necessary. This may provide a new paradigm for mainstream fashion in Australia and facilitate greater competitiveness of local products.

The erosion of an Australian-based TCF manufacturing industry (Parliament of Australia 2012) has meant that there are few options when it comes to sourcing locally. Many businesses within the TCF sector are forced to source textiles and manufacturing services from overseas suppliers. These overseas suppliers are generally located in developing countries where labour and environmental regulation is less stringent than those set out under Australian law (Diviney and Lillywhite 2007). The distance between Australian business and these suppliers also introduces issues with regard to transparency and traceability in the manufacturing and production process.

In comparison with overseas markets such as the USA and Europe, the Australian TCF industry is challenged by limited supply pull and influence with overseas manufacturers. This lack of pull, for example, impacts on the ability of Australian 'fast fashion' brands to access quick run and production turnaround times to meet demand. While this issue of supply pull affects the way the sector does business, it also has an impact on the amount of influence the sector has over supply chain practices and performance (Diviney and Lillywhite 2007). There is a growing body of work which provides good evidence that large multinationals can successfully collaborate with overseas suppliers to positively influence their ethical and sustainability performance. One example in particular is Marks & Spencer's Plan A, which details the company's eco and ethical programme.[18]

To date, efforts by individual businesses in the Australian TCF sector to engage overseas suppliers to enhance ethical and sustainable performance have not been hugely successful (e.g. see Diviney and Lillywhite 2007). Given the size of the Australian TCF manufacturing industry, is there an opportunity to mainstream garments produced offshore using ethical labour, such as the award-winning fairtrade clothing label 3Fish?[19] This would suggest that, since becoming aware of the ECA programme, industry's consciousness of the treatment of workers in their offshore supply chains has been raised. However, if brands,

18 www.marksandspencer.com, accessed 26 September 2012.
19 www.3fish.com.au, accessed 25 September 2012.

manufacturers and retailers can move from traditionally competitive positions to pursue collaborative approaches (and thereby increase supply pull), they may achieve more improvement in labour rights and environmental outcomes in overseas supply chains. Larger retailers, brands and institutional buyers (i.e. governments) could also utilise their market power domestically to require changes in local production.

Consumer trends in Australia, and the rest of the developed world for that matter, are challenging for the ethical and sustainable production of fashion. Over the past two decades we have seen the rise of hyper-consumerism and fast fashion trends (Financial Review 2012). It is no longer the case that consumers add a few key pieces to their wardrobe each season. The availability of cheap goods and the strength of branding and marketing campaigns have helped to drive consumers towards complete replacement of their wardrobe each season. It appears that there is a rise in consumers placing more value on range, accessibility and price of goods (Weller 2007b).

There is a growing market segment that is searching for ethical and sustainable fashion, and traditional quality and premium fashion items continue to have a place in the market. However, it would be naïve to believe that engaging the mainstream consumer market on the ethical and sustainability impacts of their purchasing decisions will be anything but a challenge for the foreseeable future.

This has been exacerbated by growing scepticism among Australian consumers about 'green' and 'ethical' claims, fuelled by highly publicised cases where such claims have been exposed as misleading (Mobium Group 2007–2010). In contrast, one of the strengths of the ECA programme is that it relies on trade union-verified certification, rather than any company self-regulated code of practice, that accredited businesses have met their obligations to workers in their supply chains. In addition ECA only accredit clothing and footwear that is 100% made (i.e. cut, make and trim) in Australia.

The high churn in fashion items produced by current consumer trends, not only puts environmental pressures on the virgin and natural resources needed to produce goods, it also introduces a number of additional ethical and sustainably challenges into the mix (Draper *et al.* 2007). This includes what to do with the clothing waste at the end of its life. While some of this clothing waste is handled through charities who redistribute goods to those in need, most of this waste is sent directly to landfill (Draper *et al.* 2007). In the case where goods are sent offshore by charitable organisations to developing countries, this may solve the immediate problem of lack of clothing; however this influx of goods may actually have negative social and economic impacts on their own primary production and TCF industries (Baden and Barber 2005). There are business opportunities for entrepreneurs and innovative brands to create value through product stewardship schemes, repurposing discarded fashion items and designing for low impact end of life disposal. TCF products and brands that seek to minimise the significant environmental impact of 'fashion use' (i.e. washing, drying) through design and customer education and engagement are also required.

12.4.2 The opportunity of 'ethical and green' fashion for the Australian fashion industry

Australia is known for its natural environment, outdoor lifestyle and the national character of openness and a 'fair go' for everyone. Perhaps there is an opportunity to reshape the Australian TCF industry around these principles. The term 'Made in Australia' may in time come to represent a set of standards that reflect the values that Australian manufacturing businesses embody. In the same way that 'Made in Italy' may represent notions of luxury and heritage, Australian made could be a marker that consumers worldwide recognise as being healthily, ethically and sustainably made.

There is an opportunity for the Australian TCF sector to pursue innovation in producing 'ethical and green' fashion for Australia and the global market. Addressing ethical manufacturing onshore through the ECA label is one pillar. Another could be to build on the known competitive advantage of producing TCF products onshore from design through to cut, sew and trim. This could potentially increase local market share, and adding value by producing 'in season', doing shorter runs and exercising more control over an onshore supply chain flow from this as business possibilities. Industry collaboration on sourcing of ethically and sustainably produced textiles would add another dimension to the 'ethical and green' story, as would collaborating to enhance environmental performance of manufacturers (both onshore and off). Pioneering business models that embrace product stewardship, support consumers to have less environmental impact in apparel use, and connect 'fashion waste' with emerging industries hungry for fibre as a resource could also shift the Australian fashion industry from survival mode to a thriving future.

12.4.3 Where to from here?

The challenges that have faced the Australian TCF industry over the last three decades, as well as continuing competitive pressures, suggest that a rethink of the made-in-Australia proposition is required to better position the sector for the decades ahead. A value proposition that links Australia's reputation for a 'fair go' with ethical and sustainable fashion production and consumption is one way to approach such a repositioning.

The recent success of the ECA label demonstrates the greatness of potential when government, industry, unions, NGOs and consumers work together. Choosing the 'ethical and green' route will demand courage and innovation, especially with the unique challenges of the Australian fashion industry. If realised, benefits could be great for business, the industry, its workers and the environment.

References

Access Economics (2010) 'Household E-Commerce Activity and Trends in Australia', www.dbcde.gov.au/__data/assets/pdf_file/0020/131951/Household_e-commerce_activity_and_trends_in_Australia-25Nov2010-final.pdf, accessed 25 September 2012.

AusIndustry (2012) 'Textile, Clothing and Footwear (TCF) Strategic Capability Program (SCP)', www.ausindustry.gov.au/programs/manufacturing/tcf-scp/Pages/default.aspx, accessed 25 September 2012.

Australian Competition and Consumer Commission (2011) 'ACCC Re-authorises Homeworkers Code of Practice', press release, 17 February 2011, www.accc.gov.au/content/index.phtml/itemId/973327, accessed 25 September 2012.

Australian Government Department of Foreign Affairs and Trade (2011) 'Trading our Way to More Jobs and Prosperity', www.dfat.gov.au/publications/trade/trading-our-way-to-more-jobs-and-prosperity.pdf, accessed 25 September 2012.

Australian Senate (2012) 'Senate Hearing, Inquiry into Fairwork Amendment (Textile, Clothing and Footwear Industry) Bill 2011', *Senate Standing Committee on Education, Employment and Workplace Relations*, Melbourne, 2 February 2012.

Baden, S., and C. Barber (2005) 'The Impact of the Second Hand Clothing Trade on Developing Countries', Oxfam, www.oxfamilibrary.openrepository.com/oxfam/bitstream/10546/112464/1/rr-impact-second-hand-clothing-trade-developing-countries-010905-en.pdf, accessed 18 October 2012.

Brown, S. (2010) *Eco Fashion* (London: Laurence King).

Department of Education, Employment & Workplace Relations (2009) 'Fair Work Principles User Guide', www.deewr.gov.au/WorkplaceRelations/Policies/FairWorkPrinciples/Pages/Publications.aspx, accessed 18 October 2012.

Department of Education, Employment & Workplace Relations (2011) 'Australia's Fair Work System: Ethical Clothing Australia Education and Compliance Program', www.deewr.gov.au/WorkplaceRelations/Programs/Pages/EthicalClothingAustraliaProgram.aspx, accessed 25 September 2012.

Diviney, E., and S. Lillywhite (2007) *Ethical Threads: Corporate Social Responsibility in the Australian Garment Industry* (Fitzroy, Victoria: Brotherhood of St Laurence, www.bsl.org.au/pdfs/DivineyLillywhite_ethical_threads.pdf).

Draper, S., V. Murray and I. Weissbrod (2007) 'Fashioning Sustainability: A Review of the Sustainability Impacts of the Clothing Industry', Forum for the Future, www.forumforthefuture.org/sites/default/files/project/downloads/fashionsustain.pdf, accessed 28 January 2012.

Financial Review (2012) 'Fast Fashion: The Squeeze Is On', Financial Review, 30 March 2012, www.afr.com/p/afrmagazine/fast_fashion_the_squeeze_is_on_3sgPhLTIfgJLClV7D McImN, accessed 25 September 2012.

Golden, J. (ed.) (2010) 'An Overview of Ecolabels and Sustainability Certifications in the Global Marketplace (interim report)', Corporate Sustainability Initiative, Nicholas Institute for Environmental Policy Solutions, Duke University, www.sustainabilityconsortium.org/wp-content/themes/sustainability/assets/pdf/Ecolabels_Report.pdf, accessed 28 January 2012.

Green, R. (2008) 'Building Innovative Capability: Review of the Australian Textile, Clothing and Footwear Industries', Commonwealth of Australia, Canberra, www.teansw.com.au/Curriculum/Textiles%2011-12/Resources/401_TCF%20review_vol1.pdf, accessed 15 April 2012.

Mobium Group (2007–2010) *Living LOHAS 3: Consumer Trends Report* (Melbourne: LOHAS).

Parliament of Australia (2012) 'Fair Work Amendment (Textile, Clothing and Footwear Industry) Bill 2011', www.aph.gov.au/Parliamentary_Business/Bills_Legislation/bd/bd1112a/12bd092, accessed 26 September 2012.

Textile, Clothing and Footwear Union of Australia (2012) 'Submission to Inquiry into Fair Work Amendment (Textile, Clothing and Footwear Industry) Bill 2011', Senate Standing Committee on Education, Employment and Workplace Relations, 11 January 2012.

Weller, S. (2007a) *Retailing, Clothing and Textiles Production in Australia* (Working Paper No. 29; Melbourne: Centre for Strategic Economic Studies, Victoria University).

Weller, S. (2007b) *Beyond 'Global Production Networks': Australian Fashion Week's Transsectoral Synergies* (CSES Working Paper No. 27; Melbourne: Centre for Strategic Economic Studies, Victoria University).

World Trade Organization (2007a) 'Trade Policy Review: Australia 2007', Government Report, www.wto.org/english/tratop_e/tpr_e/tp279_e.htm, accessed 26 September 2012.

World Trade Organization (2007b) 'Trade Policies by Sector Report', www.wto.org/english/tratop_e/tpr_e/s178-04_e.doc, accessed 18 October 2012.

Cameron Neil has worked with governments, businesses and community sector organisations for more than a decade on various social and environmental sustainability initiatives. He worked with Fairtrade Certification for 7 years in Australia and New Zealand, and is passionate about linking sustainable production and consumption, especially in the food, fashion and forest industries.

Eloise Bishop has worked in communications and corporate social responsibility for the past decade and a half, with her main focus now on sustainable and ethical fashion. Her work in this area includes collaborating with Australian designers and manufacturers, building strategic consumer awareness campaigns, developing industry seminars and events, as well as teaching sustainability in fashion at TAFE.

Kirsten Simpson has over a decade of professional experience managing and implementing sustainability initiatives across the corporate sector. Kirsten has extensive experience in environmental management, corporate performance reporting assurance and audit. She holds an honours degree in Earth Sciences from Monash University and a Master's of Environment from Melbourne University.

13

'Sustainability isn't sexy'
An exploratory study into luxury fashion

Carla-Maria Streit and Iain A. Davies
University of Bath, School of Management, UK

The fashion industry has received surprisingly little attention from thought leaders and academics interested in sustainability and ethics. There is no question that there are people out there producing exciting and exquisite fashion items with a strong sustainable edge. However in a market obsessed with self-expression and identity (Mason 1992; Groth and McDaniel 1993; Vickers and Renand 2003; Vigneron and Johnson 2004), is there space, or interest, in consuming fashion for altruistic purposes?

There has been recent debate on the role of sustainability and ethics in luxury markets within the commercial and consumer press (Bendell and Kleanthous 2007; DeBeers 2009; Ageorges 2010; La Tribune 2010, 2011). However, most academic literature on ethical consumption focuses on commodity products—food, beverages, cosmetics and high street clothing (Sriram and Forman 1993; Strong 1996; Auger *et al.* 2003, 2008; Vermeir and Verbeke 2006; McGoldrick and Freestone 2008)—with comparatively little written about ethical luxury products in academic journals (Joergens 2006). The few empirical studies which do exist are limited to counterfeiting (Arghavan and Zaichkowsky 2000; Wilcox *et al.* 2009) and consumer studies suggesting a 'fallacy of clean luxury', indicating that, by their very nature, luxury products are perceived to be sustainable (Davies *et al.* 2012: 46). This chapter is therefore an exploratory study into the high-end luxury fashion market drawn from interviews with industry insiders such as designers, purchasers and consultants about their perception of the role of sustainability and ethics in their industry. First, however, we provide a brief overview of the rising interest in ethical luxury consumption.

13.1 Ethical luxury

The extent to which ethical luxury goods such as sustainable prestige fashion items are desirable in the market is unclear despite strong popular press attention (Ageorges 2010; La Tribune 2010, 2011). In Davies *et al.*'s (2012) 'Do Consumers Care About Ethical Luxury', consumers are presented as having far less concern about ethics in luxury purchases than in day-to-day commodity purchases. They propose a **fallacy of clean luxury** where luxury products are perceived as devoid of ethical issues based purely on the price tag or brand name on the label. Davies *et al.* also suggest that even if customers are aware of potential ethical issues they are unlikely to consider them at their 'moment of truth' (Carrington *et al.* 2010) when purchasing a luxury item. Yet, conversely, reports by WWF-UK and DeBeers (Bendell and Kleanthous 2007; DeBeers 2009) suggest consumers are ready for sustainability to emerge as a competitive offering in the $120 billion luxury goods market. With such wildly differing views on the consumers' ability to identify 'sustainable' vs. 'unsustainable' products and willingness to seek out information on what happens behind the label, it is highly uncertain how successful the sustainability message will be in the luxury fashion market.

The fashion industry is just as susceptible to breaches in ethics as many other industries: for example, the employee abuses and health risks associated with leather production, the extensive use of animal pelts, exploitation of (especially younger) models, conflict diamonds which are mined and sold from war zones to fund military campaigns, or the displacement of communities, contaminated drinking water and environmental damage caused by the gold mining industry (Tibbetts 2007; DeBeers 2009). Luxury brands themselves have come under the media spotlight for breaching the law or codes of conduct: examples include luxury cosmetic firm, Garnier, which was found guilty of racial discrimination; LVMH, owners of Louis Vuitton and TAG Heuer, which was de-listed from the FTSE4Good index as a result of poor compliance with supply chain requirements; and the exploitation of illegal Chinese immigrant workforces in Italian sweatshops by Prada (or even what 'Made in Italy', or 'Made in France' actually represents when mostly complete articles are shipped in from Asia). Despite this mounting evidence of unethical practices by luxury brands, there are few NGOs dealing in these markets, few labelling or certification systems in place to audit them and limited research being published concerning producers' or consumers' views of sustainability and ethics in luxury markets.

Despite these apparent disadvantages, ethical fashion is coming. Luxury brands such as Jérôme Dreyfuss, Vivienne Westwood, Stella McCartney and 'Petit h' by Hermès, as well as industry initiatives such as Swan-marked diamonds and Fairtrade gold, are sowing the seeds of producer interest in the potential of more ethical fashion items. However we know from extensive work in the consumer behaviour field that consumers are looking for a distinctly different set of benefits when buying luxury products compared with their commodity purchases (Arghavan and Zaichkowsky 2000; Vigneron and Johnson 2004; Ward and Chiari 2008). Therefore research into sustainable consumption based on food, cosmetics and sportswear (Sriram and Forman 1993; Strong 1996; Auger *et al.* 2003, 2008; Vermeir and Verbeke 2006; McGoldrick and Freestone 2008), or eco-labels (Anderson and Hansen 2004; Bjørner *et al.* 2004) and fairtrade (Elliott and Freeman 2001; De Pelsmacker *et al.* 2005; Loureiro and Lotade 2005) are unlikely to provide a strong basis for predicting or understanding the underlying rationales for luxury fashion purchases.

Consumer behaviour research into luxury consumption suggests there are three interrelated perspectives of what consumers look for in a luxury purchase such as fashion items: the economical view, the psychological view and the marketing view (de Barnier *et al.* 2006).

- The economical view distinguishes between luxury and necessity where luxury goods do not fill an elementary need, but a realm of desire (Mortelmans 2005). This is embodied in Groth and McDaniel's (1993) exclusive value principle which states that a luxury product's market price is the sum of its pure utilitarian value (e.g. quality, aesthetic design, excellence of service, etc.) and exclusive value premium (e.g. external factors such as advertising)

- The psychological view explores the intra- and inter-personal context of luxury consumption, particularly around peer and self-perception (Mason 1992; Vickers and Renand 2003; Vigneron and Johnson 2004). Vickers and Renand (2003) suggest that luxury goods are symbols of consumer identity, characterised by the dimensions of experimentalism and symbolic interaction. As a consequence, the primary value for luxury goods is psychological in terms of how this positions the consumer within society

- The marketing view is a combination of the above (de Barnier *et al.* 2006) where the motivation for luxury consumption is tied to the nature of the financial, individual and functional utilities of a brand (Wiedmann *et al.* 2007). Therefore consumers not only desire to impress other people or display status and success, but also form a semantic network of non-personal perceptions including conspicuousness, uniqueness and quality, and personal perceptions encompassing hedonism and the extended self (Vigneron and Johnson 2004). Thus self-pleasure or self-gift giving (de Barnier *et al.* 2006) is an essential aspect for many luxury good consumers

According to the psychological view one could expect that consumers who can afford more luxury goods would pay more attention to ethics, either to feel good about themselves (self-identity) or to impress others (peer identity). Conversely, if luxury good consumption is about hedonism and self-pleasures, in line with the marketing view, it is less likely that altruism would override hedonistic desires. We therefore have a very limited and conflicting basis for building a theoretical framework for understanding the role of sustainability in the fashion industry. As such we take a very exploratory approach to this area of research.

13.2 Methods

In the absence of extant empirical research on which to base this study an unstructured approach is required through which insight can be allowed to emerge from the data (Glaser 1992; Goulding 2000). Therefore the research takes a grounded, interpretivist, inductive approach to allow for the data to lead the research process.

Theoretical sampling is used in this research and is defined by Glaser (1992: 101) as 'the process of data collection for generating theory whereby the analyst jointly collects, codes and analyses his data and decides what data to collect next and where to find them, in order to develop his theory as it emerges'. Theoretical sampling begins with a sample in which the process of interest is transparently observable and ends when each category is saturated, elaborated and integrated into the emerging theory (Glaser 1992).

The virtue of theoretical sampling is the ability to take advantage of fortuitous events (Corbin and Strauss 2008) such as the launch of Pure Premium, a new section at the Pure London Fashion Show, dedicated to high profile contemporary womenswear where contacts were made for the research. Hoping to gain an invaluable and unbiased insight into the industry we interviewed eight active and regular high-end luxury clothing consumers aged between 21 and 55 (code C1–C8), 14 luxury brand clothing designers (seven traditional luxury brands, code LB1–LB7 and seven ethical brands, code EB1–EB7 varying in size from small boutiques to household names), three buyers for independent high-end retailers (code R1–R3) and three industry consultants on sustainability in the textile and fashion industry (code O1–O3). As grounded research is not bound by discipline or data collection and allows for multiple data sources (Glaser 1992), promotional material such as leaflets, event guides, etc. are considered as integral to the data collected.

In line with a naturalistic analysis, one-on-one in-depth interviews were conducted. This strategy eliminates the limitations of traditional surveys where the relevance of ethical issues is overemphasised, in addition to the clouding of true preferences through false information (Auger and Devinney 2007). We recorded all interviews enabling high levels of detail and accuracy while allowing for superior interaction through eye contact and body language (Liamputtong and Ezzy 2005). Following a semi-structured approach, the interviewer remained flexible and became a co-participant, thereby realising their role as an actor, director and choreographer (Berg 2007). Using a very brief interview guide (Bryman 2004), open, broad and exploratory themes were used to initiate conversation and encourage storytelling. This offered the greater breadth of data necessary in exploratory research while allowing data and themes to emerge (Glaser 1992; Fontana and Frey 2000). As suggested by Liamputtong and Ezzy (2005), a journal was kept, which allowed the researcher to return to questions and avoid interrupting and tampering with initial responses. Memos were written immediately after each interview as means of documenting the researcher's impressions and description of the situation (Goulding 2000). In order to saturate categories relevant to the emergent theory, theoretical sampling provides the grounded direction to the next samples and more focused questions. Analysis was carried out through an inductive process, in accordance with Spiggle (1994), whereby data is coded and recoded before being fed into the next round of interviews.

13.3 Findings

Central to the findings, are the assumptions and expectations which consumers hold of luxury fashion brands. In the next section we document a lack of awareness or fundamental interest in ethical luxury fashion from nearly all actors (consumers, designers, representatives). We then corroborate the concept of the *fallacy of clean luxury* by demonstrating that even insiders take the assumption that quality infers ethics, and are unwilling to invest time in finding otherwise. Finally, we investigate the emergent finding that those inside the fashion establishment appear to find sustainability or ethics at odds with the ideals of fashion, to the extent that anything to do with ethics must be treated in a very light touch manner, and certainly could be not relied on to open new markets or launch new brands in luxury fashion.

13.4 Who cares about ethics?

Similar to research in the extant luxury literature we identify that ethics is of very limited importance to designers or fashion consumers. When reflecting on past luxury fashion purchases or fantasising about upcoming ones, consumers listed countless criteria, which were important when making a purchase decision such as quality, materials, timelessness and identity creation:

> I would say a higher quality product. So, with better fabrics, meaning longer life time and also more attractively looking. I think it's also some kind of identity, because you buy the brands you like and you can actually suit yourself to that so it's like an image almost. You can create your own image, so for me personally it's very much about all that… I like to look a bit better than the average brand, and that's the reason why I mostly buy luxury goods (C4).

> When I buy a luxury brand it is definitely better quality than the high street alternative. Say, an investment. So if I buy something luxury I would expect to wear it more often and longer. And the cut would be better than on the high street so it's sort of more exclusive. Also, the experience of the brand and its individuality, because every item has had more attention from the designer and from the producer (C1).

While C4 places a lot of emphasis on identity creation, C1 hopes to distance herself from the high street and sees a luxury fashion purchase as an investment. Therefore, different criteria become more or less important depending on the wants and needs of the consumer. Nevertheless, a closer examination of all purchase criteria pointed towards three (design, quality and price), which were mentioned most frequently and were common across all interviewees.

1. **Design**. The design of a luxury fashion good often inspired buyers to compromise on other criteria such as price and frequently functioned as a gateway criterion. Therefore, good design often sufficed when justifying a purchase or deliberating over whether to make one:

   If it comes to shoes, as long as I like them, that's it (LB5).

   You like it, you buy it. That's it. It's the first…you know, the first sight that counts (C2).

   Now it's all about the detail, which is good for us because as a brand, we are all about detail (LB3).

2. **Quality**. While it allows consumers to differentiate between luxury and high street fashion, it also provided them with the desired longevity and physical durability of the product:

   Once I buy it, I never throw it out. I use it for a very long time… If it does break, or there is a problem, I just take it to the vendor and they, without any problem, they fix it (C8).

   I think quality is important when you're spending so much money because places on the high street like Zara…they can do a good replica of a Chloé dress but then the quality is not good at all. If it's long lasting, you can argue it's an investment (LB4).

3. **Price**. According to LB3, this is becoming increasingly important for consumers during the recession:

   Right now after the financial crisis people are much more price driven but they have a certain wealth that allows them still to treat themselves. Maybe not as much as before, but they definitely don't stop shopping… It's a bit more of an investment to them (LB3).

Nevertheless, exceptions are made by interviewees when they wish to buy something special as described by C7 who allocated an unlimited budget for his dream Saville Row suit or C5 outlines how she would spend more on a purchase that is really necessary:

   If I'm just buying something for jokes, like I don't really need it, I just like it, I wouldn't spend over a certain amount. But if I'm buying something I need, for work or for an occasion then I am willing to spend more.

With design, quality and price being the main criteria when shopping, it is evident that luxury fashion consumers did not care about ethics when making a purchase decision. 'I'm not sure what the response would be if I asked about it because I have never asked' (C4). With the exception of five interviewees (LB2, EB1, EB2, O2 and O3) who all worked within the ethical fashion industry, none of the participants brought up ethics as a criterion. As such, ethics were described as a bonus, unimportant, secondary or last on the list when participants were specifically asked.

> Actually the fair-trade and ethical stance is something, maybe a secondary thing where they go, oh that's great. It's a bonus (EB4).

> When you have to sort of list it to yourself, it's almost like the ethics of the company are almost at the bottom because that is what it is like for most of our customers. But for us, as a business, it's very important (EB7).

> To be honest it's not the first thing that pops into my head... It kind of just comes as a bonus if, you know, a brand works towards creating good ethics (LB4).

> Ethics is just not something I'm bothered about when I shop for clothes. All companies practise unfair practices in some way if you know what I mean. From that point of view you shouldn't buy from anywhere (C2).

> I'm not so worried about how or what it's made of (LB5).

> I guess it's just not one of the things I care about when I buy clothes. So this would be very, very far down on my priority list and I don't see how... when I'm talking about my enjoyment and buying something and wearing a nice thing, then I would not get additional enjoyment from knowing that the cotton I'm wearing is organic (C1).

While interviewees listed innumerable factors which impacted on their buying behaviour, it was felt that only three showed consistency across all participants. The main criteria were thus identified as design, quality and price. Unfortunately, only five participants spontaneously mentioned having ever considered ethics when buying a luxury fashion good. Once the topic was addressed, consumers admitted that little attention was paid to ethics and that they would not consciously consider it as an important criterion. Therefore it can be concluded that ethics is not a key criterion for consumers when making a luxury fashion purchase.

13.5 Luxury means ethics...right?

With the aim of exploring factors that hinder ethics from becoming a criterion, the focus was drawn to the problems faced by consumers and how they dealt with them. During a discussion on ethical issues, interviewees demonstrated a great breadth of awareness of ethical issues such as the environment, sweatshop labour and both social and environmental damage caused by gold, ivory, leather and textiles industries. However, examples were limited to commodities such as food and high street chains. When exemplifying their arguments, almost all respondents referred to cases such as Primark, Topshop, H&M, Next, Gap, Nike, BHS and Nestlé.

Although all interviewees worked within the industry, only LB7, who studied ethics at university, was able to provide information regarding ethical issues within the luxury fashion industry. Furthermore, only four interviewees (LB7, LB3, LB6 and O3) referred to ethical fashion designers such as Katharine Hamnett, Stella McCartney and Vivienne Westwood. On the contrary, the majority explained they were not aware of ethical issues within the luxury fashion industry, and many respondents (LB1, LB2, C1, C2, C3, C4, C6 and C8)[1] automatically assumed and expected that luxury fashion brands did not engage in questionable ethics.

> I have never come across any of these high luxury brands needing to market themselves as ethical (C8).

> I'm not really aware of any ethical issues within the luxury fashion industry. I haven't really looked into it much either…but you don't hear of Burberry sweatshops (C6).

While LB1 and LB2 romanticised about the manufacturing process at Hermès, C2 explained how the craftsmanship at Louis Vuitton is often passed from father to son.[2] Similarly, C1 describes her view of her favourite brands:

> I wouldn't imagine Prada employing child labour in Bangladesh.[3] Because you would think you're paying for the quality. And Bangladesh and child labour is not associated with quality. So if you say Prada or Gucci, I imagine one of these Italian factories where there are skilled workers who are making the clothes. I would expect and assume that. I trust these brands and you would think that the reputational damage if that is not the case would be too large (C1).

Consumers in particular therefore suffer from what Davies *et al.* (2012) refer to as the fallacy of clean luxury. Where, despite underlying knowledge of problems in the gold, ivory, leather and textiles industries, these are disassociated from the gold, ivory, leather and textiles in composite products the moment a label is added.

13.6 And anyway, it's not my fault—no one told me!

Despite this trust in the label, C6 points to a 'lack of information. I don't know which designers are ethical and which ones aren't. I wouldn't even know where to start'. Consequently, the lack of awareness was blamed as a major barrier. Most importantly, interviewees described how the lack of awareness was hindering them from making an educated purchase decision.

---

1 Note this includes all but two of the consumers.
2 Although LV now manufactures many part and fully finished bags in India.
3 Although Prada was accused of using illegal immigrant workforces under sweatshop conditions in Italy.

I don't really know what the issues are and what the implications might be. For instance with food, I know that if I buy some bean sprouts from Kenya then they're flown across the world and you're polluting the air. Then you can make a conclusion out of that fairly easily. I need more information with clothes (C4).

When you know about the child labour and you know what goes on, you can make up the decision for yourself but I think people are very blind to what goes on in factories, and how things are produced. I think more information should be available to the consumer (LB6).

Interestingly, all interviewees were in agreement with LB6 and argued that there was a clear need for more information. Furthermore, there was a strong desire for the media and educational system to provide more information and educate consumers. The role of the media was widely discussed by interviewees such as O2 who argued that 'there just needs to be more press awareness! And, I think the magazines and designers need to work together with NGOs to actually track and trace their supply chains.' Furthermore, there was a strong belief that the media would be capable of creating change as 'people only change if they get caught' (LB1). Similarly, C3 argues that '9 times out of 10 things do improve when the media gets hold of it'. This was exemplified by C8 who worked with large US retail labels such as Gap and witnessed changes in both labour conditions and the attention paid to environmental issues as a result of high media pressure. The media also changed LB5 and LB6's attitudes towards Primark who were 'quite disgusted' and 'put off' from the brand by the media coverage.

In addition to the media, many interviewees felt that ethics should be more available as a topic at school or university. According to LB6 'it's just about planting seeds everywhere. If there are no seeds, then there's no growth'. Similarly, O2 argued that 'it's just about schools and assemblies and inspiring kids to learn more'. A positive attitude towards education was also evident from interviewees who had learned about ethics at school or university such as LB1: 'I was surprised and it opened up my mind'. Comparably, LB2's education helped her 'understand these issues' while C8 now visits the Labour Behind the Label website quite regularly after using it as an information source for an assignment at university. However, C8 goes on to argue 'if I didn't have to do the research, I wouldn't know, because the company or university forced me to do it'. Thus it became apparent that none of the interviewees was willing to deal with their lack of awareness using their own motivation.

I'm in my own little bubble to be honest with you. So unless I'm really interested in a particular brand, unless they bring that forward and I hear and see that, then it doesn't hit on me (R1).

I probably wouldn't [research a brand] to be fair. I probably wouldn't think, let's check where it's made or how it's made and who makes it. But if it was put in front of me, then that would be different (LB5).

I guess you could go on the website, but I wouldn't bother. Generally wouldn't bother. So, they'd have to get it across in another way for me to actually realise (C6).

While all interviewees argued that a lack of awareness posed a major barrier for them, none was willing to act on it. Akin to C6 (above), this irony was best explained by C5 who described herself as 'lazy, very lazy' or C4 who claimed he was 'not really bothered'. Nevertheless, this further confirms that ethics is not an import criterion for consumers when making a luxury fashion purchases.

13.7 And isn't ethics at odds with what it means to be 'fashionable'?

What became increasingly apparent was that using ethics or sustainability as the main marketing proposition did not appeal to the interviewees at all. According to LB4, high-end fashion 'doesn't tie in so well with ethics in that way. It's not so glamorous... You know, it doesn't have that edge'. Or R3 who stated: 'Lets face it Sustainability isn't sexy! Fashion is sex! Sustainability is a hemp grocery bag and no makeup'. As a result, brands such as EB3 who mix new and old fabrics prefer the term 'upcycling' as opposed to recycling given that 'expensive clothing and recycling sound at odds'. C8 furthers this when arguing that 'people in the luxury brand sector don't want to use the word organic because it might reduce the value of the clothing, in the sense that it doesn't sound good'. LB4 goes further stating: 'organic makes you think of soil and dirt—why would I want people to look at my clothes and think of dirt.'

This theme emerged repeatedly as the seven 'ethical' designers explained the struggles they faced in promoting brands. Particularly EB3 who had just moved into the luxury sector was finding it difficult to get a story published in fashion magazines:

> A friend of mine has pitched us a few times as a story to write to magazines. And it never gets accepted. And he was like 'I'm gonna pitch it as, this is a really cool label and then at the end mention the ethics'. And you're more likely to get accepted among the trendy magazines... It sort of feels like just another eco story otherwise. You've got to be more than just another eco story... That is the key... There's just not really anybody who's doing something that people can really jump on and be like, this is really fucking cool and it's sustainable.

The reality appears to be that ethics is fundamentally too boring, virtuous or pedestrian to be of interest to any designer:

> Dresses don't sell because they're ethical; they sell because they are fabulously designed. Whatever causes a woman to fall in love with a piece of clothing, it certainly isn't the garment's ethical credentials! ...If ethical fashion is to become the norm, creative design must be the USP! (EB7)
>
> Sustainability is not edgy enough for them. It's design first! It's got to look cool. One hundred percent! One hundred million, trillion percent! (EB3)
>
> It's the design first not the ethics. The whole ethical movement in my opinion needs to be rebranded (O1).

O3, an expert in the field of marketing for ethical fashion designers, explained the difficulty of fashion being at odds with marketing the ethical side of a product.

> The soul of fashion is about being rebellious. It's an art form that's plugged into that part of culture. So all real successful fashion has been sort of zeitgeisty, a reflection of what's going on politically and culturally. Like punk, like heroin chic. People wear clothes to make fashion statements and communicate something powerful... At its root, people really respond when it's sort of bad. So that young people can use it to rebel. And you can't [rebel] with ethical fashion. That's good, that's got a halo on it and that is instantly at odds with this kind of concept. They can work, but you have to kind of do it right... That sort of explains why ethical products don't fly off the shelf if you use the ethics as your number one marketing tool.

As a result designers such as EB3 and EB5 are trying to move out of the 'eco ring':

> The reason why I set up the business is because I feel really passionate about [ethics], but to push that forward to people [*click of the tongue*] you don't want to concentrate too heavily on it (EB3).

> You don't sell the ethics to a [retail] purchaser unless they ask. It can only ever cause problems otherwise... They might think you are accusing other designers of being unethical (EB5).

This was confirmed by O3:

> If the designer isn't known, you need to work out which product attributes you can use as a marketing tool and I've always found that the ethical side of it is not that simple. It has to be wrapped up in a story. It has to be part of why the product is of better quality. That is very sellable. People do nowadays want a story.

In summary it is therefore apparent that sustainability and ethics could actually be detrimental to a luxury brand if utilised in the wrong way. Big named designers can use their influence to try to change the market—but they are successful because they are already a major brand, famed for fabulous design—not because they are more sustainable.

13.8 Discussion

Sproles *et al.* (1978) argued that efficient decision-making requires consumers to be fully informed; however Boulstridge and Carrigan (2000) found that most consumers lack information to distinguish whether a company has or has not behaved ethically. In this research we further this by suggesting that even industry insiders lack the knowledge about their own industry and are unwilling to seek out information about sustainability. The fashion industry works in parallel with many industries for which there are well-known issues of ethical breaches and abuses. Participants are even aware of the systematic abuses in similar industries such as sportswear and high street fashion, yet take the automatic assumption that these abuses are not prevalent within their own industry. There is therefore a strong 'fallacy of clean luxury' within the fashion industry, supporting the proposition of Davies *et al.* (2012).

What drives this fallacy is not necessarily clear. Although there does appear to be a pervasive believe that if something is high quality, it must by nature have been made with care and attention to all details—including sustainability. In practice this is the flip side of the separation fallacy (Freeman 1994; Harris and Freeman 2008) where in consumers' minds there is a separation between ethics and business leading to the misapprehension that ethics always costs more. In fashion consumption the aspirational and prestige elements of the brands are supported by an already high price which in turn conveys the perception of ethics. For many participants the perception of the consequences to the luxury brand of being 'found out' breaching ethics was perceived as too potentially damaging. However in reality is it that damaging?

If Bhattacharya and Sen (2004) and Auger *et al.* (2008) find commodity consumers unwilling to sacrifice quality for ethics, then luxury consumers will be even more stringent on their brand choices. If fashion items are bought primarily because of design, quality and price, then the desire to boycott a product for an ethical breach is likely to be very low. Indeed, if you look at the impacts of media exposure from ethical breaches of fashion brands, such as those discussed in the chapter, it is hard to see any impact on consumption levels at all.

Looking across the industry more generally it appears that breaching ethics can at most produce a hiccough to the people exposed and in other cases lead to huge success. Looking at the ongoing success of certain models, for instance, scandals such as cocaine abuse by Kate Moss, Jodie Kidd's body mass index (BMI) of 13, and Naomi Campbell's convictions for assault suggest that being a bad role model can actually assist in building and maintaining careers in this industry. This suggests that there are institutional issues within the fashion industry that encourage the aspiration to be bad, and if caught the offender is not institutionally punished. It is certainly not punished by consumers, who happily turn a blind eye to ethical issues in search of that perfect dress.

This study even goes so far to suggest sustainability and ethics can be a detrimental product attribute to luxury fashion success because ethics, virtue and sustainability are simply not rebellious enough, not sexy and not aspirational. This creates a clear barrier for the use of sustainability as a unique selling proposition in the high end of the luxury fashion market, thus making it difficult for breakthrough ethical luxury designers to gain a foothold in the market.

It is also relatively clear that unlike commodity markets where there is a large(ish) ethical niche of radical and pragmatic customers willing to champion a more sustainable brand (Renard 2005; Beji-Becheur *et al.* 2008; Golding 2009), industry insiders believe luxury fashion markets simply don't have this niche market. In fact the overriding issue is that sustainability will simply not sell unless it is wrapped up in exclusive design, with high-quality materials and helps build the story of why the product is exclusive. The sustainable component should allow the design of the product to shine in order to fulfil the primary criteria of luxury fashion consumers. This is particularly important when the designer is yet to establish their name within the industry as it allows them to build credibility and a reputation for cutting edge design. Finally, it is crucial that the ethical component is wrapped up in a larger story which both humanises the brand and brings the consumer closer to the designer and the cause.

13.9 Conclusions

In this chapter we have provided an initial exploration of the potential role for sustainability brands in the luxury fashion market. We are able to confirm Davies *et al.*'s (2012) concept of the fallacy of clean luxury in a different context and using a different methodology, suggesting the potential pervasiveness of this concept. Fundamentally both industry insiders and consumers disassociate luxury brands from abuses they know exist in similar/associated industries. We call this a fallacy because it is clear that many materials used within fashion items are liable to come from these associated industries, unless there is an active pursuit of transparent supply chains. We are also aware of abuses within specific luxury brands but these have failed to seep into industry representative or customer consciousness at the 'moment of truth' (Carrington *et al.* 2010).

Our results also confirm suggestions in the literature about the lack of interest in pursuing information regarding sustainability. The lack of information is clearly blamed for lack of action, although this appears a weak argument for two reasons. First, respondents clearly had no interest in finding out about sustainability issues within the industry. And, second, even if they had good information about ethical abuses it is unlikely to dissuade luxury fashion consumers from shopping because of the strong hedonistic aspects associated with luxury fashion consumption. This is evidenced by the experience of our ethical designers, who found that being vocal about sustainability is often a hindrance in this marketplace and must be utilised sparingly. The undercurrent driving this is the pervasive belief that sustainability is simply not sexy enough for luxury fashion items. Virtuousness is at odds with rebellion, and rebellion is the heart of good fashion.

In fashion you've got to be bad to be good!

References

Ageorges, D. (2010) *Luxe Et Développement Durable Au Palais De Tokyo Pour Parler Avenire* (Paris: Agence France Presse).

Anderson, R.C., and E.N. Hansen (2004) 'Determining Consumer Preferences for Ecolabelled Forest Products', *Journal of Forestry* 102.4: 28-32.

Arghavan, N., and J.L. Zaichkowsky (2000) 'Do Counterfeits Devalue the Ownership of Luxury Brands', *Journal of Product and Brand Management* 9.7: 485-97.

Auger, P., and T.M. Devinney (2007) 'Do What Consumers Say Matter? The Misalignment of Preferences with Unconstrained Ethical Intentions', *Journal of Business Ethics* 76: 361-83.

Auger, P., P. Burke, T.M. Devinney and J.J. Louviere (2003) 'What Will Consumers Pay for Social Product Features?', *Journal of Business Ethics* 42.3: 281-304.

Auger, P., T.M. Devinney, J.J. Louviere and P.F. Burke (2008) 'Do Social Product Features have Value to Consumers?', *International Journal of Research in Marketing* 25.3: 183-91.

Beji-Becheur, A., V. Diaz Pedregal and N. Ozcaglar-Toulouse (2008) 'Fair Trade: Just How "Fair" are the Exchanges?', *Journal of Macromarketing* 28.1: 44-52.

Bendell, J., and A. Kleanthous (2007) 'Deeper Luxury', www.wwf.org.uk/deeperluxury/_downloads/DeeperluxuryReport.pdf, accessed 4 May 2009.

Berg, B.L. (2007) *Qualitative Research Methods for the Social Sciences* (Boston, MA: Pearson, 6th edn).

Bhattacharya, C.B., and S. Sen (2004) 'Doing Better at Doing Good: When, Why, and How Consumers Respond to Corporate Social Initiatives', *California Management Review* 47.1: 9-24.

Bjørner, T.B., L.G. Hansen and C.S. Russell (2004) 'Environmental Labelling and Consumers' Choice: An Empirical Analysis of the Effect of the Nordic Swan', *Journal of Environmental Economics and Management* 47.3: 411-24.

Boulstridge, E., and M. Carrigan (2000) 'Do Consumers Really Care about Corporate Responsibility? Highlighting the Attitude–Behavior Gap', *Journal of Communication Management* 4.4: 355-68.

Bryman, A. (2004) *Social Research Methods* (Oxford, UK: Oxford University Press, 2nd edn).

Carrington, M., B. Neville and G. Whitwell (2010) 'Why Ethical Consumers Don't Walk Their Talk', *Journal of Business Ethics* 97: 139-58.

Corbin, J., and A. Strauss (2008) *Basics of Qualitative Research* (Thousand Oaks, CA: Sage Publications, 3rd edn).

Davies, I.A., Z. Lee and I. Ahonkhai (2012) 'Do Consumers Care About Ethical Luxury', *Journal of Business Ethics* 106: 37-51.

de Barnier, V., I. Rodina and P. Valette-Florence (2006) *Which Luxury Perceptions Affect Most Consumer Purchase Behavior? A Cross-Cultural Exploratory Study in France, the United Kingdom and Russia* (working paper; Grenoble, France: University Pierre Mendes).

De Pelsmacker, P., L. Driesen and G. Rayp (2005) 'Do Consumers Care about Ethics? Willingness to Pay for Fair Trade Coffee', *Journal of Consumer Affairs* 39.2: 363-85.

DeBeers (2009) *Luxury: Considered* (London: Ledbury Research).

Elliott, K.A., and R.B. Freeman (2001) *White Hats or Don Quixotes? Human Rights Vigilantes in the Global Economy* (Cambridge, MA: National Bureau of Economic Research).

Fontana, A., and J.H. Frey (2000) 'The Interview: From Structured Questions to Negotiated Text', in N.K. Denzin and Y.S. Lincoln (eds.), *The Handbook of Qualitative Research* (Thousand Oaks, CA: Sage Publications, 2nd edn).

Freeman, R.E. (1994) 'The Politics of Stakeholder Theory: Some Future Directions', *Business Ethics Quarterly* 4.4: 409-22.

Glaser, B.G. (1992) *Basics of Grounded Theory Analysis: Emergence vs. Forcing* (Mill Valley, CA: Sociology Press).

Golding, K. (2009) 'Fair Trade's Dual Aspect: The Communications Challenge of Fair Trade Marketing', *Journal of Macromarketing* 29.2: 160-71.

Goulding, C. (2000) 'Grounded Theory Methodology and Consumer Behaviour, Procedures, Practice and Pitfalls', *Advances in Consumer Research* 27.1: 261-66.

Groth, J., and S.W. McDaniel (1993) 'The Exclusive Value Principle: The Basis for Prestige Pricing', *Journal of Consumer Marketing* 10: 10-16.

Harris, J.D., and R.E. Freeman (2008) 'The Impossibility of the Separation Thesis', *Business Ethics Quarterly* 18.4: 541-48.

Joergens, C. (2006) 'Ethical Fashion: Myth or Future Trend?', *Journal of Fashion Marketing and Management* 10.3: 360-71.

La Tribune (2010) 'Luxe et développement durable peuvent-ils faire bon ménage?' La Tribune, 6 May 2010, www.latribune.fr/green-business/20100506trib000506311/luxe-et-developpement-durable-peuvent-ils-faire-bon-menage-.html, accessed 26 September 2012.

La Tribune (2011) 'Développement Durable et Luxe Sont-ils Compatibles?' La Tribune, 23 February 2011, www.latribune.fr/entreprises-finance/publi-redactionnel/abc-luxe/20110223trib000603700/developpement-durable-et-luxe-sont-ils-compatibles-.html, accessed 26 September 2012.

Liamputtong, P., and D. Ezzy (2005) *Qualitative Research Methods* (South Melbourne, Victoria: Oxford University Press).

Loureiro, M.L., and J. Lotade (2005) 'Do Fair Trade and Eco-Labelling in Coffee Wake up the Consumer Conscience?', *Ecological Economics* 53.1: 129-38.

Mason, R.S. (1992) 'Modeling the Demand for Status Goods', *Association for Consumer Research Special Volumes*: 88-95.

McGoldrick, P.J., and O.M. Freestone (2008) 'Ethical Product Premiums: Antecedents and Extent of Consumers' Willingness to Pay', *International Review of Retail, Distribution and Consumer Research* 18.2: 185-201.

Mortelmans, D. (2005) 'Sign Values in Processes of Distinction: The Concept of Luxury', *Semiotica* 157.1/4: 497-520.

Renard, M.-C. (2005) 'Quality Certification, Regulation and Power in Fair Trade', *Journal of Rural Studies* 21: 419-31.

Spiggle, S. (1994) 'Analysis and Interpretation of Qualitative Data in Consumer Research', *Journal of Consumer Research* 21.3: 491-503.

Sproles, G.B., L.V. Geistfeld and S.B. Badenhop (1978) 'Informational Inputs as Influences on Efficient Consumer Decision-Making', *Journal of Consumer Affairs* 12: 88-103.

Sriram, V., and A.M. Forman (1993) 'The Relative Importance of Products' Environmental Attributes: A Cross-Cultural Comparison', *International Marketing Review* 10.3: 51-70.

Strong, C. (1996) 'Features Contributing to the Growth of Ethical Consumerism: A Preliminary Investigation', *Marketing Intelligence and Planning* 14.5: 5-13.

Tibbetts, G. (2007) 'Unethical Luxury Brands Criticised by WWF', The Telegraph, 29 November 2007, www.telegraph.co.uk/earth/earthnews/3316454/Unethical-luxury-brands-criticised-by-WWF.html, accessed 10 January 2011.

Vermeir, I., and W. Verbeke (2006) 'Sustainable Food Consumption: Exploring the Consumer "Attitude–Behavioral Intention" Gap', *Journal of Agricultural and Environmental Ethics* 19: 169-94.

Vickers, J.S., and F. Renand (2003) 'The Marketing of Luxury Goods: An Exploratory Study, Three Conceptual Dimensions', *Marketing Review* 3.4: 459-78.

Vigneron, F., and L.W. Johnson (2004) 'Measuring Perceptions of Brand Luxury', *Brand Management* 11.6: 484-506.

Ward, D., and C. Chiari (2008) 'Keeping Luxury Inaccessible', MPRA, www.mpra.ub.uni-muenchen.de/11373/1/MPRA_paper_11373.pdf, accessed 2 August 2009.

Wiedmann, K.P., N. Hennings and A. Siebels (2007) 'Measuring Consumers' Luxury Value Perception: A Cross-Cultural Framework', *Academy of Marketing Science Review* 7: 1-21.

Wilcox, K., H.M. Kim and S. Sen (2009) 'Why Do Consumers Buy Counterfeit Luxury Brands?' *Journal of Marketing Research* 46: 247-59.

Carla-Maria Streit is a brand executive for one of the world's top FMCG (fast-moving consumer goods) companies. She is a graduate of both the University of Nottingham and the University of Bath and was the 2010 Procter & Gamble 'Best Overall Performance' prize winner.

Dr **Iain A. Davies** specialises in marketing fairtrade and ethical luxury items. He explores the assimilation of ethics within business networks drawing on his experience working in the fairtrade sector since the 1990s. His research is well read, with the most downloaded articles in *Business Ethics: A European Review* in 2010 and *Journal of Business Ethics* in 2011/2012 and has published in *Harvard Business Review*.

Ethical fashion in Western Europe

A survey of the status quo through the digital communications lens

Ilaria Pasquinelli and Pamela Ravasio

texSture, UK

Understanding cross-border diversity in consumer behaviour, advertising, sales and marketing management is a core area of research of international marketing. The impact of cultural differences has been studied particularly in the field of business negotiations, advertising, consumer behaviour and marketing research. Looking at the differences between high-context and low-context cultures in business negotiations (Herbig 2003) is useful for our purposes because of the impact on the quality and quantity of information businesses are willing to share. In high-context cultures, most of the information is either in the physical context or initialised in a specific person, while very little is in the explicit, transmitted part of the message. High-context cultures have a strong sense of tradition and history, and they assume the listener/reader already knows everything. In low-context cultures, rules are important, knowledge is publicly accessible, the message is carried more by verbal than non-verbal means. Italy and Spain are typical high-context countries, France and UK have got elements of the two but France tends to be more a high-context country, Germany, Denmark and Sweden are low-context countries.

Different cultures mean different approaches to ethics in business. Ethics in business evolves over time as a result of historical, political and socioeconomic drivers

(Argandonga and Hoivik 2009). Literature on corporate social responsibility (CSR) shows that firms from the more liberal market economies where English is the primary language and with British cultural influence (e.g. USA, UK) score higher on most dimensions of CSR than firms in the more coordinated market economies in continental Europe (e.g. Jackson and Apostolakou 2010). German corporations for instance, are tied to tight social and environmental regulations; therefore CSR activities are regulated by law (Ethical Corp. 2011). This result lends support to the view that the voluntary CSR practices in liberal economies are but a substitute for institutionalised forms of stakeholder participation.

Sustainability communication can be a source of differentiation and competitive advantage (UNEP 2006). It increases the brand's equity in the long run (Morgan *et al.* 2011). Deciding what type and level of accuracy of information to disclose is therefore a strategic decision as it has a direct impact on the brand's image and on the stakeholders' engagement. It was further shown that when companies want to communicate with stakeholders about their CSR initiatives, they need to involve those stakeholders in a two-way, carefully crafted and increasingly sophisticated communication process (Morsing and Schultz 2006). If successful, this will result in a heightened corporate image, strengthened stakeholder–company relationships and enhanced stakeholders' advocacy behaviours (Du *et al.* 2010).

For the purpose of this chapter, we apply the term 'ethical fashion' as defined by the Ethical Fashion Forum (EFF 2004). The majority of academic research in ethical fashion originates from either UK (e.g. Pretious and Love 2006; Williams 2009) or US (e.g. Stanforth and Hauck 2010) universities and research centres, or collaborative projects between a UK and a continental European partner (e.g. Aspers 2006; Joergens 2006; Cervellon *et al.* 2010). The focus of these projects thereby revolves around:

- The ethical consumer, only rarely of fashion specifically: the buying patterns that can be identified in order to explain their purchasing decisions and the importance of ethical issues in this respect (Dickson 2000; Ozcaglar-Toulouse *et al.* 2006)

- Ethical and environmental labelling systems in the fashion industry (Aspers 2008)

- Human rights issues in the fashion supply chain, in combination with case studies on how to make supply chains more sustainable (Hale and Willis 2005; De Brito 2007)

- Unethical practices in the high-street fashion industry, particularly in the UK (UCA 2006; Labour Behind the Label 2011)

A much larger body of research results and publications stems, however, from non-academic organisations such as NGOs, international organisations, labelling bodies, multi-stakeholder groups and trade unions. It is these results that serve as the primary point of reference to fashion industry professionals in the realm of their professional practice. Examples of recent publications are:

- Sweatshop conditions in the factories supplying high-street retailers (e.g. ActionAid 2010; Labour Behind the Label 2011) and in specific sourcing countries (e.g. ITGLWF 2011)

- The health risk of specific treatments for garments and harmful substances (e.g. Ferrigno 2005; Labour Behind the Label 2010; Greenpeace 2011)

- Working conditions in the cotton industry (e.g. EJF 2010)

In summary, it can be said that while there is an abundance of CSR and fashion supply chain-related research results, there is a lack of research with regard to the communication side of ethical fashion, i.e. how fashion brands communicate their commitments and achievements to a wider public. It is our aim hence to lay a foundation stone by looking at different European markets and market segments, and how specific fashion companies currently communicate with their consumers and business stakeholders.

14.1 Method

14.1.1 Selection of countries

The countries selected were chosen from across Western Europe as the topic of sustainability is more advanced in these areas of Europe. Further, we selected the countries such that they not only represent the most important fashion markets on the continent, but also that their cultural identity differences would be taken into consideration. The markets selected were: Spain and Italy (South); France and Germany (Centre); Sweden and Denmark (Scandinavia); and the UK (North).

14.1.2 Brand selection

For each of the selected markets, we surveyed sustainability communications across different market segments through individual brand case studies. The market segments were chosen so as to represent the whole width and breadth of commercial offerings available, and were represented by brands or enterprises (Table 14.1), each belonging to one of the following categories: (Cat. 1) international brand with a turnover of at least several tens of millions euros and a leader market position; (Cat. 2) couture fashion brand; (Cat. 3) medium-priced, ready-to-wear fashion brand retailed in specialist boutiques; (Cat. 4) low-price segment fashion brand commonly available on the high-street; (Cat. 5) multi-brand luxury department store; (Cat. 6) multi-brand, medium-priced department store.

Brands/retailers were selected in the first instance to be as perfect as possible a representation for their market segment. For certain categories, such as category no. 1 or 5, this already determined—in all cases but the UK—the specific company, as the options within the markets were minimal.

Table 14.1 **Brands selected to represent each of the analysed national markets, by country and market segment**

Country	Cat. 1	Cat. 2	Cat. 3	Cat. 4	Cat. 5	Cat. 6
Italy	Gucci	Zegna	Benetton	Original Marines	Coin Group	Luisa Via Roma
Spain	Adolfo Dominguez	Loewe	Pikolinos	Inditex	Eks & Ekseption	El Corte Inglés
France	LVHM	Lancel	Les Fées Du Bengale	Monoprix	Galéries Lafayettes	La Redoute
Germany	Rena Lange	Wunderkind	Inka Koffke	C&A	KaDeWe	Galeria Kaufhof
Denmark	Vero Moda	Noir	Modstrom	Coop Danmark	Lubarol	Illum
Sweden	Odd Molly	Lars Wallin	Tiger of Sweden	H&M	NK	Ahlens
UK	Vivienne Westwood	Hemyca	Good One	Tesco Fashion	Harvey Nichols	John Lewis

For each category where we had more than a single candidate to choose from, a minimal engagement with sustainability is what we required for our evaluation. This engagement was confirmed through links to organisations such as the Ethical Trading Initiative (UK), Initiative Clause Sociale (France), Danish Ethical Trading Initiative (Denmark), Business Social Compliance Initiative (BSCI) and others. If this was not possible, the presence of other elements was assessed such as: sustainability/CSR report, or other documented commitments around sustainability. This information was collected online on the brand's or its holding's websites. Information from third party sources was collected for reference purposes.

14.1.3 Brand and retailer survey

Since corporate communications is recognised as a managerial and strategic function, there reigns an agreement among researchers that the discipline is operationally highly relevant as the interface between the organisation and its stakeholders. In short, it serves to gather, relay and interpret information from, and to represent the organisation towards, the outside world (Vercic and Grunig 2000; Cornelissen *et al.* 2006).

If we accept corporate communications as the interface between a brand's or retailer's corporate world and that of society at large, then it becomes clear that corporate communications is completely adapted to the cultural norms and barriers, preferences and taboos of a specific country. It follows that all of these aspects can be traced though publicly available corporate communication documents of each company, such as websites, Facebook profiles or digitally available articles by reputed publishing outlets such as *Drapers, Corriere Della Sera, El Pais, The Guardian* or *Frankfurter Allgemeine*, specifically through the following dimensions (Wanderley *et al.* 2008): customer segment(s), engagement and focus; wording used, linguistic style and vocabulary; archetypes and metaphors employed; quantity and quality of information; accuracy and verifiability of information; engagement with social stakeholders.

In addition, while existing research results focus on the differences between 'ethical' consumer characteristics of different European market economies (e.g. Cervellon 2010), we required basic, overarching characteristics of the national market to better understand the strategic communication choices made by individual brands. For that, we assessed: the reputation of ethical fashion with national consumers from public digital media; the key concepts referred to; the estimated market share of ethical fashion if available; the type of media that published ethical fashion related content, their linguistic style and the occasion of the publication.

English (UK, Denmark, Sweden), Spanish, Italian, French and German resources were analysed based on their native language version. Two reviewed Danish brands presented themselves in English (Vero Moda, Noir); for the remaining—Coop, Lubarol and Illum—Danish–English translations were used alongside originally English language resources. The same applies to Sweden, where Swedish–English translations were used for Nk and Ahlens.

In order to investigate the mentioned dimensions, the following survey checklist was compiled:

- Key sustainability concepts referred to by the brands themselves

- Communication style: engaging–boring; subjective–objective/informative; emotional–rational; direct–indirect

- Quantity of general brand and 'ethical fashion' information provided

- Quality, degree of detail and verifiability of information of ethical practices (supply chain and general business practices)

- Principal market segments, principal consumer profile

- Type, quantity, detail and verifiability of media content available about the brand, and the subset about sustainability

- Additionally (if available): size of the brand; turnover of brand; (local) community involvement; information available in how many languages? Trade fair participation: what fairs, in what section? Stockists: where and what type of stockists? 'About' online page: content and detail of brand story from 'self' point of view

- Survey of geographical markets: consumer reputation of ethical fashion in national market; focus of ethical fashion in the market: social, environmental, quality, recycling, consumerism; estimated market share of ethical fashion (if available); ethical fashion in the media: what, when, how and why?

14.2 Results: Ethical fashion and corporate communications in the principal European fashion markets

14.2.1 Italy

In Italy, 'ethical fashion' (*moda etica*) is still an empty term for the majority of end consumers (Mora *et al.* 2011). Fashion brands are not taking the initiative to increase consumers' awareness. In fact, it is difficult to find any specific information about their business ethics or their engagement at all. From the analysed brands, it becomes clear that ethical commitment is equivalent to philanthropy and local community involvement aimed at preserving local and national skill-sets and craftsmanship. This responds to a common fear and a public need for keeping production and know-how in the country. And indeed, luxury brands such as Zegna and Gucci, but also Benetton, are working with local and national communities towards this.

The surveyed brands do not seem to treat sustainability as an integral part of their business practices. The quantity of information provided varies from brand to brand, but global brands with high brand equity such as Benetton and Gucci do much better than national brands such as Original Marines or the COIN Group.

With regard to the supply chain, its traceability and impact, there was very little data available. Well-structured codes of conduct, if extant, are not published, and only Benetton displays initial tracking efforts.

Across all surveyed brands, the communication style is traditional, subjective, not factual and only little information is made available. This results in a complete lack of transparency—not surprising in a country where consumers are traditionally sceptical about advertising and corporate communication.

14.2.2 Spain

Spain shares one important characteristic with Italy: the sustainability concept is still new to Spanish consumers, and does not have much resonance. The term is not established as of yet, however, and is currently mostly associated with *comercio justo* (fair trade) (Burgos 2011). Thanks to a few brands at the forefront, e.g. Pikolinos or the IOU project, there is a probability, however, that the discussion will be led from more of a design angle than in other European geographies.

At present, ethics-related efforts are mostly found in the larger organisations such as El Corte Inglés or Inditex. Our survey suggests that there is a correlation between the target market of a company, and its public face commitment to ethics: Information available about, for instance, Inditex is abundant and fairly concrete; but there are few specifics available from exclusive Loewe.

The language adopted by the large companies reviewed is both suggestive and factual, with the former covering up for where the facts cannot be verified. The reviewed small and medium-sized enterprises (SMEs; EC 2003) engage with their customers more emotionally, often by means of case stories.

Commitment to sustainability in our sample of large corporations seems to be down to legal or political pressure, while in SMEs it has become a personal issue. The large companies make, if extant at all, strategic documents (e.g. codes of conduct) publicly available, yet it is difficult to ascertain how these are being enforced. The reviewed SMEs adopt a more personal communication style, choosing to depict workers and manufacturing sites through, for example, imagery or interviews.

14.2.3 France

In France, ethical fashion is primarily about *commerce équitable* (fairtrade) and *développement durable* (sustainable development): 77% of consumers state that for 'ethical fashion', 'no child labour' is an important criterion; and 58% feel that 'respect employees' working conditions and pay them a decent wage' is key. Furthermore 60% of consumers say it is all about 'help develop underprivileged populations' (IFM 2009).

However, looking into the specific initiatives by the surveyed brands, it is evident that their engagement is quite broad and also includes ecological elements. Across all market segments, business ethics is not normally on the agenda of French fashion players, or at least, they do not communicate it, a fact perhaps rooted in the prevalent sceptical consumer attitudes (IFM 2009). Reviewed brands that are part of big corporate groups seem to treat sustainability just as part of their 'corporate policy' but do not seem willing to engage in a more active debate. Communications is entirely product focused with an emphasis on collections, styles and design. Iconic and historic brands (e.g. Louis Vuitton or Lancel) focus their communication on their heritage and importance in the international fashion arena. The prevailing communication style is emotional and subjective; storytelling, combined with significant visuals, is a common technique applied.

Aware of the fact that consumers are sceptical of the ethical claims of high-street retailers, Monoprix has made extensive information available to the end consumers. The company also prides itself in organising online and offline initiatives to foster consumer awareness. Its communication style is participative, and it clearly seeks the consumers' active participation, which it considers essential in order to attain its sustainability objectives.

14.2.4 Germany

The German fashion market has become increasingly quality oriented over recent years (FU 2007; NewsAT 2011). Communications hence consistently include the quality attribute, and the primary addressees are professional women in their late 20s to 50s. Owing to the national importance of Stiftung Warentest, a not-for-profit organisation founded in 1964 specialising in the evaluation of consumer goods, quality, health and safety, and environmental issues are the consumers' primary concern. This is reflected in the reviewed fashion companies' communications: the spotlight is on environmentally friendly quality products made from organic cotton and other natural fibres.

With 1.4% of the market, the German 'eco' fashion market is currently estimated to be Europe's largest (Urbanek 2010). Yet all reviewed fashion companies have to strike a fine balance in order to reach an affluent consumer segment for which 'ethical' is of interest, without associating themselves with the unattractive 'charity' cliché of the past (Brodde 2009).

Reviewed ethical fashion-related information is overall subdued, understated, minimal and factual, and often only accessible to those actively looking for it. The more a brand or retailer caters towards the luxury sector, the less it publicly refers to sustainability and ethics in any way at all. The lower the price segments and larger the retailer the more information is available, although verifiability of claims and published achievements remains a challenge. Finally, from the reviewed brands, it seems that 'Made in Germany' and local craftsmanship are overall less appreciated than elsewhere in Europe.

14.2.5 Denmark

The growing Danish fashion industry, positioned as 'accessible luxury', is committed to sustainability and many brands put this even at the core of their strategy (CSRwire 2012). At the same time, department stores and pure retailers do not communicate commitments, unless they are multi-brand retailers stocking ethical fashion brands exclusively.

The analysed brands talk about sustainability from a perspective that suggests that doing business ethically has already become the norm. According to the analysed brands and retailers, sustainability always encompasses labour issues, supply-chain management and responsible production. In addition, animal rights are also mentioned prominently, in contrast to the other countries of this survey. Information about business ethics is easy to find on a brand's website; the vocabulary and stylistics are concrete and direct; facts are openly available without embellishment; and concise statements outline achievements, ongoing challenges and continuing improvements. The type of language used does not differ on the B2C (business-to-consumer) and B2B (business-to-business) websites and this may mean that the companies are targeting a well-informed segment of consumers.

Reviewed Danish brands have joined the Danish Ethical Trading Initiative and support the UN Global Compact. Importantly, and possibly the most visible sign of their commitment, most of them also collaborate with each other and follow recognised best practices in their initiatives.

14.2.6 Sweden

Sweden, in contrast to other European fashion markets, lacks a tradition of luxury goods consumption. Its fashion market is defined by a democratised, authentic, practicality fashion culture, most recently characterised by the 'Swedish Denim Miracle' (West 2011). Consumer ethics is considered an integral part of being a 'good and valuable citizen'. Brands as well as consumers present innovative, future-oriented behaviour, manifested among other ways in the above-mentioned Denim Miracle.

Brands are proud of their 'Made in Sweden' credentials (e.g. Odd Molly or H&M), even if in fact their supply chain is located abroad. This leads to the issues of ethics in fashion being invariably linked to the 'Made in Sweden' discussion. While efforts related to environmental sustainability are considered a given, documentation made publicly available by the reviewed brands themselves, as well as their partnering organisations, primarily relates to responsible manufacturing. The information is factual, accurate and available in adequate amounts. Manufacturing-related codes of conduct, or commitments with NGOs such as the Clean Clothes Campaign, are common and the audit results made publicly available without further ado.

Sweden is, together with Denmark, the only market we have encountered where a few among the reviewed brands made their ethical credentials available in a user-friendly format. Ethics, hence, is well on the way to becoming accepted into the mainstream.

14.2.7 United Kingdom

The British fashion landscape is a paradox: there is no other European market where fast fashion is more commonplace (Brodde 2009). Equally, there is no other country where the direct consequence of said consumption pattern has raised more concern on a political level (UK Parliament 2012). As a consequence, even strategic policies (Defra 2011) are being developed to curb the impact; leading high-street retailers have committed publicly to sustainability (M&S 2012) and supply chain transparency (M&S 2011); and within the realms of ethical fashion, the higher educational institutions are also engaged through high-profile researchers and research institutions.

Being open, or even proactive, about ethical commitments as a fashion brand or designer, remains however a luxury enjoyed only by the well established, as it carries a whole range of negative connotations and clichés, which only high-profile brands such as Vivienne Westwood have managed to overcome thanks to the designer's public image.

From a communication point of view the public messaging of reviewed brands is approached from either of two principal angles: focus on the uniqueness, quality and technical ingenuity of the designs—'Made in Britain', craftsmanship—for up and coming brands; and public profiling of individual projects and achievements by well-established brands and retailers such as Tesco, John Lewis, Harvey Nichols or Vivienne Westwood.

For the established retailers we reviewed, the width of information made available to the public is considerable; for the reviewed fashionable high-end brands the information is scarce and focused on specific products and product ranges; and for up and coming brands relevant information is often only accessible through personal connections.

14.3 Discussion

In this section we discuss the insights gained in our research. Differences and commonalities across markets are summarised and examined in further depth. While the differences are important and substantial, the commonalities among reviewed markets lead to a more rounded, consolidated picture of the current state of ethical fashion in Western Europe.

14.3.1 Differences

- **Consumers' opinions do have a positive impact on the development of an ethical fashion agenda**. It is important to state that a corporate lack of interest in the sustainability agenda correlates with a limited number of extant activist NGOs and consumer interest groups in markets such as Italy or Spain. While correlation evidently does not imply causality, it is reasonable to assume that the two factors are connected: while consumers do not demand transparency and 'better fashion' on their own behalf, and hence do not exert pressure onto fashion producers and retailers, there is little benefit for the latter to engage with the topic in any substantial way. The fact that consumer demand and pressure indeed do have an important and tangible impact on how consumer-faced enterprises conduct their core business, cannot be overstated

- **Each market has its own priorities with regard to the ethical fashion agenda**. Across Western Europe, each individual geographical (ethical) fashion market comes with its own flavour and historical development that influences the way the sustainability discussion is perceived in society at large. While the Scandinavian markets have adopted a more integrated, proactive and, notably, factual approach, other European markets 'specialise' in one aspect or another of the full spectrum, the most popular ones being either fairtrade or the environment.

- **The North–South divide does exist**. The divide (Welford 2005) is apparent in the degree to which sustainable fashion has penetrated into the spotlight and the public awareness in each individual country. Importantly though, in the South, notably Italy and the Iberian Peninsula, the discussion has been all but launched, and it remains to be seen in which way it will ultimately develop.

14.3.2 Commonalities

- **SMEs' lack of resources undermines their communication.** When rating the quality, quantity and accessibility of the information made available by the different companies in the public domain, the reviewed SMEs overall lose out against the large/er corporations. In fact, the fashion SMEs that are known for their engagement at every step of their core business, such as Good One or Inka Koffke, do not exploit their achievements in any way attractive to the consumer. In contrast, the large corporations such as C&A, Tesco or Inditex, have done a thorough job in extracting the essence from their sustainability initiatives and present it to their stakeholders, including consumers, in a way most beneficial for their public image and sales targets. The most logic explanation at hand for this phenomenon is the lack of resources in SMEs, which is in stark contrast to the teams of expert communication professionals available to large corporations.

- **Internationalisation favours engagement with sustainability.** The more international the reviewed company, and hence in the more countries it operates, the more active it is in the area of ethical fashion. This underlines the key role consumers and consumer perception play for the success in a market, and it suggests that companies adapt and scale their efforts up in order to be ready for all eventualities of the public's and customers' demands and scrutiny.

- **Size correlates with more well-rounded engagement, but initiatives at the heart of core business processes still take a back seat**. The larger the reviewed corporation, the wider their engagement portfolio. For the very big ones, the range encompasses initiatives in all primary areas: environment, communities, diversity and labour rights. However, it must be stated that few, if any, of these undertakings are located right at the heart of core business processes.

- **At present, publicly available information in relation to CSR and/or ethical fashion is usually B2B**, hence targeting trade contacts, not end-consumers, in the first instance. The type of available and reviewed information often only makes sense to industry insiders or to the very informed consumer. Publicised details are mostly related to compliance breaches (e.g. regarding labour rights in a factory), which pose a substantial risk to the brand's name, value and public image.

- **Publicly available information on a company's ethical fashion practices is presented unattractively,** and does not lend itself to be taken in easily. The design of ethical fashion-related websites and documents is dry, uninviting and in most cases scattered across the reviewed brand's and its parent company's websites. It does not accomplish the task of inviting the reader to actively deal with the topic and content at hand, or to read it in its entirety. In selected cases, such as Vivienne Westwood or H&M, multimedia material is made available; however, their content is invariably related to a low number of specific projects rather than to overarching company policies.

- **Craftsmanship and 'Made In ...' are mostly absent topics in the published materials**. This fact casts a dubious light onto the reviewed fashion companies, notably those that amply exploit said concepts in their marketing and brands messaging, and have officially made it part of their brand's core values.

- **The luxury sector—with exception of big international consumer brands— does not engage with the topic,** or else keeps purposely mute. Which of the two possibilities is the accurate interpretation of the results, we do not know, as there are arguments in favour of both hypotheses. But in summary it can be stated that the high-end luxury sector is notably absent in the bigger picture of ethical fashion.

- **There reigns a lack of verifiability with regard to actual achievements and results**. In our research, we found that the majority among reviewed brands provide only small quantities of information on their sustainability initiatives, and even less hard data which would allow consumers to verify their 'ethical' claims. In the presence of a code of conduct for suppliers for, for example, John Lewis or Galeria Kaufhof, either no evidence as to how implementation is effectively controlled is provided, or if audits were in place, no indication was given whether these were announced or not, and what the outcome of the audits was. Hence, the absence of concrete and verifiable results is of such prominence that substantiated doubts as to the effectiveness and impact of any of the practised initiatives seem justified. The lack of verifiable facts suggests that the biggest challenge remaining for the reviewed fashion companies of all sizes and flavours is to commit wholeheartedly to transparency in their core business processes, and to recognise that it is in their own interest and benefit to disseminate results, including challenges, factually and accurately. Selected industry examples (e.g. Levi Strauss 2011) prove the strategic as well as economic viability of the concept, but leading companies such as these are far ahead from what can be considered the norm.

14.4 Conclusion

For our research we surveyed 42 European fashion brands' and retailers' communication strategies with respect to their ethics and sustainability commitments. Geographical markets specifically looked into were: United Kingdom, Germany, France, Italy, Spain, Sweden and Denmark. The differences and commonalities between countries were highlighted, and where possible hypotheses as to their origins discussed.

Our research builds on and extends the existing body of work by looking into and determining the status quo of communication strategies and messages in the realm of ethical fashion specifically, notably across Western European fashion consumer markets.

Our research shows that while there are important differences between the individual markets—notably the existence of a North–South divide in relation to how integrated ethical considerations are in the consumers' buying decisions—there are equally important commonalities.

Most prominently the following four points proved to hold true for the surveyed companies and geographies:

1. Lack of verifiability: hardly any verifiable information is made available with regard to companies' results and achievements in the ethical fashion arena.

2. NGO, consumer interest group and mass communication media pressure indeed do have a direct impact on how 'good' a company is and presents itself in public.

3. The myth of 'badly designed' ethical fashion may at present have less to do with the facts and more to do with the lack of communication resources available among small brands, and consequently their inadequate public representation.

4. The luxury sector overall proves to be the most conservative and the least engaged market segment, with initiatives only taking place in multinationals.

While we have looked at ethical fashion-related corporate communications from the consumer and stakeholder point of view, and the underlying brand strategies, further research is needed into the reason for and approaches to how brands design and determine their ethical fashion-related communication. Also, there is a need for quantitative rather than qualitative research about consumers' ethical fashion buying criteria and spending behaviour.

References

ActionAid (2010) 'Asda, Poverty Guaranteed: Why Asda Should Pay Women Clothing Workers a Living Wage', www.actionaid.org.uk/doc_lib/asda-poverty-guaranteed.pdf, accessed 30 January 2012.

Argandona, A., and H. Hoivik (2009) 'Corporate Social Responsibility: One Size Does Not Fit All. Collecting Evidence from Europe', *Journal of Business Ethics* 89.3 (November 2009): 221-34.

Aspers, P. (2006) 'Ethics in Global Garment Market Chains', in N. Stehr, C. Henning and B. Weiler (eds.), *The Moralization of Markets* (London: Transaction Press): 289-309.

Aspers, P. (2008) 'Labelling the Fashion Industry', *International Journal of Consumer Studies* 32: 633-38.

Brodde, K. (2009) *Saubere Sachen: Wie man grüne Mode findet und sich vor Öko-Etikettenschwindel schützt* (Munich, Germany: Ludwig Verlag).

Burgos, R. (2011) 'Una economista entre maasai', El Mundo, 6 September 2011, www.elmundo.es/elmundo/2011/09/05/alicante/1315220480.html, accessed 29 January 2012.

Cervellon, M.C., E. Hjerth, S. Ricard and L. Carey (2010) 'Green in Fashion: An Explanatory Study of National Differences in Consumers' Concerns for Eco Fashion', paper presented at the *9th International Marketing Trends Conference*, Venezia, 21–23 January 2010.

Cornelissen, J., T. van Bekkum and B. van Ruler (2006) 'Corporate Communications: A Practice-based Theoretical Conceptualization', *Corporate Reputation Review* 9: 114-33.

CSRwire (2012) 'BSR, Danish Fashion Institute Launch "NICE Consumer" Project to Define a Sustainable Future for Fashion', CSRwire, www.csrwire.com/press_releases/33862-BSR-Danish-Fashion-Institute-Launch-NICE-Consumer-Project-to-Define-a-Sustainable-Future-for-Fashion-, accessed 10 April 2012.

De Brito, M.P. (2007) 'Towards Sustainable Supply Chains: A Methodology', paper presented at *Symposium on Production, Logistics and International Operations (SIMPOI/POMS)*, Rio de Janeiro, Brazil, 8–10 August 2007.

Defra (Department for Environment, Food and Rural Affairs) (2011) 'Sustainable Clothing Action Plan', www.defra.gov.uk/publications/2011/03/30/pb13206-clothing-action-plan, accessed 29 January 2012.

Dickson, M.A. (2000) 'Personal Values, Beliefs, Knowledge, and Attitudes Relating to Intentions to Purchase Apparel from Socially Responsible Businesses', *Clothing and Textiles Research Journal* 8: 19-30.

Du, S., C. Bhattacharya and S. Sen (2010) 'Maximizing Business Returns to Corporate Social Responsibility (CSR): The Role of CSR Communication', *International Journal of Management Reviews* 12: 8-19.

EC (European Commission) (2003) 'Small and Medium-Sized Enterprises (SMEs): What is an SME?' Enterprise and Industry, www.ec.europa.eu/enterprise/policies/sme/facts-figures-analysis/sme-definition/index_en.htm, accessed 10 April 2012.

EFF (Ethical Fashion Forum) (2004) 'What is Ethical Fashion?' www.ethicalfashionforum.com/the-issues/ethical-fashion, accessed 10 April 2012.

EJF (Environmental Justice Foundation) (2010) 'White Gold: Uzbekistan, A Slave Nation for Our Cotton?' www.ejfoundation.org/sites/default/files/public/ejf_uzbek_harvest_WEB.pdf, accessed 6 October 2012.

Ethical Corp. (2011) *The State of Responsible Business in Europe* (London: Ethical Corporation).

Ferrigno, S. (2005) *Moral Fibre: A Beginner's Guide to the UK Market* (London: Pesticide Action Network UK).

FU (Fashion United) (2007) 'Verbraucher setzten wieder vermehrt auf Markenware', www.fashionunited.de/News/Leads/Verbraucher_setzten_wieder_vermehrt_auf_Markenware_200712061369, accessed 10 April 2012.

Greenpeace (2011) 'Dirty Laundry: Unravelling the Corporate Connections to Toxic Water Pollution in China', www.greenpeace.org/international/en/publications/reports/Dirty-Laundry, accessed 30 January 2012.

Hale, A., and J. Willis (eds.) (2005) *Threads of Labour, Garment Industry Supply Chains from the Workers' Perspective* (Oxford, UK: Blackwell Publishing).

Herbig, P.A. (2003) *Marketing Interculturale* (Milan: Apogeo).

IFM (Institut Français de la Mode pour le défi) (2009) 'Mode et Consommation Responsable: Regards des Consommateurs', www.ethicalfashionshow.com/efs1/ifm_defi.html, accessed 30 January 2012.

ITGLWF (International Textile Garment & Leather Workers' Federation) (2011) 'An Overview of Working Conditions in Sportswear Factories in Indonesia, Sri Lanka & the Philippines', www.itglwf.org/lang/en/documents/ITGLWFSportswearReport2011_000.pdf, accessed 30 January 2012.

Jackson, G., and A. Apostolakou (2010) 'Corporate Social Responsibility in Western Europe: An Institutional Mirror or Substitute?' *Journal of Business Ethics* 94.3 (July 2010): 371-94.

Joergens, C. (2006) 'Ethical Fashion: Myth or Future Trend?' *Journal of Fashion Marketing and Management* 10.3: 360-71.

Labour Behind the Label (2010) 'Killer Jeans: A Report on Sandblasted Jeans', www.labour behindthelabel.org/join/item/download/145, accessed 30 January 2012.

Labour Behind the Label (2011) 'Let's Clean Up Fashion', www.labourbehindthelabel.org/ news/itemlist/category/220-clean-up-fashion, accessed 30 January 2012.

Levi Strauss (2011) 'Levi Strauss & Co. Supplier List', www.levistrauss.com/sustainability/ product/supplier-list, accessed 29 January 2012.

M&S (Marks & Spencer) (2011) 'Marks & Spencer Signs Traceability Deal With Historic Futures', Press Release, 4 August 2011, www.corporate.marksandspencer.com/page.aspx? pointerid=e1eee46c65894637800c237915923bf0, accessed 29 January 2012.

M&S (Marks & Spencer) (2012) 'Plan A', www.plana.marksandspencer.com, accessed 29 January 2012.

Mora, E., M.C. Cervellon and L. Carey (2011) 'I consumatori di mode sostenibile hanno i pannelli solari e non fanno sesso', in M. Ricchetti and M.L. Frisa (eds.), *Il bello e il buono. Le ragioni della moda sostenibile* (Milan: Marsilio Editori spa): 101-105.

Morgan, J., M. Dylan, M. Strong, P. Thigpen and K.O. Hanson (2011) 'CSR as Reputation Insurance: Primum Non Nocere', *California Management Review*, 1 May 2011.

Morsing, M., and M. Schultz (2006) 'Corporate Social Responsibility Communication: Stakeholder Information, Response and Involvement Strategies', *Business Ethics: A European Review* 15: 323-38.

NewsAT (2011) 'Geiz ist nicht mehr geil: Deutsche Konsumenten achten wieder auf Qualität', News Networld Internetservice GmbH, www.news.at/articles/1105/30/288081/geiz-deutsche-konsumenten-qualitaet, accessed 10 April 2012.

Ozcaglar-Toulouse, N., E. Shiu and D. Shaw (2006) 'In Search of Fair Trade: Ethical Consumer Decision Making in France', *International Journal of Consumer Studies* 30.5: 502-14.

Pretious, M., and M. Love (2006) 'Sourcing Ethics and the Global Market', *International Journal of Retail and Distribution Management* 34.12: 892-903.

Stanforth, N., and W. Hauck (2010) 'The Effects of Ethical Framing on Consumer Price Perceptions', *Journal of Fashion Marketing and Management* 14.4: 615-23.

UCA (University of Cambridge) (2006) *Well Dressed? The Present and Future Sustainability of Clothing and Textiles in the United Kingdom* (Cambridge, UK: University of Cambridge Institute for Manufacturing, www.ifm.eng.cam.ac.uk/uploads/Resources/Reports/UK_ textiles.pdf, accessed 6 October 2012).

UK Parliament (2012) 'All-Party Parliamentary Group on Ethics and Sustainability in Fashion', Register of All-Party Groups, www.publications.parliament.uk/pa/cm/cmallparty/ register/ethics-and-sustainability-in-fashion.htm, accessed 10 April 2012.

UNEP (United Nations Environment Programme) (2006) 'Sustainability Communications: A Toolkit for Marketing and Advertising Courses', Division for Technology, Industry and Economics, www.unep.fr/shared/publications/pdf/DTIx0886xPA-EducationKitEN.pdf, accessed 10 April 2012.

Urbanek, J. (2010) 'Das Gewand des guten Gewissens', Wiener Zeitung, 8 October 2010, www.wienerzeitung.at/nachrichten/kultur/mehr_kultur/36148_Das-Gewand-des-guten-Gewissens.html, accessed 29 January 2012.

Vercic, D., and J.E. Grunig (2000) 'The Origins of Public Relations Theory in Economics and Strategic Management', in D. Moss, D. Vercic and G. Warnaby (eds.), *Perspectives on Public Relations Research* (London: Routledge): 9-58.

Wanderley, L., R. Lucian, F. Farache and M. Sousa (2008) 'CSR Information Disclosure on the Web: A Context-Based Approach Analysing the Influence of Country of Origin and Industry Sector', *Journal of Business Ethics* 82.2: 369-78.

Welford, R. (2005) 'Corporate Social Responsibility in Europe, North America and Asia: 2004 Survey Results', *Journal of Corporate Citizenship* 17 (Spring 2005): 33-52.

West, C. (2011) 'The Swedish Denim Miracle', Swedish Institute, www.sweden.se/eng/Home/Lifestyle/Fashion-design/Reading/The-Swedish-denim-miracle, accessed 29 January 2012.

Williams, D. (2009) 'Volume 2.0: Centre for Sustainable Fashion: Fashioning the Future', University of the Arts London, www.ualresearchonline.arts.ac.uk/2749, accessed 29 January 2012.

Ilaria Pasquinelli is a marketing specialist for the fashion industry with over a decade of experience in managing strategic projects at a global level, particularly for sustainable fashion businesses. She is a managing director of texSture, the leading sustainability advisory and think-tank for the fashion and textiles industry.

Pamela Ravasio is a strategy specialist with a PhD from the Swiss Federal Institute of Technology, Zurich, Switzerland. She has 15 years of international, cross-continental industry and research experience. She is a managing director of texSture, scientific committee member for the executive education in CSR at the University of Geneva, a regular contributor to *Ecotextile News*, and winner of a 2011 Observer Ethical Award.

15

Effectiveness of standard initiatives

Rules and effective implementation of transnational standard initiatives (TSI) in the apparel industry: An empirical examination

Claude Meier

University of Zurich and University of Applied Sciences Zurich (HWZ), Switzerland

In our globalised world new forms of governance have come into existence. The reason is that many issues have transboundary causes and effects (e.g. climate change, migration) which cannot be solved by territorially defined nation-states (Rosenau and Czempiel 1992: 3f., 7; Weiss 2000). 'Governing beyond the nation state' is being established at the global level whereby states may or may not be engaged (Zürn 1998; Zangl and Zürn 2004). Important non-state actors from the societal sectors of business and civil society have gained more authority and often are involved in these new forms of governance (Rosenau and Czempiel 1992: 3; Brütsch and Lehmkuhl 2007: 2f.). In particular, the influence of transnational companies (TNCs)[1],

---

1 The abbreviation thus stands for **transnational companies** and not as usual for transnational corporations. In this way, in addition to large corporations, SMEs (small- and medium-sized enterprises) can also be considered. For readability in the following, generally the word 'company', meaning TNC, is used.

which are not bound territorially, has increased in the last two decades of globalisation (Rondinelli 2002; Post *et al.* 2002; Kahler and Lake 2004; Scherer and Palazzo 2006: 81). It is characteristic of these new forms of governance that they are voluntary (not mandatory like state laws) and vary concerning the issue, their rules and actor participation. These new 'systems of rule' (Rosenau 1995: 13) are subsumed in this chapter under the term **transnational standard initiatives** (TSIs). The aim of the chapter is to examine how effectively two TSIs concerned with labour rights in the garment industry contribute to a solution of labour rights issues.

15.1 Research problem

Very little empirical-analytical research about how different TSIs work in the real world has been conducted (e.g. Messner and Nuscheler 2003; Dingwerth and Pattberg 2006a, b; Rasche 2009b: 195, 2009a: 22). Or in other words, until now it has remained largely unclear how TSIs work in the context of their concrete implementation, which mostly takes place among TNCs, and what the results thereof are (Abbott and Snidal 2009: 63ff.). Börzel and Risse (2005: 196) state that too little empirical investigation concerning the effectiveness of TSIs has been done and that further studies are of importance. Therefore this chapter, which is part of an ongoing study, is aimed at finding answers to the question of how effective TSIs are, concerning their implementation in TNCs in the garment industry.[2]

The TSIs chosen for the empirical investigation are the **Business Social Compliance Initiative** (BSCI) and the **Fair Wear Foundation** (FWF). Both are social TSIs committed to the achievement of a bundle of the same International Labour Organisation (ILO) core conventions[3] in the apparel industry. Their implementation is studied in two internationally known Swiss apparel companies, for which a significant proportion of their production takes place in China, a so-called risk country.[4] In these empirical cases it can be seen how a TSI's institutional design

---

2 Exceptions of empirical-analytical work referring to effective implementation are Rieth (2009), who examines why companies implement TSIs, Starmanns (2010), who examines how companies in the apparel industry define, implement and legitimise corporate social responsibility approaches, and Kolk and Van Tulder (2002a), who investigate how actors 'deal with child labour in their codes' (2002a: 291). See also e.g. Kolk and Van Tulder 2002b, 2005; Van Tulder *et al.* 2009.

3 For example, Hours of Work Convention no. 1; Minimum Wage Fixing Convention no. 131.

4 Definition by BSCI: 'The classification as a risk country is, in addition to the field experience of sourcing companies, based on the Human Development Index of the UN and the Corruption Index of Transparency International' (BSCI 2011). FWF defines *low* risk countries 'by the presence and proper functioning of institutions (trade unions [etc.]), which can guarantee the compliance with basic [labour] standards' (FWF 2009d). All other countries are risk countries.

(i.e. its rules) leads to an implementation that contributes to effectively solving the issue of labour rights (e.g. Abbott and Snidal 2009: 66ff.).

This chapter first presents how the question about effective implementation will be investigated in a systematic way through an analytical framework. After that, a short introduction to the guiding methods is given. Finally, preliminary results are presented before a short conclusion is drawn.

15.2 The analytical framework

The analytical framework should enable a systematic investigation of the research problem. It consists of two parts. The first is a **phase-model** conceptualising the idea of the assumed 'general' causal process that leads to effectiveness. The second part contains the **theoretical considerations** and the derived **hypotheses**, which should help in explaining under what conditions one can expect effectiveness. Figure 15.1 depicts the whole phase-model including the theoretical considerations which are explained in Section 15.2.2.

15.2.1 The phase-model

The purpose of the phase-model is to structure the causal process. It is sectioned into the three phases: **output**, **implementation** and **outcome**. And, it is oriented on models in public policy research in political sciences as well as on models investigating effectiveness of environmental governance systems (e.g. Easton 1965; Sprinz and Helm 1999; Miles *et al.* 2002; Jann and Wegrich 2007; Mitchell 2008; Jann and Wegrich 2009; Howlett *et al.* 2009). The phase-model shows a time-determined causal chain that begins with the phase output which (should) influence implementation which (should) influence the outcome. Although these phases are separated conceptually, empirically they are at least partly overlapping. In the following a short description of the three phases of the analytical framework is given.

15.2.1.1 Output

Miles *et al.* (2002: 5) define output, the first element of the phase-model, as 'the formal output of a decision-making or regime-formation process (that is, the norms, principles, and rules constituting the regime itself)'. For the purpose of this work the term 'regime'[5] is to be exchanged by TSI. Correspondingly, the output is understood as consisting of different established and thus given dimensions of what I call

---

5 One of the most common definitions understands regimes as 'implicit or explicit principles, norms, rules, and decision-making around which actors' expectations converge in a given area of international relations' (Krasner 1983: 2). Sometimes also formal organisations belonging to regimes (e.g. the WTO).

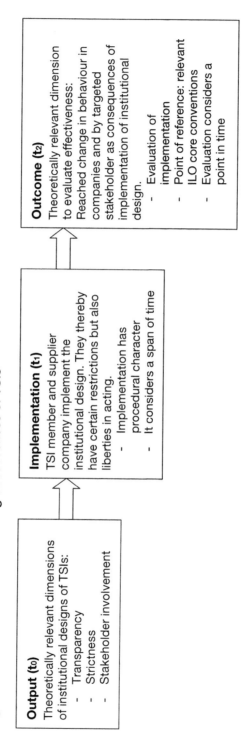

Figure 15.1 **Phase-model concerning effectiveness of TSIs**

institutional design constituting the formal norms, rules and the intended policy of a certain TSI (Miles *et al.* 2002: 24ff.).

15.2.1.2 Implementation

Implementation, the second element in the causal chain, has two different facets. First, the way an implementation is done is influenced and (partly) predetermined by the foregoing process of policy and rule formation and thus by the output. Simply put, the previously established rules structure how the implementation is done (Sabatier 1986: 20f.). Second, the companies in which the implementation is performed in effect have a certain scope and can modify and elaborate the rules. Hence it can influence to some extent how implementation is done, and therefore influence subsequent consequences directly (Hill and Hupe 2009: 6f.). Intra-organisational characteristics, for example management systems and values of these companies, play crucial roles for the implementation of the institutional design (e.g. Lipsky 1980: xxi; Greenwood and Hinings 1996: 1031; Campbell 2004: 77ff.; Abbott and Snidal 2009: 65; Park-Poaps and Rees 2010: 308). Finally, implementation is procedural in its character; it is dynamic and not static. To be able to assess this procedural and dynamic character a certain span of time (i.e. not only a point in time) has to be considered.

15.2.1.3 Outcome

Outcome is the last element of the phase-model. It is understood as an immediate outcome[6] which generally is seen as a behavioural change in addressees of TSIs, i.e. companies and targeted stakeholders (e.g. Jann and Wegrich 2009: 83). Outcome is considered as 'change in the human behaviour targeted by the [TSI]' (Underdal 2008: 64). Although it is not easy in every case to separate implementation and outcome, behavioural change is understood as the result of implementation. Miles *et al.* (2002: 6) state that outcomes are 'the consequences in the form of changes in human behaviour…flowing from the implementation and adaption to [a] [TSI]' (see also Biermann and Bauer 2004: 191).

Hence, effectiveness can be assessed by looking at behavioural change referring to a point of reference (in this case ILO core conventions) that is causally linkable to output and implementation. Outcome corresponds to effectiveness. The evaluation of the outcome mainly determines how a TSI has fared (Vedung 1997: 3; Howlett *et al.* 2009: 178). Outcome therefore can be considered as the end state of the implementation (Lane in Hill and Hupe 2009: 59). The outcome consequently is a 'reached state' and is therefore static: It has to be assessed at a certain point in time.

---

6 In the sense that it follows chronologically and causally immediately after the precursory phases. It is not the long-term outcome which some scholars call impact or ultimate outcome (Vendung 1997: 5; Miles *et al.* 2002: 7; Underdal 2008: 63f.).

15.2.2 Theoretical approaches

As already mentioned, theoretical considerations and hypotheses should help to explain what conditions influence an effective implementation. In the following the theoretical presumptions are presented. They refer to the institutional design which constitutes the phase of output which is the first element of the causal phase-model (as depicted in Figure 15.1; see also Section 15.2.1.1 Output).

15.2.2.1 Transparency

The phase-model mentioned that companies have a scope of action during implementation. This scope has impacts on the outcome. It enables a gap between the intentions of a TSI and the practices of an implementing company. This intention-gap with its proximate consequences for a TSI's effectiveness can be explained through agency theory. It provides explanations of why the intention-gap exists, and how effectiveness may be enhanced by modifying the gap.

Basically, agency theory 'is directed at the ubiquitous agency relationship, in which one party (the principal) delegates work to another (the agent), who performs that work' (Eisenhardt 1989: 58). In its best-known form it is a neoclassical theory in economic science used to explain the relationship between managers (agents) and shareholders (principals) (e.g. Jensen and Meckling 1976; Fama 1980; Fama and Jensen 1983a, b). But it has been expanded for example to sociology and political science (e.g. Mitnick 1975; McCubbins and Schwartz 1984; Waterman and Meier 1998; Shapiro 2005; Blum and Schubert 2009). There are diverse contexts in which the theory can contribute to explaining social and economic relationships, such as for example between 'doctors and patients, teachers and pupils, workers and management' (Power 1991: 33).

In this chapter I consider stakeholders such as the organisational organs of a TSI (i.e. boards, bureaus, employees) and other relevant stakeholders (e.g. affected groups and individuals such as workers and customers) as the principals (e.g. Hill and Jones 1992; Shankman 1999). The implementing company I take as the agent: it is in its hand to 'perform the work'. Hence, a separation between rule-establishing and rule-implementing actors exists. The agency problem lies in the difficulty for the principals to verify activities of the agent. It depends on the contract between the parties how efficiently a principal can verify the agent's behaviour (Fama 1980: 289ff.; Eisenhardt 1989: 58; Hill and Jones 1992: 132f.). The intention-gap between principals and agent manifests itself as follows: The stakeholders' interest is that the requirements of the TSI are implemented in the most effective way. The primary interest of the company, which adopts a TSI voluntarily (it is not a state law), is to reach at least a minimum return that allows survival. This is true even if the company seriously wants to implement the requirements of a TSI (Rondinelli 2002: 410) (also Carroll 1991). The institutional design of the TSI can be taken as the contract between the TSI-establishing stakeholder(s) and the implementing company.

A central role for overcoming differences in interest is played by a contract's arrangement concerning information asymmetry: Agents know about their activities, but principals have this information only incompletely. The agency problem can be reduced by lowering the information asymmetry (e.g. Spence 1973; Fama and Jensen 1983b: 310f.; Power 1991: 32; Hill and Jones 1992: 140). Thereto an institutional design of a TSI needs to include an information system that transfers information about what the implementing company is doing to the relevant stakeholders ('signaling') (Spence 1973; Eisenhardt 1989: 60f.; Power 1991: 36). In other words, the agency-problem can be reduced and thus effectiveness increased when transparency towards the principal is enhanced. This leads to the following hypothesis:

H1: The more transparency demanded by the institutional design of a TSI, the more effective the TSI

15.2.2.2 Strictness of rules

In this chapter, strictness of rules is understood in the sense that the institutional design of a TSI is well-elaborated, clear and strong (not necessarily or only in a quantitative sense) (Kolk and Van Tulder 2002a: 296f.; Fransen and Kolk 2007: 54; Underdal 2008). It is thought to have an impact on effectiveness. It consists of two elements: **Preciseness** (well-elaborated, clear) and **strength** (restriction of choices: strong rules). They are described in the following.

Underdal (2008: 54) states concerning strictness: 'the strength of a [TSI] is usually defined in terms of the extent to which it constrains the freedom of legitimate... choice open to the individual member'. This statement is about strictness in the meaning of the strength of a TSI's institutional design: Strong designs have high set aims and therefore restrict the pool of possible activities. To achieve high set aims only certain and few (and not other) activities are expedient, while for achieving lower aims more alternatives exist. The stronger the rules of a TSI, the smaller the choice for alternative actions to fulfil them.

Second, strictness can be understood in the meaning of clearness and being precise. Some managers interviewed by Jamali and Basiou (2009: 14) mentioned that a main weakness of voluntary standards is that they are too general as they 'lack... clear and practical guidelines'. Kolk and Van Tulder (2005: 9) state that specific standards for responsibility can be better monitored and measured than unspecific ones. These argumentations about strictness lead to the following hypothesis:

H2: The stricter the institutional design of a TSI, the more effective the TSI

15.2.2.3 Role and involvement of stakeholders

Scholars speak mostly of multi-stakeholder initiatives (MSI) or use similar terms when they talk about whether stakeholders from different societal sectors are involved in the establishment and governance of a TSI (e.g. Utting 2002; Benner *et al.* 2004; Fransen and Kolk 2007). The discussion then is mainly about stakeholder involvement in the phase of TSI-establishment and governance. In contrast, this chapter focuses primarily on the aspect of stakeholder involvement in the implementation phase.

During implementation, actors called stakeholders are quite closely tied to a concrete company: for example its workers and the local unions as well as the local community.[7] All of them are affected by the activities of the company. Freeman's (1984: 46) classic definition reflects this view: 'Stakeholders are any group or individual who can affect or are affected by the achievement of the organisation's objectives'.

For an effective implementation, it is essential that a TSI's institutional design involves various relevant stakeholders (in this chapter stakeholders regarding labour rights and rules of BSCI and FWF). Kolk and Van Tulder (2002a: 298) state that resolution of issues, for example child labour, can only be achieved when relevant local and transnational stakeholders from outside the business (and state) sectors are involved. Moreover, stakeholders generally contribute resources to the company in the widest sense (e.g. know-how, capital, acceptance, workforce) (Post *et al.* 2002: 19; Sachs and Rühli 2011: 114ff.) (also Freeman 1984; Carroll and Näsi 1997; Banks and Vera 2007; Freeman *et al.* 2010). These resources normally are used for economic aims, but can also be brought in for the implementation of TSIs. Sachs and Rühli (2011: 58) state concerning stakeholder involvement: 'it is most important that corporate relations with multiple stakeholders are seen as constitutive to maintain and increase the corporation's abilities to create wealth'. This means that more interactions between company and stakeholders lead to more wealth for both. Wealth here is to be understood in a wider sense than only financial terms and also includes, for example, good working conditions of labour (e.g. Sachs and Rühli 2011). These considerations lead to the following hypothesis:

H3: The more involvement of issue-relevant stakeholders the institutional design of a TSI requires for implementation, the more effective the TSI

15.3 Methods and data

As mentioned above, the research problem under investigation concerns the issue of labour rights in the apparel industry. The chosen empirical cases are the Business

---

7 At the governance level of a MSI companies themselves are just one stakeholder group among others (from e.g. state or civil society): An issue then (e.g. labour rights), not companies themselves, is at the centre. In this sense it can be said that companies *are* stakeholders concerning the governance level, and they *have* stakeholders referring to the level of implementation (e.g. Roloff 2008: 238; Sachs *et al.* 2011).

Social Compliance Initiative (BSCI) and the Fair Wear Foundation (FWF) as well as two internationally known Swiss companies in the apparel industry. One of them is a BSCI-member, the other a FWF-member.

The investigation is being done through a qualitative comparative case study. Case studies can provide explanations that help us to come to a deeper under-standing of a phenomenon or case (Creswell 2003: 88, 181f.; Yin 2003: 15; Blatter *et al.* 2007: 127). According to Yin (2003: 15) the most important application of case studies 'is to explain the presumed causal links in real-life interventions that are too complex for survey or experimental strategies'. Moreover, case studies include contextual conditions ('real-life') (Yin 2003: 13; George and Bennett 2005: 21). They enable us to judge whether hypotheses are plausible concerning their arguments about causality, at least for the empirical cases chosen. This means that the results cannot be generalised and are not representative for the whole population of TSIs (e.g. George and Bennett 2005: 25). Done in a comparative way, the plausibility of hypotheses can be enhanced through a higher credibility of results.

The case selection is oriented (as far as possible) towards the ideal of a control-led comparison, which means that cases are similar in many contextual aspects but differ concerning some few characteristics (e.g. Przeworski and Teune 1970; Lijphart 1971: 687ff.; Blatter *et al.* 2007: 142f.). BSCI and FWF are both concerned with labour rights in the apparel industry and they have similar aims (achieving ILO core conventions). Additionally both have sophisticated monitoring systems as well as audit processes and both provide training for workers and managers. But they vary in different ways in terms of the institutional design (transparency, strict-ness and stakeholder involvement). The two selected companies are both Swiss, are of similar size (revenue) and a more or less similar percentage of their production takes place in China. They differ concerning their membership in TSIs (one BSCI, one FWF) as well as concerning intra-organisational characteristics. Moreover, the inclusion of the context as done in case studies also enables us to detect induc-tively explanations that are not considered in the hypotheses (George and Bennett 2005: 21, 179; Mahoney and Goertz 2006: 245; Bennett and Elman 2006: 254). For these reasons a qualitative comparative case study is an appropriate method for this chapter: the cases of TSI rules implemented by companies are too complex to be examined in a quantitative way, therefore including the context is essential (e.g. Yin 2003: 215; George and Bennett 2005: 21, 181).

15.4 Preliminary results

Preliminary results are based on data already collected in interviews with BSCI- and FWF-experts as well as with implementation experts of the two Swiss TSI member companies in the apparel industry. Moreover, they are based on the rule documents (i.e. institutional designs) from BSCI and FWF. Data collection for the study is still ongoing.

15.4.1 Institutional designs of BSCI and FWF

15.4.1.1 Transparency

The required information transfer between member companies, their suppliers, the auditors and the TSIs' organisational organs is overall similar between BSCI and FWF. This is also true for the confidential handling of competition-relevant data. Differences can be found regarding outside communication, i.e. the communication with external stakeholders (e.g. customers).

FWF declares transparency as one of its underlying principles. Three reports are required to be published, which contain certain internal data and hence concern member companies[8] directly. First, FWF requires its members to publish a social report annually. In this report, insights concerning the achievements of FWF-relevant ILO core conventions are to be published. Information about the monitoring system applied by a member and its outcomes per country and supplier factory (made anonymous) are also part of the report, as well as information about training and capacity building. Finally, information about transparency and communication are also parts of the report (FWF 2009a: 5, 2009b).

Second, FWF publishes Management System Audits (MSA), which contain information about the implementation of management system requirements in member companies. The report contains conclusions, requirements and recommendations (FWF 2009–11).

And, third, FWF publishes reports about complaints filed with FWF. In addition to the accused party (normally a supplier of a member company) the involved member company is also named, and case-relevant information is given (corrective action plan, verification, conclusions) (FWF 2009c).

Additionally, FWF publishes an annual report (FWF 2008–10). In this report FWF's current status concerning achievements, activities and positions are at the centre. FWF also publishes country studies (FWF 2004–11). These studies contain primarily information about country-specific problems regarding the relevant ILO core conventions. Finally, FWF publishes sporadic resources for example guidance or definition papers (e.g. FWF 2012).

Member companies of **BSCI** are not required to publish (social) reports, with or without internal data. BSCI requires outside communication when it concerns the SA8000 social standard certification system, which is recognised by BSCI as best practice (BSCI 2009d: 9). In this case the supplier, not the member company 'must…report on its social policy, via reviews and monitoring activities' (BSCI 2009b: 78). Additionally, a responsible person for outside communication must be appointed in the supplier company.

BSCI publishes an annual report (BSCI 2010), highlighting its current achievements, activities and positions, but internal data of specific member companies is

---

8 Because FWF and BSCI members are predominantly companies, in the following often only the word 'member' is written.

not included. Additionally, BSCI publishes sporadic resources, for example position papers (e.g. BSCI 2009c).

15.4.1.2 Strictness

The main differences between the investigated TSIs along the two dimensions of strictness are discussed in the following.

FWF requires the payment of a living wage (FWF 2009a: 14).[9] This is strict in the sense that it restricts the freedom of choice of the company.

Further, FWF requires the member company 'to adjust their management system in order to allow effective implementation of the Code of Labour practices' (FWF 2009a: 9). The strictest restriction in the freedom of choice is that the member has to establish its own system for monitoring supplier factories. This means a significant part of the responsibility for implementation is imposed on member companies. Through FWF's Management System Audit (MSA), this adjustment is controlled. Audits carried out in relation to this monitoring system are generally paid for by the member company. Additionally, FWF carries out audits on its own in randomly or specifically selected supplier factories.

FWF requires especially meticulous and detailed audits when they are conducted by FWF-trained audit teams. The duration of the audit reflects this: depending on the size of a factory it takes from 6 days to 13 days (FWF 2011). Besides FWF-trained teams, FWF also accepts certain audit companies.

FWF's strictness in the sense of being precise is generally high. But it is limited in the sense that it does not have a clear graduation system for audit results. The results are given primarily in a comprehensive qualitative form. These results are indeed very detailed but not very practical when one wants to have a systematic and simple overview.

BSCI requires the payment of a legal minimum wage. Beyond that it requires the payment of an industry standard wage,[10] if it exists and if it is higher than the legal minimum wage. Each member can pursue a living wage on a voluntary basis. The TSI SA8000, which is accepted as best practice by BSCI, requires the payment of a living wage (BSCI 2009c: 2). This concerns strictness in the sense of the freedom of choice of the company. Because the living wage is voluntary, the freedom of choice in this area remains in large part in the hands of member companies.

BSCI requires the supplier companies to establish 'a management system to ensure that the requirements of the BSCI Code of Conduct can be met' (BSCI 2009a: 3).

---

9 Definition from FWF: 'A wage which provides for the basic needs…of an average family unit in a country divided by the average number of adult wage earners in the family unit' (FWF 2009a: 16). Definition from BSCI: 'A living wage is one that is adequate for someone to support himself and his family [i.e.] to be able to cover basic needs and to have at least some discretionary income' (BSCI 2009a).

10 Definition from BSCI: 'Local social partners (trade unions and employers) define the industry wage' (BSCI 2009c: 1).

Hence, primarily supplier companies have to adopt their management system: a considerable part of the implementation responsibility is imposed on them. The audit of the suppliers' factories can be requested by member or supplier companies. It is to be carried out exclusively by accredited auditing companies.[11] Audits last from 1.5 to 4.5 days, depending on the size of a factory. All this concerns strictness in the meaning of freedom of choice.

BSCI has a high level of strictness concerning precision in the definition of terms and concepts. BSCI has a graduation system regarding audit results. It has four clearly defined levels (BSCI 2009b: 25).[12] The audit reports are practical conceptualised forms. They contain fairly detailed qualitative data which serve as a basis for judgements expressed by the four graduation levels. Every single point of requirement is judged. They are summed up then to a total in one of the four graduation levels.

15.4.1.3 Stakeholder Involvement

As mentioned above, the stakeholder involvement considered in this chapter is primarily about implementation and not about TSI rule establishment or governance.

FWF cooperates in producing countries with stakeholders that have an impact on or responsibility for labour conditions (business associations and manufacturers, trade unions and workers, relevant NGOs, (semi) governmental organisations). The cooperation is particularly 'for consultation of FWF policies and on local labour conditions' (FWF 2009a: 5, 7). Stakeholders can also, for example, provide policy advice to FWF, suggest candidates for FWF audit teams and be involved in capacity building programmes of FWF such as training (FWF 2009a: 7).

In the home countries of member companies, FWF organises stakeholder meetings. The members and stakeholders can exchange information and hold discussions on the implementation of labour rights.

In production countries **BSCI** works together with stakeholders in dialogue forums such as round tables (BSCI 2009d: 7). Representatives of different stakeholders, for example unions, employers, the government and academia, come together to discuss subjects such as wages. The subjects are discussed normally on a national and general level. Representatives do not occupy themselves with questions concerning concrete cases. Sometimes work groups are established.

BSCI also organises meetings of member companies in their own countries. The members can exchange information at these meetings in a confidential environment.

Table 15.1 lists important differences between BSCI and FWF

---

11 Audit companies have to be accredited by Social Accountability Accreditation Services (SAAS) to be accepted by BSCI for conducting audits.

12 From best to worst: 'good', 'improvements needed', 'non-compliant', 'not applicable' (BSCIb 2009: 25).

Table 15.1 **Comparison of BSCI and FWF**

Subject	BSCI	FWF
Wage level required	Legal minimum wage or, if higher, industry standard wage	Living wage
Allowed audit teams	Only auditing companies accredited by Social Accountability Services (SAAS)	Staff of the member company Auditing companies FWF audit teams Quality level implied in the Audit Manual is the required standard for audit programmes
Thresholds for audit process over time	After 3.5 years, 2/3 of buying volume or 2/3 of supplier factories in risk countries must have been audited. And 1/3 of the volume/suppliers must be rated with 'good' or 'improvements needed' (not lower) After 5.5 years still 2/3 of the volume/suppliers must have been audited. But now 2/3 must be rated with 'good' or 'improvements needed'	At the end of the 1st year of membership: 40% of the production commissioned by the member must originate from audited supplier factories (or from low risk countries) At the end of the 2nd year of membership 60% And after the 3rd year 90%
Number of members	Around 800*	75
Costs for audits	Payment of costs has to be negotiated between member and supplier company. In principle, the cost for audits should be borne by the companies audited. But it is up to the member to decide that in detail	Costs are generally carried by the member companies
Financing	Two main sources: Membership fees (in 2010, 89% of the income) Audit fees (in 2010, 11% of the income)	Membership fees are one basic financial resource (amount is based on member's turnover) and count for about 25–30% of the FWF budget Additional funding from different (often Dutch) stakeholder organisations, e.g. NGOs
Duration of audit	Depending of factory size: from min. 1.5 days to max. 4.5 days	Depending on factory size (and audit team): from min. 6 days to max. 13 days

Subject	BSCI	FWF
Responsibility and actors	The supplier factories have to adapt their management system according to BSCI requirements in order to implement the labour standards. The member has to heighten the suppliers' awareness of social responsibility	The member itself has to adapt its management system according to the FWF requirements. It is also responsible for monitoring the activities concerning implementation of labour standards in the supplier factories
	Primarily the supplier factories are responsible for a successful implementation of labour standards	The supplier has to inform workers about the different aspects of FWF rules and to implement the required social standards
		Member and supplier are responsible for a successful implementation of labour standards

* BSCI is a TSI not only for the garment industry but also for other industry goods (e.g. toys) as well as food products. This may contribute to why BSCI has so many members.

15.4.2 Implementation and effectiveness

15.4.2.1 Transparency

According to most interviewed representatives of TSI member companies, transparency plays an important role for effective implementation. If employees of a company know for example that their company publishes an annual social report (voluntarily or required), this exerts pressure on those employees who have to contribute to it. They know that they have to present what they have done during the year in this field. So the pressure to write for the social report leads to an effort to contribute something substantial for effective implementation of TSI requirements. The condition is that the social report is not purely a PR measure but is committed to contain substantial socially relevant information.[13] The interviewed BSCI member company, which voluntarily published a social report, stated that it did so because of pressures from external stakeholders such as end-consumers, journalists and even clients (generally retailers).

This leads to the preliminary conclusion that having to publish (because of external pressures or TSI requirements) leads to internal pressure on key employees to really do what is expected, and hence that transparency influences effectiveness.

13 For example, how much and in which country the company produces.

15.4.2.2 Strictness

First, we look at strictness in the sense of being precise. On the one hand, the interviewed FWF member company criticised that there is no graduation system for audit results. The qualitative description in FWF audit reports is indeed comprehensive. But it is not easy to recognise where a supplier of a member company actually stands. On the other hand, a BSCI expert criticised the four levels of graduated audit results in BSCI. Clearly delimited levels lead to threshold effects and a pass-or-fail mentality: if the threshold of a certain level (e.g. 'improvements needed') is overcome, there is no longer an incentive for a supplier company to improve inside this level because this does not lead to a higher ranking. To reach the next level very large efforts would be necessary.[14] According to the expert, BSCI has recognised the problem and is looking for a solution. A middle way between what BSCI and FWF actually do could point to an appropriate solution: more delimited levels with shorter value intervals.

Another point of being precise concerns definitions of terms and concepts. Overall, BSCI and FWF are precise in this meaning. According to the interviewed FWF member company, being precise is important in order to know exactly how to act regarding certain points (e.g. the mentioned graduation system, but also some definitional points). The BSCI member company expressed that some range in interpretation is important for a company. Overall and based on the data at hand, it seems that preciseness and clearness in the rules of TSIs play a role for effective implementation.

A point concerning strictness in understanding the restriction of choices of companies, in which BSCI and FWF clearly differ, is the demand for a living wage: FWF requires it; BSCI leaves it up to its members. The interviewed BSCI member company thinks that BSCI could be more demanding on this point. It also conducted its own investigations to get information about the situation in its supplier companies. According to the interviewed FWF member company, the problem is not the living wage as such but the preciseness of its definition. FWF established a wage ladder tool, which, according to the member company, is an applicable instrument in practice. Overall, it seems that more demanding rules lead to more efforts to reach the declared aims of a TSI. This is true regarding FWF and the investigated member company in the area of living wages. The investigated BSCI member company, which has the freedom of choice, said that it felt pressured to seek living wages by an NGO campaign demanding them. More choice-restricting rules of TSIs—or, and that was not hypothesised, campaigns—seem indeed to lead companies to make more efforts in this direction. But there is also the assumption that more demanding rules in fields which are demonstrably difficult to influence

---

14 Whether the average work time per week in a factory is for example 65 or 80 hours does not matter because both numbers of hours belong to the same level. To reach the next level, 60 hours or below would be necessary.

(e.g. freedom of association and collective bargaining) may not lead to a more effective implementation. In order to get sounder results, more data must be collected and analysed.

To establish and maintain the monitoring system led by the member company as required by FWF, the member must provide many resources. But, according to statements from interviewed persons it is important that the different relevant actors work together and each contributes its part to achieve the desired labour conditions. With the current status of the study it is too early to present more detailed results thereto.

15.4.2.3 Stakeholder involvement

Primarily the TSIs themselves are working together in producing countries with local stakeholders as mentioned above. The interviewed member companies do not cooperate extensively with stakeholders in producing countries. But they participate in stakeholder and member meetings in their home countries. Both companies stated that the exchange on the implementation of TSI requirements with other member companies (thus also competitors), NGOs and representatives from the administration as well as with other stakeholders is important and helpful to them. This leads to the preliminary conclusion that a well-elaborated stakeholder involvement policy on different levels (geographic, thematic etc.) supports more effective implementation.

15.4.3 Additional preliminary findings

The following problems are structured according to the groups of actors affected by them.

- **Market power**. Concerns particularly member companies. Often one single company simply orders too little from a supplier to put pressure on it to change its behaviour. More cooperation between companies could help

- **Multiple audits** in supplier factories are mainly a problem for member and supplier companies. There are many TSIs and little coordination among them. A best practice or certificate accepted by all TSIs (e.g. SA8000) could be a solution

- **Country-specific problems** or those ILO conventions that are difficult to achieve are a concern for TSIs and member companies. For companies it is important to have their own employees on site and hence to be present; for TSIs it is important to have, for example, their local round tables

- **Training and capacity building** becomes more important for effective implementation; audits alone are not enough. Establishing effective training systems concerns TSIs, members and suppliers

15.5 Conclusion

In this chapter the question of effective implementation of the institutional designs of the TSIs BSCI and FWF in two Swiss member companies has been examined. Through an analytical framework consisting of a phase-model and theoretically drawn hypotheses, I tried to find responses in a systematic way.

On the basis of the data already in hand, it can be preliminarily concluded that, as hypothesised, transparency plays a role for effective implementation. This is because the pressure for responsible employees to publish what they have done concerning the requirements of a TSI pushes them to perform activities relating to effective implementation. Responses concerning the second hypothesis regarding strictness are more complex. Strictness, as precise and clear definitions and operationalisation of concepts and terms, leads to a clear picture of what to do. But if requirements are too detailed the necessary flexibility for interpretation gets lost. Rules that are strict in the sense of restriction of choice can lead to more effort to reach declared aims. Pressures from external campaigns can lead to similar efforts. But at the same time, rules that are too demanding, especially concerning ILO conventions that are difficult to control, may not lead to more effectiveness. Stakeholder involvement happens in different ways. For TSI member companies the most effective way is to meet with other member companies and stakeholders in home countries for an exchange of views. Contacts with stakeholders in producing countries are administered mainly by TSIs themselves. It can be preliminarily concluded that an elaborate stakeholder involvement policy can lead to effectiveness.

Overall, for more sound results more empirical data has to be collected and analysed; however the preliminary results allow some first insights in the examined area.

Future research may apply the analytical framework with other TSIs in industries other than the garment industry. More case studies would help to recognise patterns which later may support a generalisation. It would also be meaningful to examine in more detail the limits of TSIs as voluntary governance systems by, for example, comparing them with state laws or rules established by international cooperation (e.g. OECD Guidelines).

References

Abbott, K.W., and D. Snidal (2009) 'The Governance Triangle: Regulatory Standards Institutions and the Shadow of the State', in W. Mattli and N. Woods (eds.), *The Politics of Global Regulation* (Princeton, NJ: Princeton University Press).

Banks, M., and D. Vera (2007) 'Towards a Typology of Stakeholder Management Strategies', paper presented at the *Academy of Management (AoM) Annual Meeting*, Philadelphia, PA, 3–8 August 2007.

Benner, T., W.H. Reinicke and J.M. Witte (2004) 'Multisectoral Networks in Global Governance: Towards a Pluralistic System of Accountability', *Government and Opposition* 39.2: 191-210.

Bennett, A., and C. Elman (2006) 'Complex Causal Relations and Case Study Methods: The Example of Path Dependence', *Political Analysis* 14: 250-67.

Biermann, F., and S. Bauer (2004) 'Assessing the Effectiveness of Intergovernmental Organisations in International Environmental Politics', *Global Environmental Change* 14: 189-93.

Blatter, J., F. Janning and C. Wagemann (2007) *Qualitative Politikanalyse* (Wiesbaden, Germany: VS Verlag für Sozialwissenschaften).

Blum, S., and K. Schubert (2009) *Politikfeldanalyse* (Wiesbaden, Germany: VS Verlag).

Börzel, T.A., and T. Risse (2005) 'Public–Private Partnerships: Effective and Legitimate Tools of Transnational Governance?', in E. Grande and L. Pauly (eds.), *Complex Sovereignty: Reconstituting Political Authority in the Twenty-First Century* (Toronto: University of Toronto Press).

Brütsch, C., and D. Lehmkuhl (2007) 'Introduction', in: C. Brütsch and D. Lehmkuhl (eds.), *Law and Legalization in Transnational Relations* (London: Routledge).

BSCI (Business Social Compliance Initiative) (2009a) 'Code of Conduct', www.bsci-intl.org/resources/code-of-conduct, accessed 18 January 2012.

BSCI (2009b) *Management Manual* (Brussels: BSCI).

BSCI (2009c) 'Position on Wages', www.bsci-intl.org/resources/bsci-positions, accessed 18 January 2012.

BSCI (2009d) 'Rules and Functioning', www.bsci-intl.org/resources/rules-functioning, accessed 18 January 2012.

BSCI (2010) 'Annual Report', www.bsci-intl.org/resources/annual-report-bsci, accessed 18 January 2012.

BSCI (2011) 'BSCI List of Risk Countries', www.bsci-intl.org/bsci-list-risk-countries-0, accessed 18 January 2012.

Campbell, J.L. (2004) *Institutional Change and Globalization* (Princeton, NJ: Princeton University Press).

Carroll, A.B. (1991) 'The Pyramid of Corporate Social Responsibility: Toward the Moral Management of Organizational Stakeholders', *Business Horizons* 34: 39-48.

Carroll, A.B., and J. Näsi (1997) 'Understanding Stakeholder Thinking: Themes from a Finnish Conference', *Business Ethics* 6.1: 46-51.

Creswell, J.W. (2003) *Research Design: Qualitative, Quantitative, and Mixed Methods Approaches* (Thousand Oaks, CA: Sage).

Dingwerth, K., and P. Pattberg (2006a) 'Global Governance as a Perspective on World Politics', *Global Governance* 12.2: 185-203.

Dingwerth, K., and P. Pattberg (2006b) 'Was ist Global Governance?', *Leviathan* 34.3: 377-99.

Easton, D. (1965) *A Systems Analysis of Political Life* (New York: John Wiley & Sons).

Eisenhardt, K.M. (1989) 'Agency Theory: An Assessment and Review', *Academy of Management Journal* 14.1: 57-74.

Fama, E.F. (1980) 'Agency Problems and the Theory of the Firm', *The Journal of Political Economy* 88.2: 288-307.

Fama, E.F., and M.C. Jensen (1983a) 'Agency Problems and Residual Claims', *Journal of Law and Economics* 26.2: 327-49.

Fama, E.F., and M.C. Jensen (1983b) 'Separation of Ownership and Control', *Journal of Law and Economics* 26.2: 301-25.

Fransen, L.W., and A. Kolk (2007) 'Global Rule-Setting for Business: A Critical Analysis of Multi-Stakeholder Standards', *Organization* 14.5: 667-84.

Freeman, E.R. (1984) *Strategic Management: A Stakeholder Approach* (Boston, MA: Pitman).

Freeman, E.R., J.S. Harrison, A.C. Wicks, B.L. Parmar and S. De Colle (2010) *Stakeholder Theory: The State of the Art* (Cambridge, UK: Cambridge University Press).

FWF (Fair Wear Foundation) (2004–11) 'FWF Country Information: Country Studies', www.fairwear.org/resources, accessed 27 May 2011.

FWF (2008–10) 'FWF Annual Reports', www.fairwear.org/resources, accessed 18 January 2012.

FWF (2009a) 'Charter [including Code of Labour Practices]', www.fairwear.org/ul/cms/fck-uploaded/documents/companies/FWFdocs/fwfcharterjanuary2011.pdf, accessed 11 January 2012.

FWF (2009b) 'BLACKOUT AG: Annual CSR Report 2009', Format Social Report Affiliates, FWF, www.fairwear.org/ul/cms/fck-uploaded/documents/companies/ManualsReports/Format socialreport2009E.pdf, accessed 18 January 2012.

FWF (2009c) 'FWF Complaints Procedure', www.fairwear.org/ul/cms/fck-uploaded/documents/complaints/fwfcomplaintsprocedurejune2009.pdf, accessed 18 January 2012.

FWF (2009d) 'Low Risk Policy: Low Risk Countries', www.fairwear.org/ul/cms/fck-uploaded/documents/companies/ManualsReports/lowriskpolicyfwf-mar2009.pdf, accessed 18 January 2012.

FWF (2009–11) 'Company Reports: Brand Performance 2011—Management System Audit (MSA)', www.fairwear.org/resources, accessed 18 January 2012.

FWF (2011) 'Terms for Audits by FWF Audit Teams', www.fairwear.org/ul/cms/fck-uploaded/documents/companies/FWFdocs/termsforFWFauditsfeb2011.pdf, accessed 20 January 2012.

FWF (2012) 'Resources: Policy Documents', www.fairwear.org/resources, accessed 25 January 2012.

George, A.L., and A. Bennett (2005) *Case Studies and Theory Development in the Social Sciences* (Cambridge, MA: MIT Press).

Greenwood, R., and C.R. Hinings (1996) 'Understanding Radical Organizational Change: Bringing Together the Old and the New Institutionalism', *Academy of Management Review* 21.4: 1022-54.

Hill, C.W., and T.M. Jones (1992) 'Stakeholder-Agency Theory', *Journal of Management Studies* 29.2: 131-54.

Hill, M., and P. Hupe (2009) *Implementing Public Policy* (London: Sage).

Howlett, M., M. Ramesh and A. Perl (2009) *Studying Public Policy: Policy Cycle & Policy Subsystems* (Toronto: Oxford University Press).

Jamali, D., and A. Basiou (2009) 'A Practitioner Lens on Global Accountability Standards', paper presented at the *AoM Annual Meeting*, Chicago, 7–11 August 2009.

Jann, W., and K. Wegrich (2007) 'Theories of the Policy Cycle', in F. Fischer, G. J. Miller and M.S. Sidney (eds.), *Handbook of Public Policy Analysis: Theory, Politics and Methods* (Boca Raton, FL: CRC Press).

Jann, W., and K. Wegrich (2009) 'Phasenmodelle und Politikprozesse: Der Policy Cycle', in K. Schubert and N.C. Bandelow (eds.), *Lehrbuch der Politikfeldanalyse* (München: Oldenbourg Wissenschaftsverlag).

Jensen, M.C., and W.H. Meckling (1976) 'Theory of the Firm: Managerial Behavior, Agency Costs and Ownership Structure', *Journal of Financial Economics* 11.4: 305-60.

Kahler, M., and D.A. Lake (2004) 'Governance in a Global Economy: Political Authority in Transition', *Political Science and Politics* 37.3: 409-14.

Kolk, A., and R. Van Tulder (2002a) 'Child Labor and Multinational Conduct: A Comparison of International Business and Stakeholder Codes', *Journal of Business Ethics* 36: 291-301.

Kolk, A., and R. Van Tulder (2002b) 'The Effectiveness of Self-Regulation: Corporate Codes of Conduct and Child Labour', *European Management Journal* 20.3: 260-71.

Kolk, A., and R. van Tulder (2005) 'Setting New Rules? TNCs and Codes of Conduct', *Transnational Corporations* 14.3: 1-28.

Krasner, S. (1983) 'Structural Causes and Regime Consequences: Regimes as Intervening Variables', in S. Krasner (ed.), *International Regimes* (Ithaca, NY: Cornell University Press).

Lijphart, A. (1971) 'Comparative Politics and the Comparative Method', *American Political Science Review* 65: 682-93.

Lipsky, M. (1980) *Street-Level Bureaucracy: Dilemmas of the Individual in Public Services* (New York: Russell Sage Foundation).

McCubbins, M.D., and T. Schwartz (1984) 'Congressional Oversight Overlooked: Police Patrols versus Fire Alarms', *American Journal of Political Sciences* 28.1: 165-79.

Mahoney, J., and G. Goertz (2006) 'A Tale of Two Cultures: Contrasting Quantitative and Qualitative Research', *Political Analysis* 14: 227-49.

Messner, D., and F. Nuscheler (2003) *Das Konzept Global Governance: Stand und Perspektiven* (Duisburg, Germany: Institut für Entwicklung und Frieden (INEF)).

Miles, E.L., A. Underdal, S. Andresen, J. Wettestad, J.B. Skjaerseth and E.M. Carlin (2002) *Environmental Regime Effectiveness: Confronting Theory with Evidence* (Cambridge, MA: MIT Press).

Mitchell, R.B. (2008) 'Evaluating the Performance of Environmental Institutions: What to Evaluate and How to Evaluate it?', in O.R. Young, L.A. King and H. Schroeder (eds.), *Institutions and Environmental Change* (Cambridge, MA: MIT Press).

Mitnick, B.M. (1975) 'The Theory of Agency: The Policing "Paradox" and Regulatory Behavior', *Public Choice* 24: 27-42.

Park-Poaps, H., and K. Rees (2010) 'Stakeholder Forces of Socially Responsible Supply Chain Management Orientation', *Journal of Business Ethics* 92: 305-22.

Post, J.E., L.E. Preston and S. Sachs (2002) *Redefining the Corporation: Stakeholder Management and Organizational Wealth* (Palo Alto, CA: Stanford University Press).

Power, M. (1991) 'Auditing and Environmental Expertise: Between Protest and Professionalisation', *Accounting Auditing & Accountability Journal* 4.3: 30-42.

Przeworski, A., and H.J. Teune (1970) *The Logic of Comparative Social Inquiry* (New York: Wiley & Sons).

Rasche, A. (2009a) 'A Necessary Supplement: What the United Nations Global Compact Is and Is not', *Business & Society* 48.4: 511-37.

Rasche, A. (2009b) 'Toward a Model to Compare and Analyze Accountability Standards: The Case of the UN Global Compact', *Corporate Social Responsibility and Environmental Management* 16: 192-205.

Rieth, L. (2009) *Global Governance und Corporate Social Responsibility* (Opladen, Germany: Budrich UniPress).

Roloff, J. (2008) 'Learning from Multi-Stakeholder Networks: Issue-Focussed Stakeholder Management', *Journal of Business Ethics* 82.1: 233-50.

Rondinelli, D.A. (2002) 'Transnational Corporations: International Citizens or New Sovereigns?', *Business and Society Review* 107.4: 391-413.

Rosenau, J.N. (1995) 'Governance in the Twenty-first Century', *Global Governance* 1: 13-43.

Rosenau, J.N., and E.-O. Czempiel (1992) *Governance Without Government: Order and Change in World Politics* (Cambridge, UK: Cambridge University Press).

Sabatier, P. A. (1986) 'Top-Down and Bottom-Up Approaches to Implementation Research: A Critical Analysis and Suggested Synthesis', *Journal of Public Policy* 6.1: 21-48.

Sachs, S., and E. Rühli (2011) *Stakeholders Matter: A New Paradigm for Strategy in Society* (Cambridge, UK: Cambridge University Press).

Sachs, S., E. Rühli and C. Meier (2011) 'Stakeholder Governance as a Response to Wicked Issues', *Journal of Business Ethics* 96: 57-64.

Scherer, A.G., and G. Palazzo (2006) 'Corporate Legitimacy as Deliberation: A Communicative Framework', *Journal of Business Ethics* 66: 71-88.

Shankman, N.A. (1999) 'Reframing the Debate Between Agency and Stakeholder Theories of the Firm', *Journal of Business Ethics* 19: 319-34.

Shapiro, S.P. (2005) 'Agency Theory', *Annual Review of Sociology* 31: 263-84.

Spence, M. (1973) 'Job Market Signaling', *The Quarterly Journal of Economics* 87.3: 355-74.

Sprinz, D.F., and C. Helm (1999) 'The Effect of Global Environmental Regimes: A Measurement Concept', *International Political Science Review* 20.4: 359-69.

Starmanns, M. (2010) *The Grand Illusion? Corporate Social Responsibility in Global Garment Production Networks* (PhD thesis; Cologne, Germany: University of Cologne).

Underdal, A. (2008) 'Determining the Causal Significance of Institutions: Accomplishments', in O.R. Young, L.A. King and H. Schroeder (eds.), *Institutions and Environmental Change* (Cambridge, MA: MIT Press).

Utting, P. (2002) 'Regulating Business via Multistakeholder Initiatives: A Preliminary Assessment', in UN-NGLS and UNRISD (eds.), *Voluntary Approaches to Corporate Responsibility: Readings and a Resource Guide* (Geneva: NGLS/UNRISD).

Van Tulder, R., J. Van Wijk and A. Kolk (2009) 'From Chain Liability to Chain Responsibility', *Journal of Business Ethics* 85: 399-412.

Vedung, E. (1997) *Public Policy and Programme Evaluation* (New Brunswick: Transaction Publishers).

Waterman, R.W., and K.J. Meier (1998) 'Principal–Agent Models: An Expansion?', *Journal of Public Administration Research and Theory* 8.2: 173-202.

Weiss, L. (2000) 'Globalization and the Myth of Powerless State', in R. Higgott and E. Elgar (eds.), *The Political Economy of Globalization* (Cheltenham, UK: Macmillan Palgrave).

Yin, R.K. (2003) *Case Study Research: Design and Methods* (Thousand Oaks, CA: Sage).

Zangl, B., and M. Zürn (2004) 'Make Law, Not War: Internationale und transnationale Verrechtlichung als Baustein für Global Governance', in B. Zangl and M. Zürn (eds.), *Verrechtlichung: Baustein für Global Governance?* (Bonn, Germany: Dietz).

Zürn, M. (1998) *Regieren jenseits des Nationalstaats. Denationalisierung und Globalisierung als Chance* (Frankfurt, Germany: Suhrkamp).

Claude Meier is a PhD student at the Institute of Political Science of the University of Zurich, where he also studied political sciences and business administration. He works as a research assistant on different projects regarding the stakeholder approach and as a lecturer at the Institute for Strategic Management/Stakeholder View at HWZ (Hochschule für Wirtschaft Zürich).

Part III
The practice in textiles and fashion

16

Corporate responsibility in the garment industry
Towards shared value*

Anna Larsson
U&We, Sweden

Katarina Buhr
IVL Swedish Environmental Research Institute and Linköping University, Sweden

Cecilia Mark-Herbert
Swedish University of Agricultural Sciences, Sweden

While materialistic consumerism has been called into question in recent years, the consumption of clothes has increased dramatically in many countries. In Sweden, the consumption of textiles and clothes increased by a staggering 40% in nine years during the first decade of the 21st century (Carlsson *et al.* 2011). Alongside this trend, 80% of consumers agree that companies have a responsibility for production that takes place in developing countries (Fairtrade International 2011). The garment and textile industry is characterised by low margins (Bremer and Udovich 2001) and labour-intensive production in low-income countries. The majority of clothes consumed in Sweden and other countries in the West are produced by independent contractors in China, Pakistan, India and Bangladesh (Ander 2010).

* This chapter builds on a study carried out at the Department of Economics, the Swedish University of Agricultural Science and IVL Swedish Environmental Research Institute. The authors sincerely thank the editors and anonymous reviewers for constructive feedback on this manuscript.

Since the early 1990s, Swedish garment retailers have come under increasing critical scrutiny by non-governmental organisations (NGOs), and have been exposed to negative media because of poor working conditions and negative environmental impacts in the complex supply chains (Wingborg 2009). These critical reviews, and an increased awareness of the ethical aspects of a purchasing role (Young and Welford 2002), have motivated garment retailers in acknowledging a corporate responsibility in the supply chain network, involving a large number of actors in the value chain (Roberts 2003; Ählström and Egels-Zandén 2008). The garment industry therefore offers a rewarding empirical setting, given experiences of addressing corporate responsibility issues of social and environmental character.

This chapter aims at providing a contextual understanding of retailers' corporate responsibility, with a focus on the value chain. Corporate responsibility in value chains is acknowledged by a majority of garment retailers, but tends to be practised mainly in the first step of the chain (Welford and Frost 2006). The comparative case study presented here is based on corporate responsibility reporting of four major garment retailers in Sweden, H&M, Lindex, KappAhl and MQ, holding 32.6% of the Swedish garment retail market (Handelns Utredningsinstitut 2010). The companies were theoretically sampled based on size, markets served and corporate responsibility communication (Eisenhardt 1989). A thematic coding of the empirical data gave rise to a categorisation of corporate responsibility context bound factors, which offered grounds to provide an overview of value chain perspectives in communication (Larsson 2011). Secondary data, such as industrial reports, web pages and newspaper articles also served as empirical data.

The chapter begins with a historical review of important stages in the process of acknowledging corporate responsibility, which provides a historical context to current actions. Focus of the empirical analysis lies on communicated corporate responsibility initiatives by the garment retailers and where in the value chain these initiatives take place. Our conclusions are concerned with present conditions for corporate responsibility in the garment industry from a retailer perspective and future expectations of sustainable value chain development.

16.1 Corporate responsibility: By whom and for whom?

The essence of corporate responsibility is to create shared value for the corporation and its stakeholders (Porter and Kramer 2011). Carroll (1991: 43) argues that the company's responsibility is to 'make a profit, obey the law, be ethical and be a good corporate citizen'. Corporate responsibility can both be considered a business case and a strategy for risk mitigation (Epstein 2008; Arvidsson 2010). Laudal (2010) even argued that a misinterpretation occurs when corporate responsibility is referred to as aspects that go *beyond* what is regulated by law in the context of garment retailers. His studies of corporate responsibility at an industrial level point to initiatives addressing basic human rights and compliance with environmental laws.

Corporate responsibility can be expressed as demanding standards for production, creating alternative business models or developing environmentally conscious products (Mamic 2004). Halme and Laurila (2009) argue that the societal and financial outcomes of corporate responsibility depend on the approach adopted by the company. To integrate it as part of the core business, for example, by developing new business models, is more likely to be sustained over time and lead to shared value between corporations and stakeholders, in contrast to a philanthropic approach which predominantly has a direct benefit to the recipient (Halme and Laurila 2009; Porter and Kramer 2011). However, corporate responsibility is not a static concept (Swedish Standards Institute 2010: 5), but 'The elements of social responsibility reflect the expectations of society at a particular time, and are therefore liable to change. As society's concerns change, its expectations of organisations also change to reflect those concerns'. Thus, the definition is contextually bound in time and space, which is also reflected in terms used to describe corporations' responsibility towards stakeholders. Corporate citizenship, corporate social responsibility, social responsibility and corporate responsibility are used synonymously in the debate. Although there is no set framework for what corporate responsibility entails (Windell 2006), corporate actions typically involve a wide range of initiatives, addressing challenges in-house as well as in the value chain (Roberts 2003; Stigzelius and Mark-Herbert 2009; Dobers 2010).

16.2 Corporate responsibility in the garment industry

Corporate responsibility is a growing concern among retailers (Frostenson *et al.* 2011), where brand reputation and corporate image are important, if not a prerequisite, for future profitability (Grafström *et al.* 2008). Branded goods retailers stand a high risk of a damaged reputation if critical issues in the value chain are revealed. In the words of Roberts (2003: 164), 'the higher the profile of a brand, the greater the scrutiny of its activities and the higher the potential of it to become a target for pressure group action'. In a retailer context, the need for a value chain perspective focusing on sustainable sourcing in the purchasing portfolio (Fang *et al.* 2010; Pagell *et al.* 2010) may be explained by the massive criticism directed towards the industry. Since the 1990s, when child labour and inadequate working conditions for factory workers in garment-producing countries was high on the agenda, NGOs and media have regularly scrutinised garment retailers for lacking responsibility in the value chain (Welford and Frost 2006). Continued responsibility expectations from consumers and NGOs include business disclosure of corporate responsibility management and performance of suppliers (Mamic 2004; Miles *et al.* 2004). Managing all aspects of upstream components in a value chain serves as a risk management strategy, aimed at precautionary damage control or, more proactively, to maximise value creation in a triple-bottom-line framework (i.e. where social, environmental and economic aspects are of equal importance) (Lyon and Maxwell 2008; Pagell *et al.* 2010).

Traditionally, garment production has been studied with a supply chain perspective focusing on economic and managerial aspects of the production. More recent perspectives, motivated by a growing interest in ethical aspects of global sourcing, motivate a customer perspective—a value chain. The value chain has its origin in branded goods retailers' needs to be accountable (Fig. 16.1).

A number of actors play important roles in the value chain of garment retailers, from the farmer providing raw materials to the consumer encountering the garment in the retail store.

Figure 16.1 illustrates a simplified, general value chain in the garment industry. The stages that make up the value chain can include dyeing, washing, printing and assembling as well as the production of raw materials. At the base of the value chain are farmers, the producers of natural raw materials for production of textiles. Cotton is only one of many raw materials used in garment production, but is the main focus of the case companies' corporate responsibility reporting. Other materials, such as polyester and wool are also used, along with newer materials such as bamboo and lyocell, but these will not be elaborated on further in this study.

Figure 16.1 **Garment value chain perspectives involving a large number of stakeholders in different parts of the world**

Source: interpretation of Roberts 2003: 165

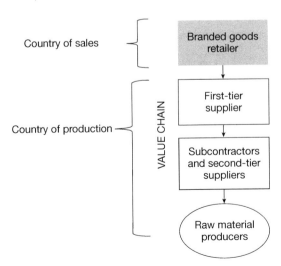

The farmers' power position is weak in relation to the brand retailer, and the production is associated with numerous environmental and social problems. Moving up the value chain, there may be as many as eight suppliers until the final product reaches the hands of a consumer. It has been argued that corporations that operate in industries in which the supply chains are long and complex have particular moral obligations as a result of their power position and the context of a market that has a relatively high awareness of sustainability issues (Roberts 2003; Mamic 2004; Laudal 2010).

16.3 Corporate responsibility in a Swedish garment retailing context

Corporate awareness of responsibility issues has gradually matured over the last two decades (Fig. 16.2). In 1996, the Swedish garment retailers, H&M, Lindex and KappAhl, formally acknowledged a responsibility for workers' rights in outsourced production of garments (Ählström and Egels-Zandén 2008). Prior to this, H&M, Lindex and KappAhl had not expressed that their responsibility as garment retailers would also include the producers. In the decades that have followed, the responsibility of garment retailers continues to receive a significant amount of attention

Figure 16.2 **Growing awareness of corporate responsibility among consumers from the 1990s was promoted by NGO actions (above the time line). Corporate actions in response to the growing concerns and expectations are illustrated below the time line**

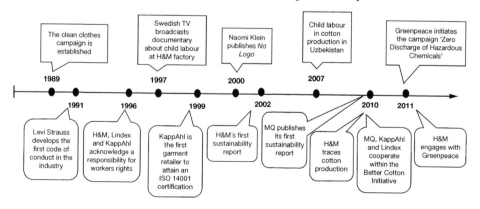

in the media. Critical reports and documentaries have been published annually, scrutinising the poor conditions for chemical management, overtime, denied right to collective bargaining and cotton production (Engwall 2008; Wingborg 2009; de Verdier *et al.* 2010; Ander 2010). However, as the time line in Figure 16.2 illustrates, several steps towards recognition of corporate responsibility have been taken among the Swedish garment retailers from the mid-1990s onwards.

Figure 16.2 shows a selection of events in the international and Swedish development of corporate responsibility. It includes corporate recognition of responsibility in the value chain, environmental certification, voluntary reporting, acknowledgement of a responsibility for cotton production and cooperation with NGOs. External pressure from NGOs and media has motivated the continued development of corporate responsibility actions (Mamic 2004; Welford and Frost 2006; Ählström and Egels-Zandén 2008) for garment retailers worldwide. The relation between private and public interests (corporations and NGOs) has also developed from antagonistic positions to realisations of public–private partnerships (Mendelson and Polonsky 1995; Rotter *et al.* 2012).

16.4 Classifying corporate responsibility actions in the value chain

Based on Robert's (2003) model and our empirical case studies of H&M, Lindex, KappAhl and MQ, the corporate responsibility initiatives have been classified into four categories in the value chain: in-house, first-tier suppliers, subcontractors and second-tier suppliers, and raw material producers (Table 16.1). It is worth pointing out that the case companies offer garments of a similar style. The garments are closely tied to a quickly changing fashion that requires cheap production and short lead times. Their markets vary in size; H&M is by far the largest corporation, with the world as its market. The other retailers are mainly acting on a European market, with major markets in Sweden and Eastern Europe.

Table 16.1 demonstrates the empirical findings for four categories in the value chain. **In-house activities** for the branded goods retailers such as an environmental management system, codes of ethics and specific policies regarding travelling, transportation, equality and diversity are communicated by all of the case companies. Initiatives relating to quality assessment, life-cycle assessment and labour rights are motivated by a strict legal enforcement, awareness of equal opportunity rights as well as by NGO and media involvement (Visser and Tolhurst 2011).

The **first-tier suppliers** represent the best chance of influencing corporate conduct for the branded goods retailers, as a formal business contract exists. Given a powerful position, this is where retailers' codes of conduct may serve as conditions for signing a contract. A code of conduct and an assessment for ensuring compliance with the code is established among garment retailers and was one of the first

Table 16.1 **Selection of retailer corporate responsibility actions directed towards the own organisation, first-tier suppliers, subcontractors and second-tier suppliers, and raw material producers**

Source: H&M 2009; KappAhl 2008; Lindex 2009; MQ 2009

	H&M	KappAhl	Lindex	MQ
In-house activities	• Code of ethics • Travel and transport • CEO Water Mandate • Climate reporting • Life-cycle assessment • Whistle-blowing policy • Paper use analysis • Policy for employees • Donations of clothes	• Management systems • Work environment • Equality and diversity • Clean Shipping Project • Climate offsetting • Life-cycle assessment • Employee survey • Donations of clothes	• Environmental policy • Travel and transport • Equality and diversity • Environmental impact and action plan • Clean Shipping Project	• Travel policy • Policies for business ethics and equality • Equality plan • Energy efficiency and recycling • Employee survey • Donations of clothes
First-tier suppliers	• Code of conduct • Management System Scorecard • Training and education • Fair Labor Association • Water footprint and wastewater management • Pilot projects • Supplier training for quality assessment of subcontractors	• Code of conduct • Environmental code • Supplier training • Database for assessment of suppliers • Business for Social Compliance Initiative	• Code of conduct • Training programme • Supplier stop list • Grading system for environmental compliance • IT system for follow-up • Business for Social Compliance Initiative	• Code of conduct • Critical violation policy • Training via Business for Social Compliance Initiative • SA8000 • Business for Social Compliance Initiative
Subcontractors and second-tier suppliers	• Code of conduct • Voluntary assessment pilot projects • Home worker policy	• No communicated initiatives	• Voluntary assessment of subcontractors	• No communicated initiatives
Raw material producers	• Better Cotton Initiative • Textile Exchange • Country of origin for cotton • Fur Free Alliance Program • Leather Working Group • Organic cotton	• Better Cotton Initiative • Animal rights policy • Organic cotton	• Better Cotton Initiative • Textile Exchange • Animal rights policy • Organic cotton	• Animal rights • Organic cotton

steps in practising this responsibility (Welford and Frost 2006; Ählström and Egels-Zandén 2008). In the studied cases H&M has its own code of conduct. In contrast, Lindex, KappAhl and MQ have joined the Business for Social Compliance Initiative, which is a business-driven organisation aiming at improving conditions in global supply chains. The codes of conduct represent expectations of minimum compliance with environmental and labour laws, and thus offer a standard for the first-tier suppliers. Training programmes aimed at local education serve as long-term investments for increased compliance with the code.

Subcontractors and second-tier suppliers are responsible for much of the environmental degradation in the production process, such as dyeing, printing and washing. This tier may represent several actors and the transparency is low, as few suppliers want to relinquish their business partners for competitive reasons (Engwall 2008). The negotiation power from a branded retailer perspective is here claimed to be weak, as no formal business contract exists (H&M 2009; Lindex 2009). From a retailer perspective, expectations on first-tier suppliers are aimed at extending the expectations on subcontractors and second-tier suppliers. H&M's auditors visit producers to assess the potential of implementing more environmentally friendly practices as part of voluntary pilot projects and training programmes (H&M 2009). Lindex also, to some extent, has projects aiming at addressing issues such as water and chemical management among second-tier suppliers and subcontractors (Lindex 2009).

Raw material suppliers in the garment industry are to a great extent cotton producers making use of large quantities of freshwater and chemicals, which may affect biodiversity, pollute groundwater and cause falling water tables (Soth *et al.* 1999). Cotton production is also known for poor working conditions and child labour has been reported in the major cotton producing country, Uzbekistan (Ander 2010). In response to reports of child labour in Uzbekistan, H&M is working on a system to be able to trace the country of origin of cotton. This system aims to avoid sourcing cotton from Uzbekistan, which to a large extent is used by suppliers in Pakistan. Lindex, KappAhl and MQ rely solely on private–public partnerships with the Better Cotton Initiative and support the Textile Exchange to improve conditions in the cotton industry and to promote organic cotton.

16.5 Retailer perspectives on conditions for corporate responsibility

Swedish retailers have addressed social issues related to their operations since the mid-1990s and also more recently environmental issues in the value chain. Pressure from external stakeholders has to a large extent motivated efforts in the sector in general and NGOs and media have played important roles (Welford and Frost 2006). The presented case studies indicate that NGOs and media continue to be important but with an extended role. They still exert pressure on corporations to be accountable, above and beyond the first-tier for the garment retailer. However, the extended role for some NGOs has developed into that of being partners in work towards sustainable business development in an international value chain. Organisations that once saw themselves as having strong conflicts of interest are increasingly finding opportunities to collaborate by seeking to create win–win situations. Yet, these alliances may cause blurred roles between corporations and NGOs that offer opportunities as well as conflicts. The challenges include finding balances and remaining true to organisational values and their identities. These partnerships are sometimes referred to as private–public partnerships and are gaining increased acceptance in international retail (Rotter *et al.* 2012) and multinational enterprise management (Mamic 2004).

H&M, Lindex, KappAhl and MQ all communicate corporate responsibility aims and performance on an annual basis. The annual reports reveal the scope and character of their responsibility, within their own organisations as well as in the value chain, with a focus on issues relating to the environment and people. However, the lack of comprehensive and stringent frameworks for corporate responsibility that prescribe how businesses should address social and environmental issues offers room for companies to decide on the focus (Grayson and Hodges 2004). The comparison of retailer initiatives in the value chain between the case studies shows common features of the corporate responsibility reporting. All case companies focus on the use of codes of conduct, standards and international cooperation. Most initiatives are addressed in their own organisation and in first-tier suppliers, levelling off further down in the supply chain.

For first-tier suppliers there are follow-up systems in place: for example, codes of conduct, which are a well-established practice to exercise demands on suppliers (Mamic 2004; Welford and Frost 2006; Stigzelius and Mark-Herbert 2009). Although the focus areas of the retailers' responsibility are similar, there are numerous ways of addressing the key issues. The systems for following up compliance include a stop list, a critical violation policy, IT systems and management system scorecards, which are all different tools for approaching the issues. Training and education is a common element, aimed at targeting areas where compliance with the code of conduct is low. The long-term aim is to attain an increased level of awareness of labour laws, the right to collective bargaining and chemical management among other challenges.

At the level of subcontractors and second-tier suppliers, less formal systems are in place. Garment retailers generally argue that they are not in a position to express demands at this part of the value chain, as no formal business contract exists (H&M 2009; Lindex 2009). However, H&M communicates that its code of conduct is also applicable to subcontractors, and Lindex and H&M communicate voluntary assessments of subcontractors and second-tier suppliers, aiming at voluntarily improving and supporting the actors at this stage of the value chain. This is a more recent approach to working with suppliers aimed at empowerment and mutual understanding. The 'inspection and auditing mentality' is judged less effective than building long-term relationships between retailers and suppliers (Welford and Frost 2006: 170).

The largest company in this study, H&M, is a high profile brand with global recognition. According to Roberts (2003) the higher the profile of the brand, the more criticism it is likely to receive and the more likely it is to take action in the value chain. Although the problem areas addressed and the actions taken by the four companies are of similar character, differences do exist. The case of H&M shows an advanced ambition to take accountability as far down in the value chain as possible. Its communicated efforts are the most extensive of the four cases and the difference becomes particularly evident further down in the value chain. H&M has taken several initiatives of its own; two examples are the initiative of applying a code of conduct for subcontractors and the tracking system to identify country of origin for cotton. The other companies, Lindex, KappAhl and MQ, communicate no initiatives of their own in the very last stage of the value chain but focus on cooperation with global NGOs. Most initiatives related to the basic level of the value chain, raw materials, are subject to cooperation, such as the Better Cotton Initiative and the promotion of organic cotton through Textile Exchange.

16.6 Towards shared value in global garment value chains

The variation in corporate responses to expectations for responsible action raises questions about current and future limitations for sustainable value chains. Truly sustainable value chains, particularly in the fashion industry, require more developed strategies than is the case today. Garment retailers often claim they have little power to influence factory owners and the production countries, but in many cases large corporations are potentially more powerful than governments where their production is outsourced. Countries in Asia depend on exporting, and hence they are in many cases willing to keep minimum wages low and compromise with labour conditions and environmental regulation to attract foreign garment retailers (Stigzelius and Mark-Herbert 2009; Fang *et al.* 2010). The character of the initiatives in the value chain also, to some extent, shows that the garment retailers are using their power, for example, by offering voluntarily initiated assessments of subcontractors and second-tier suppliers.

The strength of the corporate responsibility strategies among the case companies is the focus on the core problems associated with their production, which is a prerequisite for shared value (Porter and Kramer 2011). H&M, Lindex, KappAhl and MQ do not focus on, for example, climate change or waste management, which is common in other sectors, but their initiatives concern key issues in the garment industry such as human rights, chemical management and cotton production. Indeed, a challenge that still needs to be addressed is to clarify the objectives of corporate responsibility. Why is it important that corporations urge factories to comply with labour laws and to not harm the local ecosystems? Business tends to be more successful where it is clear why these issues are addressed, such as in the relationship between retailers and suppliers. The retailer runs a lower risk of being criticised by stakeholders and the factory manager will run a business where human rights and planetary boundaries are respected. In the long run such strategies will be the strategies that lead to competitive advantage.

When ethical and environmental considerations are taken in the production of garments it creates shared value (Porter and Kramer 2011). Shared value can, for example, be created when the factory worker is working under conditions that comply with international labour laws and local environmental laws, and receives a living wage. Taking a wider perspective, shared value has been created in the local community, providing job opportunities but not at the expense of the local environment. Value has also been added to the garment, produced without harming the environment and people, bought by a consumer in Sweden creating a market for ethical products.

Changes for the better have taken place in the garment industry during the last few decades, and they deserve to be recognised. Nevertheless, many issues remain to be resolved, and quite a few of these issues have ethical dimensions that imply trade-offs, focusing on some stakeholders' needs at the expense of others and dealing with a particular problem at the expense of other problems. For the garment industry to become sustainable there is a need to focus on production and on what is happening at the geographical locations where the clothes are produced. Attention also needs to be directed towards alternative materials and consumer behaviour that promotes socially and environmentally sustainable value chains.

16.7 Conclusions

The aim of this chapter was to provide a contextual understanding of garment retailers' corporate responsibility in the value chain. We have argued that a fundamental condition for garment retail initiatives is related to external expectations of accountability as motives for creating changes towards sustainable business development. H&M, Lindex, KappAhl and MQ have, to a varying degree, developed strategies and methods to deal with challenges in the upstream value chain, where raw materials are processed to garments. This is an attempt at being accountable: that is, a willingness to take responsibility for the sourcing, above and beyond the first-tier supplier that the branded goods retailer faces in its procurement process. Accountability incorporates the entire value chain including the many subcontractors for the suppliers in the value chain.

Among the range of corporate responsibility initiatives identified among the case companies in this study, we have identified a number of common denominators:

- **Codes of conduct**. Internal control, a part of a management system
- **Standards and labels**. Certification through third-party audits
- **International collaboration with NGOs**. To address issues in the value chain
- **Educational efforts**. Aimed at increasing the awareness of environmental and social issues among actors in the supply chain

It is also clear that a contextual account offers grounds for an understanding of how initiatives are tailored to each retailer's identified needs and resources. A large corporation will have more resources to become a role model, which may inspire other corporations to follow. Branded goods retailers have the greatest opportunities to influence the first-tier level because of their ability to exercise power on those actors. However, the cases also show that the garment retailers are using their position to exert pressure on other actors in the value chain, with initiatives adapted to the character of the problem and organisational resources.

Corporations that attempt to make a difference further down in the value chain may fill a void in countries with weak legal enforcement. This is where standards and corporate codes of conduct can make a difference—but the cost of assurance with legal compliance rests with the corporations. Although such initiatives may blur the boundaries between governmental and corporate responsibility, they also raise questions on the extent to which social and environmental issues can be seriously tackled if they remain a sole responsibility of corporations. Business initiatives of good practice in the value chain may open up for changes that later develop into a standard and a formal requirement that leads the way for legislation.

This chapter is concluded with a reflection on whether we should expect to recognise the findings of our study when examining the garment industry in other countries. We have argued that external pressures provide a rationale for corporations to invest in an extended responsibility in the global garment supply chain. Some of these pressures are of relevance for corporations in many countries, such as international labour agreements, or local institutional systems where the garment production takes place. Other external pressures, including consumer responses to labelling, media's portrayal of the garment industry and increased demand for external reporting by NGOs are, to a greater extent, country-specific. National pressures may also depend on the presence of a large resourceful company that takes a lead. Hence, despite a similar industry structure, in which corporations in the West sell textiles produced in low-income countries, we can expect that today's commonplace corporate responsibility initiatives in the garment industry are influenced by both international and national factors.

Conservative economic perspectives will argue that it is not in the retailer's interest to be accountable in a value chain perspective. From a sustainability perspective it would be argued that it is a moral obligation to continue the path embracing the obligations of extended value chain responsibility. These two seemingly contrasting perspectives may approach each other when considering shared value as a potential corporate objective. Interests may be redefined, as corporations further explore the potential that lies in extending their responsibility in the value chain.

References

Ählström, J., and N. Egels-Zandén (2008) 'The Process of Defining Corporate Responsibility: A Study of Swedish Garment Retailers' Responsibility', *Business Strategy and the Environment* 17: 230-44.

Ander, G. (2010) *Bomull: En solkig historia* (Stockholm, Sweden: Ordfront).

Arvidsson, S. (2010) 'Communication of Corporate Social Responsibility: A Study of the Views of Management Teams in Large Companies', *Journal of Business Ethics* 96.3: 339-54.

Bremer, J., and J. Udovich (2001) 'Alternative Approaches to Supply Chain Compliance Monitoring', *Journal of Fashion Marketing and Management* 5.4: 333-52.

Carlsson, A., K. Hemström, P. Edborg, Å. Stenmarck and L. Sörme (2011) *Kartläggning av mängder och flöden av textilavfall* (SMED Rapport Nr 46 2011; Norrköping, Sweden: Swedish Meteorological and Hydrological Institute).

Carroll, A.B. (1991) 'The Pyramid of Corporate Social Responsibility: Towards the Moral Management of Organizational Stakeholders', *Business Horizons* 34.4: 39-48.

Dobers, P. (ed.) (2010) *Corporate Social Responsibility: Challenges and Practices* (Stockholm, Sweden: Santérus Academic Press).

Eisenhardt, K. (1989) 'Building Theories from Case Study Research'. *The Academy of Management Review* 14.4: 532-50.

Engwall, M. (2008) *Den blinda klädimporten. Miljöeffekter från produktionen av kläder som importeras till Sverige* (Stockholm, Sweden: Swedwatch).

Epstein, M.J. (2008) *Making Sustainability Work: Best Practices in Managing and Measuring Corporate Social, Environmental and Economic Impacts* (Sheffield, UK: Greenleaf Publishing).

Fairtrade International (2011) *Globescan Konsumentundersökning 2011* (Stockholm: Fairtrade Sverige, www.fairtrade-scratch.spacedout.se/wp-content/uploads/2012/07/globescan. pdf, accessed 2 October 2012).

Fang, T., C. Gunterberg and E. Larsson (2010) 'Sourcing in an Increasingly Expensive China: Four Swedish Cases', *Journal of Business Ethics* 97.1: 119-38.

Frostenson, M., S. Helin and J. Sandström (2011) 'Organising Corporate Responsibility Communication Through Filtration: A Study of Web Communication Patterns in Swedish Retail', *Journal of Business Ethics* 100: 31-43.

Grafström, M., P. Göthberg and K. Windell (2008) *CSR: Företagsansvar i förändring* (Malmö, Sweden: Liber AB).

Grayson, D., and A. Hodges (2004) *Corporate Social Opportunity! Seven Steps to Make Corporate Social Responsibility Work for your Business* (Sheffield, UK: Greenleaf Publishing).

Halme, M., and J. Laurila (2009) 'Philanthropy, Integration or Innovation: Exploring the Financial and Societal Outcomes of Different Types of Corporate Responsibility', *Journal of Business Ethics* 84: 325-39.

Handelns Utredningsinstitut (2010) *Guiden över detaljhandelns branscher: Branschfakta 2010* (Stockholm, Sweden: AB Handelns Utredningsinstitut).

H&M (2009) 'Style with Substance: Sustainability Report 2009', www.about.hm.com/content/ dam/hm/about/documents/en/CSR/reports/Style%20&%20Substance%20Sustainability% 20Report%202009_en.pdf, accessed 2 October 2012.

KappAhl (2008) 'Miljö och socialt ansvar', www.kappahl.com/Documents/Miljo_o_CSR/ Miljo%20och%20socialt%20ansvar%20-%20SE.pdf, accessed 1 May 2011.

Larsson, A. (2011) 'Assessment Methods for Corporate Responsibility on the Fashion Scene: A Case Study of Hennes & Mauritz, Lindex, KappAhl and MQ', IVL Swedish Environmental Institute, Report B2010, www.ivl.se/publikationer/publikationer/assessmentmethods forcorporateresponsibilityonthefashionsceneacasestudyofhennesmauritzlindexkappahl andmq.5.50a499dd132037d524e80008130.html, accessed 1 April 2012.

Laudal, T. (2010) 'An Attempt to Determine the CSR Potential of the International Clothing Business', *Journal of Business Ethics* 96.1: 63-77.

Lindex (2009) 'CSR-Rapport 2009', Lindex, www.lindex.com/Archive/pdf/CSR_Report_SE_2009.pdf, accessed 4 May 2011.

Lyon, T.P., and J.W. Maxwell (2008) 'Corporate Responsibility and Environment: A Theoretical Perspective', *Review of Environmental Economics and Policy* 2.2: 240-60.

Mamic, I. (2004) *Implementing Codes of Conduct: How Business Manage Social Performance in Global Supply Chains* (Sheffield, UK: Greenleaf Publishing).

Mendelson, N., and M.J. Polonsky (1995) 'Using Strategic Alliances to Develop Credible Green Marketing', *Journal of Consumer Marketing* 12.2: 4-18.

Miles, M.P., L.S. Munilla and J.G. Covin (2004) 'Innovation, Ethics and Entrepreneurship', *Journal of Business Ethics* 54.1: 97-101.

MQ (2009) 'Urban Passport: MQ Sustainability Report 2009/2010', www.mq.se/media/sustainability_report_eng.pdf, accessed 19 October 2012.

Pagell, M., Z. Wu and M. Wasserman (2010) 'Thinking Differently about Purchasing Portfolios: An Assessment of Sustainable Sourcing', *Journal of Supply Chain Management* 56.1: 57-73.

Porter, M.E., and M.R. Kramer (2011) 'The Competitive Advantage of Corporate Philanthropy', *Harvard Business Review* 80.12: 56-69.

Roberts, S. (2003) 'Supply Chain Specific? Understanding the Patchy Success of Ethical Sourcing Initiatives', *Journal of Business Ethics* 44: 159-70.

Rotter, J., N. Özbek and C. Mark-Herbert (2012) 'Private–Public Partnerships: Corporate Responsibility Strategy in Food Retail', *International Journal of Business Excellence* 5.1/2: 5-20.

Soth, J., C. Grasser and R. Salemo (1999) *The Impact of Cotton on Freshwater Resources and Ecosystems: A Preliminary Synthesis* (Gland, Switzerland: WWF).

Stigzelius, I., and C. Mark-Herbert (2009) 'Tailoring Corporate Responsibility to Suppliers: Managing SA8000 in Indian Garment Manufacturing', *Scandinavian Journal of Management* 25.1: 46-56.

Swedish Standards Institute (2010) *Guidance on Social Responsibility. ISO 26000:2010* (Stockholm: Swedish Standards Institute).

de Verdier, M., C. Riddselius and S. Chudy (2010) *Har modet modet? En rapport om nio klädföretagsarbete med etik och miljö i leverantörsleden* (Stockholm, Sweden: Fair Trade Center).

Visser, W., and N. Tolhurst (ed.) (2011) *The World Guide to CSR: A Country-by Country Analysis of Corporate Sustainability and Responsibility* (Sheffield, UK: Greenleaf Publishing).

Welford, R., and S. Frost (2006) 'Corporate Social Responsibility in Asian Supply Chains', *Corporate Social Responsibility and Environmental Management* 13.3: 166-76.

Windell, K. (2006) *Corporate Social Responsibility under Construction: Ideas, Translations, and Institutional Change* (doctoral thesis No.123; Uppsala, Sweden: Department of Business Studies, Uppsala University).

Wingborg, M. (2009) *Vägar till ett bättre arbetsliv. Tre svenska företags försök att skapa bättre villkor på fabriker i Iniden och Sri Lanka* (Stockholm, Sweden: Swedwatch).

Young, W., and R. Welford (2002) *Ethical Shipping* (London: Fusion Press).

Anna Larsson is an associate partner of the environmental consultancy group U&We. Her specialisation is in business management and corporate responsibility. She holds a BSc in business administration from Mälardalen University and an MSc in environmental science from the Swedish University of Agricultural Sciences.

Katarina Buhr is a researcher at IVL Swedish Environmental Research Institute and the Centre for Climate Science and Policy Research, Linköping University. Her work revolves around environmental management and policy, with particular focus on climate change. She received her PhD from Uppsala University and her MSc from the Swedish University of Agricultural Sciences, both in business administration.

Cecilia Mark-Herbert is an associate professor at the Department of Economics at the Swedish University of Agricultural Sciences. She works as a researcher and lecturer in marketing. Her specialisation is in corporate responsibility and most of her research is related to economic, environmental, social and ethical aspects of marketing management.

17

Zigzag or interlock?
The case of the Sustainable Apparel Coalition*

Kim Poldner
University of St Gallen, Switzerland

'What happens when you put executives from Walmart and Patagonia in a room? This isn't the start of a bad joke, it's how the Sustainable Apparel Coalition (in short 'coalition') was born' (Schwartz 2011). In February 2011, 30 large fashion companies launched a multi-stakeholder alliance with the aim to draft a set of sustainability indicators for use across the entire garment industry (Moore 2011). With members accounting for 60% of global sales (Zeller 2011), the initative seemed to be a groundbreaking step forward in an attempt to green textile supply chains. Especially as it was the first grass-roots collaboration coming from the corporates themselves instead of initiated by NGOs or enforced by governments. At the same time, the new platform was critically received as just another 'greenwashing initiative'. Many questioned the efficacy of quantifying and reducing negative social and environmental impact done within the boundaries of big—and thus bad per se?—business. Seen as an antithesis to a growing focus on local production and (re)valuation of resources and communities (McDermott 2011), the formation of the coalition could possibly endanger existing work done by organisations such as Textile Exchange and Made By. Greenpeace, which has been campaigning to push

* The author would like to thank Ishwari Thopte for her important contribution to the development of the study. Financial support from the Swiss National Science Foundation is gratefully acknowledged.

companies manufacturing in China to eradicate the release of toxics into rivers, said it would 'keep a close eye on how the coalition works in practice' (Cooper 2011).

Traditionally perceived as an industry not known for its transparency, a thought-provoking question could be how members seek equilibrium between their own interests and the ambitions of the coalition. Most of them have their own sustainability initiatives and one might wonder how far they go in bringing these best practices to the table of the coalition. Additionally it is interesting how members view the existence of earlier initiatives and the foresight of collaboration with these institutions. Will the coalition become a strong multi-stakeholder initiative that really furthers innovation towards more sustainable business practices (O'Connor 2011)? Or will it end up being a loosely coupled network of companies that prioritise advancement of their own brands over real industry change? In other words: will the coalition turn out to be an interlock that ties together best practices in a solid framework or will it rather be a zigzag stitch[1] that allows companies to bend the rules to their own good? After this introduction of the research question, the literature review problematises the relevant discourse around strategic alliance networks and is followed by a short explanation of the methodology and analysis and a presentation of the findings. I summarise the answer to the research question in the conclusion leaving space for discussion and reflection.

17.1 Literature review

Strategic alliances are increasingly gaining popularity in the global economy (Elmuti and Kathawala 2001). The father of modern management, Peter Drucker, states that 'the greatest change in corporate culture, and the way business is being conducted, may be the accelerating growth of relationships based not on ownership but on partnership' (Drucker 1996). This study uses the umbrella term 'strategic alliance' when referring to the different kinds of collaboration formed by companies, non-profit organisations and universities such as the Sustainable Apparel Coalition. Strategic alliance can be defined as 'a relationship between one or more organisations that—through the combination of resources, can create significant and sustainable value for everyone involved' (Steinhilber 2008: 2). Spekman *et al.* (2000: 37) further classify an alliance as a 'close, collaborative relationship with the intent of accomplishing mutually compatible goals that would be difficult for each to accomplish alone'. Thus, strategic alliances help both or all of the participating organisations to achieve mutually profitable goals by collectively using the available resources in the best of each company's interest, creating value in the process. Statistics show that more than 2,000 strategic alliances are launched worldwide each year and these partnerships are growing at a rate of 15% annually (Cools and Roos 2005). Yet, despite all the

---

1 A zigzag stitch is mostly used for stretch fabrics allowing the fabric freedom to move, while interlock is a stitch used for garments that will see a lot of tear and wear such as towels and jeans.

growth and headlines, a little more than half of the strategic alliances fail (Geringer and Hebert 1991; Mohr and Spekman 1994; Kale *et al.* 2002).

Strategic alliances include an assortment of collaborative forms and different studies analyse them based on different criteria. These include classification based on the area of collaboration (Coopers & Lybrand 1997; Elmuti and Kathawala 2001; Grant and Baden-Fuller 2004) and the level of integration in the collaboration (Robinson and Clarke-Hill 1994; Gomes-Casseres 2003; Johnson *et al.* 2005). According to Grant and Baden-Fuller (2004), the activities covered in an alliance range from outsourcing agreements, supplier–buyer partnerships, joint research projects, technical collaboration and shared new product development, to common distribution agreements, shared manufacturing arrangements, cross-selling arrangements and franchising. These activities enable organisations to develop competitive advantage by supplementing the skills and competence of its partners to improve the performance of its value chain (Spekman *et al.* 2000). Nevertheless, resource dependency theory (Pfeffer and Salancik 1978) illustrates that a majority of organisations are not capable of delivering the resources required to build competitive advantage by themselves. On the other hand, Varadarajan and Cunningham (1995: 287) identify alliance strategy as a mechanism of change, where firms 'make a conscious attempt to influence their environment through their exchange and inter-firm relationships'.

The Sustainable Apparel Coalition can be perceived as an example of an 'alliance group' or 'alliance network' which is a specific type of strategic alliance. Casseres (2002) describes these 'alliance networks' as companies linked together for a common purpose. This form of alliance has evolved from the traditional two-company group to a dynamic multi-company network. It is referred to in different ways—networks, clusters, constellations or virtual corporations—and consists of companies joined together in a larger overarching relationship. The individual companies in any group may differ in their size and product offerings, but they fulfil specific roles within their group. In addition, the companies may be individually linked to one another through various kinds of alliances, ranging from the formality of an equity joint venture to the informality of a loose collaboration. The idea of network alliances arose for two main reasons: 1) influence of the global economy; and 2) growing complexity of products, services and their design, production and delivery. Several studies on alliance networks have explored how the structure and partner substitutability (Bae and Gargiulo 2004) or diversity of an alliance (Goerzen and Beamish 2005) affect the economic performance of the individual firms. A more recent study examined the influence of the structure and composition of a firm's alliance network on the creation of novel knowledge, meaning knowledge non-inherent in the company (Phelps 2010). Some of these studies have looked into the density of the alliances pointing to the connectedness of the different members and the intensity of their interactions (Goerzen and Beamish 2005). Intensity is understood as the level of engagement of the coalition members in the work of the coalition. To my knowledge, no research on strategic alliance groups or networks has examined how the *density* of the collaboration affects competitiveness of the alliance itself—not of the individual members. I chose the case of the Sustainable Apparel Coalition as the activities of this initiative are comparable to the work done by other organisations that strive for the same goals. As such I aim to address this gap in the literature.

17.2 Methodology and analysis

Triangulation of methods safeguards credibility (Flick 2006)[2] of the findings thus this chapter draws on a variety of qualitative sources. It is grounded in a longitudinal research project of the ethical fashion industry that started in 2008. During this time, the author has had numerous formal and informal conversations with representatives of companies that are now coalition members as well as with non-profit experts. This has advanced a broad understanding of the context in which the coalition was spawned. For this chapter, semi-structured interviews with a selection of members have been undertaken thereby focusing on the involvement of these actors with the coalition. To get a more general perspective of the coalition, the author also interviewed experts from the non-profit sector who are closely involved with activities related to developing a more sustainable apparel industry. Companies ranged from large fashion retailers in Western countries to companies that work at farm, fabric mill and manufacturing level in developing countries. This enabled the researcher to get a broad impression of the coalition (Eisenhardt 1989), which was chosen to be approached as a single case study (Yin 2003). All interviews were done with the companies' representatives—often the CEO or CSR manager—and took place over the phone or Skype for a duration of 45 to 60 minutes. In addition, websites of the companies and organisations, as well as auxiliary web-sources such as blogs, press releases and articles, have been examined. The interviews were transcribed and analysed with the research question as a guiding thread. The patterns that surfaced from that qualitative data were verified with the respondents to secure credibility. To preserve dependability, quotations from the research informants have been cited (anonymously) and reviews from the editors have been incorporated into the manuscript.

17.3 Exploring the field

The past decade has seen a surge in initiatives that support the development of more sustainable textile supply chains. The coalition is thus operating in a crowded domain of organisations and programmes aiming for similar goals. Table 17.1 gives a non-comprehensive overview of some of the organisations whose work could possibly be jeopardised by the activities of the coalition.

---

2 I have applied the four alternative quality criteria developed by Lincoln and Guba (1985) and fleshed out by Flick (2006).

Table 17.1 **Overview of organisations/programmes that provide services similar to activities of the Sustainable Apparel Coalition**

Source: based on the review of compliance programmes in Gertsakis and Neil 2011

Organisation	Country of origin	Intervention approach	Emphasis on consumer/ industry	Industry focus
Sustainable Apparel Coalition (SAC)	USA	Business engagements + tools and projects	Industry (consumer)	Apparel supply chains
Fair Wear Foundation (FWF)	Netherlands	Code of conduct	Industry	Apparel cut make trim
Fair Labor Association (FLA)	USA	Code of conduct	Industry	Textile manufacturer and apparel cut make trim and other goods
Textile, Clothing, Footwear & Associated Industries Award	Australia	Government legislation	Industry	TCF manufacturing
Nordic Initiative Clean and Ethical (NICE)	Scandinavian countries	Business support and engagement + tools and projects	Industry and consumer	Apparel supply chains
DFID	UK	Government funding programme	Industry	Apparel cut make trim
Eco Index	USA	Assessment tool	Industry	Apparel supply chain
Defra's Sustainable Clothing Action Plan	UK	Government programme	Industry	Apparel supply chain
Bluesign	Switzerland	Business tools	Industry	Textile supply chain
Ethical Clothing Australia	Australia	Company accreditation	Consumer	TCF manufacturing

Organisation	Country of origin	Intervention approach	Emphasis on consumer/ industry	Industry focus
Global Organic Textile Standard (GOTS)	USA, Japan, UK, Germany	Product certification	Consumer	TCF supply chain
Made-By	Netherlands	Product certification	Consumer	TCF supply chain
Worldwide Responsible Accredited Production (WRAP)	USA	Product certification	Consumer	General manufacturing (apparel cut make trim focused)
Oeko-Tex 100, 1000, and 100+ standards	Austria, Germany, Switzerland	Product certification	Consumer	Textile manufacture and apparel cut make trim

TCF: textile, clothing, footwear

From the 44 programmes reviewed in this study, I have only selected those initiatives that work at an industry and/or consumer level focusing on the apparel/textile industry.

The overview shows the variety of organisations: from governmental bodies to commercial start-ups. Three of the initiatives are government programmes that operate on a national scale in the UK and Australia. NICE is founded by a former fashion editor together with representatives from Nordic fashion schools and fashion weeks. Its website and events aim to inform and inspire industry professionals and consumers, but it does not provide labelling or have industry members like the coalition does. The two Dutch initiatives are both member organisations that up to now have attracted mainly smaller brands such as Switcher (FWF) and G-Star (Made-By). Whereas Fair Wear Foundation concentrates on improving labour conditions in the garment industry, Made By aims to address both social and environmental concerns. FWF is a verification initiative that monitors the progress its members make in complying with the eight labour standards that form the core of the Code of Labour Practices. Made By offers tools such as a scorecard, a track and trace system and a blue button label that enable members to communicate their dedication to sustainability to the consumer. Ethical Clothing Australia[3] assists the local fashion industry to ensure Australian workers receive fair wages and decent conditions and thus has a very local focus compared with the coalition's global reach. Even though WRAP[4] and the Fair Labor Association (FLA) include other industries, their focus is on ethical and labour conditions in the apparel industry. With headquarters in Switzerland, Bluesign serves the need to advance the sustainability practices of global players such as Nordstrom and Patagonia, two companies that are also coalition members. GOTS (Global Organic Textile Standard) and Oeko-Tex are worldwide recognised product certification labels that show consumers which fabrics are either organic or free of harmful substances or both. As we will learn, the Eco Index has already been integrated in the development of the coalition's own index.

In addition to these 13 initiatives, another two programmes need to be mentioned. Textile Exchange (former Organic Exchange) is a global membership organisation that serves as an expertise centre for sustainable textiles. Celebrating its tenth birthday in 2012, the organisation has evolved from creating knowledge on mainly organic cotton to covering all kinds of sustainable fibre. Although some interviewees perceive this as a loss, others stress the advantages of this new approach. The strength of the organisation is bringing together many different actors from the supply chain: during its conference in September 2011 many side discussions between different actors took place parallel to the main programme. The Global Social Compliance Programme is an industry consortium that collaborates on improving supply chains of global buying companies. Although not focused solely on textile supply chains, the GSCP is another important player and several of its affiliates (for example Adidas and C&A) are also members of the coalition.

3 www.ethicalclothingaustralia.org.au/home/home, accessed 13 April 2012.
4 Worldwide Responsible Accredited Production, www.wrapapparel.org, accessed 13 April 2012.

17.4 Stitching sustainable change?

This section explores the structure of the coalition and describes its main project after which I turn to the most relevant themes that emerged from the data. As this chapter presents only a snapshot in time, it is important to mention the theoretical process approach that has been adopted, which is embodied in the titles of the different sections[5] and the way the story is narrated.

17.4.1 Fabricating the coalition

Golden *et al.* (2011) argue that industry consortia are the main drivers behind green product design and sustainable value chains. After the launch of the Global Social Compliance Programme (in 2006) and the Sustainability Consortium (in 2009), the Sustainable Apparel Coalition was the next alliance group that was founded by some of the global corporate giants. Just like the other consortia, it came into being on the basis of shared beliefs and a common vision. Coalition members are convinced they cannot solve social and environmental challenges in textile supply chains on their own, but that they need to join forces to avoid more unnecessary harm in the future. They also acknowledge that current challenges are both a business imperative and an opportunity. Building on each other's strengths and knowledge—instead of every company having to (re)invent the wheel by itself—can help to free technical, financial and knowledge resources that can take innovation to a new level (Sustainable Apparel Coalition 2011). During the first year of its existence, the coalition has focused on a number of key activities. After bringing together the 30 founding circle members, they have divided into working groups and sub-groups according to interest and expertise such as a social working group and a communication group. Each working group regularly meets through webinars, while the entire coalition comes together four times per year, up to now in cities such as Seattle and Stockholm. The communication group launched the coalition while the governance group has been developing a model for the new organisation. As a concrete result, the coalition hired an executive director in late 2011 who has quickly built an entire team operating from San Francisco. The systems working group has been working on mapping out the software needs to manage the future index. Since the beginning of 2012, the coalition has opened membership to other participants.

17.4.2 Developing an index

The sustainable apparel index is the first major project initiated by the coalition. Designed as a common, industry-wide tool for measuring environmental and social performance, the index consists of an assessment model that is applied on

---

5 See for example Weick 1995, which argues for the use of verbs instead of nouns when studying organisations.

three different levels: brand level, supplier level and product level. It is built on the Eco Index framework of the Outdoor Industry Association and the Apparel Environmental Design tool developed by Nike. While these earlier indices have been almost fully integrated into the coalition index, the working group has decided to add the brand level because,

> we won't have any sustainable products if we don't have the corresponding strong progress at brand level. So it really all fits together (CSR manager, global sports brand).

The first problem that may arise from building on these two indices is that they are focused on the outdoor/ sports industry, which might be difficult to adapt to other sectors such as high fashion or footwear. Second, these indices have been developed with criteria that have been highly criticised, such as the acceptance of certain chemicals by one certification body that were absolutely prohibited by another institution. Although the index is not just piloted by the members, but also by other companies and is reviewed by an external panel of experts, the credibility of its measurements remains questionable. While version 1 of the index (V1.0) was launched in July 2012 as the Higg Index,

> we that are involved in the version 2, we're already rolling up our sleeves and learning everything we can about metrics and lifecycles (Head of Sustainability, global sports brand).

The ambition of the coalition is to include social and labour indicators and develop a footwear and consumer index as well, although this will take a couple of years. According to some interviewees the development of an index should be an academic endeavour instead of taking time away from actually implementing the criteria.

17.4.3 Getting involved

The way most companies have become involved with the coalition is by being asked by other stakeholders to get on board. After Patagonia and Walmart had successfully collaborated on a sustainability assessment tool, they decided to start working on a larger index for the industry. In autumn 2009, they invited the CEOs of 12 companies to help found the coalition and soon thereafter they started approaching other big players to join (Schwartz 2011), a call that was answered with widespread enthusiasm.

> It was something that we thought 'Wow this makes a lot of sense for us', since it is where we are in our journey as well (CSR manager, global retailer).

Soon the big brands and retailers realised they had to involve companies that were working in other parts of the supply chain. For these companies, it was a pleasant eye-opener to be invited.

> A few years ago they wondered why would they talk with us, but now they want to know what we're doing and maybe it is also to secure supply of fabrics, which will be more important in the future (Head of marketing, manufacturing company).

At the end of 2011, the founding circle consisted of stakeholders representing different parts of the supply chain ranging from multinational stakeholders to large suppliers and manufacturers while an NGO and several universities support the coalition work on a content level. Interestingly, many of the founding members already had engagements with other initiatives. Nike was for example one of the first Textile Exchange Members, Adidas is also an affiliate of the FLA and Nordstrom and Patagonia are both accredited by Bluesign.

> I remember when I was still working for…and we became a member of… and all those big guys were there… I soon found out they also did not know what they were doing (former CSR manager of a fashion brand and currently CSR consultant).

It appears that companies are searching for different avenues to improve their supply chains. Some outsource research to universities while others hire communication specialists. Some become a member of several organisations in order to gain knowledge in different areas and others attend large conferences to exchange expertise. Whereas the annual membership fee was very high at the outset, it has now been adapted to the sales volume of the company. This has enabled smaller brands to get on board that are likely to contribute just as much in terms of verve and expertise. Nevertheless, the strength of the coalition is that it encompasses so many huge players in the textile industry, some of which have been under fire for their unsustainable practices. The changes they can make, because of their size, *could* have far-ranging ripple effects (McDermott 2011).

17.4.4 Affecting processes

Even though the coalition is still in its infancy, company representatives stress the impact it has already had on their companies. Such impacts range from the establishment of a sustainability unit with three employees servicing well over 100 employees to hiring life-cycle specialists that bring new knowledge to the organisation. As up to now most of the work has been backstage, mainly consisting of developing the V1.0, the companies stress the internal effects of their involvement with the coalition. The testing and piloting of the index has sharpened companies' awareness regarding which aspects of their operation deserve more attention.

> After joining the coalition we have started a painstaking process of evaluating our utilities, all the way down to the machine level (CEO, global manufacturer).

Distinctive to the coalition is that it engages not solely one company representative, but a variety of employees.

> Because there are a lot of working groups, it has been involving a lot of
> colleagues… There starts to be consensus on that it makes a lot of sense
> to have this life-cycle focus (CSR manager, global retailer).

Aside from empowering colleagues, it also helps to push decision-makers to put
sustainability more prominently on the agenda.

> The formation of the coalition shows our board that sustainability is not
> disappearing anymore, but that it will play a big role in our work in the
> future (Head of marketing, manufacturing company).

A heightened awareness of colleagues about the importance of sustainability has
an impact in many ways.

> For us it was a confirmation that we're on the right track, we did the right
> things in the past. It also means not to stop with our activities: while the
> industry is picking up on more sustainable practices, we need to keep on
> developing our projects (Head of marketing, manufacturing company).

This can be interpreted as follows: member companies value their involvement
with the coalition as being 'ahead of the game', which might lead to a competitive advantage. While company representatives were overall positive about the
effects of their engagement in the coalition, other interviewees were more critical.
Some said that it is not realistic to apply the LCA (life-cycle assessment) approach
to fashion products that are constantly changing: by the time one assessment has
been done, a new product needs to be launched to satisfy the savvy consumer. The
strong focus on LCA also takes resources away from the companies and slows them
down, especially when companies take on an attitude of 'let's wait until the coalition has done the work'. After one year of existence, the strategy and the impact
of the coalition had not become really visible at all for outsiders. Some argue that
this quiet beginning—the index was only made public in January 2012—'belies the
impact it is poised to bring to the industry' (Ruvo 2012).

17.4.5 Learning by doing

During its first year the coalition has been managed by a sustainability consultancy
that organised the quarterly meetings and coordinated the many online discussions.
They have set the standard for systemising processes, something that is essential
with such a large group of stakeholders that are often competing with each other.

> The coalition doesn't work too long on a topic, they try to get a decision,
> knowing that it might be only an 80-20 solution. But this way they can
> save time and then afterwards there is always time to improve and do
> things better. But they take the decision altogether and then go to the next
> step (Head of marketing, manufacturing company).

Some express the true excitement they derive from their work as pioneers in
sustainability, both as individual companies as well as being a part of the multi-
stakeholder initiative.

> Somehow it is a bit like being Columbus or Vasco da Gama to find out the maps of good products and life-cycles... Traditional life-cycle methodologies just don't do the trick anymore (CSR manager, global retailer).

Although our non-profit experts share the excitement and see advantages in the forming of the coalition, they also doubt its effectiveness.

> The LCA discussions are very complicated and show large differences between the European and the American perspectives... My impression is that they have not come up with anything new yet (sustainable textiles expert).

The pragmatic governance structure encourages members to contribute their knowledge on specific issues. While some working groups were defined from the start, others have come into being over time as a response to a need to specialise on certain topics. All members have pledged to share best practices in order to improve supply chain performance industry-wide, but the question is how far they go in this endeavour. Sports retailers such as Puma, Adidas and Nike are sitting together, but naturally they want to develop their own products to be different from their competitors.

> Innovation has to be on a basic level where everybody can benefit from. For example the detox program which they agree to work on to avoid chemicals which are toxic. This could be a project that is of use for the whole industry (sustainable textiles expert).

This could be interpreted as follows: there is only a limited transparency, even though it is already looking much better than it ever was before, something that is acknowledged by the non-profit interviewees.

17.4.6 Becoming comparables?

The other open issue is how members deal with other players in the market. These players are often member-based organisations as well that are dependent on payment from the same companies that have now initiated the coalition. The fear some interviewees have is that some of the members will cut their budget for such earlier engagements leading to a loss of resources for the more 'neutral' players in the field. The reasoning of coalition members is that other initiatives have always only managed to cover certain parts of the supply chain, which made it very difficult to find the right organisation that could help on all levels.

> The coalition has a holistic approach, they cover everything and of course they focus more on their own needs, from the brand and retail perspective (Head of marketing, manufacturing company).

According to some interviewees this holistic approach is an interesting way to see it...

> ...because on the other hand they say 'we can't work without synthetic
> fibres, as we are dependent on oil' so the only option to make it look green
> is to recycle it from for example plastic bottles, but they don't think about
> how to recycle it further. To me this is greenwashing (sustainable textiles
> expert).

In addition the companies had to certify all their operations and had to pay for
every bit of certification. As such it is no surprise that the coalition has come into
being, while at the same time interviewees view the different initiatives as being
very complementary. Over the years a lot of knowledge has built up in such organisations and they can be very helpful on the content side, for example when it
comes to sourcing raw material or signalling fabric trends. The question remains
how the coalition will deal with competition. Will companies really share their best
practices in a border-crossing manner thereby moving from being competitors to
realising that they are all in the same boat?

> There is a lot of openness and sharing and the atmosphere has been good
> which I think has been helpful to be as fast as it has been (CSR manager,
> global retailer).

And will the coalition itself evolve into becoming comparable with, or equal to,
the earlier initiatives instead of a possible threat? These queries continue to exist
and necessitate at least another three years of operation before a proper judgement
can be made.

17.4.7 Fashioning the future

All members are convinced that sustainability will become mainstream in the
future, but they allude to different catalysts for that change. Ten years down the
line there will be a much larger group of people that wants to consume more, better
and more fashionable clothes. At the same time it is expected that environmental
consciousness that many consider a luxury good, will come to the fore.

> Sustainability is an issue of growing importance, it will be much more part
> of the DNA of the fashion industry, especially when the customer asks for
> it. Since fashion is in the end a reflection of society (CSR manager, global
> retailer).

There are going to be a lot of resource challenges in trying to fulfil that demand
and sustainability is expected to be more on people's minds than it has in the decades gone by. The coalition's goal is that the sustainable apparel index will become
the key measurement tool to evaluate products and it will be used industry-wide.

> It [the index] will lead to a consumer label so finally on the package of a
> T-shirt, like with food, you will have written the CO_2 emissions, the water
> emissions etc. so that you can compare products regarding their environ-
> mental impacts (head of marketing, manufacturing company).

Non-profit experts are not convinced that the index will become the main measurement tool and are of the opinion that companies will still have to comply with standards that are already out there such as GOTS. At the moment the majority of the members are headquartered in the Western world thereby not taking pressing issues in developing countries into account such as lack of power supply and polluted groundwater. The coalition's focal point is developing cost-saving technologies that improve sustainability: when fewer resources such as water, energy and material are being used, a product should become cheaper. At the same time, externalities such as clean air are not included in prices and people expect this will change in the future.

> Products will become more expensive, as somebody has to pay for it. At the moment nobody wants to pay for it, but at one point the industry has to decide how to share the costs (CEO, global manufacturer).

Even though the holistic 'systems' approach aims to bundle the fortes of the different members and move the industry towards a green future, the lack of a clear strategy makes the work of the coalition less credible than would be wished for.

17.5 Conclusion

This chapter has aspired to answer how the competitive impact of alliance networks is affected by the density of the alliances between the network's partners. First of all we need to evaluate whether the members of the sustainable apparel coalition have really been able 'to share insights and drive innovation in managing the environmental and social impacts of their products' (O'Connor 2011). The index has been developed expanding on and integrating two earlier measurement tools built by individual companies, which can be viewed as a standard for other members to be just as transparent in sharing their knowledge. The pledge to share best practice information appears not to be just a matter of rhetoric. People are impressed with the speed of achieving coalition objectives, the way work gets done and the atmosphere in which all of that takes place. Innovation mainly comes to the fore through the holistic approach of the coalition that aims to integrate all aspects of the supply chain. This has not only become visible in the way the founding circle has been formed, inviting companies that were not part of the conversation before, but also in how the index evaluates on a product, facility but also brand level. This has never been done before in a similar way, by such a group of heavyweights. Despite criticism from non-profit interviewees, the coalition seems to bring something new to the field, especially with regard to the density of their interactions.

It is exactly this density that will decrease the competitive impact on the work of like-minded initiatives. Work done by other organisations is acknowledged, just as is the realisation that the coalition could become a serious competitor for some of them. For now the interviewees view the activities of these stakeholders as complementary and they point to the conversations that have already taken place on a content level. We have seen that most companies are already involved in other initiatives whether through accreditation, membership or as an affiliate. The data shows that they 'shop around' in search of knowledge on how to green their supply chains. So far it appears that not one organisation has been able to give comprehensive answers to the many complicated questions that arise when evaluating processes. This leads us to the counterintuitive hypothesis that the more closely coalition members work together on projects such as the development of an index, the more knowledge they will be able to bring into the prevailing initiatives. Instead of pushing these initiatives out of the market, they will benefit from the work that is being done within the coalition. Thus the competitive impact of the coalition as an alliance network will *decrease* with the density of alliances between the network's partners. In précis, it looks like the coalition is on its way to becoming a strong interlock that can really drive change in the industry. If the current trust, positive energy and constructive peer-monitoring attitude persist, the coalition might really embody its name and sustain[6] a more sustainable apparel industry.

17.6 Discussion and reflection

Weaknesses of this study are that only a limited number of interviews have been undertaken thus showcasing the views of a select number of coalition members and outside experts. In addition to the qualitative data collection methods it would have been good to conduct a survey to be able to back up the findings with quantitative numbers. This is a clear suggestion for future research projects. My own role as a researcher-practitioner has had a significant impact on the interpretation of the data (Ybema *et al.* 2009). First of all it might have endangered confirmability (Flick 2006) as I was not a neutral outsider to the field of study and thus have most probably integrated biased assumptions. On the other hand, my data—audio-recorded interviews, transcriptions and web-sources—is available for any third party to do a neutrality check. Second, my optimistic nature has possibly influenced my perception of the coalition as an organisation that can really make a difference. On the other hand, I have been critical about the numerous initiatives that have sprung up since my involvement in the field back in 2005, which might have sharpened my senses during this study. It has been confusing to be confronted with so many different non-profit projects aimed at certification and raising awareness. Learning more about the apparel coalition has given me new hope that the fashion industry is really going through a major transformation thereby becoming the frontrunner as predicted by McDonough and Braungart (2002): 'Just like the first industrial revolution started in the fashion industry, so will the second that leads us to sustainability'.

---

6 Here I refer to the meaning of the verb sustain as in 'support' instead of 'maintain'.

References

Bae, J., and M. Gargiulo (2004) 'Partner Substitutability, Alliance Network Structure and Firm Profitability in the Telecommunications Industry', *Academy of Management Journal* 47.6: 843-59.

Casseres, B. (2002) 'Group vs Group: How Alliance Networks Compete', in *Harvard Business Review on Strategic Alliances* (Boston, MA: Harvard Business School).

Cools, K., and A. Roos (2005) *The Role of Alliances in Corporate Strategy* (Boston, MA: BCG).

Cooper, B. (2011) 'The Sustainable Apparel Coalition's Collective Efforts', Just-Style Management Briefing, www.just-style.com/management-briefing/the-sustainable-apparel-coalitions-collective-efforts_id111816.aspx, accessed 11 January 2012.

Coopers & Lybrand (1997) 'Strategic Alliances', Coopers & Lybrand Trendsetter Barometer, www.barometersurveys.com/vwAllNewsByDocID/EDF934133F547E8D85256BA1007A F1AF/index.html, accessed 19 October 2012.

Drucker, P. (1996) 'Non Profit Prophet', www.allianceanalyst.com, accessed 12 April 2012.

Eisenhardt, K. (1989) 'Building Theories from Cases', *Academy of Management Review* 14.4: 532-50.

Elmuti, D., and Y. Kathawala (2001) 'An Overview of Strategic Alliances', *Management Decision* 39.3: 205-17.

Flick, U. (2006) *An Introduction to Qualitative Research* (London: Sage).

Geringer, J., and L. Hebert (1991) 'Measuring Performance of International Joint Ventures', *Journal of International Business Studies* 22.2: 249-63.

Gertsakis, J., and C. Neil (2011) *The Feasibility of a Voluntary Ethical Quality Mark for the Australian Textile, Clothing and Footwear Industries* (Fitzroy, Victoria: Ethical Clothing Australia).

Goerzen, A., and P. Beamish (2005) 'The Effect of Alliance Network Diversity on Multinational Enterprise Performance', *Strategic Management Journal* 26: 333-54.

Golden, J., V. Subramanian and J. Zimmerman (2011) 'Sustainability and Commerce Trends', *Journal of Industrial Ecology* 15: 821-24.

Gomes-Casseres, B. (2003) 'Competitive Advantage in Alliance Constellations', *Strategic Organization* 1.3: 327-35.

Grant, R., and C. Baden-Fuller (2004) 'A Knowledge Accessing Theory of Strategic Alliances', *Journal of Management Studies* 41.1: 61-84.

Johnson, G., K. Scholes and R. Whittington (2005) *Exploring Corporate Strategy* (Harlow, UK: Financial Times Prentice Hall, 7th edn).

Kale, P., J. Dyer and H. Singh (2002) 'Alliance Capability, Stock Market Response, and Long-Term Alliance Success: The Role of the Alliance Function', *Strategic Management Journal* 23.8: 747-67.

Lincoln, Y., and E. Guba (1985) *Naturalistic Inquiry* (London: Sage).

McDermott, M. (2011) 'Sustainable Apparel Coalition Plans Industry-Wide Eco-Index', Treehugger, www.treehugger.com/style/sustainable-apparel-coalition-plans-industry-wide-eco-index.html, accessed 11 January 2012.

McDonough, W., and M. Braungart (2002) *Cradle to Cradle: Remaking the Way We Make Things* (New York: North Point Press).

Mohr, J., and R. Spekman (1994) 'Characteristics of Partnership Success: Partnership Attributes, Communication Behavior, and Conflict Resolution Techniques', *Strategic Management Journal* 15.2: 135-52.

Moore, B. (2011) 'Partnerships: The Sustainable Apparel Coalition', Ethical Fashion Forum, www.source.ethicalfashionforum.com/article/partnerships-the-sustainable-apparel-coalition, accessed 11 January 2012.

O'Connor, M.C. (2011) 'Major Clothing Lines Launch Sustainable Apparel Coalition', Earth Island, www.earthisland.org/journal/index.php/elist/eListRead/sustainable_apparel_coalition_launches_beta_version_of_apparel_index, accessed 11 January 2012.

Pfeffer, J., and G.R. Salancik (1978) *The External Control of Organizations: A Resource Dependence Perspective* (New York: Harper & Row).

Phelps, C. (2010) 'A Longitudinal Study of the Influence of Alliance Network Structure and Composition on Firm Exploratory Innovation', *Academy of Management Journal* 53.4: 890-913.

Robinson, T., and C. Clarke-Hill (1994) 'Competitive Advantage through Strategic Retailing Alliances: A European Perspective', paper presented at the *Recent Advances in Retailing and Service Science Conference*, Alberta, Canada, May 1994.

Ruvo, C. (2012) 'Sense and Sustainability', Wearables, www.wearables-digital.com/publication/frame.php?i=97014&p=56, accessed 16 April 2012.

Schwartz, A. (2011) 'Patagonia, Adidas, Walmart Team Up on Sustainable Apparel Coalition', Fast Company, www.fastcompany.com/1731780/patagonia-hm-walmart-team-up-on-a-sustainable-apparel-index, accessed 11 January 2012.

Spekman, R., L.A. Isabella and T.C. MacAvoy (2000) *Alliance Competence: Maximizing the Value of Your Partnerships* (New York: Wiley).

Steinhilber, S. (2008) *Strategic Alliances: Three Ways to Make Them Work* (Boston, MA: Harvard Business Press).

Sustainable Apparel Coalition (2011) 'About Us', www.apparelcoalition.org/about-us, accessed 21 January 2011.

Varadarajan, P., and M. Cunningham (1995) 'Strategic Alliances: A Synthesis of Conceptual Foundations', *Journal of the Academy of Marketing Science* 23.4: 282-96.

Weick, K. (1995) *Sensemaking in Organizations* (Thousand Oaks, CA: Sage).

Ybema, S., D. Yanow, H. Wels and F. Kamsteeg (2009) *Organizational Ethnography: Studying the Complexities of Everyday Life* (London: Sage).

Yin, R. (2003) *Case Study Research: Design and Methods* (Newbury Park, CA: Sage).

Zeller, T. (2011) 'Clothes Makers Join to Set "Green Score"', New York Times, www.nytimes.com/2011/03/01/business/01apparel.html, accessed 11 January 2012.

Kim Poldner is a doctoral researcher at the University of St Gallen, Switzerland, and founder of the website Eco Fashion World. Her research interests include entre- and intra-preneurship in sustainable fashion, the tension between fashion, organisation and self-design and the use of narrative methodologies and video-ethnography in doing research.

18

Garments without guilt?

A case study of sustainable garment sourcing in Sri Lanka

Patsy Perry

George Davies Centre for Retail Excellence, Heriot-Watt University, UK

Any discussion of sustainable production in the garment and textile industry must also consider how the process of turning raw materials into finished garments impacts on labour conditions in supplier facilities. A dynamic, challenging global industry, the high-street fashion industry is characterised by complex global sourcing networks and faces simultaneous pressure for short lead times and low costs (Bruce *et al.* 2004; Masson *et al.* 2007). As a high-profile consumer industry, the fashion sector has become a focal point for the debate on the socioeconomic impact of the global shift of garment production to lower labour-cost countries (New 1997; Maitland 1997; Adams 2002), in terms of sweatshops, child labour and worker exploitation (Smestad 2010). Therefore, in order to address sustainability in the garment sector, there is a need to understand how to safeguard the notion of ethics despite the existence of commercial pressures which conflict with the notion of corporate social responsibility (CSR). The concept of CSR contributes to sustainable development in the fashion industry by promoting social goals alongside environmental goals and economic growth.

This chapter reports on a case study of Sri Lankan export garment manufacturers, in order to understand how suppliers in one of the world's top garment sourcing locations have succeeded in creating a global reputation for ethical garment manufacture alongside developing long-term sourcing relationships with key global fashion retailers and brands, despite the existence of commercial pressures.

The chapter is structured as follows: a literature review provides an overview of the issues in fashion supply chains which jeopardise CSR implementation at factory level. The findings of the case study are then presented and conclusions are made on how CSR is supported in the Sri Lankan context. Despite the challenging competitive context of the fashion industry, there is potential to address CSR issues as well as commercial demands by adopting supply chain management principles which promote trust, commitment and long-term mutual benefits for both supply chain partners. Full package suppliers that provided differentiated value-added services to retail customers had more opportunities to implement CSR initiatives than contract manufacturers.

18.1 CSR issues in the fashion supply chain

In the fashion supply chain, the social issues of CSR concern worker welfare and can be broken down into three main areas of wages, working hours and working conditions (Sethi 2003). Fashion retailers have been accused of chasing cheap labour across the globe as well as:

> failing to pay their workers a living wage, using child labour, turning a blind eye to abuses of human rights, being complicit with repressive regimes in denying workers the right to join unions and failing to enforce minimum labour standards in the workplace (Maitland 1997: 593).

Poor CSR practices in subcontractor facilities can result in bad publicity, consumer boycotts and loss of retail brand value in the home market, while industrial action at subcontractor facilities and supplier relationship problems disrupt the smooth flow of product through the supply network and increase supply chain risk (Waters 2007). Companies are not only held responsible for social practices within their own premises, but increasingly for the social performance of their suppliers, and ultimately for the entire supply chain (Wong and Taylor 2000; Andersen and Skøtt-Larsen 2009). Developments in telecommunications and Internet technology have increased awareness of ethical issues in fashion supply chains, and there is evidence of emerging consumer demand for low-cost fashionable clothing sourced through ethical supply chains (Adams 2002; Frenkel and Scott 2002; Shaw *et al.* 2006, 2007; Gilbert 2006).

There can be clear benefits for companies to implement CSR initiatives. In addition to delivering societal benefits, CSR initiatives can also serve the firm's strategic commercial interest (Porter and Kramer 2006; Welford and Frost 2006) through 'image and reputation management, the manipulation of stakeholders and the integration of the organisation into its host community' (Hemingway and Maclagan 2004: 41), as well as the development of 'long-term loyalty, legitimacy, trust or brand equity that reinforce the corporation's other strategic objectives' (Godfrey and Hatch 2007: 88). CSR thus represents the business response to minimising the negative societal impact of global business operations.

However, the very nature of the fashion supply chain with its pressure on cost and lead time compromises CSR implementation at factory level. In recent times, retailers have developed ethical sourcing policies and codes of conduct to address issues of worker exploitation in supplier factories; however, the effectiveness of these may be debated as the media continue to report on sweatshop scandals: in 2011, Zara faced negative media publicity after inhumane working conditions were discovered in a subcontractor facility in Brazil (BBC News 2011); while in 2010, Gap, Next and Marks & Spencer faced similar accusations concerning their operations in India (Chamberlain 2010).

18.2 Fashion supply chain characteristics

The clothing sector faces continual downward price pressure (Masson *et al.* 2007), with long-term deflation experienced in the UK garment market year on year from 1998 to 2008 (Verdict 2010). Additionally, the sector is characterised by short product life-cycles, high product variety, high levels of impulse purchasing and may be described as 'fickle, volatile and unpredictable', since garment product life-cycles average six weeks but may be as short as three weeks for high-fashion items (Lowson 2003; Masson *et al.* 2007: 239). The fast fashion phenomenon has shifted competitive advantage from a price focus to a focus on quick response to consumer demand for the latest fashion trends at an ever-increasing pace (Barnes and Lea-Greenwood 2006). As retailers demand greater variety from manufacturers, the traditional two-season purchasing calendar has been augmented with the addition of mid-season purchasing (Tokatli *et al.* 2008), while fast fashion retailers may count as many as 20 planned seasons per year (Christopher *et al.* 2004). Retailers thus face an ongoing challenge of balancing flexibility against sourcing cost to achieve success in the highly competitive mid-market sector (Hines and McGowan 2005).

With the relatively small amounts of skill and capital investment required and the enduring labour-intensive nature of the manufacturing process (Jones 2006; Abernathy *et al.* 2006), competitive advantage in garment manufacture has shifted from economically advanced nations to developing countries with large pools of labour resources. Since the process of sewing makes up around 30% of the wholesale garment cost (Jones 2006), the impact of the labour cost differential between developed and developing countries is significant and the global shift of the garment manufacturing function to lower labour cost countries thus allows Western fashion retailers to cut supply chain costs. Over the years therefore, garment production by developed country producers has continued to decline, in some cases to the point of absolute decline, and has shifted to lesser-developed countries, particularly East Asian ones (Dicken 2007).

Notwithstanding some well-known examples of vertically integrated fashion businesses such as Benetton, Zara and American Apparel, the mid-market sector tends to be structured according to a design, source and distribute business model whereby retailers and brands outsource the manufacturing function to subcontractors in lower labour-cost countries. For mid-market firms, there are no artisan skills involved in production therefore there is no advantage in increased levels of control that come with vertical integration. They can take advantage of the cost efficiency and flexibility offered by operating as supply chain networks and subcontracting garment manufacture to lower labour-cost countries. The trend towards vertical disintegration, combined with the dual pressure for low cost and short lead time (Adams 2002; Welford and Frost 2006; Masson *et al.* 2007), results in complex globally dispersed fashion supply chains (Gereffi 1999). In practice, fashion retailers source garments in three ways: via third party specialists or directly from suppliers via (a) their own headquarters or (b) overseas sourcing hubs (Fernie *et al.* 2009). Suppliers can be further defined as:

- Contract manufacturers, who cut, assemble and ship finished garments from imported inputs under the buyer's brand name. They may also be referred to as CMT or subcontractors

- Full-package suppliers, who coordinate the entire production process on behalf of the buyer, from procurement of raw materials through to manufacture and shipping (Neidik and Gereffi 2006)

A typical fashion supply chain, which may be spread across several countries, is shown in Figure 18.1.

Figure 18.1 **Global garment supply chain**

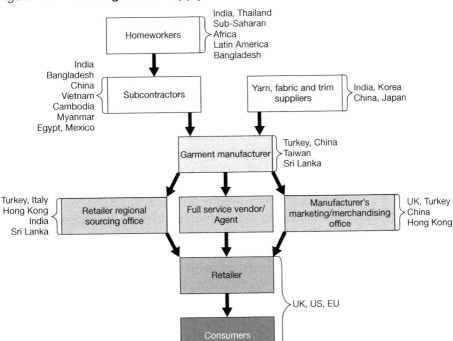

18.3 Impact of fashion supply chain characteristics on CSR

As fashion supply chains become more complex and geographically dispersed, visibility and control of CSR issues in each successive supplier tier becomes more difficult. Supply chain complexity is further exacerbated by retail buying practices which attempt to address price deflation and demand for quicker production turnaround in the sector (Hearson 2009). In a study of the garment industry in Bangladesh, FIDH (2008) concluded that social auditing efforts were largely undermined by downward price pressure and demand for shorter lead times. Industry evidence suggests that retail buyers are unwilling to increase prices paid to suppliers to reflect the increased cost of ethical production (Welford and Frost 2006; Daniel 2009; Ruwanpura and Wrigley 2011). Hearson (2009) argued that the competing demands of the fashion business model—low prices, quick turnarounds and greater uncertainty—were in fact incompatible with demands for good labour standards in the supply chain.

Furthermore, the nature of trading relationships, which were traditionally adversarial, price-focused and short-term (Crewe and Davenport 1992; Jones 2006; Barnes and Lea-Greenwood 2006), add greater complexity to global sourcing networks. A Primark shareholder reported in 2005:

> Key to Primark's business model is the sourcing of products from the cheapest possible supplier. Primark has used hundreds of suppliers located across the world. Relationships with suppliers can be short and variable, sometimes even changing mid-season (Newton Responsible Investment 2005: 21).

Palpacuer (2006: 2281) thus described the nature of fashion retailers' sourcing networks as 'fragmented and unstable' and the conflicting pressures of cost and lead time therefore continue to present a challenge to the success of CSR implementation in fashion supply chains. International risk consultancy Acona (2004) found that three areas in the fashion supply chain negatively affected the supplier's ability to uphold ethical requirements: lead time, flexibility and cost. As buyers seek to reduce their risk of under- or over-buying by placing orders as close to the season as possible, short lead times and unrealistic delivery schedules increased the likelihood that suppliers would have to work overtime to complete orders on time. Lack of advance commitment to orders and requirement for supplier flexibility affects the supplier's ability to plan the business and recruit permanent employees, while encouraging the use of temporary workers who may also belong to vulnerable social groups such as economic migrants. Pressure to reduce garment cost could force the supplier to lower wages, not pay overtime and use vulnerable workers such as economic migrants. Furthermore, payment terms vary widely in the industry, from 30 to 160 days, which puts pressure on CMT suppliers that need to pay wages on time as well as on full package suppliers that must pay for fabric and trims in advance. Acona (2004: 35) concluded that: 'There are profound and complex connections between the normal commercial buying practice of a company and its suppliers' ability to meet required ethical standards'.

18.4 The contribution of supply chain management principles to CSR

Supply chain management (SCM), as 'a set of approaches utilised to effectively integrate suppliers, manufacturers, logistics and customers for improving the long-term performance of the individual companies and the supply chain as a whole' (Hong and Jeong 2006: 292), shifts the focus from short-term adversarial transactions based on price, to longer-term partnership relationships based on total cost. SCM initiatives such as supply chain integration and supply base rationalisation support the implementation of CSR and the maintenance of ethical standards in the garment manufacturing process. Buyer–supplier relationship management is also an antecedent of CSR implementation within the fashion supply chain as it shifts focus onto long-term goals (Welford and Frost 2006).

There is evidence of increased retailer preference for full package supply rather than CMT production (Lezama *et al.* 2004; Palpacuer *et al.* 2005). As such, many larger apparel retailers are removing extra tiers of suppliers as part of a strategic manoeuvre towards a smaller supplier base, in order to reduce costs and develop closer partnership relationships with a fewer number of better suppliers (Palpacuer *et al.* 2005; Welford and Frost 2006). As well as the drive for cost reduction and continuous quality improvement and innovation, this move can also be explained by the realisation that there is a limit to the extent to which multiple supplier relationships can be effectively managed (Christopher and Jüttner 2000). The benefit of rationalisation is that it increases visibility and facilitates CSR management through the supply chain (Welford and Frost 2006).

In terms of trading relationships and CSR, Hughes (2005) concluded that arm's length relationships were not conducive to achieving good levels of social compliance in supplier facilities, whereas close inter-firm relationships and strong social ties enabled tighter retailer control over the supply chain. Frenkel and Scott's (2002) study of Asian athletic shoe manufacturers similarly discovered that collaborative trading relationships were dynamic and promoted joint learning and innovation, whereas in compliance-type relationships the setting of functional targets merely resulted in their achievement and maintenance, rather than a push for further improvement. Supply chain integration and the requisite development of closer trading relationships reduce the need for excessive monitoring of activities and can thus reduce the cost of CSR implementation (Vachon and Klassen 2006).

Additionally, implementing efficiency-boosting measures may also support CSR, as evidenced by UK fashion retailers such as New Look, Marks & Spencer and George at Asda, who pioneered boosting factory productivity to increase operator wages

(Martowicz 2009; Just-style 2010). Finally, using technological advances to speed up the concept-to-production cycle time reduces the effect of lead time pressure on the supply chain. Product life-cycle management (PLM) software improves communications between buyers and suppliers during product development to speed up the process (Şen 2008), while inventory management tools such as VMI (vendor-managed inventory), where the buyer shares demand information to allow the supplier to take responsibility for managing the buyer's inventory replenishment, enhance responsiveness to reduce lead time (Yao *et al.* 2007; Waller *et al.* 1999).

These factors suggest that implementing SCM initiatives in fashion supply chains could enable buyers and suppliers to better manage commercial pressures of cost and lead time, in addition to supporting implementation of CSR in garment factories.

18.5 Case study of Sri Lankan export garment suppliers

A qualitative case study approach was selected in order to gain greater depth of understanding of CSR in fashion supply chains; specifically, to explore from a managerial perspective the impact of negative and positive forces within the fashion supply chain on CSR implementation, with a view to understanding how CSR implementation could be reconciled with the competitive challenges of the fashion sector. Sri Lanka was selected for the study as it is a key global garment sourcing location (KSA 2009) and has a reputation for high levels of social responsibility and compliance with norms of ethical sourcing (Ruwanpura and Wrigley 2011; Loker 2011). Included in buyer-driven networks since the 1980s (Knutsen 2004), the country produces mainly casualwear, sportswear and lingerie for many global brands and retailers including Victoria's Secret, Liz Claiborne, Pierre Cardin, Nike, Gap, Tommy Hilfiger, Polo Ralph Lauren, Next and Marks & Spencer (BOI 2012). Sri Lanka has a long history of corporate philanthropy and CSR was identified by many business leaders as a historical practice that had been modernised to suit local needs (International Alert 2005; Loker 2011). Additionally, the 'Garments Without Guilt' campaign was launched by the national garment and textile industry body, in 2006. This initiative aimed to promote the country's ethical credentials by assuring buyers that garments produced in Sri Lanka were made under ethical conditions. Fieldwork was conducted within seven case study companies which were theoretically sampled to represent the range of business sizes and models (full package supply or contract manufacture) in the export garment manufacturing sector. Data collection methods included on-site, face-to-face, semi-structured interviews with key informants and non-participant observation within factory environments. Analysis of interview transcripts was conducted manually, using Eisenhardt's (1989) method of within-case and cross-case analysis, and triangulated with observational data and documentary evidence. Table 18.1 provides a breakdown of the case study companies.

Table 18.1 **Case study company breakdown**

Co.	Employees in Sri Lanka	Factories in Sri Lanka	Business model	Date set up	Customers
A	25,000	24	FPS	1969	Gap, Old Navy, M&S, Next, Lands' End, Abercrombie & Fitch
B	10,000	12	CM	1979	George (Asda), M&S, Gap, Intimissimi, Tesco, Warner Bros.
C	15,000	21	FPS	1946	Eddie Bauer, Liz Claiborne, Levi's, Tesco, M&S, BHS, Matalan, Asda
D	5,200	7	FPS	1991	Gerry Weber, Esprit, Chaps Ralph Lauren, Betty Barclay
E	5,000	4	FPS	1978	Tommy Hilfiger, Nike, Polo Ralph Lauren, Liz Claiborne
F	300	1	CM	2000	Noni B
G	300	1	CM	1995	Reborn, Macy's

There was clear evidence of sunken CSR in many of the companies; that is, informal, unstructured CSR that is deeply embedded within corporate strategies and behaviours (Jenkins 2004; Perrini *et al.* 2006). Many factories had practised CSR activities, such as providing free breakfast and transport for workers, donating to local causes and promoting diversity in the workplace, long before the advent of retailer codes of conduct in the 1990s. Historically strong labour laws provided a foundation on which to progress the CSR agenda with retail buyers. 'Some [labour laws] are even tighter than international requirements. Most of our labour law requirements are tighter than the vendor requirements' (Senior Manager, Company A).

In terms of the business benefits, CSR was perceived by senior management as a form of national competitive advantage and a means of differentiation against other lower labour-cost countries: 'We are using (CSR) as a weapon. We have clean factories; we have superb manufacturing management compared to other neighbours in this part of the world' (Senior Manager, Company A).

In addition, CSR was understood by factory management as a key contributor to sustainable business development in a labour-intensive industry sector:

> Most of the businesses especially in apparel they are looking for a sustainable business. They do understand that unless you pay enough and look after your employees enough then ultimately you will not have enough people to work in your business (Senior Manager, Company A).

Factory management recognised that good CSR standards contributed to worker welfare and resulted in productive, efficient and committed employees, reducing labour turnover and contributing to business success and sustainability:

> When we are taking care of our employees…there will also be a return
> to the business, people are very committed, they are loyal to the com-
> pany and they do whatever maximum they can contribute' (Compliance
> Manager, Company A).

> We have about 60% employees who have worked here more than five
> years; out of that 60% another 60% is more than ten years (HR Manager,
> Company E).

In terms of the issues in fashion supply chains, downward price pressure was
evidenced in an increase in payment terms: for example from 30 days to 45 days, or
up to 90 days from some buyers. However, the larger full package suppliers had key
supplier status with certain brands and retailers and therefore trading relationships
tended to be long term and collaborative rather than short term and adversarial.
Therefore, downward price pressure had less of a negative effect as both parties
were able to work together to achieve a mutually acceptable solution. For example,
the practice of open-book accounting between Company A and one of its key buyers was perceived by factory management to be a positive 'win–win solution' that
enabled buyer and supplier to work together to achieve target costs, thereby supporting relational continuity. By seeing a precise cost breakdown, the buyer was
able to suggest to Company A where cost savings could be made.

In general, pressure on lead times was less of an issue in Sri Lanka because suppliers produced core basic items with relatively long shelf-lives and simple construction, rather than fast fashion garments. On long-running orders, workers were
able to achieve a level of efficiency that would be difficult to achieve with greater
levels of style changes that are characteristic of fast fashion. This enabled them to
earn production bonuses and increase their monthly salary to levels higher than
those stipulated either by national legislation or industry regulations. For example,
Company A's VMI arrangement with Gap for men's casual bottoms (chinos) enabled the supplier to gain greater visibility of retail demand and thus become more
proactive in terms of planning ahead for factory scheduling and capacity loading,
in addition to benefiting from a faster payment cycle.

Full package suppliers fostered strong relationships with retailers over considerable periods of time (10–20 years) and collaborated on initiatives to increase efficiency and agility, such as cost reduction and vertical integration of pre-production
activities, which reduced the negative influence of cost and time pressure on CSR
implementation:

> We have a very very close established relationship and most of all it's the
> trust. We were never let down by anyone so far, our relationships are excel-
> lent and we are in continuous progress that we are making with each and
> every customer (Director, Company E).

Larger companies who had invested in industrial upgrading, via backward integration and integration of pre-production activities with their buyers, felt that this
provision of higher value-added services helped to ensure the continuation of long-
term buyer–supplier relationships. Although there was little evidence of formal

commitments for future orders, there was an unwritten assumption of continuity based on the duration of the relationship and satisfactory past performance: 'With the service we are giving they wouldn't do that' (go to another supplier) (Company C).

Some of the companies had invested in garment and textile production facilities outside of Sri Lanka, for example in India or Vietnam, in order to offer their buyers the benefits of lower labour costs alongside fabric sourcing and thus to retain the trading relationship in the face of competition from other countries' suppliers. Others had invested in sophisticated product development centres, where buyers were able to work with the production team on pre-production activities such as design and product development in order to cut lead times.

However, smaller contract manufacturers without value-added services were unable to develop strong collaborative relationships with buyers which would enable greater investment in CSR implementation, and experienced greater difficulties with regard to sustaining cash flow following last-minute order changes or cancellations:

> We get reasons like the buyer cancels the orders, the fabric did not come on time, trims did not come on time, quality problems with fabrics, things like that...sometimes we have idle time, then we are going at a loss if we couldn't manage to fill up the gap (Managing Director, Company G).

Indeed, the strategic benefits of long-term orientation and shared goals between buyers and suppliers to successful CSR implementation were confirmed by the Head of Sustainable Business at Marks & Spencer: a co-defined approach to CSR that recognised the opportunity for shared learning and mutual benefit produced better results than a coercive, compliance-based approach that stifled innovation and creativity. Some of the larger companies had developed their own CSR initiatives based on buyer CSR programmes, such as Marks & Spencer's 'Marks & Start' programme, which aims to promote diversity in the workplace. This demonstrated how best practice in CSR was not only cascaded through the supply chain but also driven forward by suppliers as a result of long-term orientation in the buyer–supplier relationship.

18.6 Conclusion

The success of CSR implementation in the Sri Lankan export garment industry was influenced by product nature, the level of service provided by the supplier and the long-term partnership approach to buyer–supplier relationship management. The core basic nature of the product meant that orders were more likely to be long-running, so manufacturers were sheltered from the unpredictability in orders and frequent style changes characteristic of fast fashion. This level of stability enabled suppliers to invest in CSR implementation. Full package suppliers fostered strong relationships with retailers over considerable periods of time (10–20 years) and collaborated on initiatives to increase efficiency and agility, such as cost reduction and vertical integration of pre-production activities. This resulted in greater opportunities to implement CSR initiatives than for contract manufacturers without value-added services, who were unable to develop such strong collaborative relationships with buyers which would have enabled greater investment in CSR implementation. Although Sri Lanka is classed as a global leader in ethical garment manufacture, much is therefore dependent on the size and provision of services offered by the supplier, which dictates the nature of the buyer–supplier relationship: vertically integrated full package suppliers had closer links with buyers than contract manufacturers and hence greater ability to drive CSR implementation through the business.

Despite downward price pressure and the shift of garment production to lower labour-cost countries such as Vietnam and Bangladesh, Sri Lanka has thus managed to carve out a unique position in the highly competitive global garment industry through industrial upgrading and building a reputation for ethical garment manufacturing. Continuous reinvestment in backward integration has resulted in the development of a sophisticated apparel industry that has moved from contract manufacturing to higher value-added total supply chain solutions (Knutsen 2004), which is able to provide a high-quality full package service for mid- to upper-market retailers who put a premium on ethical compliance (Montlake 2011). Echoing Loker (2011), ex-VF Corporation senior executive, Jeff Streader, notes: 'Sri Lankans aren't the cheapest guys. It's for people who are trying to differentiate their product' (cited in Montlake 2011). For large mid-market global retailers with strong brands and reputations to uphold, risk-free sourcing becomes more important, especially as labour rates in China and Bangladesh increase. Indeed, Sri Lanka's reputation as a low-risk sourcing destination was highlighted in 2010 after retailers moved to transfer production from Bangladesh following the bloody riots over minimum wage levels (Oxberry 2010; Samaraweera 2010).

The benefits of strategic CSR provide a clear justification for CSR implementation in globally dispersed fashion supply chains, in terms of risk reduction and protection of brand image as well as in terms of ensuring supplier business sustainability. By adopting supply chain management principles, fashion retailers can reap the rewards of improved supply chain performance without compromising CSR at factory level. By building closer relationships with fewer suppliers, sharing information and integrating pre-production activities such as product design and development, fashion retailers can reduce time-to-market without compromising worker welfare in factories. Adopting supply chain management principles thus overcomes the negative effects of retail buying practices. It also progresses supplier CSR performance beyond that which is achievable via a coercive, compliance-based model: in particular, the principles of shared goals and collaborative ways of working moves the focus onto the long-term and a partnership way of working as distinct from a short-term adversarial approach that tends to breed distrust. This encourages suppliers to be innovative and take ownership of CSR, driving it through their businesses to cascade best practice throughout the supply chain. The inherent conflict between CSR implementation and the characteristics of fashion supply chains may be reconciled by moving away from traditional adversarial supply chain relationships and adopting the SCM philosophy of long-term orientation and shared goals between trading partners.

References

Abernathy, F.H., A. Volpe and D. Weil (2006) 'The Future of the Apparel and Textile Industries: Prospects and Choices for Public and Private Actors', *Environment and Planning A* 38: 2207-32.

Acona (2004) *Buying Your Way into Trouble? The Challenge of Responsible Supply Chain Management* (London: Acona).

Adams, R.J. (2002) 'Retail Profitability and Sweatshops: A Global Dilemma', *Journal of Retailing and Consumer Services* 9.3: 147-53.

Andersen, M., and T. Skøtt-Larsen (2009) 'Corporate Social Responsibility in Global Supply Chains', *Supply Chain Management* 14.2: 75-86.

Barnes, L., and G. Lea-Greenwood (2006) 'Fast Fashioning the Supply Chain: Shaping the Research Agenda', *Journal of Fashion Marketing and Management* 10.3: 259-71.

BBC News (2011) 'Fashion Chain Zara Acts on Brazil Sweatshop Conditions', www.bbc.co.uk/news/world-latin-america-14570564, accessed 24 August 2011.

BOI (Board of Investment of Sri Lanka) (2012) 'Key Sectors for Investment: Apparel', www.investsrilanka.com/key_sectors_for_investment/apparel_overview.html, accessed 5 October 2012.

Bruce, M., L. Daly and N. Towers (2004) 'Lean or Agile: A Solution for Supply Chain Management in the Textiles and Clothing Industry?' *International Journal of Operations and Production Management* 24.2: 151-70.

Chamberlain, G. (2010) 'Gap, Next and M&S in New Sweatshop Scandal', The Observer, www.guardian.co.uk/world/2010/aug/08/gap-next-marks-spencer-sweatshops, accessed 24 August 2011.

Christopher, M., and U. Jüttner (2000) 'Developing Strategic Partnerships in the Supply Chain: A Practitioner Perspective', *European Journal of Purchasing & Supply Management* 6: 117-27.

Christopher, M., R. Lowson and H. Peck (2004) 'Creating Agile Supply Chains in the Fashion Industry', *International Journal of Retail and Distribution Management* 24.2: 50-61.

Crewe, L., and E. Davenport (1992) 'Changing Buyer–Supplier Relationships within Clothing Retailing', *Transactions of the Institute of British Geographers* 17.2: 183-97.

Daniel, D. (2009) 'Extension of GSP Plus Concessions: Apparel Exporters Pin Hopes on Government', www.island.lk/2009/09/05/business1.html, accessed 20 November 2009.

Dicken, P. (2007) *Global Shift: Mapping the Changing Contours of the World Economy* (London: Sage).

Eisenhardt, K.M. (1989) 'Building Theories from Case Study Research', *Academy of Management Review* 14.4: 532-50.

Fernie, J., P.A. Maniatakis and C.M. Moore (2009) 'The Role of International Hubs in a Fashion Retailers' Sourcing Strategy', *International Review of Retail, Distribution and Consumer Research* 19.4: 421-36.

FIDH (International Federation for Human Rights) (2008) *Bangladesh: Labour Rights in the Supply Chain and Corporate Social Responsibility* (Paris: FIDH).

Frenkel, S.J., and D. Scott (2002) 'Compliance, Collaboration and Codes of Labour Practice: The Adidas Connection', *California Management Review* 45.1: 29-49.

Gereffi, G. (1999) 'International Trade and Industrial Upgrading in the Apparel Commodity Chain', *Journal of International Economics* 48: 37-70.

Gilbert, H. (2006) 'Sourcing Good CSR', *Supply Management* 11.7: 28-29.

Godfrey, P.C., and N.W. Hatch (2007) 'Researching Corporate Social Responsibility: An Agenda for the 21st Century', *Journal of Business Ethics* 70: 87-98.

Hearson, M. (2009) *Cashing In: Giant Retailers, Purchasing Practices, and Working Conditions in the Garment Industry* (Amsterdam: Clean Clothes Campaign).

Hemingway, C.A., and P.W. Maclagan (2004) 'Managers' Personal Values as Drivers of Corporate Social Responsibility', *Journal of Business Ethics* 50.1: 33-44.

Hines, T., and P. McGowan (2005) 'Supply Chain Strategies in the UK Fashion Industry: The Rhetoric of Partnership and Power', *International Entrepreneurship and Management Journal* 1: 519-37.

Hong, P., and J. Jeong (2006) 'Supply Chain Management Practices of SMEs: From a Business Growth Perspective', *Journal of Enterprise Information Management* 19.3: 292-302.

Hughes, A. (2005) 'Corporate Strategy and the Management of Ethical Trade: The Case of the UK Food and Clothing Retailers', *Environment and Planning A* 37.7: 1,145-63.

International Alert (2005) *Peace through Profit: Sri Lankan Perspectives on Corporate Social Responsibility* (London: International Alert).

Jenkins, H. (2004) 'A Critique of Conventional CSR Theory: An SME Perspective', *Journal of General Management* 29.4: 37-57.

Jones, R.M. (2006) *The Apparel Industry* (Oxford, UK: Blackwell).

Just-style (2010) 'Bangladesh: Retailers Must Play a Part in Wage Issue says ETI', www.just-style.com/news/retailers-must-play-a-part-in-wage-issue-says-eti_id108640.aspx, accessed 2 December 2010.

Knutsen, H.M. (2004) 'Industrial Development in Buyer-Driven Networks: The Garment Industry in Vietnam and Sri Lanka', *Journal of Economic Geography* 4.5: 545-64.

KSA (2009) *Global Sourcing Reference: Cost Comparison Handbook for the Retail and Apparel Industry* (Manchester, UK: KSA).

Lezama, M., B. Webber and C. Dagher (2004) *Sourcing Practices in the Apparel Industry: Implications for Garment Exporters in Commonwealth Developing Countries* (London: Commonwealth Secretariat).

Loker, S. (2011) 'The (R)Evolution of Sustainable Apparel Business: From Codes of Conduct to Partnership in Sri Lanka', www.jaafsl.com/news/500-the-revolution-of-sustainable-apparelbusiness-from-codes-of-conduct-to-partnership-in-sri-lanka, accessed 1 August 2011.

Lowson, R.H. (2003) 'Apparel Sourcing: Assessing the True Operational Cost', *International Journal of Clothing Science and Technology* 15.5: 335-45.

Maitland, I. (1997) 'The Great Non-Debate over International Sweatshops', in T.L. Beauchamp and N.E. Bowie (eds.), *Ethical Theory and Business* (Upper Saddle River, NJ: Prentice Hall): 593-605.

Martowicz, M. (2009) 'Boosting Productivity, Rewarding Your Workers!' Impactt, www.impacttlimited.com/2009/12/02/boosting-productivity-rewarding-your-workers, accessed 2 December 2010.

Masson, R., L. Iosif, G. MacKerron and J. Fernie (2007) 'Managing Complexity in Agile Global Fashion Industry Supply Chains', *International Journal of Logistics Management* 18.2: 238-54.

Montlake, S. (2011) 'Brandix Adapts to Sri Lanka's Post-Civil War World', Forbes, www.forbes.com/global/2011/1205/companies-people-ashroff-omar-brandix-apparel-sri-lankan-montlake.html, accessed 5 December 2011.

Neidik, B., and G. Gereffi (2006) 'Explaining Turkey's Emergence and Sustained Competitiveness as a Full-Package Supplier of Apparel', *Environment and Planning A* 38.12: 2,285-303.

New, S.J. (1997) 'The Scope of Supply Chain Management Research', *Supply Chain Management* 2.1: 15-22.

Newton Responsible Investment (2005) *Corporate Governance and SRI: Q4 2005* (London: Newton Investment Management Ltd).

Oxberry, E. (2010) 'More Price Rises Ahead as Bangladesh Riots Continue', Drapers, www.drapersonline.com/multiples/analysis/more-price-rises-ahead-as-bangladesh-riots-continue/5014751.article, accessed 12 January 2012.

Palpacuer, F. (2006) 'The Global Sourcing Patterns of French Clothing Retailers: Determinants and Implications for Suppliers' Industrial Upgrading', *Environment and Planning A* 38.12: 2271-83.

Palpacuer, F., P. Gibbon and L. Thomsen (2005) 'New Challenges for Developing Country Suppliers in Global Clothing Chains: A Comparative European Perspective', *World Development* 33.3: 409-30.

Perrini, F., S. Pogutz and A. Tencati (2006) *Developing Corporate Social Responsibility: A European Perspective* (Cheltenham, UK: Edward Elgar).

Porter, M.E., and M.R. Kramer (2006) 'Strategy and Society: The Link between Competitive Advantage and Corporate Social Responsibility', *Harvard Business Review* 84.12: 78-92.

Ruwanpura, K., and N. Wrigley (2011) 'The Costs of Compliance? Views of Sri Lankan Apparel Manufacturers in Times of Global Economic Crisis', *Journal of Economic Geography* 11: 1031-49.

Samaraweera, D. (2010) 'Sri Lanka: China-Bangladesh Overflow Boosts Exports', www.just-style.com/news/china-bangladesh-overflow-boosts-exports_id109825.aspx, accessed 12 January 2012.

Şen, A. (2008) 'The US Fashion Industry: A Supply Chain Review', *International Journal of Production Economics* 114: 571-93.

Sethi, S.P. (2003) *Setting Global Standards: Guidelines for Creating Codes of Conduct in Multinational Corporations* (Hoboken, NJ: Wiley).

Shaw, D., G. Hogg, E. Wilson, E. Shui and L. Hassan (2006) 'Fashion Victim: The Impact of Fair Trade Concerns on Clothing Choice', *Journal of Strategic Marketing* 14: 427-40.

Shaw, D., E. Shiu, L. Hassan, C. Bekin and G. Hogg (2007) 'Intending to be Ethical: An Examination of Consumer Choice in Sweatshop Avoidance', *Advances in Consumer Research* 34: 31-38.

Smestad, L. (2010) 'The Sweatshop, Child Labour, and Exploitation Issues in the Garment Industry', *Fashion Practice* 1.2: 147-62.

Tokatli, N., N. Wrigley and O. Kizilgun (2008) 'Shifting Global Supply Networks and Fast Fashion: Made in Turkey for Marks & Spencer', *Global Networks* 8.3: 261-80.

Vachon, S., and R.D. Klassen (2006) 'Extending Green Practices across the Supply Chain: The Impact of Upstream and Downstream Integration', *International Journal of Operations and Production Management* 26.7: 795-821.

Verdict (2010) *UK Clothing Market 2010: Issues and Opportunities* (London: Verdict).

Waller, M.A., M.E. Johnson and T. Davis, T. (1999) 'Vendor-Managed Inventory in the Retail Supply Chain', *Journal of Business Logistics* 20.1: 183-203.

Waters, D. (2007) *Supply Chain Risk Management* (London: Kogan Page).

Welford, R., and S. Frost (2006) 'Corporate Social Responsibility in Asian Supply Chains', *Corporate Social Responsibility and Environmental Management* 13: 166-76.

Wong, E., and G. Taylor (2000) 'An Investigation of Ethical Sourcing Practices: Levi Strauss and Co', *Journal of Fashion Marketing and Management* 4.1: 71-79.

Yao, Y., P.T. Evers and M.E. Dresner (2007) 'Supply Chain Integration in Vendor-Managed Inventory', *Decision Support Systems* 43.2: 663-74.

Dr **Patsy Perry** is a Lecturer in Management and Deputy Programme Director of the MSc International Fashion Marketing at Heriot-Watt University in Edinburgh, UK. She completed her PhD on corporate social responsibility in the fashion supply chain in 2011 and is a regular contributor to the Ethical Fashion Forum's online Source magazine.

Next one, please: Integrating sustainability criteria in the procurement of operating-room textiles

The case of Germany

Edeltraud Günther
Technische Universität Dresden, Germany

Holger Hoppe
SCHOTT Solar, Germany

Gabriel Weber
ENT Environment & Management, Spain

Julia Hillmann
Technische Universität Dresden, Germany

The concept of sustainable development and its integration in daily operations has been widely discussed. This chapter analyses the integration of sustainable development in a standard decision process in organisations. We take the perspective of a procurer and focus on procurement of operating-room (OR) textiles in hospitals. We directly evaluate the information available for OR textiles and assess it in terms of sustainable development on the level of supply management, which is a 'set of purchasing policies held, actions taken, and relationships formed in response to concerns associated with the natural environment' (Zsidisin and Siferd 2001: 69).

In Section 19.1 the concept of sustainable development is defined. In Section 19.2, the relevance of procurement as an important factor for integrating sustainable development in business operations is outlined. Section 19.3 describes the integration of sustainable development into the procurement of OR textiles. A decision support tool to integrate the dimensions of sustainable development in procurement processes is presented in Section 19.4, followed by some conclusions in the final section.

19.1 Sustainable development and organisations

Sustainable development can be defined as development that meets the needs of the present without compromising the ability of future generations to meet their own needs (WCED 1987). At present, the principle of sustainability is not achievable without the integration of organisations (Drenk 2005: 5). There have been great efforts towards useful legislative pressure, as well as support to make organisations consider their environmental aspects (Wingard 2001: 65). Well-known systems for better environmental performance in firms are environmental management systems, such as ISO 14001. There are numerous tools focusing on environmental performance such as life-cycle assessment (LCA), ecological footprinting and more (Robèrt 2000). This chapter aims at providing a holistic assessment method for integrating sustainability aspects in the procurement of OR textiles.

19.2 The relevance of procurement for sustainable development and vice versa

The need for integrating sustainability aspects into procurement decisions is stressed by the European Commission, which intensively promotes green procurement (European Commission 2004). Almost 16% of the EU's gross national product was spent on public procurement in 2009 (PriceWaterhouseCoopers 2009: 13); thus, a high environmental impact exists.

The integration of specific criteria in procurement as a function of supply management is important for the realisation of sustainable development in business decision-making. Following the definition of Korhonen (2004), procurement is a means to realise the concept of sustainability by setting principles (e.g. environmentally friendly products) and defining specific actions to reduce environmental impacts (Bowen *et al*. 2001; Koplin *et al*. 2007). Procurement also has the potential to influence the production process, the application phase and the end-of-life of goods and services by determining environmental and economic aspects over the whole life-cycle of a product. Organisations have only started to include these aspects into their supply processes (Kolk and van Tulder 2002: 260). Studies have observed that many hurdles exist within procurement processes, especially when it comes to the integration of sustainable development dimensions (Günther and Scheibe 2005: 123f.).

The hospital itself consumes material and resources and must follow legal requirements (e.g. Act for Promoting Closed Substance Cycle Waste Management and Ensuring Environmentally Compatible Waste Disposal). Since the first priority within German law on waste management is the avoidance of waste, the procurement of products has considerable influence on this issue. Therefore, procurers need to integrate holistic criteria including sustainability aspects. Nevertheless, the costs are crucial for the final decision. One approach which combines costs with the life-cycle perspective is the life-cycle costing (LCC) method. LCC is particularly applicable when dynamics and interdependences, affecting performance, costs and time, are incorporated into decision-making processes (Wübbenhorst 1986: 88). The LCC approach observes cash flows over time, including more than simply the costs for purchasing (Gluch and Baumann 2004: 573).

These cash flows can be considered from a customer or a producer's point of view. In our case the hospitals act as consumers as they procure OR textiles. For the customer, LCC serves as an ad hoc basis for decisions that refer, for example, to alternative products, machines, installations, maintenance strategies and suppliers.

Figure 19.1 shows the trade-off between initial investment and subsequent costs. If a customer knows the total life-cycle costs of alternatives, he or she can evaluate

Figure 19.1 **Trade-offs between initial investment and subsequent costs**

Source: Burstein 1988: 257, IMA (Institute of Management Accountants, www.imanet.org); adapted with permission

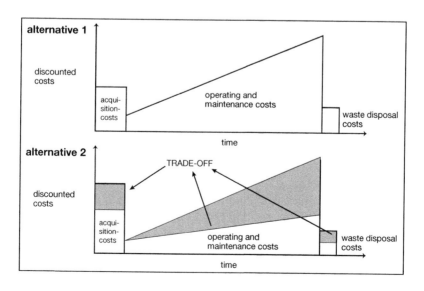

trade-offs between initial investment and follow-up costs, and choose the better alternative.

Therefore, relevant data has to be provided: for example, cash outflows for the goods, timing and amount of payment, and so forth. In this regard the basic accounting systems of a company have to provide sufficient data for LCC as a method for planning, assessing and comparing investment alternatives as well as analysing a product's profitability (e.g. Wübbenhorst 1986). The results of a LCC study are 'highly dependent on the accessibility, quality and accuracy of input data', thus dependent on the accounting system (Cole and Sterner 2000; Lindholm and Suomala 2005). Data collection is considered as the most time and resource-intensive step (Elmakis and Lisnianski 2006). Still, this is necessary in order to be able to make an optimal purchasing decision.

19.3 Integration of sustainable development into the procurement of OR textiles

In 2010, almost 14 million operations were performed in German hospitals. All of them applying OR textiles and causing related energy, material and financial flows. Assuming that four gowns and four drapes are used in each operation, about 56 million gowns and drapes are used annually, which indicates the large scale of environmental aspects.[1]

However, OR textiles may not only be assessed from the environmental perspective. Hygiene is a central criterion as the risk of surgical site infections is always present in an operation. Approximately 2% of all surgeries are estimated to result in infection in Germany (Gastmeier and Geffers 2006: 3). According to Plowman *et al.* (1999: 6), a case with an infection costs, on average, 2.9 times more than a case without infection. Therefore, the avoidance of surgical site infections is important from a medical and an economic point of view. One means of reducing the risk of a surgical site infection is the use of innovative OR textiles with special barrier-effect against pathogens (e.g. Feltgen *et al.* 2000; Rutula and Weber 2001). The introduction of the 'diagnosis related groups' in Germany put further economic pressure on hospitals and made full cost accounting a vital tool. The assessment of different alternatives for OR textiles, along with the specific requirements for linen management at the hospital, is part of that economic analysis. Clearly, all this leads to the conclusion that OR textiles have to be analysed and compared from a hygienic, an economic and an environmental perspective, as exhibited in Figure 19.2.

Our analysis distinguishes between single-use and re-usable products and their individual life-cycles, including all stages through which an OR textile passes (i.e. from production and use to disposal).

---

1 This assumption is based on our observation within the two case study hospitals.

Figure 19.2 **Criteria of a life-cycle oriented analysis**

Source: compiled by the authors

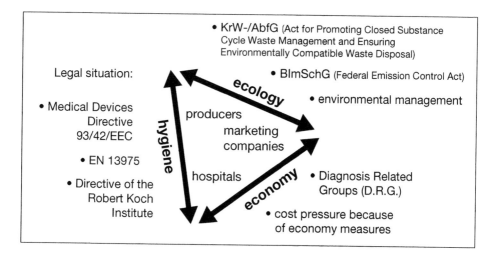

Based on those ideas, four factors have been identified that are important for the realisation of sustainable development in procurement, which focus on the environmental aspects and impacts caused by the product. These aspects are relevant for all procurement processes and are explained below.

19.3.1 Development of decision criteria and assessment framework

This section identifies important criteria to assess OR textiles from a theoretical point of view and to develop an assessment framework by focusing on product relevant criteria.

Very often only the purchase price is considered for the procurement of OR textiles, as detailed information on the economic consequences is missing. However, the other important criteria when procuring OR textiles have already been pointed out. Besides the hygienic criterion, the criteria of comfort and quality are also relevant. Other criteria which need to be included are related to hospital activity. These are shown in Figure 19.3.

For example, the assessment of environmental aspects of re-usable textiles in particular includes the steps of sterilisation and laundry. A decision-maker might set up an assessment framework as presented in Figure 19.5 in order to assess different OR textiles and services provided by the distributors. This framework should be implemented in hospitals by means of procurement models (see for example Humphreys *et al.* 2003).

Figure 19.3 **Assessment framework for OR textiles**
Source: compiled by the authors

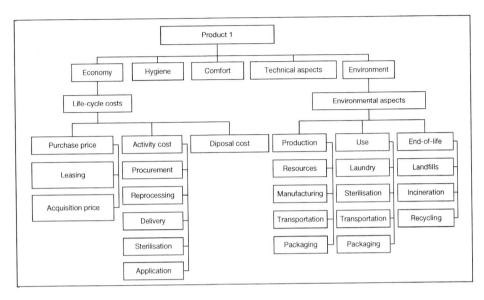

In order to evaluate all criteria for the decision-making process, appropriate instruments have to be selected, such as life-cycle costing (LCC) and activity-based costing (ABC), for the evaluation of economic criteria and technical analysis, as well as user surveys to assess hygienic and technical criteria. Ideally, the selection of data follows the assessment method.

19.3.2 Data availability of sustainable development related information

When the assessment framework and methods are defined, the identification of data is necessary. For this process the range of internal and publicly available information is evaluated. In this section, focus is laid on the availability and acquisition of sustainability-related information.

Concerning economic data, the acquisition price is normally available from offers of possible suppliers of OR textiles. When collecting further economic data, a decision-maker has to consider a wide range of information such as types of OR textiles, infrastructure of the hospital and type of linen management.

Moreover, before procuring OR textiles, the fundamental question of whether to use single-use or re-usable textiles has to be taken into account. Both types can be mainly distinguished by the applied textile management: single-use textiles are disposed of while re-usable textiles are reprocessed after their use. In addition,

Figure 19.4 **Types of linen management**

Source: based on Rothfuß 2004

		Re-usable OR textiles				Single-use OR textiles
		Owned by hospital	Commission	Rental	Full service	Delivery
Acquisition	Procurement					
	Investment in textiles					
Use	Disposition					
	Stock keeping					
	Internal logistics					
	OR use					
	Investment into machinery					
	Reprocessing					
	Sterilisation					
	Repair					
End-of-life	Disposal					
Related activities	Cost control					
	Cost allocation					

there are many possibilities to design the linen management for both types. Figure 19.4 gives a general overview of different types of linen management that might be applied by a hospital. Grey fields indicate a process done at a hospital; dotted fields show processes that might be part of the linen management by a hospital; and white fields indicate processes outsourced to textile service providers.

To achieve a process-oriented comparison of different offers, the availability of data concerning internal processes of the hospital is vital. Thereby, internal data availability is highly dependent on the design and performance of the cost accounting system applied within an organisation. To realise an economic evaluation by means of life-cycle costing, the points discussed in Section 19.2 have to be taken into consideration.

As OR textiles are a minor cost factor in hospitals, the level of information available is low. A decision-maker might therefore turn towards publicly available information; but information in journals on this topic is scarce. Many publications were published by companies selling OR textiles or by consulting companies that have to be contacted in order to obtain a detailed report, thus limiting the general accessibility. We could identify only nine publications analysing the economic consequences of the use of OR textiles. The majority of these sources identify single-use textiles as the most cost-efficient variant (see Table 19.1). Concerning the technical and hygienic criteria, the decision-maker can rely on DIN EN 13975, which defines the properties OR textiles have to fulfil.

Nevertheless, the decision on whether 'standard' or 'high' performance OR textiles should be used has to be made by the procurer. The evaluation of subjective criteria such as comfort is not as easy. Therefore, a practical test is often applied in which the criteria are rated by the OR personnel. The results of such tests are subjective and therefore not always unanimous. Those tests are seldom published; therefore, many hospitals perform their own tests.

Table 19.1 **Comparison of economic studies**

Source: compiled by the authors

Source	Object	Single use	Combined	Re-usable (Leasing)
KMC GmbH 2006a	Drapes	100%	102%	130%
KMC GmbH 2006b	Gowns	100%	156%	n.a.
Martec 2001	Gowns (hospital > 500 beds)	100%	n.a.	Micro-fibre: 106% Laminates: 125%
Martec 2001	Drapes (hospital > 500 beds)	100%	n.a	111%
Boisvert 2002	Drapes	100%	n.a.	82%–230%
Vincent-Ballerau et al. 1989	Gowns	100%	52%–74%	75%–100%
Riegl 2000	Gowns	100%		107%–161%

Note: Study results are normalised for the cost for single-use textiles

19.3.3 Evaluation of the acquired data

Public data on the technical properties of OR textiles is only available in a limited number of sources (see e.g. Feltgen *et al.* 2000). However, a complete assessment of OR textiles under practical conditions is still missing.

The economic data available is characterised by a lack of a detailed description concerning the methods applied for evaluation as well as for data used or assumptions applied. For this reason, the results are not generalisable and mostly serve as benchmarks. The data evaluation for OR textiles should be based on the two instruments of ABC and LCC, where ABC provides the internal cost data needed for LCC. The instrument of LCC allows a direct connection to the environmental criteria as it is also based on the life-cycle of the object of investigation. Based on the data availability described above, a hospital has to collect a large amount and variety of in-house data.

19.3.4 Legal framework

When the above-mentioned problems of criteria identification are overcome and the decision-maker has a profound understanding of the criteria for a holistic procurement decision, his or her knowledge still has to be applied and integrated into the tendering process, which is still determined by the possibilities offered by the legal framework, requiring special know-how. The EU hereby suggests where to include environmental aspects in tenders (see European Commission 2004: 14ff.). In the case of OR textiles there is no decision aid supporting the integration of environmental aspects, presenting another hurdle for a holistic procurement decision. Still, the legal framework differs in every country and thus forms part of the following guideline for sustainability-oriented procurement.

19.4 Guideline for sustainability-oriented procurement

Based on the case study regarding the integration of sustainability criteria into the procurement of OR textiles, we developed a management process scheme for sustainable procurement (see Fig. 19.5). The process scheme consists of six elements: 1) hurdle analysis; 2) life-cycle analysis; 3) market research; 4) life-cycle costing; 5) legal analysis; and 6) stakeholder management.

We have tested most of the elements of the guideline for sustainability-oriented procurement decisions either in case study hospitals or in similar environments. For example, we performed a simplified life-cycle assessment in the case study hospitals and used the insights for a systematic review of existing life-cycle assessments of OR textiles (see Nowack *et al.* 2012). By applying activity-based costing we calculated life-cycle costs of single-use as well as re-usable surgical gowns and drapes (see Günther *et al.* 2007). We performed a legal analysis in the two hospitals. Based on that we developed, together with lawyers specialised in procurement law, standardised specimen procurement documents (Schneider and Siewert 2009). Other elements of the guideline have not been applied in the case study hospitals; however, we used them in other contexts. For example, we have applied the hurdles analysis widely in other organisations such as municipalities or federal agencies (see Günther and Scheibe 2005). In several studies we have investigated the role of stakeholder management for organisations (see Weber *et al.* 2011).

Figure 19.5 **Sustainability-oriented procurement process**
Source: compiled by the authors

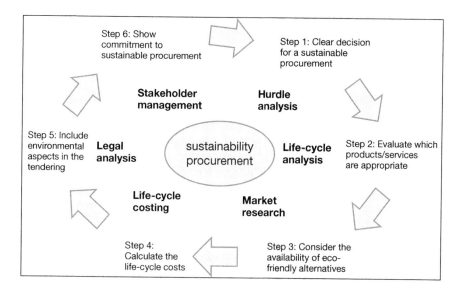

We found that proactive stakeholder management is a key element of environmental performance and therefore highly recommend it to practitioners in hospitals.

The guideline integrates sustainability aspects in the procuring process and provides practitioners with a decision-support tool. It can be applied for the procurement of OR textiles as well as other low-value products and is explained below.

1. **Decision for sustainable procurement**. Top management commitment to sustainable development is a precondition of sustainable procurement, so that procurers do not have to legitimate their environmentally friendly decisions. To cope with different departments and the discussion of environmentally friendly procurement, hurdles have to be assessed. The hurdle analysis method can assist organisations in identifying and discovering reasons for their emergence (Günther and Scheibe 2005: 115ff.)

2. **Evaluate which products and services are appropriate**. Procurers should compare the environmental performance of products and services to be able to choose the least burdensome. For the evaluation of the environmental impacts of products to be procured, a life-cycle assessment is promising

3. **Consider the availability of environmentally compatible alternatives**. After evaluating the environmental impact of purchasing products or services, procurers should consider the availability of environmentally compatible alternatives. For procurers it is very helpful to do market research to ensure a sustainable procurement decision. Pertinent publications and websites such as www.eco-label.com can be used as a decision support

4. **Calculate the costs over the whole life-cycle of products and services**. Another requirement for a sustainability-oriented procurement decision is an examination of the product's whole life-cycle. In the case of energy-saving lamps, for example, eco-friendly alternatives are more expensive but have a longer lifespan and lower disposal costs. Hence, it is promising to use life-cycle costing to evaluate the alternatives

5. **Include environmental aspects in the tendering**. Public procurement law is very sophisticated. For many procurers it is difficult to assess whether and how to integrate environmental criteria in the particular phases of the tendering. European law offers a broad scope for sustainability-oriented tendering. This particularly means the definition of contract purpose, the disposition of technical specification and the choice of tenderers, the acceptance of a tender and the preconditions of a contract's conformance

6. **Communicate your commitment to sustainable procurement**. The last step is to communicate commitment to stakeholders, such as through publicity or media. An exchange of know-how with other procurers as important stakeholders is also possible

19.5 Conclusion

Integrating environmental aspects into procurement decisions is extremely impor-tant. The necessity to do so has been described in this chapter in general and espe-cially in the case of OR textiles. The integration of sustainable aspects into the decision-making process was explained by using an adequate method which com-bines environmental aspects and costs, which can be seen in life-cycle costing. LCC provides decision-related information and meets the requirement to think beyond prices and costs, including costs for the usage phase of the purchased product. Furthermore, a framework for procurement decisions was derived based on the observations within the two hospitals. This decision framework is also applicable for other low-value products and shows avenues for sustainable procurement in hospitals which can be transferred to other procurement decisions.

References

Boisvert, H. (2002) 'The Economics of Linen', *CMA Management* 76.2: 40-44.

Bowen, F., P.D. Cousins, R.C. Lamming and A.C. Faruk (2001) 'The Role of Supply Chain Management Capabilities in Green Supply', *Production and Operations Management* 10 (Summer 2001): 174-89.

Burstein, M.C. (1988) 'Life Cycle Costing', in National Association of Accountants Conference Proceedings (eds.), *Cost Accounting for the '90s: Responding to Technological Change* (Montvale, NJ: Institute of Management Accountants, www.imanet.org).

Cole, R.J., and E. Sterner (2000) 'Reconciling Theory and Practice of Life-Cycle Costing', *Building Research & Information* 28.5/6: 368-75.

Drenk, D. (2005) 'Sustainable Business: A Success Story for Small and Medium Sized Enter-prises?' paper presented at the *45 Congress of the Regional European Science Association (ESRA)*, Amsterdam, Netherlands, 23–27 August 2005.

Elmakis, D., and A. Lisnianski (2006) 'Life Cycle Cost Analysis: Actual Problem in Industrial Management', *Journal of Business and Economics and Management* 7.1: 5-8.

European Commission (2004) *Buying Green! A Handbook on Environmental Public Procure-ment* (Luxembourg: European Commission, www.ec.europa.eu/environment/gpp/pdf/buying_green_handbook_en.pdf, accessed 30 January 2012).

Feltgen, M., O. Schmidt and H.-P. Werner (2000) 'The Human Being in the Spotlight: Surgical Drapes and Surgical Gowns are Medical Devices', *Infection Control and Healthcare* 25 (Suppl. 2).

Gastmeier, P., and C. Geffers (2006) 'Nosocomial Infections in Germany: What are the Num-bers, Based on the Estimates for 2006?' *Dtsch Med Wochenschr* 133.21: 1,111-15.

Gluch, P., and H. Baumann (2004) 'The Life Cycle Costing (LCC) Approach: A Conceptual Discussion of its Usefulness for Environmental Decision-Making', *Building and Environ-ment* 39: 571-80.

Günther, E., and L. Scheibe (2005) 'The Hurdles Analysis as an Instrument for Improving Environmental Value Chain Management', *Progress in Industrial Ecology: An Interna-tional Journal* 2.1: 107-31.

Günther, E., H. Hoppe and G. Weber (2007) 'Sustainable Development and its Integration in Business Decisions: The Case of the Procurement of Operating-Room Textiles in German Public Hospitals', *Conference Proceedings, Corporate Responsibility Research Conference 2007*, Leeds, 15–17 July 2007.

Humphreys, P.K., Y.K. Wong and F.T.S. Chan (2003) 'Integrating Environmental Criteria into the Supplier Selection Process', *Journal of Materials Processing Technology* 138: 349-56.

KMC GmbH (2006a) *Studie über den wirtschaftlichen Einsatz von steriler OP-Wäsche – Vergleich unterschiedlicher Abdecksysteme* (Wunstorf, Germany: Klinik Management Consulting).

KMC GmbH (2006b) *Studie zur Kosten- und Prozessoptimierung der Wäscheversorgung eines Schwerpunktkrankenhauses* (Wunstorf, Germany: Klinik Management Consulting).

Kolk, A., and R. van Tulder (2002) 'The Effectiveness of Self-Regulation: Corporate Codes of Conduct and Child Labour', *European Management Journal* 20: 260-71.

Koplin, J., S. Seuring and M. Mesterharm (2007) 'Incorporating Sustainability into Supply Management in the Automotive Industry: The Case of the Volkswagen AG', *Journal of Cleaner Production* 15: 1053-62.

Korhonen, J. (2004) 'Industrial Ecology in the Strategic Sustainable Development Model: Strategic Applications of Industrial Ecology', *Journal of Cleaner Production* 12: 809-23.

Lindholm, A., and P. Suomala (2005) 'Present and Future of Life Cycle Costing: Reflections from Finnish Companies', *LTA* 2: 282-92.

MARTEC GmbH (2001) *Vergleichende Kostenstudie zum Gebrauch von Mehrweg- und Einweg-OP-Kitteln und –Abdecktüchern* (Offenbach, Germany: MARTEC GmbH, www.molnlycke.com/Global/Surgical_Products/DE/Infektionskontrolle/04%202000_Martec_Studie.pdf, accessed 21 January 2012, no longer available).

Nowack, M., H. Hoppe and E. Günther (2012) 'Review and Downscaling of Life Cycle Decision Support Tools for the Procurement of Low-Value Products', *International Journal of Life Cycle Assessment* 17.6: 655-65 (doi 10.1007/s11367-012-0401-3).

Plowman, R., N. Graves, M. Griffin, J.A. Roberts, A.V. Swan, B. Cookson and L. Taylor (1999) 'The Socioeconomic Burden of Hospital Acquired Infection', Health Protection Agency, www.dh.gov.uk/assetRoot/04/08/97/25/04089725.pdf, accessed 23 January 2012.

PriceWaterhouseCoopers (2009) *Collection of Statistical Information on Green Public Procurement in the EU: Report on Data Collection Results* (Brussels: European Commission; www.ec.europa.eu/environment/gpp/pdf/statistical_information.pdf, accessed 29 January 2012).

Riegl, F. (2000) 'Wirtschaftlichkeitsreserven locken überall', *Führen und Wirtschaften im Krankenhaus* 17.3: 280-84.

Robèrt, K.-H. (2000) 'Tools and Concepts for Sustainable Development, How Do They Relate to a General Framework for Sustainable Development, and to Each Other?' *Journal of Cleaner Production* 8: 243-54.

Rothfuß, T. (2004) 'Textilservice – ein Gewinn?' *Infodienst Berufsverband Hauswirtschaft* 5: 13-16.

Rutula, W.A., and D.J. Weber (2001) 'A Review of Single-Use and Reusable Gowns and Drapes in Health Care', *Infection Control Hosp. Epidemiology* 22.4: 248-52.

Schneider, M., and J. Siewert (2009) 'Musterausschreibung für Operationstextilien', in C. Cherif, E. Günther, L. Jatzwauk and S. Mecheels (eds.), *Evaluierung von OP-Textilien – Ergebnisse einer Untersuchung nach hygienischen, öknomischen und ökologischen Gesichtspunkten* (Dresden, Germany: addprint AG): 129-38.

Vincent-Ballerau, F., J. Trevidic, M. Lafleuriel and C. Merville (1989) 'Comparative Economic Evaluation of Nonwoven and Traditional Woven Textiles in Operating Rooms', *Annales de Chirurgie* 43.4: 275-78.

WCED (World Commission on Environment and Development) (1987) *Our Common Future* (Oxford, UK: Oxford University Press).

Weber, G., E. Günther, R. Scheel and L. Buscher (2011) 'The Role of Stakeholders in Disseminating Environmental Performance Data', short paper presented at the *3rd Annual Content Analysis Professional Development Workshop at Academy of Management Conference*, San Antonio 2011.

Wingard, H.C. (2001) *Financial Performance of Environmentally Responsible South African Listed Companies* (PhD thesis; Pretoria: University of Pretoria, www.upetd.up.ac.za/thesis/available/etd-08312001-154421, accessed 30 January 20120).

Wübbenhorst, K.L. (1986) 'Life Cycle Costing for Construction Projects', *Long Range Planning* 19.4: 87-97.

Zsidisin, G., and S. Siferd (2001) 'Environmental Purchasing: A Framework for Theory Development', *International Journal of Purchasing and Supply Management* 7: 61-73.

Edeltraud Günther received her doctorate in Environmental Accounting from the Universität Augsburg and holds the Chair in Environmental Management and Accounting at the Technische Universität Dresden. She is also Visiting Professor of Commerce at the University of Virginia. Her teaching and research interests are for example the fields of sustainability management and environmental performance measurement. Her most recent work focuses on developing climate change adaptation scenarios for different industries in Germany.

Holger Hoppe studied Economics and Engineering at the Technische Universität Dresden and Dublin City University. He recently received his doctorate in Environmental Management and Accounting at the Technische Universität Dresden. During the PhD his research focused, for example, on environmental performance measurement and its relation to financial performance. He is now working for SCHOTT Solar as Head of Sustainability and EHS.

Gabriel Weber has a PhD in Environmental Management and Accounting (TU Dresden, Germany), an MA in Public and Private Environmental Management (FU Berlin, Germany) and an MBA (HTW, Berlin). His research at TU Dresden includes climate change mitigation and climate policy as well as environmental and economic assessment in the health sector. Gabriel is now working as Marie Curie Post-Doc Fellow at ENT Environment & Management, Vilanova i la Geltrú, Barcelona.

Julia Hillmann studied Business Administration at the Technische Universität Dresden. She is currently a PhD student at the Chair of Environmental Management and Accounting at the Technische Universität Dresden. She is also working on the project developing climate change adaptation scenarios for different industries in Germany. Her research interests are, for example, strategic management and environmental strategies.

Development and the garment industry
Commonwealth of the Northern Mariana Islands

Sarah E. Heidebrecht
Alumna, Kansas State University, USA

Joy M. Kozar
Kansas State University, USA

The purpose of this chapter is to examine the effects of colonisation, development and globalisation in the Commonwealth of the Northern Mariana Islands (CNMI), with specific focus on the garment industry. This industry is analysed largely because garment manufacturing has historically been the most important industry on the islands since the Second World War, accounting for approximately 40% of the CNMI's gross domestic product (GDP) in 2002 (USGAO 2006). However, beginning in 2005, a sharp decline in garment production has occurred in the Marianas, coinciding with the final phase-out of the Multi-Fibre Arrangement (MFA). The MFA, enforced from 1974 to 2004, imposed quota limits on apparel and textile goods. This chapter will address the economic implications of this decline as seen through garment factory closures, lost revenue and a shift in guest worker populations on the Marianas.

The topic of this research is important as it lends insight into the effects of dependency on the garment industry as a main source of revenue. In the CNMI this dependency is seen through the use of garment manufacturing as a means to enter the world market economy, which, owing to the nature of the garment industry, allows for poor, under-developed nations to vie for market space with relative ease by investing minimally in resources and subsequently obtaining swift growth (Nordas and WTO Secretariat 2004). This study is relevant to other newly developed and developing countries as increasing competition from China and India in garment production is realised. A genuine fear exists that these competitive countries, which have abundant human capital, stable economies and significant infrastructure, will continue to gain unfair portions of the global market economy (Curran 2008). A case in point shows that clothing market shares for the United States tripled from China (16% to 50%) and quadrupled from India (4% to 15%) after the elimination of the MFA (Nordas and WTO 2004: 30). Owing to the economic decline that has occurred on the CNMI since the phase-out of the MFA, this chapter seeks to investigate data reported by the United States Census Bureau (USCB) and Office of Textiles and Apparel (OTEXA), as well as other legal documents, academic journals and literature. The chapter is organised as follows: Sections 20.1 and 20.2 provide a basic overview of the MFA and the development of the CNMI; Section 20.3 presents a summary of results for quantitative statistical measures utilising economic and population demographics; and Section 20.4 includes a case study of Mauritius (for comparison purposes) and discussion of future implications and predictors for the CNMI economy and its people.

20.1 Multi-Fibre Arrangement

The MFA was created in 1974 as a protectionist measure to stabilise the growth of imports and exports throughout the world and to shield the vulnerable textile and apparel industries in developed countries from over-saturation of low-cost goods into the marketplace from other producer nations (Curran 2008). Historically, this protectionism was accomplished by placing quota restrictions on various supplier nations. Leading garment producer nations such as the Asian 'tigers'—Hong Kong, South Korea, Taiwan and Macau—typically received the highest quota restrictions in the past; more recently, China has emerged as a strong contender in the export market. Through the restrictions placed on the leading producer nations, the MFA inadvertently pushed the textile industry to internationalise and diversify. For instance, when supplier nations expended their quota allowance, they would access quota from another country, thus spreading garment production to an ever-expanding network of countries (2008). The CNMI became intertwined in this worldwide system of garment production soon after the establishment of the MFA in the late 1970s and early 1980s as a means to develop the economy on the islands.

Quota reduction and elimination for apparel goods have long been issues in worldwide trade negotiations. The Uruguay Round of trade negotiations lasted from 1986 to 1995 and ended with the formation of the World Trade Organisation (WTO). One of the key focuses of these negotiations was to eliminate quotas on apparel goods, which had the potential to benefit developing countries that at the time constituted the bulk of production. By giving developing countries easier access to overcome trade barriers, the intention was to allow substantial growth of the garment manufacturing industries within these countries, capitalising on their expansive, yet relatively unskilled labour force. Beginning in 1995, quotas on apparel goods were phased out over a 10-year period, ending on 1 January 2005. The formation of the Agreement on Textiles and Clothing, the body responsible for overseeing the MFA phase-out, was viewed by many as a positive step in allowing developing countries unbiased access to the free market. However, fears also existed that larger, competitive countries such as China and India, which have the capacity, stable economy and labour force to out-produce any small economy, would gain unfair portions of market growth (Curran 2008).

To inhibit this immediate growth by China at the close of 2005, several initiatives were negotiated by WTO member countries to ease the access of China into the new global market. Aside from the MFA, which ended at the beginning of 2005, the following safeguards were developed: the China Textile Safeguards (CTS), which lasted through 2008, and the China Product-Specific Safeguards (CPSS), to be reviewed again in 2013 (Kim and Reinert 2007). The CTS and CPSS provided safeguard provisions which impede market disruption or the situation when 'a significant cause of material injury, or threat of material injury to the domestic industry occurs due to the rapid increase…of imports of an article' (Kim and Reinert 2007: 162). Beginning with the expiration of the MFA, imports to the United States from China witnessed close to a 40% drop in the cost of clothing and textile goods as well as over a 600% volume increase from these Chinese imports (*Southwest Farm Press* 2008). These initial figures not only signified the need for continued safeguard measures, but this challenging import situation also encouraged further discussions on anti-dumping policies and negotiating of a bilateral trade agreement with China (*Southwest Farm Press* 2008).

Based on this new landscape of post-MFA trade, the significance of the phase-out of the MFA on the CNMI is noteworthy. Although the CNMI is a territory of the United States, the Marianas are not protected as an autonomous country under WTO provisions. This is important as the CNMI has benefited from quota-free and duty-free trade with the United States. However, with the elimination of the MFA, the CNMI's garment industry is now facing heightened and intense sourcing competition from other producer countries, namely China (USGAO 2006). A comprehensive introduction to the colonisation and development of the Marianas is discussed in subsequent sections followed by a review of the garment industry in the CNMI.

20.2 Commonwealth of the Northern Mariana Islands

20.2.1 Colonisation and development

The Commonwealth of the Northern Mariana Islands is a collection of 14 islands in the far North Pacific Ocean. Sometimes referred to as 'Saipan', which is actually the capital, the Marianas consist of three main islands, Tinian, Rota and Saipan. Approximately 90% of the inhabitants of the CNMI live on Saipan (USCB 2008). The islands have had a long history of colonisation and military presence which have shaped their modern political and economic structures.

In the 20th century, after nearly three decades of Japanese control, the CNMI was developed to a level deemed adequate to participate in regional and global trading systems, specifically agriculture and manufacturing. Sugarcane, holding over 60% of revenues, was the predominant industry and flourished under Japanese rule (Frith 2000; Lonely Planet 2006). Japan's initiative to modernise the Marianas through trade and infrastructure development set the stage for the island's later expansion to a garment manufacturing hub.

The Marianas entered into the world's political and military scene after the attack by Japan on Pearl Harbor in December 1941. From 1941 to 1944, 'most Islanders spent the war years working to meet Japanese military needs. Military construction forced many to relocate. Property was confiscated, families disrupted, schools and churches closed' (Poyer *et al.* 2001: 309). The Second World War brought lasting change to the islands. During the battle for Saipan on 9 July 1944, over 30,000 Japanese soldiers, 3,500 Americans and 400 Saipanese were killed. Neighbouring Tinian Island also sustained mass casualties and became known as the launching pad of both atomic bombs which were bound for Hiroshima and Nagasaki (Lonely Planet 2006). The transition from Japanese ownership to American control at the close of the Second World War resulted in a complete change of political, social, economic and cultural agendas (Poyer *et al.* 2001; USCB 2008).

On 18 July 1947, President Harry Truman and the US Congress approved a joint resolution and trusteeship with the United Nations (UN) called the United States Trust Territory of the Pacific Islands (TTPI) (Poyer *et al.* 2001; USCB 2008). From the 1950s to 1970s development often encompassed foreign aid from the US Government as opposed to wide-scale plans to foster economic independence (Lonely Planet 2006). Micronesians hoped to regain their pre-war standard of living such as they knew under Japanese rule. However, American policy decisions, administrative choices and racial attitudes such as 'primitive peoples...should be content with a subsistence economy' slowly deteriorated hopes of revival (Poyer *et al.* 2001: 314). The CNMI shifted from a post-war development focus to a globalisation focus after it formed with the United States into a trusteeship on 1 January 1978, which disbanded the existing TTPI agreement and reorganised the nation as the Commonwealth of the Northern Mariana Islands (CIA 2008; USCB 2008).

Efforts to invest in capital and technological development such as tourist resorts, garment factories and commercial fishing in the CNMI and surrounding islands slowly came from 'outside the region in the form of foreign investment and foreign-owned enterprises...[where] only a small percentage of the value of local resources is retained by Pacific Island nations' (Lockwood 2004: 21). Owing to this influx of foreign capital and development, islanders became increasingly dependent on outside influences such as imported foods based on a Western diet as well as consumer items not originally available. Since then, Western foods have caused a 'rapidly growing rate of heart disease and diabetes among islanders' (Lockwood 2004: 21). At the close of 1986 on 3 November, President Ronald Reagan finally proclaimed the Marianas an official commonwealth of the United States (USCB 2008).

20.2.2 Economy and garment industry

The commonwealth status of governance in the CNMI was solely based on the United States' constitution except for special exclusions in customs, wages, immigration laws, taxation and voting rights. Indigenous inhabitants qualified as American citizens; however, still to this day, they are not allowed to vote in United States elections (CIA 2008). These constitutional exclusions allowed for capital investment to flow into the Marianas during the 1980s and 1990s, which developed the island's economy into two main industries: garment production and tourism. Approximately 85% of economic activity in the CNMI was contributed from garment manufacturing and tourism combined, and garments accounted for 96% of exports from the island (USGAO 2006).

The garment industry, the most important industry on the Marianas, was able to expand through abundant, low-skilled and low-cost labourers. Although considered American soil, half of the population in the Marianas is Asian (56.3%), one-third is Pacific Islander (36.3%), mainly of Chamorro descent, and a minute number is Caucasian/other/mixed (7.4%) (CIA 2008). The total population in 2008 was estimated to be 86,616 (USCB 2008). In July 2010, the CIA (2010) estimated a significant population drop to 48,317. Owing to the garment industry, the CNMI has long been a destination for guest workers from South Asian countries, predominately from the Philippines and China. Evidenced by the 2000 census, the population comprised nearly 28,000 foreign labourers, which is roughly one-third of the total population (CIA 2008). In order to maximise the economic advantage of its constitutional amendments, which have allowed special provisions for these labourers, the guest worker programme has provided access to thousands of Chinese and Filipina women to take part in the formation of a new international division of labour (NIDL) on the CNMI. The NIDL as defined by McMichael (2008: 96) began to occur in the 1970s and is 'the relocation of deskilled tasks to lower-wage regions of the world'. As a result of this development and repositioning of the new labour force, opportunities for offshore sourcing arose through the increase of transportation operations and information technology transfers. With ease of movement, both in human and knowledge capital, the shift of global production systems to remote regions of the world was achieved on the CNMI (McMichael 2008).

The special constitutional exclusions, for example garments made in the CNMI that were not composed of foreign materials valued at more than 70% of the garment's worth, were exempt from US quotas and customs duties if exported to the US (USGAO 2000). This allowed for duty-free and quota-free trade, specialised labour provisions such as a low minimum wage, and immigration laws allowing foreign labourers which all contributed to CNMI's comparative advantage over other island nations and Asian countries involved in garment production. For instance,

China, which had an ample, cheap labour force, was still faced with taxation, quotas and tariffs (Clarren 2006). However, more recently, with the phase-out of the MFA, the CNMI garment industry has no longer been able to compete with low-wage, high producing countries such as China. In fact, according to the Department of Labour (DOL), with quota and duty advantages lessened by the phase-out, the manufacturing industry on the islands lost more than 3,800 garment jobs from 2004 to 2006 (USGAO 2006).

In 2000, the island region had a GDP of nearly $900 million and a per capita GDP of $12,500, which included subsidies from the United States Government (USG) (CIA 2008). Unlike other US territories which grew in GDP from 2002 to 2007 (American Samoa, 0.4%; Guam, 1.8%; Virgin Islands, 2.9%), the Marianas declined by an average annual rate of −4.2% compared with mainland US which also grew (2.8%) (The Associated Press 2010). According to the CIA's criteria for GDP, this designates the Marianas as a 'developed country' (GDP of approximately $12,200 or higher) for fiscal qualifications; however, close to half of the population (41%) lies below the poverty line (DOC-CNMI 2007, 2008; CIA 2009b). This *developed country* designation is debatable by other quality of living scales such as the Human Development Index (HDI), which takes into account several different criteria (life expectancy, literacy, and per capita GDP). The HDI ranks countries in world order where a perfect score for the criterion is 1.00 and a lack of any presence for the criterion is 0.00 (CIA 2009b). The CNMI ranked 72nd (HDI = 0.875) on the HDI scale alongside 71st Latvia (0.876) and 73rd Turks & Caicos Islands (0.873). In comparison, mainland US is ranked 31st (HDI = 0.953) (Hastings 2009). These data describe the significant difference between the CNMI and mainland US with special regard to monetary differences. The income gap between $12,500 and $45,020 has posed a dilemma that the islands should be reclassified as a 'developing country'.

> Firth (2000: 191) states that the development classification for the Pacific Islands has long been a sign of contention between the island governments 'because to be classified by international organisations as a Least Developed Country brings benefits and concessions even in a rapidly globalising world'. These advantages can be seen in the continuous flow of United States subsidies that continue to necessitate island dependence on the mainland. This dependence also has been fostered by an unequal distribution of income between the wealthy and the impoverished on the Marianas and a large immigrant labour force which imparted a large percentage of their income towards remittances or overseas income transfers back to their home countries. In addition, one factor that has kept the income gap secure in the past was the low minimum wage which was $3.05 in 2006, well below the 2006 mainland American wage of $5.15 (Clarren 2006). In 2007, Congress passed a new law for the islands raising the hourly minimum wage to $7.25 in a schedule of four stages by 2014 which corresponds to mainland United States law (McPhetres 2008; Chen 2010). This mandated increase in worker wages has garnered criticism and backlash from business owners who have threatened to depart from the islands completely while workers insist a living wage is long overdue (Chen 2010).

Another competitive advantage over countries in central and southern Asia, most notably China and India, is the geographic position of the CNMI. The islands lie practically due south of Japan and east of the Philippines making them a prime location for transportation and port facilities. Although the islands are surrounded by other South Pacific nations, the CNMI's only major export trading partner has been the United States, and its sole export, apparel commodities. At the peak of its economic prosperity, the CNMI's garment industry in the late 1990s exported about $1 billion worth of wholesale garments to the United States annually. This amount equalled well over $2 billion worth of retail-valued garments (Clarren 2006). More recently, however, as increasing competition from China and India has occurred, a decline in garment production in the Marianas has been evident. For instance, in 2007 wholesale apparel goods to the US declined by over two-thirds ($307 million) from $1 billion (OTEXA 2008).

Minimal trading partners and a lack of diverse commodities has left the Marianas at the mercy of the world market economy. The CNMI has been reliant on offshore business interest and the strength of the US dollar to stabilise and grow its economy. Moreover, these circumstances have created a great reliability on the United States' economy and subsidies. Since the future of the CNMI seems uncertain, an analysis of the phase-out of the MFA on the Marianas is needed, particularly as total garment production output continues to decline. The findings of this chapter will lend insight into the long-term impact of the MFA phase-out on the CNMI economy and its people. In order to explore this topic further, both pre- and post- MFA figures from OTEXA will be examined to analyse shifts in export values by US dollar, occurring over a 10-year period from 2000 to 2009. In addition to garment industry complications, the CNMI experienced social development issues with regard to its migrant population and its poorly managed economic structure, which will be discussed further in the next section.

20.2.3 Garment industry turmoil and current conditions

Other issues have surfaced over time through the development of the garment industry on the CNMI and by nature of the guest worker programme, including the prevalence of sweatshop conditions in garment manufacturing facilities. Unpaid, forced overtime or by contrast, no overtime, used as a source of punishment, have been common practices on the Marianas. Many women sought to work overtime for a number of reasons, including repaying recruitment fees necessary to obtain a job on the islands and sending money home to families in the form of overseas remittances (Clarren 2006). Labour unions were not allowed in many factories and employers regularly threatened deportation if workers did not follow orders. Health insurance and other benefits were usually not provided and forced abortions and/ or pregnancy-related terminations of work have been common (Clarren 2006).

As of 15 January 2009, the last remaining factory, Uno Moda, closed its doors, leaving the CNMI without a garment industry and now more than ever heavily reliant on its second major industry, tourism (Saipan Factory Facts 2009). Originally, approximately 35 factories existed in the Marianas during its 30-year period of garment production (McPhetres 2008). In an interview conducted by the Australian Broadcast Corporation, Richard Pierce, Special Assistant to the Governor for Trade Relations and Economic Affairs on the Marianas, stated that not only has Saipan 'lost about 30 percent of its population…[subsequently] revenue streams have decreased about 45 percent in the last three years' (Mortensen 2009). It is obvious that the shrinking of the garment manufacturing sector as a result of the phase-out of the MFA has affected the CNMI's overall economy.

The CNMI has seen the full-circle effects of development from colonialism to globalisation through foreign market investment in the garment industry. Sachs (2005) stated that economies which are dependent on one product for export experience high volatility and uncertainty in the world market. With the fall of the garment industry, the CNMI could potentially revert back to a basic state of development, particularly with the absence of a major industry to support the economy and subsequently its people. Outcomes of this shift include a lack of employment opportunities, an increase in crime, flight of native residents to the United States, and an increase of informal activity jobs such as prostitution and domestic service (McPhetres 2008). The Results section will capture the data gleaned from the United States Census Bureau (USCB) and Office of Textiles and Apparel (OTEXA), as well as other legal documents, academic journals and literature to examine the effects of colonisation, development and globalisation in the Commonwealth of the Northern Mariana Islands, focusing specifically on the garment industry as a source of development. Future implications for the economy and outcomes for the people of the Marianas as the garment industry deteriorated were also included in this examination.

20.3 Results

Through the data analysed in this chapter and as confirmed by other news sources, '"[i]t seems the now desperate CNMI economy must now, more than ever, find some way to reinvent itself. And the possibilities for this are increasingly slim", said Dr Leroy O. Laney, economic adviser to the First Hawaiian Bank' (Eugenio 2009). Included in this section is a discussion of the impact of the MFA phase-out on the CNMI garment industry.

20.3.1 MFA phase-out

Considerable evidence reveals that the garment industry in the CNMI has experienced a market collapse. Results for garment export value (Fig. 20.1) and from the *Major Shippers Report* (Fig. 20.2) quite clearly show that the economy of the CNMI can no longer rely on garment manufacturing, which was its most important industry before the phase-out of the MFA in 2005. From 2000 to 2004, prior to the final phase-out of the MFA, garment export values declined slightly, but not to the

Figure 20.1 **Garment export value**

Source: OTEXA 2008

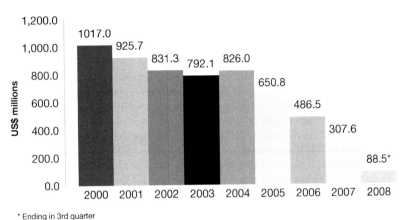

* Ending in 3rd quarter

Figure 20.2 **Major Shippers Report: CNMI**

Source: OTEXA 2008

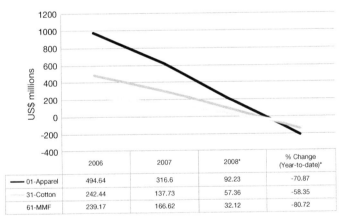

	2006	2007	2008*	% Change (Year-to-date)*
━━ 01-Apparel	494.64	316.6	92.23	-70.87
⋯⋯ 31-Cotton	242.44	137.73	57.36	-58.35
61-MMF	239.17	166.62	32.12	-80.72

* Year-to-date through September 2008

same extremes as seen after 2005. In fact, Figure 20.1, which highlights the period from 2000 to 2007, reveals that in 2004 garment export value actually increased (4.28%) from the previous year. However, in 2005 exports plunged by –21.21% based on 2004 levels and in subsequent years garment export values have continued to erode. From 2004 to 2007, total garment exports declined by two-thirds (–62.76%) from $826.0 million to $307.6 million. The percentage change in export value from 2007 to 2008 (3rd quarter) shows a –71.23% decline (DOC-CNMI 2003, 2006, 2008).

As for imports to mainland US from the CNMI, the Office of Textiles and Apparel (OTEXA) *Major Shippers Report* (see Fig. 20.2), which highlights the period from 2006 to 2008, shows that Category 1-Apparel has fallen by nearly three-quarters (–70.87%) since 2006 through 2008 (year-to-date). In dollar amounts, this accounts for a $402,418,000 loss within two years. In 2006, total garment shipments from the CNMI to the US totalled $494,643,000; by 2008, total garment shipments to the US amounted to only $92,225,000. Shipments have also fallen dramatically from 2006 to 2008 in Category 31-Cotton Apparel (–58.35%) and Category 61-Man-made Fibre Apparel (–80.72%). Clearly, these figures substantiate a resounding decline in CNMI's total garment exports (OTEXA 2008). Furthermore, news reports confirmed that 'the three remaining garment factories on Saipan will survive long enough to meet their obligations to their buyers' (Erediano 2008: 1).

In a smaller cross-section of the CNMI's economy, the manufacturing sector on the CNMI accounted for nearly half of the employed population on the islands. As shown by the data in Table 20.1, the apparel manufacturing sector in 2002, pre-MFA phase-out, encompassed almost all of the manufacturing sector with regard to sales/revenues, annual payroll and number of employees. With the demise of the garment industry, the major provider of legitimate employment on the CNMI, over 17,000 people, predominately women, are now either unemployed or struggling to find another means of living (see Fig. 20.3). Additionally, in the 2007 *Economic Census of Island Areas* report, post-MFA phase-out, apparel manufacturing establishments fell by almost 50%, sales/revenues decreased by nearly 75% as did annual payroll, and number of employees dwindled to 60% of that reported in the 2002 *Economic Census of Island Areas* report (USCB, DOC 2004, 2010a).

The most significant factor leading to the demise of the garment manufacturing industry on the CNMI was the phase-out of the MFA in 2005. The MFA was created to stabilise the growth of imports and exports throughout the world by placing quota restrictions on supplier nations. It aided smaller producer nations by protecting them from over-saturation of low-cost goods into the marketplace by larger, more developed nations such as China and India. The intent of the 2005 MFA phase-out was to provide freer trade around the world; yet, the CNMI, a smaller producer nation, was devastated from lost garment export revenues by the close of 2009.

Table 20.1 **Economic factors in 2002 and 2007 for apparel manufacturing, the manufacturing sector and total sectors of the CNMI economy**
Source: USCB, DOC 2004, 2010a

	Year	Establishment #	Sales/Revenues (US$)	Annual payroll (US$)	Employee #
Apparel manufacturing	2002	42	639,357,000	177,781,000	16,351
	2007	25	160,032,000	47,852,000	6,374
Manufacturing sector	2002	78	665,774,000	184,706,000	16,941
	2007	59	189,715,000	56,565,000	7,094
Total sectors	2002	1,276	1,832,130,000	381,575,000	32,790
	2007	1,191	1,284,188,000	246,133,000	22,622

Figure 20.3 **Employed civilian population 16 years and over by male and female (total employed versus manufacturing sector)**
Source: USCB, DOC 2003

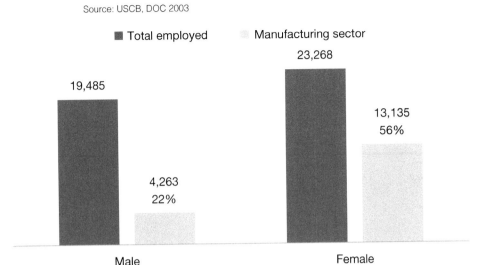

To expand on the effect of the MFA phase-out on the CNMI's economy, further evidence was reported from the *US Possessions Report* published by OTEXA (Table 20.2). These data conveyed that pre-MFA phase-out (2000–2004), imports into the United States from the CNMI totalled over $4,411,166,305 and post-MFA phase-out imports (2005–2009) totalled just $1,596,799,434. In total, a decline of -99.53% occurred in this 10-year period from 2000 to 2009. By 2009, imports into the US from the CNMI accounted for $4,649,067 and a –95.53% loss from the previous year (OTEXA 1995–2009). The *Economic Indicator Report* from the Central Statistics Division of the CNMI's Department of Commerce also had similar findings (Table 20.3). In the post-MFA period (2005–2009), export values from the CNMI to the US fell most dramatically from 2008 to 2009, which recorded $0 in exports by the second quarter of 2009 (DOC-CNMI 2000, 2006, 2009). These findings substantiate the theory that the demise of the garment industry on the CNMI was in fact a result of the phase-out of the MFA in 2005. This phase-out and shift in trade preferences left the small island nation in a state of disarray and financial instability. A result of this garment industry collapse was the reliance on the CNMI's next largest industry, tourism. In the wake of the post-MFA phase-out, the tourism industry on the Northern Mariana Islands has not emerged as the hoped-for solution of economic stability and business growth on the islands. Evidence of a declining industry exists in the business gross revenue reported by the CNMI's Department of Commerce, which recorded a –6.9% change between 2005 and 2009 (DOC- CNMI 2010). With this decline, the working women on the CNMI have faced increasing challenges for employment and survival. A discussion illustrating the effects of the MFA phase-out on women's development on the CNMI is included in the next section of this

Table 20.2 **Total textile and apparel imports by value from 2000 to 2009 (imported by the US from CNMI)**

Source: OTEXA 1995–2009

	Year	Value (US$)	Change to previous year (%)
Pre-MFA phase-out	2000	1,024,985,293	-2.16
	2001	946,597,374	-7.65
	2002	815,310,842	-13.87
	2003	817,151,189	0.23
	2004	807,121,607	-1.23
Post-MFA phase-out	2005	676,915,602	-16.13
	2006	494,724,334	-26.92
	2007	316,602,740	-36.00
	2008	103,907,691	-67.18
	2009	4,649,067	-95.53

Table 20.3 **Total exports from the CNMI from 2000 to 2009**

Source: DOC-CNMI 2000, 2006, 2009

	Year	Export value* (US$)	Change to previous year (%)
Pre-MFA phase-out	2000	1,017,000,000	-4.24
	2002	831,300,000	-18.26
	2003	792,100,000	-4.72
	2004	826,000,000	4.28
Post-MFA phase-out	2005	650,800,000	-21.21
	2006	486,500,000	-25.23
	2007	307,570,000	-36.78
	2008	145,780,000	-52.60
	2009.1	3,140,000	-97.85
	2009.2	0	-100.00

*For the years 1999–2000, the *Economic Indicator Report* attributed this category to 'Total Exports' only. However, the 2002–2009 reports stated 'Garment Exports Value'[1]

1 Ivan Blanco (personal communication, 15 November 2010), Director of the CNMI Commerce Department's Central Statistics Division stated this discrepancy as '99% of CNMI exports from the years you're looking at 1999–2009 was Garment… We do a little export in other commodities but they are not significant and are on an inconsistent basis to capture in our economic indicator reports'.

chapter. Additionally, a comparison of Mauritius, another small island nation, will address how a nation similar to the CNMI has handled development and the MFA-phase out. The chapter will conclude with an exploration of development in the garment industry and future consequences for the CNMI's economy and people.

20.4 Implications

20.4.1 Women as human capital in the garment industry

Human development specifically involving women as human capital is a common practice in the garment industry throughout the world. In order to maintain low production costs, largely an unskilled and uneducated labour force is needed and comprises the majority of the workforce in the garment manufacturing industry. On the CNMI, data from Figure 20.3 illustrate that women and men were equally represented in the total labour market on the Marianas. However, by contrast, in the manufacturing sector, which includes the garment industry, women labourers outnumbered men by 3:1 (USCB, DOC 2003). These data validate the fact that human capital consisted predominantly of women on the CNMI, which is consistent with characteristics of the garment industry. As reported by Bonacich (2002: 126), 'employers claim they prefer young women because of their hand-eye coordination…who are shy and soft-spoken, who have never heard the word *union*, and who respect male authority'. These findings capture the unique characteristics of gender-specific jobs that the garment industry brought to the CNMI which were geared towards women workers. These data also illustrate that the reverberations from the demise of the garment industry have affected women far more than men.

Future policy considerations for the Government of the CNMI should include a focus on women's development. With the disbandment of the garment industry and the downturn of the economy, many positions traditionally held by women in garment manufacturing have created a need in policy development for expanded opportunities in education and technical skills training. Training in higher level skills such as sourcing, trading, marketing, cooperative and fairtrade practices would be an excellent start. Also, development in products that require a higher initial value such as leather manufacturing for accessories like handbags, gloves and shoes could be a potential niche market for the CNMI. By training and educating women in a skill set that is higher than their previous guest worker standard, the government would be creating a new tier of workers, benefiting both individual lives and the country's economic situation. Also, investment in women's training and skill development will provide new human capital investment that could yield positive results for the country's economy and social environment by expanding product manufacturing potentials and new industry segues into technology and communication hubs. Such examples of development in a small island nation can be seen through the development of Mauritius as outlined in the following section.

20.4.2 Mauritius, another small island nation

The garment industry has been vital to the development of market economies for newly developed and developing nations around the globe, and as trade policies and agreements are modified, the effects reverberate throughout the world by impacting markets of scale. As such, another developing small island nation that has also been affected by the phase-out of the MFA is Mauritius. Mauritius stands as one of the most developed southern African nations. With a population of nearly 1.3 million, the island nation has grown from a low-income, agriculturally based economy to a middle-income development state which incorporates industry, tourism and financial investment (CIA 2009a). At its independence in 1968, per capita income was approximately $260. Today, it has grown to nearly $12,400 which is the second highest in Africa (World Bank 2008; CIA 2009a).

Mauritius is similar in its colonial development to the Commonwealth of the Northern Mariana Islands. However, its economy has most recently been based on four pillars: sugar, tourism, economic processing zones (EPZs) and financial services. A plan called the *Economic Agenda for the New Millennium (2001–2005)* also identified an additional 'pillar' of growth within Mauritius which is the information and communication technology sector (African Development Bank Group 2009). This additional pillar has guided Mauritius's development away from dependence on its initial colonial economic sources such as sugar production while providing 'greater diversification, hoping to make it more resilient to shocks and increase its competitiveness in world markets' (Mauritius Economy: Outlook 2009: para. 1). Out of the above pillars, sugarcane accounts for 15% of Mauritius's export earnings and approximately 90% of cultivated land use. Additionally, food processing, textiles and garment manufacturing, mining and chemicals are part of the industry sector. The services sector, making up almost three-quarters of the GDP (70.6%), has continued to attract upwards of 32,000 outside foreign investment companies which gain advantage from the banking sector and commerce in India, South Africa and China (CIA 2009a). Investments in education and infrastructure continue to play an important role to provide adequate facilities and increased human capital for the services sector on Mauritius (Mauritius Economy: Outlook 2009).

Unlike the CNMI, EPZs have long been a part of Mauritius's model of development. The CNMI represented an EPZ by definition, but it bound itself to only a small segment of garment trading with the US. EPZs as defined by Kinunda-Rutashobya (2003: 227) are 'geographically or juridically bounded areas in which free trade, including duty free import of intermediate goods, is permitted provided that all goods produced within the zone are exported'. Major incentives for EPZs are 'economic development via export development, growth of manufactured products, creation of employment, technology transfer and better use of domestic resources' (Kinunda-Rutashobya 2003: 227). Beginning in 1970, Mauritius founded Africa's first EPZ which today exports the likes of textiles, apparel, flowers, optical goods, jewellery and toys. In the late 1990s, clothing accounted for nearly 80% of EPZ exports and of those exports one-half went to two countries: France and the UK (Brautigam 1999). However, even with the success of the Mauritian EPZ model which increased foreign investment, capital and manufactured exports, the country has recently found itself challenged by a declining export market and the downturn of the Mauritian rupee from the late 2000s worldwide financial crisis. Mauritius was diversified and specialised within garment manufacturing and other industries; yet instead of losing a foothold in trade, it continued to explore new ways to grow its internal economy through foreign direct investment (FDI).

Mauritius mimicked the CNMI's business boom closely in the mid-1980s. Yet, the Mauritius model was firmly grounded in export-led industrialisation as a means to create economic growth. This export-led development facilitated investment from outside businesses particularly from European countries that had reached their quota limits and were exploring cheaper sources of labour. In addition, local domestic capital derived mainly from the sugar oligarchy was also invested back into the EPZs which accounted for approximately 50% of ownership (Meisenhelder 1997). Less dependence on foreign investment and a furthering of development for internal banks and lenders has given Mauritius an advantage over other African countries that do not have such a diverse range of capital. Of the foreign investors that have taken part in the Mauritian economy, Hong Kong and China have been the predominant force behind FDI (Brautigam 1999). As a result of this EPZ expansion early on in Mauritius's export history, key infrastructure development and worldwide trading networks contributed to and provided for the stability of the country's economy. In order to add more diversity in foreign investment strategies, one solution that Mauritius considered was to bolster EPZs by focusing on a 'higher value-added production while moving lower-skill production to neighboring countries with cheaper labour' (Brautigam 1999: 230).

Mauritius has excelled at developing FDI through its use of EPZs in the past two decades to develop a stable and growing economy. As necessity for factory investments has declined, Mauritian businesses and their government have been creative in seeking out offshore production capacities as a model of 'value-added' production. These economic policies have led the country into a network of globalisation and support, forming a regional economic integration (REI) and regional trade agreements (RTAs) with several southern African nations. These nations may be better equipped to handle world market shocks and unforeseen factors in globalisation because they have in a sense pooled their resources as one, while still maintaining individualised goals and niches in the marketplace.

Aside from FDI in the Mauritian economy as shown above, capital has also been invested across southern Africa by private enterprises, mainly in sugar and other agro-industries but also in the garment industry. Côte d'Ivoire, Tanzania, Madagascar and Mozambique have been recipients of this REI (Lincoln 2006). REI as defined by Buckley *et al.* (2001: 252) is 'a way of increasing the preference of multinational enterprises (MNEs) for local production within the integrating area, and of increasing relative discrimination against firms outside the area of integration'. This allows for countries to reap the economic benefits of a larger geographical area, in effect increasing the 'size' of a country, without reliance on only one autonomous nation. REI and RTAs indeed create stability in a region; however, they also have the potential to exhibit protectionist measures by limiting global trading systems to operate without hindrances. Ultimately, Mauritius has positioned itself in an ideal place to begin branching out from its initial focus on sugar production and garment and textile manufacturing.

REI and RTAs have exhibited both political and economic significance for the region and '[t]odays RTAs go beyond simple trade liberalization of goods to incorporate comprehensive agreements on services, investment, customs procedures, and reach behind borders to harmonize domestic policies on standards, intellectual property, procurement etc.' (Close 2006: 867). An important consideration, however, is that REI must take place between countries at a similar development stage or the gap between economies and technologies may be an upward challenge that causes more frustration than benefit (Close 2006). Ultimately, REI and RTAs have the potential to provide technology transfers and government reform through the use of trade and capital.

As the Government of the Commonwealth of the Northern Mariana Islands looks to the future, evidence of increased regional economic integration and regional trade agreements should be a prime focus. Formation of REI and RTAs present a huge possibility for the CNMI. With close proximity to Guam, the Marshall Islands, Solomon Islands and Micronesia, the CNMI is situated to expand into a regional bloc for manufacturing and trade alliances. With the termination of garment production contracts, new inventiveness is necessary in order to transition into a different industry. Mauritius has been proactive by developing its fifth pillar, the information and communication technology sector, and it has been creative in exploring new processes for sugar production such as alternative fuel energy. The small island of Mauritius positioned itself in a stronger economic position after the 2005 MFA phase-out than that in which the CNMI now finds itself. This ingenuity and motivation are ultimately the first steps to cultivating a nation with strong, stable and lengthy economic growth possibilities and a positive human capital development factor.

20.4.3 Development and the garment industry

The long-term impact of the MFA phase-out has not yet been seen, but in the short term it has caused terrible consequences for the CNMI's island economy and its people. Clearly the CNMI's cost of living is inflated as noted in statistics from the consumer price index in Figure 20.4, which shows that the costs for housing and utilities, food and transportation have escalated since 2005. In the case of housing and utilities, the cost of living has risen by over 40% after the phase-out of the MFA (DOC, CNMI 2009). In addition, the International Data Base, published by the USCB, predicts a levelling off of population growth by 2025 which does not bode well for labour-intensive industries such as manufacturing and service sectors that support tourism (USCB, DOC 2010b). Another factor for the people of the CNMI that has complicated their future development is the complete federalisation of the island's governance given over to the US Government. In a broadcast interview by PRI's The World (2010: 3), Magistrad, the reporter, stated:

Figure 20.4 **CNMI consumer price index comparison for 2000, 2005 and 2009 in the 4th quarter**

Source: Department of Commerce, Commonwealth of the Northern Mariana Islands 2009 (DOC-CNMI 2009)

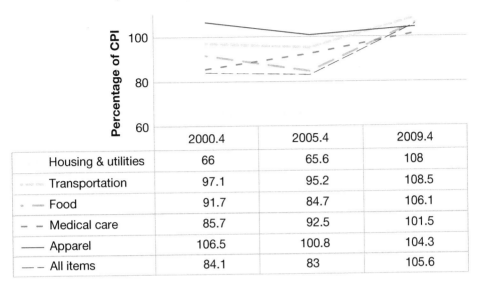

	2000.4	2005.4	2009.4
Housing & utilities	66	65.6	108
Transportation	97.1	95.2	108.5
Food	91.7	84.7	106.1
Medical care	85.7	92.5	101.5
Apparel	106.5	100.8	104.3
All items	84.1	83	105.6

> [A native islander]…says he grew up in a very different Saipan, a quieter and friendlier Saipan and looking around at the Chinese hookers in micro-minis, the abandoned garment factories, the casinos and endless poker parlors, he says we don't need more of this stuff.

Another participant followed up with,

> Bank robbery. It was unheard of when I was growing up. We lost that community spirit on our island, the way we developed. We choose to be part of the United States but we're not an industrial society. We are islanders (PRI's The World 2010: 3).

The turn to US federalisation has given responsibility to the USG to control immigration rules and non-immigrant status for eligible aliens. The circumstances which led to the development of the Marianas resulted from a key decision taken by the US Administration after the close of the Second World War. An economic survey of the island conducted in 1946 gave recommendations for the economic stability of the CNMI which the USG should abide by for the sake of the island's natives. This document, *Planning Micronesia's Future*, reveals the challenging circumstances that the islands and their inhabitants were left in after devastation from the war (Oliver 1946). Because of the USG's responsibility for the islands, Oliver (1946: 28) found that:

> [n]atives lost the economic advantages of their previous income levels through no fault of their own… The American Administration must assist

in organizing the framework of finance and, like previous administrations, it must continue to provide financial assistance not only for recovery of native economic life but also for its continuation after recovery. That is one of the inescapable costs of holding the islands.

One recommendation from the US Office of Insular Affairs' government report, *Economic Impact of Federal Laws on the Commonwealth of the Northern Mariana Islands*, was that the US should amend the covenant originally binding the two countries together. For factors such as minimum wage and immigration laws, this could be an avenue into self-governance for the CNMI. But for practical purposes, this recommendation could also deplete any financial support and security that the US currently provides to the islands which would leave them in an even worse condition (McPhee *et al.* 2008).

The question remains to be answered if the garment industry is in fact a positive factor in the development of small nations such as the CNMI and regions with little to no previous manufacturing and trading experience. The paradox remains that the USG allowed and encouraged factors such as exclusions to immigration and minimum wage laws which allowed the CNMI to prosper in garment manufacturing and to develop large amounts of economic and capital gain. Based on the Human Development Index discussed in Section 20.2.2, the income gap between the CNMI and the mainland US is $12,500 to $45,020. With this in mind, the CNMI should be given special considerations for a *developing country* and the US as administrator should be responsible for its state of development. However, with the instatement of the USG as sole administrator of governance for the CNMI's immigration and constitutional amendments that occurred in late 2009, the CNMI has once again found itself where it was over 60 years ago—at an economic disadvantage to the United States and in extreme dependence on the US in matters of financial assistance and future rule and guidance.

Subsequently, the most significant implication of this study was the recognition of the lack of planning executed by the USG to grow a robust and diverse economy on the CNMI. As noted by Sachs (2005), economies which manufacture and export a singular commodity do not fare well in the global marketplace and face great uncertainty and even greater dependence in times of trial. The 'dependency theory' derives from a view that the failure of development in underdeveloped countries is a result of capitalistic ventures which strip the underdeveloped country of its own natural capital while making developed countries wealthier (Peoples 1978). The outcome of the CNMI, according to the dependency theory, shows that technology and investment in capital and skills given to an underdeveloped society cannot in and of themselves create economic growth. However, depletion of vital resources, human capital, labour manipulation and exploitation are common consequences of failing development in small island nations with little economic power (Peoples 1978). More forethought and care should be executed by governments, businesses and investors towards a country and its people who will ultimately be most affected by change through development, growth and/or decline. The USG on all accounts should be responsible for the state of the CNMI today and support the country with its autonomous desires for self-governance.

The garment industry as a catalyst for development and change is certainly a viable means for low-income, underdeveloped countries to vie for a part of the world economy. This industry brings countries with little or no infrastructure into the world market with a capitalistic structure based on Western methods of business—profit equals development and an upward movement of social status change. The garment industry is also a form of comparative advantage that allows for economic growth which in turn encourages a country's development and initiates outside trading exchanges in the world marketplace. Multiple factors are required to sustain this development such as an expansive network where garment manufacturing can flourish and lead to new tiers of increased opportunity by developing higher skill sets, educational initiatives and the ability to create innovative practices while having the capacity to risk undertaking them.

20.4.4 Recommendations for future research

Ongoing research is needed to examine the continued outcomes for the economy and people of the CNMI as a result of the garment industry collapse. Additionally, further research is recommended for studying the effects of the MFA phase-out on smaller regions and countries such as the CNMI and Mauritius where the garment industry was integral to the development of a market economy and the formation of the present-day country as a whole. Also, as the CTS and the CPSS safeguards, which give regimented protection from Chinese exports, come to an end by 2013, continued research on the effects of the garment industry on developing nations will be an important topic. Given that these Chinese safeguards still exist, they provide some protection to smaller garment producing nations. The outcomes of their complete removal are unknown and a completely free quota system in the garment industry will continue to change and influence global markets and economies.

References

African Development Bank Group (2009) 'Mauritius', www.afdb.org/en/countries/southern-africa/mauritius, accessed 23 April 2009.

Bonacich, E. (2002) 'Labor's Response to Global Production', in G. Gereffi, D. Spencer and J. Bair (eds.), *Free Trade and Uneven Development: The North American Apparel Industry after NAFTA* (Philadelphia, PA: Temple University Press): 123-35.

Brautigam, D. (1999) 'Mauritius: Rethinking the Miracle', *Current History* 98.628: 228-31.

Buckley, P., J. Clagg, N. Forsans and K. Reilly (2001) 'Increasing the Size of the "Country": Regional Economic Integration and Foreign Direct Investment in a Globalised World Economy', *Management International Review* 41.3: 251-74.

Chen, M. (2010) 'Minimum Wage, and Controversy, Reaches Distant U.S. Islands', In These Times, www.inthesetimes.com/working/entry/5858/minimum_wage_and_controversy_reaches_distant_u.s._islands, accessed 19 April 2010.

CIA (Central Intelligence Agency) (2008) 'Northern Mariana Islands', The World Factbook, https://www.cia.gov/library/publications/the-world-factbook/geos/cq.html, accessed 11 November 2008.

CIA (2009a) 'Mauritius', The World Factbook, https://www.cia.gov/library/publications/the-world-factbook/geos/mp.html, accessed 16 February 2009.

CIA (2009b) 'Appendix B: International Organizations and Groups', The World Factbook, https://www.cia.gov/library/publications/the-world-factbook/appendix/appendix-b.html, accessed 19 March 2009.

CIA (2010) 'Northern Mariana Islands', The World Factbook, https://www.cia.gov/library/publications/the-world-factbook/geos/cq.html, accessed 12 August 2010.

Clarren, R. (2006) 'Paradise Lost', *Ms. Arlington* 16.2: 34-41.

Close, P. (2006) 'Regional Adaptive Synergies in the World Trading System', *Journal of World Trade* 40.5: 865-87.

Curran, L. (2008) 'Forecasting the Trade Outcomes of Liberalization in a Quota Context: What Do We Learn from Changes in Textiles Trade After the ATC?' *Journal of World Trade* 42.1: 129-50.

DOC (Department of Commerce) CNMI (2000) 'Economic Indicator', Fourth Quarter, Central Statistics Division, www.commerce.gov.mp/wp-content/uploads/2010/08/EI-2000.4.pdf, accessed 13 August 2010.

DOC-CNMI (2003) 'Economic Indicator', Fourth Quarter, Central Statistics Division, www.commerce.gov.mp/wp-content/uploads/2010/08/EI-2003.4.pdf, accessed 11 November 2008.

DOC-CNMI (2006) 'Economic Indicator', Fourth Quarter, Central Statistics Division, www.commerce.gov.mp/wp-content/uploads/2011/09/E.I.-4th-QTR-2006.pdf, accessed 13 August 2010.

DOC-CNMI (2007) 'Economic Indicator', Fourth Quarter, Central Statistics Division, www.commerce.gov.mp/wp-content/uploads/2011/09/EI_2007.4-2.pdf, accessed 6 March 2008.

DOC-CNMI (2008) 'Economic Indicator', Third Quarter, Central Statistics Division, www.commerce.gov.mp/wp-content/uploads/2010/08/EI-2008.4.pdf, accessed 11 November 2008.

DOC-CNMI (2009) 'Consumer Price Index', Third & Fourth Quarter, Central Statistics Division, www.commerce.gov.mp/divisions/central-statistics/consumer-price-index, accessed 20 November 2010.

DOC-CNMI (2010) 'Economic Indicator', Third & Fourth Quarter, Central Statistics Division, www.commerce.gov.mp/wp-content/uploads/2011/05/EI-2010-Q3.pdf, accessed 13 August 2010.

Erediano, E.T. (2008) 'Saipan Has 3 Garment Factories Left', Marianas Variety News, 17 October 2008, www.mvariety.com/cnmi/cnmi-news/local/11784-saipan-has-3-garment-factories-left, accessed 16 October 2008.

Eugenio, H.V. (2009) 'CNMI economy bleaker', Saipan Tribune, 28 April 2009, www.saipantribune.com/newsstory.aspx?newsID=89774&cat=1, accessed April 28, 2009.

Firth, S. (2000) 'The Pacific Islands and the Globalization Agenda', The Contemporary Pacific 12.1 (Expanded Academic ASAP via Gale, www.scholarspace.manoa.hawaii.edu/bitstream/handle/10125/13505/v12n1-178-192-dialogue.pdf?sequence=1, accessed 10 November 2008): 177-92.

Hastings, D.A. (2009) 'Filling Gaps in the Human Development Index', Findings from Asia and the Pacific, UNESCAP Website, www.unescap.org/pdd/publications/workingpaper/wp_09_02.pdf, accessed 4 October 2012.

Kim, S.J., and K.A. Reinert (2007) 'Textile and Clothing Safeguards: From the ATC to the Future', *Estey Centre Journal of International Law and Trade Policy* 8.2: 155-74.

Kinunda-Rutashobya, L. (2003) 'Exploring the Potentialities of Export Processing Free Zones (EPZs) for Economic Development in Africa: Lessons from Mauritius', *Management Decision* 41.3: 226-32.

Lincoln, D. (2006) 'Beyond the Plantation: Mauritius in the Global Division of Labour', *Journal of Modern African Studies* 44.1 (doi: 10.1017/S0022278X05001412, accessed 17 February 2009): 59-78.

Lockwood, V. (2004) *Globalization and Culture Change in the Pacific Islands* (Upper Saddle River, NJ: Pearson Education, Inc.).

Lonely Planet (2006) *Northern Mariana Islands Chapter Guide* (Victoria, Australia: Lonely Planet Publications, 3rd edn).

McMichael, P. (2008) *Development and Social Change: A Global Perspective* (Los Angeles: Pine Forge Press, 4th edn).

McPhee, M.D. & Associates, and D. Conway (2008) *Economic Impact of Federal Laws on the Commonwealth of the Northern Mariana Islands* (Office of the Governor, The Commonwealth of the Northern Mariana Islands by the Office of Insular Affairs, US Department of the Interior; Sequim, WA: M.D. McPhee & Associates).

McPhetres, S.F. (2008) 'Commonwealth of the Northern Mariana Islands', *The Contemporary Pacific* 20.1 (Expanded Academic ASAP via Gale, www.find.galegroup.com/itx/start.do?prodId=EAIM, accessed 10 November 2008): 204-209.

Mauritius Economy: Outlook (2009) 'Mauritius Economy: Outlook – Moving to a Services-Orientated Economy', ABI/INFORM Global database, www.search.proquest.com.er.lib.k-state.edu/abicomplete/docview/466458246/abstract/139C661854C14F03ED1/1?accountid=11789, accessed 10 April 2009.

Meisenhelder, T. (1997) 'The Development State in Mauritius', *Journal of Modern African Studies* 35.2: 279-97.

Mortensen, M. (2009) 'Demise of Last Three Garment Factories on Saipan', Pacific Beat Home, transcript of radio broadcast 14 January 2009, Australian Broadcasting Corporation, www.radioaustralia.net.au/pacbeat/stories/200901/s2466051.htm, accessed 14 January 2009.

Nordas, H.K., and WTO Secretariat (2004) *The Global Textile and Clothing Industry Post the Agreement on Textiles and Clothing* (Geneva, Switzerland: WTO Secretariat).

OTEXA (Office of Textiles and Apparel) (1995–2009) 'U.S. Possessions Report: Commonwealth of the Northern Mariana Islands', Dataset, *Department of Commerce* (Washington, DC: OTEXA, datasets by Keith Daly).

OTEXA (2008) 'Major Shippers. Country: Northern Marianas', Department of Commerce, www.otexa.ita.doc.gov/nmar/v9610.htm, accessed 11 November 2008.

Oliver, D.L. (1946) *Planning Micronesia's Future: A Summary of the United States Commercial Company's Economic Survey of Micronesia* (Cambridge, MA: Harvard University Press).

Peoples, J.G. (1978) 'Dependence in a Micronesian Economy', *American Ethnologist* 5.3: 535-52.

Poyer, L., S. Falgout and L. Carucci (2001) *The Typhoon of War: Micronesian Experiences of the Pacific War* (Honolulu, HI: University of Hawaii Press).

PRI's The World (2010) 'Saipan's Garment Factories', PRI's The World: Global Perspectives for an American Audience, radio broadcast, 19 February 2010, www.theworld.org/2010/02/19/saipans-garment-factories, accessed 19 February 2010.

Sachs, J.D. (2005) *The End of Poverty: Economic Possibilities for Our Time* (New York: Penguin Group).

Saipan Factory Facts (2009) 'Saipan Factory Facts: Information on the Rise and Fall of the Garment Industry', www.saipanfactorygirl.com/facts, accessed 15 April 2009.

Southwest Farm Press (2008) 'U.S. Seeks Monitoring of Chinese Textile Imports', *Southwest Farm Press* 35.20.

The Associated Press (2010) 'GDP Estimated for US Territories for 1st Time', *The Seattle Times*, 5 May 2010, www.seattletimes.com/html/businesstechnology/2011790841_apusgdpterritories.html?syndication=rss, accessed 10 May 2010.

USCB, DOC (United States Census Bureau, Department of Commerce) (2003) *2000 Census of Population and Housing, PHC-4-CNMI: Commonwealth of the Northern Mariana Islands* (Washington, DC: US Government Printing Office).

USCB, DOC (2004) *2002 Economic Census of Island Areas: Geographic Area Studies, IA02-00A-NMI: Northern Mariana Islands* (Washington, DC: US Government Printing Office).

USCB, DOC (2008) 'Puerto Rico and the U.S. Island Areas. Overview: The Commonwealth of the Northern Mariana Islands', www.census.gov/population/www/proas/pr_ia_hist.html, accessed 11 November 2008.

USCB, DOC (2010a) '2007 Economic Census of Island Areas: Sector 00: IA0700A01: All Island Area Sectors: Geographic Area Series: Comparative Statistics by Kind of Business for American Samoa, Guam, Northern Mariana Islands, Puerto Rico, and U.S. Virgin Islands: 2007 and 2002', American FactFinder, www.factfinder2.census.gov/bkmk/table/1.0/en/ECN/2007_IA/00A01/0400000US69/naics~ALL, accessed 18 September 2010.

USCB, DOC (2010b) 'Country Summary: Northern Mariana Islands', International Data Base, www.census.gov/population/international/data/idb/region.php?N=%20Results%20&T=13&A=separate&RT=0&Y=2010&R=-1&C=CQ, accessed 5 December 2010.

USGAO (United States Government Accountability Office) (2000) *Report to the Ranking Minority Member, Subcommittee on International Security, Proliferation and Federal Services, Committee on Governmental Affairs, U.S. Senate: Northern Mariana Islands: Procedures for Processing Aliens and Merchandise* (GAO/GGD-00-97; Washington, DC: US Government Accountability Office).

USGAO (2006) *Report to the Committee on Energy and Natural Resources, US Senate. US Insular Areas: Economic, Fiscal, and Financial Accountability Challenges* (GAO-07-119; Washington, DC: US Government Accountability Office).

World Bank (2008) 'Mauritius: Country Brief', www.web.worldbank.org/WBSITE/EXTER-NAL/COUNTRIES/AFRICAEXT/MAURITIUSEXTN/0,,menuPK:381984~pagePK:141132~piPK:141107~theSitePK:381974,00.html, accessed 16 February 2009.

Sarah Heidebrecht graduated from Kansas State University with a MS in Apparel & Textiles and a focus on development in the apparel industry. She currently resides in Madison, Wisconsin, as a Product Buyer for SERRV International, one of the first recognised fairtrade non-profit organisations in the world.

Joy M. Kozar is an associate professor in the Department of Apparel, Textiles, and Interior Design at Kansas State University. Her research activities include an examination of issues pertaining to social responsibility and labour exploitation in the production of apparel and textile goods.

Part IV

Consumer: purchase, identity, use and care of clothing and textiles

Young academic women's clothing practice

Interactions between fast fashion and social expectations in Denmark

Charlotte Louise Jensen and Michael Søgaard Jørgensen

Department of Development and Planning, Aalborg University, Denmark

Clothing is one of the sectors in which substantial parts of production in industrialised countries have been outsourced to newly industrialised countries. Cleaner technology and eco-labelling initiatives in the industrialised countries have been launched more or less parallel to this outsourcing of production. Furthermore, the frequency of design of new products has increased through industry's and retailers' so-called 'fast fashion' strategies (Bhardwaj and Fairhurst 2010), and consumption of clothing in industrialised countries has grown (see for example Hille 1995 and Behrendt *et al.* 2003). This chapter contributes to the development of knowledge about how female clothing practices in industrialised countries are shaped by social aspects and by the dynamics of the global supply chains and the fashion strategies. Furthermore, the chapter contributes to analyses of the conditions for development of clothing practices in industrialised countries with fewer environmental effects. The chapter is based on an ethnographic study of the clothing practices among a small group of young Danish academic women (Jensen 2010). The chapter also draws on experiences from several case studies of environmental management in companies and product chains in the Danish clothing sector (Stranddorf *et al.* 2002; Kawansson and Roy 2002; Forman *et al.* 2003; Forman and

Jørgensen 2004; Jørgensen 2006; Thomsen 2007; Jørgensen *et al.* 2010). Denmark is interesting to analyse as it is one of the countries in the European Community with the highest number of EU flower eco-labelled products on textiles and clothing, both in absolute and relative terms.

21.1 Practice theory

Sociological studies of women's relationship with clothes show that women often create identity and express themselves through their clothes (Guy *et al.* 2001; Woodward 2008). In analyses of women's use of clothing from an environmental perspective, it is interesting to look into factors which shape these practices, especially the social dimensions of self-expression.

The dynamics behind the daily practices of buying clothes and choosing what to wear and what not to wear have been analysed through a practice theory perspective, which focuses on the shaping of everyday life activities. Practice theory suggests that our actions have social meaning. Practice theory related to consumption studies mainly draws on practice theory as articulated by Schatzki and Reckwitz (Gram-Hanssen 2011) and focuses on understanding routines in everyday life. Both authors emphasise the collective aspect of practices. Reckwitz focuses on individuals acting as carriers of practices, meaning that everyone *performs* practices as part of their everyday life by having a certain way of enacting and articulating things. Because we perform the practice, the practice exists. Schatzki focuses on practices as coordinated entities that are unfolded temporarily, consisting of people's 'doings and sayings' (Gram-Hanssen 2011), also meaning that practices exist *because* we enact and verbalise certain things in our everyday life that through our doings and sayings become socially accepted and even socially dominant. According to Røpke (2009), 'individuals face practices-as-entities as these are formed historically as a collective achievement; and through their own practices-as-performance, individuals reproduce and transform the entities over time'. Individuals thus act as 'carriers of practices' (Røpke 2009). Dressing yourself as everyday activity is seen as a practice with certain norms and routines that are acted out when a person chooses what to buy and what to wear. Performing a certain practice in daily activities does not necessarily make people aware of the fact that when performing the practice they consume resources (Røpke 2009). People focuses on what performing the practices means to them (Røpke 2009). This implies that activities such as buying and wearing clothes are not necessarily seen as consumption of resources materialised in clothes, and people do not therefore necessarily see their clothing practice as having environmental impacts. Røpke (2009) points to the importance of analyses of the *shaping* of practices through co-evolutionary studies of the changing configurations of practices, modes of provision and global supply chains.

21.2 Methodology for analyses of clothing practices

A statistical analysis of the changes in average annual private purchase of clothing and footwear among Danish consumers in 2000–2007 was carried out in order to assess the recent trends in clothing practices. (Since it was not possible to obtain data for only clothing, the combination of purchase of clothing and footwear had to be chosen.) In order to get knowledge about individual clothing practices and their shaping, an ethnographic study of six young women's clothing practices was carried out. The women chosen for this study were all between 25 and 30 years old, all enrolled in higher education or had just finished it. The type of education that all women had acquired included some level of environmental education or basic environmental knowledge. The women are analytically seen as critical cases in the sense that, as well-educated women, they should be more likely than the average consumer to consider environmental concerns in their clothing practices. This implies that if these women are only showing limited environmental concerns in their clothing practices it is likely that Danish consumers in general show limited environmental concerns in their clothing practices.

When studying practices, it may be relevant to make use of ethnographic research approaches. Ethnography is a well-known approach in social sciences and is about studying *culture*. From being a method that has mostly been used to explore cultures in 'far-off' places that has almost been regarded as 'detached', it has become more and more widely used to understand ourselves in multicultural societies (Spradley 1979). When doing ethnographic interviews, the interviews are qualitative and open-ended, only guided by a semi-structured interview guide (Spradley 1979) that helps the interviewer and the interviewee to keep 'on track', but is by no means supposed to confine the interview process, if the informant puts emphasis on aspects related to the topic which are not included in the interview guide.

In our study (Jensen 2010), we have mainly used the ethnographic research approach in order to try to uncover and understand social dimensions that shape women's relationship with clothes.

The study comprised a number of individual interviews based on a semi-structured interview guide. Prior to the interviews, the women were asked to write a diary for a week, describing their choices of what to wear and what not to wear, what inspired those choices, and how they made them. The diaries were handed back to the researcher, and then read prior to the interviews. The individual interview was based on a common interview guide (see Jensen 2010) but accompanied by questions that had arisen when reading the particular informant's diary. The diaries were included in the research process to make the women reflect on their clothing processes, *before* knowing what the interviews were going to focus on. In this case, aspects that each woman found relevant for her clothing practice could be included in the interview. In this way the researcher was also able to see whether any environmental issues as well as aspects about resources and amounts of clothes were included in each woman's *own initial* reflections.

During the individual interviews, each woman was asked to talk about her wardrobe, while showing it to the interviewer, very much like a 'guided tour' around the wardrobe. Each woman could choose by herself what she felt important to talk about when going through the wardrobe. The session was called 'show me your wardrobe' and was done in correspondence to Spradley's (1979) suggestions on including descriptive questions in the interview. This enables the interviewee to talk about her practice in her own words, emphasising what she finds important.

After the individual interviews, a focus-group interview was conducted with the same women. The focus group interview is not an ethnographic approach, but it can help the researcher to uncover and understand the social dimensions of aspects covered in the focus-group interview. When people are put together to discuss an aspect the social orders of the group as well as the social aspects of the topic may be better uncovered, than when doing individual interviews (Halkier 2008). The focus-group interview was specifically about environmental aspects of clothing, and the women were asked through a very confined number of questions to discuss how they think clothes influence the environment. Afterwards, the women were asked to individually rank a number of approaches to 'greener' clothing practices (eco-labelling etc.), and afterwards explain their ranking, which immediately led to a discussion of the different options among the women.

Before presenting the findings of the ethnographic study, some overall dynamics of production and consumption of clothing will be described to contextualise the women's clothing practices.

21.3 Overall dynamics of production and consumption of clothing

The clothing sector is a very distributed and heterogeneous industrial sector with a globalised structure in large parts of the sector where production and consumption take place in different countries and possibly different continents. The clothing product chains are composed of a wide number of subsectors covering the entire production cycle from the production of raw materials (fibres) to semi-processed products (yarn and fabrics with their finishing processes) and final/consumer products. Around 55% of the world production of fibres for clothing and textiles are synthetic fibres and around 45% are different types of natural fibre (mainly cotton) (Allwood *et al.* 2006).

An increasing portion of the clothes sold in Denmark is manufactured in Eastern Europe and in newly industrialised countries in Asia. Furthermore, an increasing part of the products exported from Denmark has been manufactured in these countries, while design takes place in Denmark (Stranddorf *et al.* 2002).

Clothing consumption in Western countries has been increasing since the 1960s. Behrendt *et al.* (2003) reported an increasing volume of clothing sales in Germany during the 1990s. Norwegian consumption of clothes and footwear grew by 21% from 1997 to 1999 within a stable part of household costs for consumption (Hille 2000), which points to a relative decrease in prices, probably due to increased outsourcing and stronger global competition. According to Allwood *et al.* (2006), the average purchased volume of clothing per capita in the UK increased by 37% from 2001 to 2005. The spending on women's clothing grew by 21% and on men's clothing by 14% despite the fact that prices went down by 14% in real terms. Analysis of the average Danish consumption of clothing and footwear showed an 11% increase in volume from 2000 to 2007. Spending increased 9% while the relative prices decreased by 2–3% (Statistics Denmark 2002-2009, 2010).

This increasing consumption has happened in parallel to changes in the innovation strategies in the clothing sector towards what is called 'fast fashion' (Bhardwaj and Fairhurst 2010). Until the mid-1980s, success in the fashion industry was based on low cost mass production of standardised styles that did not change frequently. However, towards the beginning of the 1990s, retailers started focusing on expansion of their product range with updated products and faster responsiveness to new fashion from the fashion shows. Bhardwaj and Fairhurst (2010) describe an addition of three to five mid-seasons, which put pressure on suppliers to deliver fashion apparel in smaller batches with reduced lead time. Retailers such as Zara and Hennes & Mauritz (H&M) changed their innovation strategies towards fast adoption of the latest fashion from fashion shows and introduced interpretations of the new designs to the stores within three to five weeks in order to attract consumers. Bhardwaj and Fairhurst (2010) argue that this change towards more frequent seasons was in contradiction to changes in the sector from the outsourcing of the production to low cost countries since the outsourcing had led to longer lead times, complicated supply chains due to geographic distances, inconsistency and variability in processes at both ends of the chain, and complex import–export procedures.

21.4 Clothing practices among young academic Danish women

In the following the study of the six women and their clothing practices is presented (Jensen 2010). The study includes an analysis of whether and how these practices affect environmental aspects in terms of resource consumption, waste, chemicals and so on, and whether environmental concerns affect the shaping of the clothing practices. Furthermore, the study focuses on the conditions for the development of more environmentally friendly ('greener') clothing practices. A number of common aspects of 'dressing' among this group of women can be deduced.

21.4.1 Getting bored with clothes

For most of the women, buying new clothes and dressing differently is closely related to having fun with clothes as well as experiencing something. Going shopping is seen as a leisure activity. Some of the women mentioned that after having worn the same piece of clothing for a while, it got boring. It could even be a dress that had only been worn once, for example at a New Year's Eve party. Next year the dress would be seen as boring.

21.4.2 Low prices motivated higher consumption

It seemed to be somewhat general that if a piece of clothing is seen as inexpensive, the women make less consideration before buying it, as opposed to the amount of consideration behind the purchase of a more expensive piece of clothing. If a piece of clothing costs 100 Danish kroner or less (approximately €15) most of the interviewed women would buy the item, even though they are unsure whether they would ever wear it. Several of them feel that if they like the piece of clothing just a little, it would be 'stupid' not to buy it when the price is that low. Furthermore, *sale* is something that made most of the women take an extra look in the shops to see whether something could be of interest because of the reduced price. Some of the interviewed women sometimes consider buying an item of clothing on sale, which they had thought about buying before the sale, but found too expensive. When on sale, how much they actually like the clothes plays a smaller role. It therefore seems fair to conclude that low prices are an enforcing factor for the consumption of clothes *not actually being used*.

21.4.3 Inactive clothes in the wardrobe

As a consequence of the above-mentioned shopping practices, all the interviewed women have amounts of inactive clothes, some more than others. Several of the women state that, because they do not have an overview of what is in the wardrobe, substantial parts of the stock of clothes are left unused. As an example, one of the women believes that she currently only is using around half of her T-shirts. However she also states that she sometimes reshuffled among the T-shirts, indicating that less than 50% is inactive. She believes that about two-thirds of her jeans are inactive, as she does not like to wear jeans but feels that she 'needs' to have some. Another of the women states that more than half of her jeans and shirts are left inactive. Two other women state that more than a third of their entire stock of clothes is inactive.

The reasons for not using the clothes seem similar. Some clothes are not used because the fashion has changed. Other clothing items seem to be inactive because they have found their way to 'the back of the closet', and therefore are out of sight. The out-of-sight-out-of-mind aspect was identified in most of the women's dressing routines. However some of the women keep the inactive clothes for their sentimental value. Some of the women particularly state that they are phasing out clothes but have difficulties discarding these clothes. Other women find it easier to clean out the wardrobe once in a while. But almost all the women keep some clothes mainly for sentimental value.

21.4.4 Expectations about the social network

All the interviewed women are concerned about how friends and colleagues perceive them and believe that the way they dress influences how they are perceived. Such concerns influence how the women dress. The three main considerations are:

- The women do not like to wear the same clothes more than once during the week *if* they meet the *same* people several times during that week. They are worried that people would find them unhygienic. It is interesting that the women do not think that anything would be wrong wearing the same clothes twice a week if they are meeting with *different* people. The women generally emphasise that they do not find it unhygienic to wear the same clothes twice a week, but fear that other people think so. It could be argued that a social practice around hygiene (Shove 2003) is influencing the clothing practice

- Other people might regard them as 'stagnating' if they are wearing the same clothes for a long time (or at two subsequent parties with people they only met at these parties)

- Fashion as a 'rule-setter': The women are influenced by new clothes they see other women wear. It could be on the streets, women they know, or female trendsetters whom one of the women follows on blogs. It seems like most of the women feel that there are certain accepted ways of dressing, and that these ways change. For instance, wearing legwarmers was accepted 15 years ago, but none of the women would even consider wearing them today

One of the women mentions that it seems to be a general expectation that people express themselves through their clothes. She is the only one of the interviewed women who strongly opposes this social expectation. She does not feel that her clothes should be the main thing reflecting her, but since she expects other people to expect that, she reluctantly feels that she needs to think about what she is wearing. She mentions that she wants to wear a kind of uniform for work, so that she does not have to think about what she expresses through her clothes, but this is not possible in her job.

The women's relationship with clothes can be described between very 'expressional' and very 'practical'. Most of these women have a highly expressional relationship with their clothes, which implies that the clothes should represent their mood and identity. Particularly the woman who expresses opposition to the idea that the clothes express you as a person has a much more practical way of relating to her clothes. In relation to a practice perspective, it seems fair to suggest that 'expressing yourself' through clothes, or that clothes can say something about you as a person (identity) or your life (stagnating or not), may characterise a general social practice around dressing—or a **practice-as-entity**, as it is termed in much practice literature (for example Shove 2003; Røpke 2009; Gram-Hanssen 2011). Women may individually perform this practice in different ways (**practice-as-per-formance**), emphasising certain aspects of the practice, or maybe even opposing it, like one of the women. The different categories mentioned above may act as differ-ent types of meaning or reasons for performing the practice. If one woman focuses on fashion and another on variation, it is different aspects which are influencing their performance, and therefore different things that are important or meaningful for them. And if opposing clothing as an expressional tool can be seen as more than merely a reflection during the interviews, but instead a protest towards the practice-as-entity, the practice-as-entity is then not reproduced by that particular woman. This is, however, not evidence of more widespread opposition to this practice, as only one of the interviewed women expresses this feeling. But this may be seen as an example of a practice-as-entity being recognised but opposed, and if more reactions against this practice-as-entity are seen, a foundation for destabilising this practice may be found. However, from this study alone, this cannot be concluded.

In relation to the environmental aspects of clothing and dressing, only one of the six interviewed women mentions something about the environment without being asked directly about it. This woman prefers organic cotton for her inner shirts, because she feels that the material is cleaner and less 'chemical'. However, this strategy is an issue of human toxicology and health, more than an issue of con-cern about the impacts to ecosystems.

21.5 Conditions for 'greener' clothing practices

During a two hour focus-group interview session, the women were asked to discuss the following topics:

- How do you think your use of clothes influences the environment?
- How can different concepts for more environmentally friendly ('greener') clothes be an alternative to conventionally produced clothes?

The women reflected on a large number of environmental aspects of their clothing practices, when asked about it. Issues included waste, use of chemicals and how the increased shopping for new clothes, because of low prices, implies an unneces-sary consumption of clothing. A throwaway mentality was also discussed, and the fact that many stores have new clothes on the racks every week was brought up, which was a new observation for most of the women.

The discussion of procurement of second-hand clothes as a strategy showed mixed experiences and opinions. Most of the women liked the concept, but few of them actually purchase second-hand clothes themselves. However, most of them hand in their own clothes for second-hand use, when discarding them.

The women also discussed issues of laundry. One of the aspects was the amount of detergent used for laundering. The women would like to see more emphasis on guidance about the right amount of detergent instead of the present focus on the temperature the laundry is done at. This implies that chemicals played a more significant role in the women's discussion than the consumption of energy from heating water for laundering.

The women were asked to reflect on a number of concepts for 'greener' clothes: for instance eco-labelling, redesign of clothes and re-use of materials from old clothes. These concepts had been identified prior to the focus-group interview through a literature review. After ranking them, the women were asked to explain why they had ranked the approaches as they did. This ranking turned out to be related to their own use of the concepts and whether they found them feasible with respect to price, costs, accessibility, accountability and so on. The 'greener' concepts discussed and the women's assessments are shown in Table 21.1.

Table 21.1 **'Greener' concepts discussed during the focus-group interview and the women's assessments of the concepts**

Source: Jensen 2010

'Greener' concepts	Women's assessments of the 'greener' concepts
Redesigning already existing clothes	Seen as too expensive, both for industry and consumers
	The women prefer new clothes
Recycled materials for production of new clothes	Most women like this idea, because it gives the possibility of buying new clothes and at the same time saving natural resources
Multifunctional clothes	Generally the women are not happy about this approach
	The women do not think that a multifunctional piece of clothing would be able to replace more than one piece of clothing
Mass-customisation (e.g. a website where one can order a specific shirt in a specific colour)	The women do not believe in this approach. They do not see it as feasible for the industry to have a very small range of variations available for the customer to choose from
	The women do not want to spend the time on choosing and 'designing' themselves
Ecological cotton	Most women would choose the organic cotton option in the stores, if they like the *design* of the piece. They would not choose the organic cotton option just *because* it is organic cotton
Less harmful dyes and chemicals in production	All the women accept this concept, as long as it would not result in *fewer* colours
Environmental labelling	Most of the women see this concept as feasible
	Some women are sceptical about labels because of a lack of transparency of the criteria
	The women do not accept that eco-labelling should restrict their possibilities for choosing between different clothes

The concepts that would require the least changes in the women's clothing practices were assessed most positively. Substitution of chemicals, organic cotton and environmental labelling were ranked highest. However, in some of the assessments it was mentioned as a condition to a positive assessment that the concept should offer the consumer the same range of designs and colours as today. The women experience the availability of environmentally friendly clothes in the stores as very limited. They had only seen environmentally friendly clothes in a certain style and shape and in few colours. The women stated that they would like to have the same wide range of styles, shapes and colours to choose from if they should use environmental labelling as a strategy in their future shopping for clothes. The concepts of redesign and multifunctionality were ranked higher by the women with a more expressional relationship with their clothing, while concepts such as environmental labelling and substitution of chemicals and dyes were ranked higher by women with a more practical relationship with their clothes (Jensen 2010). The preference for alternatives which fit the existing practice seems to confirm the difficulties in disrupting (unsustainable) practices (Røpke 2009).

21.6 Environmental aspects of clothing practices

None of the women relates her daily performances-of-practice to environmental aspects. However, these practices *have* environmental impacts. Wardrobe dynamics such as size, turnover of clothes and how frequently a person is doing laundry are all influencing the environment. The women's wardrobe sizes varied, but an average of 30–40% of inactive clothes characterised the women's practices. Inactive clothing represents clothes that are still in the wardrobe but are rarely or never used. The reasons for the clothes to be inactive varied, but one aspect that seems applicable for some of the women is an 'out-of-sight-out-of-mind' issue. When the women have a lot of clothes in the wardrobe they are not able to see all the clothes in the wardrobe. Another aspect that seemed to leave some clothes inactive was that a lot of the women seemed to fall back on trusted and safe combinations of clothes that they knew fit for various occasions. The daily clothes are rarely selected from the whole range of clothes in the wardrobe. All in all this implies that women consume more resources for clothes than their actual needs for different clothes demand. How often the women do their laundry is not obvious from the research, but they refer to social expectations which make them wash their clothes rather frequently.

21.7 Discussion

The combination of statistical analysis of Danish clothing consumption, the ethnographic study and the analysis of strategies in the clothing sector indicates that the increasing clothing consumption is influenced by interactions between low price strategies on clothing from the increased outsourcing of clothing production to low-income countries, fast fashion business strategies, and concerns about increasing social expectations among colleagues and friends about frequent changes in clothing. This conclusion is in line with Bhardwaj and Fairhurst (2010), who mention the *combination* of low price strategy and fast fashion as an important recent driving force in the clothing sector. Røpke (2000) argues that, besides fast changing fashion, product diversification is also a driver behind increased consumption. Christensen *et al.* (2007) describe industry's rapid product innovation and individualisation among citizens as important drivers of increasing consumption. Schor (2005) shows how falling goods prices in department stores in the US, like apparel prices, based on import from countries with low labour costs has contributed to increasing consumption.

Co-shaping mechanisms similar to those we have identified can be assumed to lie behind the increasing clothing consumption in other Western countries mentioned in the beginning of the chapter. Woodward (2008), who analysed 27 British women's relationships with their clothes, also concludes that the amount of clothes in wardrobes overwhelm the women when they select clothes for dressing. The women tend to fall back on 'safe' clothes, which are trusted to express the intended style of the women. The women therefore have a lot of unused clothes.

Earlier studies of corporate environmental management in Danish clothing companies show that the increasing consumption of clothing, and thereby increasing resource consumption, is not addressed by public regulation or by Danish companies (Stranddorf *et al.* 2002; Kawansson and Roy 2002; Forman *et al.* 2003; Jørgensen 2006; Thomsen 2007; Jørgensen *et al.* 2010). Only the environmental impacts *per item of clothing* (for example the use of hazardous chemicals) are addressed through cleaner technology and eco-labelling, and only in some companies. How increasing clothing consumption more precisely influences the environmental impacts in the production of clothing depends on whether and how environmental concerns have been included in the design and production of the clothes. Studies of corporate environmental management in the Danish clothing sector have identified four product-related environmental strategies (Stranddorf *et al.* 2002; Kawansson and Roy 2002; Forman *et al.* 2003; Jørgensen 2006; Thomsen 2007; Jørgensen *et al.* 2010):

- Non-public environmental criteria with chemical restrictions for all products
- Market-oriented strategy with eco-labelling of all products
- Market-oriented strategy with eco-labelling of limited part of the product portfolio
- No environmental criteria applied

The study of the Danish women's clothing practices (Jensen 2010) indicates that those corporate strategies which address *all* products and not only a limited part of a company's product portfolio are more likely to reach even this educated group of consumers since they do not want eco-labelling to limit their possibilities for choosing among different clothes when shopping. Christensen *et al.* (2007) describe how sustainable consumption policies can be undermined by the gradual changes of what is considered to be normal everyday practices: in our study the large variety of clothes from which to choose and the frequent purchase of new clothes. Since several companies in the Danish market only sell *some* of their products eco-labelled it is therefore likely that eco-labelling only has a limited impact on the clothing market in Denmark. This corresponds to Scherlofsk (2007) who concludes that eco-labelled clothes only have a small market share of the clothing market, although it is not possible to obtain exact figures. This implies that corporate strategies based on chemical restrictions to all products reduce the environmental impacts more than eco-labelling—unless all products in the product portfolio are eco-labelled.

The chapter has focused on Denmark, a Western industrialised country. However, the identified co-shaping mechanisms between production and consumption can probably also be found among middle-class people in other countries, for example newly industrialised countries. Despite a low average ecological footprint per citizen in countries such as Brazil (around 2.5 global hectares per person) and China (around 2 global hectares per person), compared with Denmark with an ecological footprint of around 8 global hectares per person, middle-class people in newly industrialised countries might have consumption patterns which are the same as those in Western industrialised countries. Elfick (2011) analyses the growing consumption and the growing consumption inequalities in China, with middle-class urban professionals as an example of a group with increasing consumption. Another indication of the increasing consumption in newly industrialised countries is the role of China, not only as a country with low labour costs to which Western production is outsourced, but increasingly also as an important market for Danish clothing and shoe companies (Jørgensen *et al.* 2007, 2010).

21.8 Concluding remarks

Statistical analyses of consumption within a consumption area combined with ethnographic studies of user practices based on a practice theory approach, such as that of Røpke (2009), and analyses of corporate environmental management enable analyses of how interactions between business strategies and social dynamics, such as workplace dress codes, shape everyday life practices. These kinds of combined analysis give knowledge about the background to increasing resource consumption for production of clothes and can support the development of better strategies for public regulation, which can encourage business strategies that are more likely to succeed in reducing resource consumption and environmental impacts from pesticides, production chemicals, etc. An important message is that general national and international restrictions to the use of chemicals in the production of clothes are more likely to reduce the environmental impacts from the increasing production of clothes than public regulation, which only focuses on setting up environmental labelling schemes and leaves the consumers with the choice between 'conventional' clothes and eco-labelled clothes. Too many companies choose not to use environmental labelling or label only a limited part of their product portfolio to make environmental labelling a successful strategy. More focus from environmental organisations and consumer organisations on the large numbers of unused clothes in wardrobes could be a way forward to increase awareness among consumers about this waste of money and material resources and support changes in clothing practices.

References

Allwood, J.M., S.E. Laursen, C.M. de Rodriguez and N.M.P. Bocken, N.M.P. (2006) *Well Dressed? The Present and Future Sustainability of Clothing and Textiles in the United Kingdom* (Cambridge, UK: University of Cambridge, Institute for Manufacturing).

Behrendt, S., C. Jasch, J. Kortman, G. Hrauda, R. Pfitzner and D. Velte (2003) *Eco-service Development: Reinventing Supply and Demand in the European Union* (Sheffield, UK: Greenleaf Publishing).

Bhardwaj, V., and A. Fairhurst (2010) 'Fast Fashion: Response to Changes in the Fashion Industry', *The International Review of Retail, Distribution and Consumer Research* 20.1: 165-73.

Christensen, T.H., M. Godskesen, K. Gram-Hanssen, M.B. Quitzau and I. Røpke (2007) 'Greening the Danes? Experience with Consumption and Environment Policies', *Journal of Consumer Policy* 30: 91-116.

Elfick, J. (2011) 'Class Formation and Consumption among Middle-Class Professionals in Shenzhen', *Journal of Current Chinese Affairs* 40.1: 187-211.

Forman, M., and M.S. Jørgensen (2004) 'Organising Environmental Supply Chain Management', *Greener Management International* 45 (Spring 2004): 43-62.

Forman, M., A.G. Hansen and M.S. Jørgensen (2003) 'The Shaping of Environmental Concern in Product Chains: Analysing Danish Case Studies on Environmental Aspects in Product Chain Relations', paper presented at *EGOS (European Group on Organisation Studies) Conference 2003*, Copenhagen Business School, Denmark, 3–5 July 2003.

Gram-Hanssen, K. (2011) 'Understanding Change and Continuity in Residential Energy Consumption', *Journal of Consumer Culture* 11.1: 61-78.

Guy, A., E. Green and M. Banim (eds.) (2001) 'Through the Wardrobe: Women's Relationship with their Clothes', in J. Eicher (ed.), *Dress, Body, Culture* (Oxford, UK: Berg).

Halkier, B. (2008) *Fokusgrupper (Focus Groups)* (Frederiksberg, Denmark: Forlaget Samfundslitteratur, 2nd edn, in Danish).

Hille, J. (1995) *Sustainable Norway: Probing the Limits and Equity of Environmental Space* (Oslo, Norway: The Project for an Alternative Future).

Hille, J. (2000) *Økologisk utsyn 2000. Økologiske konsekvenser av Norges økonomiske utvikling det siste året (Ecological Outlook 2000: Ecological Consequences of Norwegian Economic Development in Recent Years)* (Rapport 3/2000; Oslo, Norway: Framtiden i våre henders forskningsinstitut [FIFI], in Norwegian).

Jensen, C.L. (2010) *Innovation, Consumption and Environment* (Master's thesis; Kgs Lyngby, Denmark: Department of Management Engineering, Technical University of Denmark.

Jørgensen, M.S. (2006) 'Sustainable Production and Consumption of Textiles: The Interaction between Fashion, Outsourcing and Cleaner Production', in M. Charter and A. Tukker (eds.), *Sustainable Consumption and Production: Opportunities and Challenges. Proceedings from the Launch Conference of the Sustainable Consumption Research Exchange (SCORE!) Network*, Wuppertal, Germany, 23–25 November 2006: pp. 113-30.

Jørgensen, M.S., U. Jørgensen, K. Hendriksen, S. Hirsbak and N. Thorsen (2007) 'Modes of Environmental Management in Transnational Product Chains', paper presented at *GIN 2007: International Conference of the Greening of Industry Network: Sustainable Ecosystem and Social Stewardship*, Wilfrid Laurier University, Waterloo, Ontario, 15–17 June 2007.

Jørgensen, M.S., U. Jørgensen, K. Hendriksen, S. Hirsbak, H.H. Thomsen and N. Thorsen (2010) 'Environmental Management in Danish Transnational Textile Product Chains', *Management Research Review* 33.4: 357-79.

Kawansson, N., and P. Roy (2002) *Eco Labelling as Part of Corporate Strategy* (Master's thesis; Lyngby, Denmark: Department of Manufacturing Engineering and Management, Technical University of Denmark).

Røpke, I. (2000) 'Forbrug' ('Consumption'), in *Dansk Naturpolitik* (*Danish Nature Policy*) *Thematic Report no. 1* (Copenhagen, Denmark: The Nature Council, in Danish): pp. 66-81.

Røpke, I. (2009) 'Theories of Practice: New Inspiration for Ecological Economic Studies on Consumption', *Ecological Economics* 68: 2490-97.

Scherlofsk, A.W. (ed.) (2007) *EU Eco-label Marketing for Products Project 2006 Final report, Work on the implementation of the EU Eco-Label Scheme in the areas of marketing, product group development and stakeholder representation* (LOT 7; Marketing of Products Service contract no 070402/2005/420195/MAR/G2 EMP Team; Vienna: EMP Team).

Schor, J. (2005) 'Prices and Quantities: Unsustainable Consumption and the Global Economy', *Ecological Economics* 55: 309-20.

Shove, E. (2003) *Comfort, Cleanliness and Convenience: The Social Organization of Normality* (Oxford/New York: Berg).

Spradley, J. (1979) *The Ethnographic Interview* (Orlando, FL: Harcourt Brace Jovanovich College Publishers).

Statistics Denmark (2002–2009) *Statistisk Årbog 2002, 2003, 2004, 2005, 2006, 2007, 2008, 2009* (*Statistical Yearbook*) (Copenhagen, Denmark: Statistics Denmark, in Danish).

Statistics Denmark (2010) *Statistisk Tiårsoversigt 2010* (*Statistical 10 Year Review2010*) (Copenhagen, Denmark: Statistics Denmark, in Danish).

Stranddorf, H., M. Forman, A. Nielsen and M. Søgaard (2002) *Miljø-, etik og arbejdsmiljøkrav i tekstilproduktkæden* (*Environmental, Ethical and Work Environmental Demands in the Textile Product Chain*) (Environmental Project no. 681; Copenhagen, Denmark: Danish Environmental Protection Agency, in Danish, www.mst.dk).

Thomsen, H.H. (2007) *Bæredygtighed på markedet for beklædning - en undersøgelse* (*Sustainability in the Clothing Market: A Study*) (Master's Thesis; Kgs. Lyngby, Denmark: Technical University of Denmark, in Danish).

Woodward, S. (2008) *Why Women Wear What They Wear* (Oxford, UK: Berg).

Charlotte Jensen has an MSc in Innovation and Environmental Management from the Technical University of Denmark. Her Master's thesis was based on a study of women and their clothing routines. Charlotte is currently a PhD Fellow, researching Transitions for Sustainability in Society, at Aalborg University Copenhagen, Department of Development and Planning. In her PhD she is applying a social practice theoretical approach to consumption as she did in her Master's thesis.

Michael Søgaard Jørgensen is an associate professor in the Department of Development and Planning at Aalborg University in Copenhagen, Denmark and earlier with the Department of Management Engineering at the Technical University of Denmark. He has an MSc in chemical engineering and a PhD in technology assessment. His research areas are sustainable transition, greening of innovation, environmental management in product chains, sustainable working conditions and social innovation. He often works with action research and community-based research.

22

Connecting meanings and materials

Identity dynamics in sustainable fashion[*]

Fernando F. Fachin

HEC Montréal, Canada

> Engaging in new ways of doing fashion with recyclable materials, I am crafting not only clothes but also who I am (Márcia Ganem 2011).

As people discover who they are through what they do (Weick *et al.* 2005), the work with materials is a key component of identity constitution processes. In sustainable fashion, designers differentiate themselves not only through symbolic but also through material processes. Differentiation, discovery and expression of self thus can rely on meanings attached to, for example, clothes made of recyclable plastic bottles (Brown 2010). In effect, the variability of the material provokes consideration of the complexity of identities and of the expression of class, sexuality, occupation, ethnicity, gender and combinations of these (Crane 2000; Sofaer 2007).

[*] I thank the designers Anabel Burin, Márcia Ganem and Anne-Painchaud-Ouellet as well as Lis Suarez and Sonia Paradis at Ethik-BGC. I also gratefully acknowledge the continuous and encouraging support and insightful feedback of Emilie Gibeau, Ann Langley and Linda Rouleau as well as the valuable comments and suggestions of the anonymous reviewers on earlier versions of this work.

However, influenced by narrative approaches, scholars pay scant attention to the material dimension of identity constitution. Indeed, studies assuming that reality is 'made real' through language have largely influenced our understanding of the construction of self (Ricoeur 1991). Barad (2003: 801), recognising the vast space occupied by the 'linguistic turn' in social sciences, puts it very well: 'Language matters. Discourse matters. Culture matters. But there is an important sense in which the only thing that does not seem to matter anymore is matter'. Although there is recognition of materiality as a part of social activity, with clothing being considered a vibrant part of culture (Küchler and Miller 2005), little is known about the diverse ways in which social relations and materials interact, particularly in the specific context of sustainable fashion.

In order to fill this gap, this chapter, with case studies with three entrepreneurial ecodesigners (ecologically oriented designers who have founded their companies), considers materials as constituents of identity. This study is not however focused on the understanding of the agency of matter over humans (Bennett 2009) or human sensory and emotional experiences of objects (Dudley 2009). Rather, the focus is on how human agents manipulate matter to socially construct and negotiate their identities. More precisely, with a sociomaterial approach (Dale 2005; Orlikowski 2007), this research explores how materiality and meaning are intertwined in identity constitution.

This study is organised as follows. In Section 22.1, considering the focus on ecodesigners who founded their own companies, a literature review on entrepreneurial identity is presented. To highlight the interaction of social and material processes, the notion of sociomateriality, linked to identity, is presented in Section 22.2. In Section 22.3 the theoretical background is followed by a case study in sustainable fashion. Finally, Section 22.4 presents a discussion of the findings, closing with contributions for theory and practice.

22.1 Identity and entrepreneurship

No concept appears more essential to understanding the self in society than identity (Mead 1934; Giddens 1991). A frame to investigate varied social phenomena, 'identities are the various meanings attached to an individual by the self and by others' (Ibarra and Barbulescu 2010: 137). In working their identities, individuals engage in forming, repairing, maintaining, strengthening or revising constructions towards a sense of coherence and distinctiveness (Snow and Leon 1987).

Within entrepreneurship literature, the interest in identity can hardly be denied. Such a concept promotes the understanding that entrepreneurship is not fixed in an individual's personality but is constituted through interaction between individual, society and culture (Cohen and Musson 2000). In this way, we gain understanding of how entrepreneurs work their identities through a set of narratives to legitimate their new ventures in a determined context (Essers and Benschop 2009).

Sensemaking and sensegiving systems of the surrounding cultural milieu impact the construction and negotiation of the identity of entrepreneurs (Hill and Levenhagen 1995; Weick *et al.* 2005). Narratives mediate sensemaking as entrepreneurs narrate meaning, resonance and coherence (Navis and Glynn 2011), tying the crafting of the new venture to the identity of the entrepreneur (Lounsbury and Glynn 2001).

The study of identities in an entrepreneurial context is mainly informed by a narrative perspective. The literature on entrepreneurial identity has advanced understanding of entrepreneurship with a more refined understanding of entrepreneurial activity. However, we lack understanding of the interaction of both social and material processes of entrepreneurial identity constitution.

22.2 Social materiality

The notion of sociomateriality has a relational understanding of social and material processes as mutually enacting (Dale 2005; Orlikowski 2007). Connerton (1989) provides an example of this intermesh in his discussion of the Victorian dress and embodied action. He explains that the heavy, constricting and complex clothing worn by Victorian women not only signalled them as being inactive, frivolous and submissive, but also created these attributes. Meanwhile, men's clothing allowed them to be serious, active and aggressive. Connerton's (1989) study demonstrates how the formal qualities of the dress can create the response and thus the identity of the person wearing it.

Also with a relational ontology, Latour (2005) argues that agency is not a human essence, but a capacity realised through the association, whether human or non-human. This approach does not favour humans or materials, as they are not treated as distinct entities. In this way, with a network understanding, Latour (2005) argues that objects take on the characteristics of humans, while humans take on the characteristics of the objects.

The social and the material thus influence identity constitution. Ecodesigners discover and affirm who they are through the creational processes. Indeed, designers or craftspeople put themselves in physical media, such as stone, metal or wood. In this way, the physical constitution of objects relies on the way they are made to 'live' by their authors through materials and techniques in which they are made (Bann 1989; Sofaer 2007).

As the social is entangled with the material (Dale 2005; Orlikowski 2007), working the self can rely on working materials, in an interpretive activity of transformation and reproduction (Snow and Leon 1987). Indeed, although material dimensions of identity have been hinted by some scholars, the narrative understanding remains dominant (Barad 2003). To further explore the interactions between materiality and meaning, this research comprises three case studies with entrepreneurial ecodesigners in the context of sustainable fashion.

22.3 Fashioning identities: Meanings and materials in sustainable fashion

22.3.1 Methodology

This chapter relies on three case studies (Eisenhardt 1989; Eisenhardt and Graebner 2007) with entrepreneurial designers in the context of sustainable fashion. Many ecodesigners create their own companies and differentiate themselves materially (e.g. with recyclable materials) and narratively (e.g. with talk about the environment) from the working conditions and waste prevalent in the fashion industry (Phizacklea 1990; Rissaen 2008). Indeed, the context of sustainable fashion is oriented towards making clothes that respect the environment. For this purpose, entrepreneurial ecodesigners use organic raw materials (such as cotton without pesticides or silk cultured on organic trees) and recycled textiles as well as avoiding harmful bleaches to colour fabrics (Brown 2010). Also, ecodesigners differentiate themselves from other ecodesigners through the exploration of new materials and meanings in their creations (Fletcher 2008). As the use of materials and their meanings are extremely rich in sustainable fashion, it makes the phenomenon 'transparently observable' (Pettigrew 1990: 275), facilitating the observation of sociomaterial aspects of identity constitution.

For these case studies, as the objective is to understand identity and differentiation through the use of materials and meanings, sampling was informed by selecting entrepreneurial ecodesigners who have a specific material as their trademark. In order to identify potential entrepreneurs for the study, Lis Suarez and Sonia Paradis from 'Ethik BGC', a boutique, showroom and incubator of entrepreneurs in sustainable fashion were consulted. From this inquiry, a list of 11 entrepreneurs was generated. An analysis of these designers using a theoretical sampling approach (Eisenhardt 1989) was done, and three designers were selected: Márcia Ganem, Anne Painchaud-Ouellet and Anabel Burin. The designers granted permission to use their real names in this chapter and authorised the use of texts and images available on their websites.

The use of the designers' names and photos, although allowing great richness of detail in exposing the identity construction through materials, impeded the anonymity of this research. According to Alvesson (2003), such a setting could prompt respondents to use the interview as a branding activity. Indeed, there can often be a positive bias in how respondents present themselves in any interview, as they are not always engaged in sharing experiences for the benefit of the interviewer and the research problem (Alvesson 2011). Such methodological difficulty was countered by triangulating different sources of materials, confronting the designers' narratives with those of collaborators and critics. In the analysis, no discrepancy was found comparing data from different respondents.

The empirical material is mainly derived from multiple qualitative data collection methods relying on semi-directed interviews, observations and documents. Primary data includes semi-directed interviews (with designers and collaborators) and

Figure 22.1 **Data as material creations and two different textual constructions**

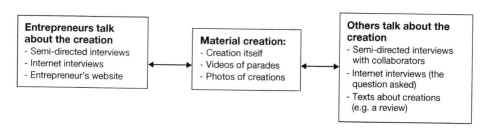

material creations (e.g. a bike tube bag). Secondary data, mainly obtained from the Internet, comprises textual and video interviews given by the designers and collaborators, textual descriptions from the designers' websites, videos of fashion parades and photos of the creations as well as textual descriptions of the designers' creations made by outsiders. This material was triangulated, as presented in Figure 22.1.

The analysis focused on understanding how materials and meanings interact, considering its cultural embeddedness. In this way, findings are based on the interpretation of these materials and analysis is done in the context of the culture in which it is practised (O'Toole and Were 2008). Theory is developed in order to understand how entrepreneurs manipulate both materials and meanings to construct their identities.

22.3.2 Findings

The analysis of the material brought to light four processes (Fig. 22.2) in a combination of bottom-up and top-down approaches (Patton 2002). **Material sense-aiming** relates to the meanings that the entrepreneur, in the material making process, wants outsiders to attach to her creation. **Material making** is the understanding of how the discovery and use of different materials and techniques lead to a creation. **Sensemaking** refers to how the entrepreneur makes sense of the creative process a posteriori based on rationalisations of a material creation. **Sensegiving** is the deliberate symbolic manipulation processes of the entrepreneurs to influence how others will interpret the creation.

The interdependence of materiality and meaning impacting identity constitution is represented in Figure 22.2. The choice of materials relies on how the entrepreneurial ecodesigner is and how he or she projects him or herself. Making sense of the material opens discursive possibilities that allow giving sense to the creation and hence the self. This interaction is explained by the four processes.

22.3.3 Material sense-aiming

Material creations receive meanings not only from the creator but also from outsiders. Creations function as signifiers in the production of meaning, and these can

Figure 22.2 **Identity construction through material and symbolic manipulation**

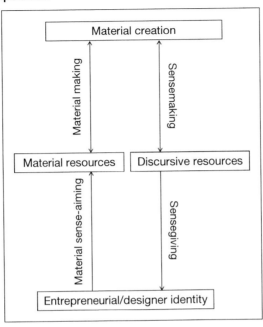

be envisaged by the actor (Becker 1982). For example, one who wears an evening dress may want to convey 'elegance', a bow tie for 'formality', jeans for 'casual', and a certain kind of sweater for 'a long romantic, autumn walk in the wood' (Hall 1997). The individual wearing the clothes generally wants to reach certain meanings to be attributed to his or her material presentation.

Likewise, in the creation process, entrepreneurial designers aim for certain meanings that they expect to be attached by other to their creations. In other words, certain materials and designs are chosen with the intention that people talk about it in a certain way, drawing on certain discourses to constitute identities. For example, Anne Painchaud-Ouellet searches for an association with ecological meanings as she uses recycled bike tubes (Ressac 2011). Had she used another material (e.g. an endangered species) in her creations, she would hardly obtain ecological constructions from others, impacting her identity. Thus, from the start, she thinks of materials and techniques that will favour certain constructions about her.

Moreover, the materials and techniques used can be explicitly linked in the narratives. In the website for Dragao Fashion Brasil, a very important fashion event in Brazil, Márcia Ganem is described as expressing 'dialog between innovation and tradition, using innovative materials and artisanal techniques' (Dragao Fashion Brasil 2011). We see how Márcia Ganem's work is constructed as innovative yet traditional. It is constructed as innovative because of the use of the materials (recycled polyamide fibre) and traditional because of the techniques (artisanal work) she uses. The choice and manipulation of materials has thus an impact on how identities are being constructed.

The usage of materials can evoke certain meanings that insert the creation/creator in a larger cultural discourse. On the Fashion File website (Pieroni 2007), the critic describes Márcia Ganem's usage of recyclable material as 'spectacular

Figure 22.3 **Márcia Ganem's creation and how others give meaning to it**

Source (photo and caption): Dragao Fashion House 2012

Photo credit: Ricardo Fernandes

[The Ciclos d'Agua collection] presents a reflection on cycles and movement through the image of water. Initiating the cycle, the sun creates a rainbow from the vapor of water. [This collection] evokes culture, religion, myths, and traditions, bringing together people and communities by connecting their beliefs and cultures with water. Márcia Ganem combines traditional artisanal techniques with innovation to talk about both continuity and permanence through the constant renewal of secular traditions.

creations that echo the Brazilian soul without becoming a caricature' and describes Márcia Ganem as the 'owner of a unique style, celebrating the richness and culture of a region'. Material creations not only differentiate the creators but also unite them with a whole culture, inscribing identities in the discourse of a broader cultural context.

The attribution of meanings to a creation is recurrent and also new meanings are attributed to different material characteristics. In Figure 22.3 we see how her diverse use of colourful textures with surfaces and reliefs, obtained through extensive research and development of techniques, can evoke meanings related to 'religion', 'myths' and 'tradition' (Dragao Fashion House 2012). The meanings attributed by outsiders complement the main theme of the collection, which invites us to reflect on water as the fundamental vehicle of life. Indeed, we can see how a wide array of meanings is 'created' by a dress.

The meanings certain material creations receive have an impact on identity constitution. Entrepreneurial ecodesigners create products aiming for the association with favourable symbols. This is done by reaching for certain discourses from the work from the start of the creative process with material. How the creations will be constructed, impacting on the entrepreneur's identity, is the search for certain meanings through the manipulation of materials beforehand.

22.3.4 Material making

The process of material making implies differentiation with the use of materials. Márcia Ganem considers researching materials the most important part of her work; she explains that she spends most of the time doing research of new materials and is deeply engaged in 'making new materials become fashion' (Márcia Ganem in semi-directed interview). Her trademark is the recycled polyamide fibre (it is copyrighted, so no one else uses it in fashion), a synthetic material with a very organic aspect. In a semi-directed interview when asked about the first encounter with this new material, Márcia Ganem says that, from the start, she wanted to have recycled polyamide fibre in her creations, although she did not know how to work it. This material that represents her went through a long physical manipulation process. A lot of research was necessary: 'the study of this fibre was made 10 years ago. We did an allergenic research to see if it would be possible to use polyamide in contact with human skin' (Márcia Ganem in Peregrino 2009). Figure 22.4 shows how research allows the designer to reach unique material constructions and thus identity differentiation.

Other creators construct their identities through different materials and techniques. In this way, new identities are created. Ressac creates bags from bikes tubes, in several steps (Fig. 22.5). Not only is the material different, but also the technique, as explained by the entrepreneurial designer Anne Painchaud-Ouellet from Ressac on her website:

> The intention to recycle inner bike tubes is one thing, but to get to a final product, several steps are necessary. The bike repair shops are the major

Figure 22.4 **Márcia Ganem's singular creations are the result of unique recyclable materials and techniques**

Source: Márcia Ganem 2011

Photo credit: Ricardo Fernandes

source of supply for the raw material. First, the tubes are cut, then cleaned and finally brushed to give them a glossy finish… A lot of imagination is required to work with bicycle inner tubes. The designer is constantly looking to develop new work methods and new products. The combination of different fabric samples with inner tubes generates unique creations.

Through the use of different materials and techniques, we can see how different entrepreneurial ecodesigners differentiate themselves through materiality. In the

Figure 22.5 **From working with bike tubes to a bike tube bag**

Source: Ressac 2011

Photo credits: Dominique Lafond

case of Márcia Ganem, recycled polyamide fibre becomes an audacious dress. With Anne Painchaud-Ouellet, an urban bag (Fig. 22.6).

The search for new materials and techniques allows the creation of something new that cannot be copied, making one recognisable anywhere by one's creations. The creations become an extension of self, and the creator is attached to and defines herself through her creations. Indeed, in Google images, typing 'Márcia Ganem', for example, the vast majority of images that appears are of those of her creations, not of her person. In effect, Márcia Ganem is engaged in copyrighting her materials and techniques so that others do not 'steal' her identity (Márcia Ganem in semi-directed interview). Indeed, as Becker (1982) points out, that is why plagiarism evokes such violent reactions; it is not just the property that is being stolen, but the basis of identity as well. Identity through the creation of new materials thus relies on what others are doing materially as well.

Thus, the process of material making involves discovering new materials and techniques, and thus the self. The experimentation with different materials and techniques is also experimentation with the self. It can be seen as an ongoing

Figure 22.6 **Identity and differentiation through different materials, design and techniques: Márcia Ganem's dress (left) and Ressac's bag (right)**

Sources: Márcia Ganem 2011; Ressac 2011

Photo credits: Ricardo Fernandes; Dominique Lafond

process of identity discovery and affirmation (Ibarra and Petriglieri 2010) through materials. The experimentation process with new materials leads to the selection of material constructions that one is engaged in maintaining. In this manner, identity construction does not rely on narrative, as it involves material experimentation and material projection, becoming an extension of self. Changing or affirming the self relies on the material and techniques that are used.

22.3.5 Sensemaking

With the case of the entrepreneurial designers in sustainable fashion, creative circumstances are turned into words, becoming narratives. The creation in a material form (e.g. a dress) becomes a means of self-understanding as designers touch and see it to understand how they had created it. Indeed, the semi-directed interviews induced their sensemaking (Weick *et al.* 2005) as they were asked questions about their creative process that they previously had not thought about. Asking the designers what a certain design, colour or texture means stimulated their reflexive understanding (Giddens 1991) of activities that lead to their creations and hence of whom they were (and are) becoming.

For example, Anabel Burin from Vuela-Vuela (in semi-directed interview) says that 'it [the creational process] depends on so many things. It comes from such a confused inspiration. I can only answer that question if I rationalize afterwards'. The creational process arises from 'confusing inspirations' that can only be made sense of after the creation is done and they are materialised in a creation. She claims that when she is creating, she is 'not fully aware of what she is doing' and had never thought (and prefers not to think) about it before the interview. Being aware of these elements (e.g. reflecting on the design of her butterfly brought back some childhood memories) influences her understanding of self as well as her approach to new creations (e.g. further exploration of childhood memories in her creations). In hindsight, the creator is making sense of the creative process when talking about it, impacting new creations.

Making sense of material creations thus allows tacit aspects of the creative activity to be brought to light, in a process of identity discovery that impacts on further creations and identity projections. In this way, the identity narrative can be shaped, altered or sustained (Giddens 1991). That only afterwards she gains more awareness of the creation process, leading to a further understanding of herself, is explained by Anabel Burin in a semi-directed interview about what she means with her material creations:

> It is the role of others to decode all these signifying elements and to combine them into a meaningful whole. When I hear interpretations of my work, I am often very surprised to see all that people can extract. There are things that I am obviously aware of, but there is also a lot of material that is beyond my control.

Sensemaking is a process of rationalisation closely tied to identity (Weick *et al.* 2005). It involves the ongoing retrospective rationalisation of peoples' actions towards activities that culminated into material creations. Making sense of material creations can thus be seen as an a posteriori understanding of identity discovery activity (Oliver and Roos 2007). Indeed, sensemaking is viewed as an important process of organising, unfolding as people concerned with identity in the social context extract cues and make sense of things retrospectively. It influences self-understanding and material projection as meanings are materialised by the creator and made sense of afterwards.

22.3.6 Sensegiving

Materials are affected by how we give sense to them. Objects do not carry their own, one true meaning, but are constantly shifting in meaning as we move through different cultures, languages and historical contexts (Hall 1997; Weick *et al.* 2005).

For example, a stone can be a stone, a boundary mark or a sculpture, depending on meanings we give to it. Sensegiving refers to the designer's deliberate efforts to influence how others interpret her creation (while sensemaking refers to the designer constructing her own interpretations and understandings of her own work).

From Ressac, the maker of bags out of bike tubes, we see the junction of narrative and material practices (Fig. 22.7). By creating from the start a bag with a large ring to combine with the product, the designer communicates what this material construction means, giving symbolic value to it. In this way, the bike tubes and metal in the form of a bag (material creation) also receive a meaning (sensegiving) of being at the same time 'chic and trendy' as well as the overall meaning of ecological fashion conveyed by Anne Painchaud-Ouellet. In this way, materials receive meanings from their creator, impacting on his or her identity.

Figure 22.7 **Material creation receiving a symbolic meaning from the entrepreneurial designer**

Source (photo and caption): Ressac 2011

Photo credits: Dominique Lafond

'With its large metal ring, I've designed this handbag thinking about the type of bag I would like to have for an important evening. Chic and trendy all at once...'

In the quotation accompanying Figure 22.7, Anne is giving sense to her creation by performing an interpretive process in an attempt to influence others through language. Similarly, Márcia Ganem, in the collection 'A declaration of faith', gives sense to 'tag', a rough organic material she introduced. This material and how it is designed represents 'the faith of poor and oppressed people, paying tribute to this inexplicable and intangible mystery of faith' (Márcia Ganem in institutional video). She materialises the culture of her region, which is very religious and of humble origin. In this way, there is a symbolic manipulation of her creation that gives meaning to herself as a creator.

The process of sensegiving, combined with material creation, is a central one in identity constitution. Making sense of the creation and constructing it narratively, there is a symbolic manipulation of the material. In this way, sensegiving and material creating are closely tied because the materials/design will have an impact on how it can be (re)constructed. As an extreme case, it is more difficult to construct an identity as being ecological using skin from crocodiles facing extinction than processing recycled plastic bottles. In this way, the role of materials is crucial in sensegiving efforts and on how the creation becomes an extension of the entrepreneurs' identities. Identities are created and maintained through the very synergy between the material creation and further sensegiving possibilities.

22.4 Discussion and conclusion

The point of departure for this chapter was the lack of studies on the material dimension of identities. To emphasise the importance of the interdependence of materiality and meaning, this research relied on three case studies focusing on the creation processes of entrepreneurial ecodesigners. With cases in sustainable fashion, this chapter extends previous work on identities in the context of entrepreneurship.

The case of entrepreneurial ecodesigners brought to light processes that consider both material and symbolic processes in the constitution of entrepreneurial identity. This chapter accounts for important aspects that influence the organisations' practices and meanings that are not grasped solely by textual descriptions. As Harquail and King (2010) point out, asking individuals to express themselves verbally will grasp only the information that they can easily put into words, while asking them to express themselves physically, followed by verbal interpretation, will reveal more complex and complete detail information. In this chapter, through processes of **material sense-aiming**, **material making**, **sensemaking** and **sensegiving**, it is demonstrated how materials are a form of expression that complete and interact with verbal expression, revealing tacit aspects of organising and of identity constitution.

Methodologically, this chapter goes beyond the talk about matter, treating materiality as a basis for, not just an effect of, construction of social differences. Indeed, this chapter considers the material as an object of analysis rather than only a subject of discussion. The study with ecodesigners focuses on specific properties of the material (e.g. recycled polyamide fibre) and how it is manipulated both physically and symbolically. In this way, with the study of material making in interaction with meaning making, this chapter opens a methodological avenue to further our comprehension of identity constitution.

Further, considering the interaction of creators with their creations (Bourdieu 1992), this study demonstrates how materials, not only narratives, can enable and constrain identity constructions. As Becker (1982) points out, artists need to mobilise resources since the materials they have access to affect the work they do. Every art form has, to different extents, artists managing resources. This chapter has demonstrated how the management and manipulation of such material resources can lead to meanings that impact on the creator's identity. In effect, the framework presented in this chapter demonstrates how working meanings and materials are intertwined with identity constitution. Also, this research demonstrates how materials and meanings are complementary. For example, the absence of certain materials may require further narrative constructions about the creation to work symbolically what was not worked materially. In sustainable fashion, the talk originated by the material or logistic process has impacts on identities, depending on how it is articulated with the designer's creative intention.

Further research could rely on ethnographic methodology (Van Maanen 1988) to grasp in further detail processes of meanings and materials. Such an approach would allow a more nuanced understanding of how eco-fashion entrepreneurs manipulate materials and imbue meaning in their creations. Also, a study of anonymous designers could lead to a more intimate understanding of material manipulation (although such a study would likely be deprived of visual images) than a more publicly held narrative, limiting potentially promotional efforts. Moreover, a longitudinal approach would further allow us to understand how meanings are changed through time along with the material changes. Indeed, a limitation of this chapter is its reliance on a posteriori accounts of the creational process, with reconstruction of events and some hindsight bias (Eisenhardt and Graebner 2007).

This chapter presents theoretical and practical contributions. At the theoretical level, this research opens a new epistemological route for studies on entrepreneurship and identity. With a sociomaterial approach, this chapter promotes a view of entrepreneurship as mobilising both material and narrative resources in material-making and sense-making/giving efforts. Indeed, this chapter attends a call for revitalisation of studies on identity (Alvesson *et al.* 2008) from methodological and epistemological standpoints. By bringing in materiality, this research opens an empirical avenue that allows an understanding of the interaction of the material and the narrative associated with it in different contexts. Promoting a new design does not manipulate meanings, but materials that will further be socially negotiated, in a process of identity constitution. At the practical level, this research can be useful to entrepreneurs and designers in that it can explain how managing both tangible and intangible elements impacts on their identities. Indeed, knowing how materials and meanings interact in creating a product is valuable in order to reach a certain market.

Furthermore, the case of sustainable fashion is an emblematic one in understanding the development of business practices oriented towards meeting the needs of the present without compromising future generations (WCED 1987). This study, with cases of entrepreneurial ecodesigners, provides an understanding of how a shift to a more sustainable way of doing business can be achieved. The success of many designers lies in how they combine technological/material innovation with the symbolic construction of their creations. They attract people who are identified with the meanings that are associated with their designs and choice of materials. In this vein, this study with entrepreneurial ecodesigners promotes an understanding between the interaction of physical reality and sense-aiming/making/giving efforts and their impact on identities.

References

Alvesson, M. (2003) 'Beyond Neopositivists, Romantics, and Localists: A Reflexive Approach to Interviews in Organizational Research', *Academy of Management Review* 28.1: 13-33.

Alvesson, M. (2011) *Interpreting Interviews* (Thousand Oaks, CA: Sage).

Alvesson, M., K. Lee and R. Thomas (2008) 'Identity Matters: Reflections on the Construction of Identity Scholarship in Organization Studies', *Organization* 15.5: 5-28.

Bann, S. (1989) *The True Vine: On Visual Representation and the Western Tradition* (Cambridge, UK: Cambridge University Press).

Barad, K. (2003) 'Posthumanist Performativity: Toward an Understanding of How Matter Comes to Matter', *Signs* 28.3: 801-31.

Becker, H.S. (1982) *Art Worlds* (Berkeley, CA: University of California Press).

Bennett, J. (2009) *Vibrant Matter: A Political Ecology of Things* (Durham, NC: Duke University Press Books).

Bourdieu, P. (1992) *Les règles d'art: Génèse et structure du champ littéraire* (Paris: Seuil).

Brown, S. (2010) *Eco Fashion* (London: Laurence King).

Cohen, L., and G. Musson (2000) 'Entrepreneurial Identities: Reflections from Two Case Studies', *Organization* 7.1: 31-48.

Connerton, P. (1989) *How Societies Remember* (Cambridge, UK: Cambridge University Press).

Crane, D. (2000) *Fashion and its Social Agendas: Class, Gender, and Identity in Clothing* (Chicago: The University of Chicago Press).

Dale, K. (2005) 'Building a Social Materiality: Spatial and Embodied Politics in Organizational Control', *Organization* 12.5: 649-78.

Dragao Fashion Brasil (2011) 'Artesanais: identidades da moda', www.dragaofashion.com.br/2011/sis.desfiles.asp?pasta=10&pagina=135&eId=8, accessed 26 April 2011.

Dragao Fashion House (2012) 'Márcia Ganem: Ciclos D'Água Coleçao 2012', www.dfhouse.com.br/dfnow-post/494/marcia-ganem, accessed 10 July 2012.

Dudley, S.H. (2009) *Museum Materialities: Objects, Engagements, Interpretations* (London: Routledge).

Eisenhardt, K.M. (1989) 'Building Theories from Case Study Research', *Academy of Management Review* 14.4: 532-50.

Eisenhardt, K.M., and M.E. Graebner (2007) 'Theory Building from Cases: Opportunities and Challenges', *Academy of Management Journal* 50.1: 25-32.

Essers, C., and Y. Benschop (2009) 'Muslim Businesswomen Doing Boundary Work: The Negotiation of Islam, Gender and Ethnicity within Entrepreneurial Contexts', *Human Relations* 62.3: 403-23.

Fletcher, K. (2008) *Sustainable Fashion & Textiles: Design Journeys* (London: Earthscan).

Giddens, A. (1991) *Modernity and Self-Identity: Self and Society in the Late Modern Age* (Cambridge, UK: Polity Press).

Hall, S. (1997) 'The Work of Representation', in S. Hall (ed.), *Representation: Cultural Representations and Signifying Practices* (London: Sage): 13-74.

Harquail, C., and A. King (2010) 'Construing Organizational Identity: The Role of Embodied Cognition', *Organization Studies* 31.12: 1619.

Hill, R.C., and M. Levenhagen (1995) 'Metaphors and Mental Models: Sensemaking and Sensegiving in Innovative and Entrepreneurial Activities', *Journal of Management* 21.6: 1057-74.

Ibarra, H., and R. Barbulescu (2010) 'Identity as Narrative: Prevalence, Effectiveness, and Consequences of Narrative Identity Work in Macro Work Role Transitions', *Academy of Management Review* 35.1: 135-54.

Ibarra, H., and J.L. Petriglieri (2010) 'Identity Work and Play', *Journal of Organizational Change Management* 23.1: 10-25.

Küchler, S., and D. Miller (2005) *Clothing as Material Culture* (New York: Berg Publishers).

Latour, B. (2005) *Reassembling the Social: An Introduction to Actor-Network Theory* (Oxford, UK: Oxford University Press).

Lounsbury, M., and M.A. Glynn (2001) 'Cultural Entreprenuership: Stories, Legitimacy, and the Acquisitions of Resources', *Strategic Management Journal* 22.6/7: 545.

Márcia Ganem (2011) 'Márcia Ganem', www.marciaganem.com.bMead, G.H. (1934) *Mind, Self and Society* (Chicago: University of Chicago Press).

Navis, C., and M.A. Glynn (2011) 'Legitimate Distinctiveness and the Entrepreneurial Identity: Influence on Investor Judgments of New Venture Plausibility', *Academy of Management Review* 36.3: 479-99.

Oliver, D., and J. Roos (2007) 'Beyond Text: Constructing Organizational Identity Multimodally', *British Journal of Management* 18.4: 342.

Orlikowski, W.J. (2007) 'Sociomaterial Practices: Exploring Technology at Work', *Organization Studies* 28.9: 1435-48.

O'Toole, P., and P. Were (2008) 'Observing Places: Using Space and Material Culture in Qualitative Research', *Qualitative Research* 8.5: 616-34.

Patton, M.Q. (2002) *Qualitative Research & Evaluation Methods* (London: Sage).

Peregrino, F. (2009) 'Inovação em produto com matéria-prima diferenciada', www.facadiferente.sebrae.com.br/2009/07/20/inovacao-em-produto-com-materia-prima-diferenciada, accessed 26 April 2011.

Pettigrew, A.M. (1990) 'Longitudinal Field Research on Change: Theory and Practice', *Organization Science* 1.3: 267-92.

Phizacklea, A. (1990) *Unpacking the Fashion Industry* (London: Routledge).

Pieroni, R. (2007) 'Muita criatividade, garra e pensamento positivo. Saiba como Márcia Ganem entrou no concorrido mercado da moda internacional e vem fazendo bonito representando o Brasil', www.oilondres.com.br/trabalho/marcia/index.htm, accessed 25 April 2011 [web page no longer active].

Ressac (2011) 'Sacs en chambres à air de vélos recyclées', www.ressac.ca, accessed 25 April 2011.

Ricoeur, P. (1991) 'Narrative Identity', *Philosophy Today* 35: 73.

Rissaen, T. (2008) 'Creating Fashion without the Creation of Waste', in J. Hethorn and C. Ulaswewicz (eds.), *Sustainable Fashion: Why Now? A Conversation about Issues, Practices and Possibilities* (New York: Fairchild): 184-206.

Snow, D.A., and A. Leon (1987) 'Identity Work Among the Homeless: The Verbal Construction and Avowal of Personal Identities', *The American Journal of Sociology* 92.6: 1,336-71.

Sofaer, J. (2007) 'Introduction: Materiality and Identity', in Sofaer, J. (eds.), *Material Identities* (Malden, MA: Blackwell): 1-10.

Van Maanen, J. (1988) *Tales of the Field: On Writing Ethnography* (Chicago: University of Chicago Press).

WCED (World Commission on Environment and Development) (1987) *Our Common Future: Brundtland Report* (Oxford, UK: Oxford Univeristy Press).

Weick, K.E., K.M. Sutcliffe and D. Obstfeld (2005) 'Organizing and the Process of Sense-making', *Organization Science* 16.4: 409.

Fernando F. Fachin is a PhD candidate in Management at HEC Montréal, Canada and a lecturer at McGill University, Canada. He completed his Master's degree at the Université du Québec à Montréal and his undergraduate degree in Brazil. His research interests include identity, sustainable fashion, entrepreneurship and materiality. He has published work in entrepreneurship, career and identity within creative industries.

23

Consumers' attitudes towards sustainable fashion
Clothing usage and disposal

Helen Goworek
Nottingham Business School, Nottingham Trent University, UK

Alex Hiller
Nottingham Business School, Nottingham Trent University, UK

Tom Fisher
School of Art and Design, Nottingham Trent University, UK

Tim Cooper
School of Architecture, Design and the Built Environment, Nottingham Trent University, UK

Sophie Woodward
School of Social Sciences, University of Manchester, UK

Environmental and social sustainability have become important issues within the fashion market, with increasing public awareness of sustainability and some increase in demand for sustainable clothing from consumers. This is evidenced by an increase in sales in this sector of the UK market from £4 million in 1999 to £172 million in 2008 (Co-operative Bank 2009). However, sustainable products still form an extremely low proportion of the clothing market (Eckhardt *et al.* 2010). Clothing consumption has significant sustainability impacts, since clothing is the second largest market sector (after food) in the UK and some of the key issues are: use of pesticides and unsustainable resources in the production of raw materials; employment rights; increasing sales of new clothing; the environmental impacts of clothing maintenance and disposal of clothing. Despite demand for sustainable clothing and interest from governments, non-government organisations (NGOs), academics and retailers, relatively little research has been published on the topics of clothing maintenance and disposal to date. However, there have been several studies on the purchase of clothing with lower sustainability impacts, prior to the use and disposal phases (for example: Carrigan and Attalla 2001; Iwanow *et al.* 2005; Connolly and Shaw 2006; Hustvedt and Dickson 2009).

The study discussed in this chapter was conducted by an interdisciplinary team from the fields of design, marketing and sociology with funding from the UK Government's Department for Environment, Food and Rural Affairs (Defra) and was published in report form (Fisher *et al.* 2008). Its main aim was to discover ways in which consumers can be encouraged to behave more sustainably towards the consumption, use and disposal of fashion products. The objectives of the chapter are, first, to focus on exploring consumers' views in relation to the sustainability of clothing maintenance and divestment and, second, to consider the potential impact of these views on the clothing and textiles industry. This chapter discusses issues relating to consumers' use, maintenance (laundry and repair) and disposal of clothing, concluding by making recommendations for companies, particularly in relation to design, manufacturing and marketing, as a consequence of the research findings.

23.1 Sustainable clothing consumption

Sustainable consumption is a major global issue, since consumption has wide-ranging negative effects on the world's resources (Low and Davenport 2006). This distancing between production and consumption has led to a growing interest by consumers in the conditions in which textiles and clothing are manufactured. Ethical consumption can be viewed as an aspect of political consumerism (Micheletti 2003) in which people seek to demonstrate their political opinions and bring about change through actions such as boycotts of products from unsustainable sources and 'buycotts', that is, buying goods only from sustainable sources. Market segmentation classifications have been developed to reflect consumers' views on environmental sustainability and the most relevant classification to this study has been developed for Defra (2008). Defra's environmental segmentation model divides consumers into the following categories, ranging from those with the most environmentally aware views (1) to those who reject such views (7):

1. Positive greens

2. Waste watchers

3. Concerned consumers

4. Sideline supporters

5. Cautious participants

6. Stalled starters

7. Honestly disengaged

It should be noted that various studies have found that although people state that they intend to behave in a sustainable manner, frequently they do not do so in practice (Eckhardt *et al.* 2010). This disconnection is referred to as the attitude–behaviour gap (Belk 1985) or the values–action gap (Yates 2008; Young *et al.* 2010). Simply providing information about sustainable products is unlikely to persuade consumers to change their actions to bridge the attitude–behaviour gap. This is because emotional appeals, rather than rational appeals, are more likely to lead to behaviour change (Eckhardt *et al.* 2010). Various studies have found that consumers typically prioritise fashionability over ethical issues in the purchase of clothing (Kim *et al.* 1999; Joergens 2006; Shaw *et al.* 2006). In view of these results, there is much potential for consumers to behave more sustainably towards clothing.

The terms 'sustainable' and 'ethical' are often used interchangeably in relation to clothing, though 'ethical fashion' can comprise a broader spectrum of issues, which are not limited to sustainability. Joergens (2006: 361) defines ethical fashion as: 'fashionable clothes that incorporate fair trade principles with sweatshop-free labour conditions while not harming the environment or workers, by using biodegradable and organic cotton'. However, since very few products meet this definition, here we take ethical or sustainable clothing to mean that which incorporates either environmentally or socially sustainable features, rarely both. It is also noteworthy that this definition relates to the production stage of clothes and the textiles which they incorporate, thereby neglecting to mention the potentially longer-term post-purchase phase and its higher sustainability impacts. Thus, this indicates that there is a potential need for a broader definition of ethical or sustainable clothing to fully encompass its life-cycle.

23.1.1 Sustainability impacts of clothing production and the sustainable fashion market

As noted above, the key social sustainability issues in the clothing market which have been widely reported relate to the working conditions of employees who produce clothing (Klein 2000; Carrigan and Attalla 2001; Iwanow *et al.* 2005; Ellis and Higgins 2006; Park and Lennon 2006; Shaw *et al.* 2006). Pressure groups appear to have targeted large companies about this issue, rather than the clothing industry as a whole, in revealing these working conditions. Their strategy has been successful in that many high-profile brands have since reassessed their sourcing policies and practice.

Widening awareness of sustainability issues could have contributed to consumers becoming more responsive to buying ethical ranges in recent years, and niche ethical clothing brands have led the way in this respect. The view that ethical clothing is not fashionable (Tomolillo and Shaw 2003) has itself become outmoded by the involvement of leading designers and specialist brands in this market. For example, the twice-yearly London Fashion Week event is now accompanied by the 'Estethica' fashion exhibition, displaying ethical fashion brands to potential retail buyers, and a number of leading designers and brands have incorporated sustainable materials into product designs. Although organic cotton and fairtrade production are the best-known ways of making garments more environmentally or socially sustainable, there are several other methods that can be used to minimise sustainability impacts, for example by recycling fibres and fabric. Collectively, such examples demonstrate that companies are increasingly considering the 'triple bottom line', where the traditionally narrow focus of business on financial sustainability is broadened so that it also takes into account social and environmental sustainability (Elkington 2004). Gwilt and Rissanen (2011: 14) call for more sustainable clothing design of the types mentioned above to become standard practice:

> The fashion industry needs to respond positively to the view that developing garments at the best possible price is not the only way to conduct business, especially when there continues to be a growth in public interest for environmentally and ethically produced goods. Our vision for the future of fashion is one where all fashion is considered sustainable, making it entirely unnecessary to label it so.

23.1.2 Use and maintenance: Laundry, storage and repair

The earlier part of this chapter relates largely to issues which affect textiles and clothing manufacture up to the point where it is purchased by consumers. Though environmental and social sustainability in the production stage have garnered more interest and discussion, the environmental impact of clothing has been found to be far more significant during the usage phase; up to 82% of the energy use during the life-cycle of a garment is caused by domestic laundering (Fletcher 2008). Despite this, there is a lack of research in relation to consumer use of clothing and the Defra study therefore sought to investigate this issue, which is reported in Section 23.3. Garment use is likely to form the longest stage of a product's purposeful life-cycle and the two major maintenance issues are the laundering and repair of clothes. Shove (2003) explores the topic of laundry, its quotidian nature making it a habitual household process, with timing and temperature bound by informal rules. The regular repetition of this mundane task suggests that it could be difficult for consumers to break ingrained habits such as washing at 40°C or tumble drying. However, as there has been a gradual movement from traditional boil-washing during the 20th century to the use of lower temperatures, it is conceivable that consumers may be persuaded to reduce temperatures further, given sufficient reasons and motivation for doing so. Perceived cleanliness is important to consumers and research by Shove (2003) indicates that clothes may be washed more frequently from habit than out of necessity. This is supported by Slater's (2003: 93) view: 'As a consequence of our current fascination for cleanliness, garments are washed or cleaned far more often than is necessary for the sake of health or even hygiene'.

New fabric finishes can help to avoid stains and reduce odours, such as nanoparticles of silver used in anti-microbial finishes, thereby minimising washing, though such treatments may have toxic effects (Dombek-Keith and Loker 2011). Tumble-drying clothes is costly and uses a substantial amount of energy, yet it is frequently used for convenience. In certain communities within the US people have little choice but to use tumble dryers since clothes lines are banned for aesthetic reasons (Dombek-Keith and Loker 2011). In addition to the impact of energy and water usage in laundering, chemical additives in detergents act as pollutants (McDonough and Braungart 2008; Dombek-Keith and Loker 2011) compounding the negative effects on the environment by curtailing the lives of fish and plants (Slater 2003). Dombek-Keith (2009) proposes the introduction of a new set of wash-care symbols to contribute to lowering the sustainability impact of laundering, for example with graphics to suggest washing only in full loads and repairing clothes. Unfortunately, dry cleaning also has environmental sustainability impacts through the manufacture of the machinery it uses and the energy it expends, as well as using solvents which can be toxic or carcinogenic (Slater 2003).

Effective storage of clothing is another maintenance issue which can contribute towards minimising sustainability impacts (Woodward 2005). For example, storing clothes with care can reduce the amount of ironing required and therefore cut down on energy usage. It appears that consumers are often reluctant to repair their clothing to extend its life, because of insufficient time or skills and the low price of replacing it (Gibson and Stanes 2011). However, garments can be designed to make them easier to repair or alter, for example by including excess fabric to accommodate this (Rissanen 2011). An approach which lacks media coverage in comparison to other techniques, but which certainly minimises sustainability impacts, is to purchase fewer, more durable clothes, which have a longer life-cycle (Blanchard 2007; Gibson and Stanes 2011). This may not be perceived as overtly 'green' behaviour by consumers, yet it is an effective strategy to combat waste. Cooper (2010: 28) advocates 'slow consumption' in preference to fast fashion and argues that: 'sustainability will only be achieved if the prevailing throwaway culture in industrial countries is transformed and there is a shift towards longer lasting products'.

Repurposing and re-using or 'upcycling' clothing offer ways of extending the usable life of clothing. For example, Del Forte denim collects and re-uses customers' jeans (Ulasewicz 2008) and Junky Styling and Traid redesign and adapt second-hand clothing. For certain consumers, shopping for second-hand clothes offers the pleasure of finding a unique item, though others may be deterred by the disorganisation of the stores in comparison with standard retailers (Gibson and Stanes 2011). As an alternative, consumers are being persuaded to participate in clothing exchanges by organisations such as Oxfam and the BBC. Hiring clothes, such as renting garments from knitwear company Keep and Share, also has a strong financial incentive and minimises sustainability impacts if the clothing is durable and enduring in style.

23.1.3 Clothing disposal

The disposal of clothing in relation to sustainability is another area in which literature is scarce. It is therefore not surprising that Birtwistle and Moore (2007) found that consumers lacked knowledge about the sustainability impacts of clothing. Their study revealed that the respondents generally dealt with clothing disposal by donating it to charity or throwing it out with refuse (particularly if it was cheap or needed repairing). A small proportion disposed of clothing by giving it to family members, exchanging it with friends or selling it, but few made use of bins intended for charity collections or recycling. Their research also revealed that clothing which charity shops have not sold is sent for recycling or for emergency relief overseas and it therefore does not go to waste. There is a tendency for consumers to buy increasing amounts of clothing and to keep it for a relatively short time until disposing of it, resulting in the widespread use of the term 'throwaway fashion', since the low price of products equates with disposability in the minds of consumers (Birtwistle and Moore 2007). This situation is exacerbated by the proliferation of low price 'fast fashion' sold by UK high-street retailers (Barnes and Lea Greenwood 2010). This has led to the normalisation of overconsumption of clothing, with Western consumers rarely owning just the bare minimum of clothing (Gibson and Stanes 2011). Domina and Koch (1999: 346) argue that 'the responsibility for lengthening product life lies as much with consumers as with manufacturers' and they stress the importance of educating consumers about the various options for textile disposal.

In the UK only 2 to 4% of clothing is recycled and clothing recycling banks operate below full capacity (Waste Online 2012). The situation is similar in the US, where a recent study found that young consumers frequently choose not to recycle because they consider it to be inconvenient. The researchers therefore recommended that recycling should be made more accessible, possibly with financial incentives (Joung and Park-Poaps 2011). It is estimated that in the UK, the average consumer disposes of 30 kg of clothing and textile waste to landfill per year (Allwood *et al.* 2006), yet the use of landfill sites is an unsustainable strategy in the UK, as their capacity will eventually run out. The disposal of products to landfill or incineration in this way is referred to as the 'cradle to grave' approach (McDonough and Braungart 2008). Some clothing has not even been worn before it is discarded, since shoppers tempted to buy clothes on impulse by low prices may never wear some of them. Additionally, upmarket clothing brands are said to have adopted a practice of cutting and disposing of unsold clothes to avoid them entering the market at low prices, to avoid devaluing the brand (BBC Radio 4 2010). If more information were provided on the consequences of textiles disposal, Morgan and Birtwistle (2009) suggest that consumers would consider changing their behaviour. In another study, donating used clothing to charity was found to be the most popular method of disposal in Scotland and Australia, with more than a third of respondents adopting this approach in both countries (Bianchi and Birtwistle 2010). However, a US study investigated consumers' motives for disposing of clothing to charity and discovered that their primary incentive was to clear space in wardrobes to make way for new clothes (Ha-Brookshire and Hodges 2009).

Therefore, the vast majority of literature on 'sustainable fashion' has focused on the production and acquisition of clothing, with recommendations for improving social or environmental sustainability in design largely made in relation to organic cotton or fairtrade supply principles. While studies relating to the sustainability impacts of clothing maintenance and its disposal and related consumer behaviour change are beginning to emerge, research here is limited and often specific to a US context. The remainder of this chapter will therefore report the results of the Defra study in relation to these issues of usage and disposal, before providing recommendations to designers and others working in the fashion industry.

23.2 Methodology

Qualitative research was conducted in Nottingham, Manchester and St Albans in the form of nine focus groups (three in each location) with 99 participants, Following these initial focus groups, 29 participants (approximately 10 from each location) were recruited to take part in a diary task and wardrobe audit, followed by three deliberative workshops. The sample was selected to include consumers representing different population segments from the Defra 'environmental segmentation model' with regard to their environmental attitudes and behaviour, as well as diversity in demographic and socioeconomic status. The first phase of focus groups sought to investigate respondents' attitudes, aspirations, assumptions and expectations in relation to the acquisition, usage and disposal of clothing. Respondents were not informed initially that the theme of the research was sustainability at this stage to avoid many of the problems encountered in researching such attitudes in relation to social desirability bias (Crane 1999). However, this was revealed towards the end of the focus group and respondents' awareness of and attitude towards sustainability issues were discussed. The second phase, consisting of a diary task and wardrobe audit, in particular was key in addressing the attitude–behaviour gap as previously discussed. Respondents were involved in a home task that involved writing a diary of their clothing practices and a reflection on a selection of three garments from their wardrobe (one used for leisure, one for work and one for special occasions). These respondents were then invited to a third phase of deliberative workshops to discuss information gleaned in the first two phases of research and specific sustainability-related issues in the acquisition, usage and disposal of clothing. These discussions were influenced by the home tasks. Group discussions were transcribed and coded to allow for comparisons across the data.

23.3 Findings

The findings reported below provide a summary across all three phases of the research. In relation to usage it is recognised that the durability or longevity of clothing is an important aspect and the relationships between the cost of clothes, their purpose, fashion and their longevity have direct implications for the potential to lessen the sustainability impacts of clothing. However, these aspects are considered (and were borne out by the respondents) to be key concerns in the acquisition stage, and as such they are omitted here to allow a focus on usage characterised by laundry and repair. Actions identified as improving sustainability impacts in relation to these areas and introduced to participants were:

Usage:

- Wash at 30°C (separate clothing)
- Wash clothes less often
- Separate out and tumble dry fewer clothes (synthetics)
- Line dry more often
- Use launderette
- Repair more at home
- Use local tailoring/alterations/repair

Disposal:

- Keep clothes as long as possible
- Sell, give away or donate unwanted clothes
- Put used clothes in recycling bank
- Reduce amount of clothing disposed
- Alter or re-use the fabric/garment

23.3.1 Usage

23.3.1.1 Laundry: washing

A largely pragmatic approach in relation to the laundering of clothes was revealed. There was an awareness of the benefits of washing at lower temperatures among some participants, although the availability of a low temperature programme on washing machines was limiting for some. Several participants said that the temperature used was linked to the reason for cleaning. For example, clothes with visible dirt or an odour (especially clothes such as sports or work clothes) were washed at a higher temperature than those that had been worn but were not visibly dirty. By contrast, other clothes, such as jumpers and items worn for a short period, were said to require 'freshening up' for which lower temperature washing was acceptable. This understanding of the relationship between types of dirt and appropriate laundry treatments led participants to distinguish between clothes needing a full wash and ones needing only a 'rinse'. Judgements about appropriate washing temperatures were made from the information provided on labels, for example by treating the temperature indications as a maximum.

As indicated by Shove (2003), participants remarked on habit as a barrier to reducing washing, many suggesting that they tended to wash clothes after a single use, perhaps confirming Slater's (2003) argument that clothes are washed more than necessary in many cases (although some reported changing these habits in their diaries). Indeed, considerable resistance was voiced to the idea of reducing the frequency of washing clothes, though several participants reported strategies to get the most out of an item before washing it, such as wearing an already used item while playing sport. This was associated with a sense of peer pressure to change clothes daily and, in the case of clothing next to skin, a fear of emitting odours. For instance, a participant 'would not put dirty clothes on after a shower or put clean clothes on without showering', thus explicitly linking washing the body and washing clothes. Participants considered hanging clothes to freshen them, rather than washing them, as was often done with dry clean-only clothes because of the expense. On the other hand, the effect of washing on putting clothes back into 'shape' was identified as a barrier to changed behaviour, exemplified by a participant who referred to the 'body-hugging' quality of newly washed clothes. Common claims about environmental impacts were not necessarily accepted by all participants. Some suggested that using a concentrated detergent may offer little benefit because people might use more, and one was even sceptical of industry's claims about washing at 30°C. Another, while mentioning that hand washing items was too time-consuming, expressed doubts as to whether it was better for the environment. The majority of participants were already aware of recent campaigns to encourage the use of lower temperatures, but many had not considered the possibility of washing less frequently.

23.3.1.2 Laundry: Drying

Many participants expressed a preference for line drying clothes, with concern over the cost of using a tumble dryer clearly influencing behaviour. Other participants preferred using tumble dryers as they were constrained by a lack of space or because of unfavourable weather conditions, particularly in winter. There was evidence of many participants separating clothes prior to washing into 'whites' and 'colours', but less knowledge about potential cost savings from separating cotton and synthetic clothing in tumble dryers. Some participants, however, spoke of sorting clothes before tumble drying by separating cottons from synthetics or removing clothes mid-cycle. However, the typical motive was to protect items that might be damaged by the dryer rather than to minimise energy consumption. For some participants such behaviour was based on a 'bad experience' where items had shrunk or deteriorated. The rationale for separating cottons and synthetics in the dryer as a way of reducing energy consumption was acceptable to some participants but may not be enough to change habits. Participants noted that an advantage of using tumble dryers over line drying was to save time, and that tumble drying was particularly effective for towels and 'small items' as an aid to keeping the house tidy. However, it was also suggested that reducing the use of tumble dryers would lessen damage to clothes and thus the need to replace them so often. Participants described routines for drying clothes in which they weighed up factors such as the smell of dried clothes, the 'wear', the feel (softness) and the cost. Environmental concerns are also relevant to some people, and there was some evidence that this coincides with segmentation: a 'concerned consumer' hinted at line drying as a moral act, albeit one subject to compromise for practical reasons.

23.3.1.3 Repair

There was little evidence of repair work being undertaken as a normal, regular activity, and most involved minor tasks such as sewing on buttons and fixing hems. As Gibson and Stanes (2011) found, participants across all groups said that repair work was undertaken less often than in the past because people lack necessary skills in contrast with previous generations. Indeed, any repairs that were claimed to be undertaken were often carried out by parents or grandparents. The fact that such skills are not taught in schools and people's lack of time and equipment were identified as barriers to repair, along with the expense of a sewing machine that might get little use and the scarcity of haberdashery suppliers. Many participants considered professional repairs expensive and this, combined with the fact that they were not always of good quality, affected the sector's reputation. Some participants associated repairs with poverty or old age and indicated that they would want to avoid clothes with visible repairs in order to protect themselves and their families from stigma. Nonetheless some participants reported a habit of repairing and altering clothes, particularly those which were expensive or to which they sensed an emotional attachment.

23.3.1.4 Product life extension

Participants in all segments spoke of 'repurposing' clothing: using clothes for dressing up, downgrading their use to decorating or gardening, or employing the cloth as cleaning rags or dusters. Some were employed in jobs that require clothing for which functionality is more important than aesthetics, such as a builder and a child minder whose work is 'hard' on clothes. A small number had dyed clothes such as trousers, tops and T-shirts, with mixed results. Other practices extend the life of clothing but are liable to be marginal in their effect on sustainability. A participant's reference to 'things for the kids' summons the idea of clothes re-used for play. Some clothes, probably not the kind used for everyday wear and perhaps sourced from charity shops, have an extended life as 'fancy dress'.

23.3.2 Disposal

23.3.2.1 Process

In terms of the process of disposal, the wearing out of clothes was only one among many reasons for disposal. Fit was frequently cited, and in many cases this concerned items bought for a particular season or occasion. Some were stored, particularly 'special' clothes (such as a prom dress), as a memento. A projected future loss of weight was also used as justification for disposing of clothes. Throwing away worn-out clothes was, for some participants, an emotional experience. As with the US consumers reported by Ha-Brookshire and Hodges (2008), the disposal of clothes was often as part of a 'spring clean'; this was sometimes referred to as a cathartic experience which related to some life change. Many participants discussed how this would be linked to a seasonal review, particularly during the summer prior to holidays, or, again, an anticipated weight loss, although sorting did not necessarily lead to disposal; clothes could be stored for a time and then later rediscovered. There did not appear to be any particular differences by segment here. Although overall few respondents discussed disposing of clothes very regularly for reasons of fashion, some participants in segments 1 and 3 (positive greens and concerned consumers), who tend to be more environmentally concerned, indicated that they are inclined to keep clothes over several seasons but nonetheless could recall isolated examples of items that became obsolete because of a short-lived style. Some participants in segments 6 and 7 (stalled starters and honestly disengaged) appeared to discard clothes relatively frequently, and references to disposal 'after a season' suggest the influence of fashion on the decision to dispose. The cheapness of some clothes reinforced this effect. While most participants appeared resigned to living in a throwaway culture, many sought to do their best to minimise their personal impact. Participants from a range of segments spoke about the need to 'recycle' (often subsuming 're-use' in using the term), and how not doing so could induce feelings of guilt.

23.3.2.2 Donating to charity

Most participants claimed that they disposed of their unwanted clothing by donating them to charity through charity shops, recycling bins at supermarkets or doorstep bag collections, consistent with the findings of previous research (Birtwistle and Moore 2007). However, several had reservations about charity donations. One participant said that unwanted clothes used to go to jumble sales and that these did not seem to take place any more. There seemed a general perception that items in poor condition, 'personal' items such as swimming costumes, socks, tights and undergarments and perhaps those which were originally very cheap should be put in a rubbish bin. Several suggested that a certain minimum level of quality was required and that damaged items were not appropriate for charity shops. There was a commonly held belief that only clothes fit to be resold could be donated to charity; there was little awareness that a charity might make decisions about whether or not an item was fit to be re-used and could still make use of items unfit for sale. One participant reported feeling obliged to wash clothes before giving them to charity shops, while others questioned whether this might offset the environmental benefit from re-use.

There was sometimes a lack of confidence that charity bag collections were from reputable organisations and were, in fact, used for commercial gain. Wearing clothes that had been used by other people was, for some participants, acceptable only if previous wearers were family members or friends. Indeed, participants reacted negatively to samples of clothes from charity shops in the final phase of the research. Some participants were unhappy to discard re-usable clothes without receiving a financial return, which has also been found to be the case with certain US consumers (Joung and Park-Poaps 2011). Several suggested that people should get money for returning used clothes, while others indicated that they try to sell their unwanted clothes.

23.3.2.3 Recycling

Participants spoke about their need for more information on how best to dispose of 'useless' items. In support of Birtwistle and Moore (2007), their awareness of clothing recycling, as distinct from re-use, appeared poor owing to a lack of information about how or where recycling can be done and there was limited awareness that once clothes are beyond repair the cloth can be recycled. Some suggested that a clothes collection bin to complement household recycling bins would be useful, and just as Morgan and Birtwistle (2009) propose, respondents stated they would consider changing their behaviour if equipped with greater knowledge. In particular participants identified as being more environmentally motivated discussed people's need for greater knowledge about clothing re-use and recycling. They felt that people have little understanding of clothes recycling and assume that charity shops are only for re-use, unaware that they may also pass on clothes for recycling. Participants in all groups questioned whether people were adequately motivated to dispose of clothing responsibly and some doubted the feasibility of a 'take back' system on the grounds that many people would lack the motivation and that transport would be a barrier. Some suggested that re-use should be made easier for households through, for example, the provision of regular used clothing collections from people's homes.

23.3.2.4 Discarding

Participants in segment 7 (honestly disengaged) spoke almost exclusively of binning clothes, at the extreme, speaking about the 'joy' of throwing clothes in the bin in such a way that there seemed a therapeutic aspect to it that could not be obtained from recycling. This joy in disposal was not shared by participants in segment 2 (waste watchers), who indicated that they feel guilty binning clothes and would re-use them for dusters.

23.3.2.5 Selling

Selling clothes was a less frequent occurrence. Relatively few participants indicated that they sold unwanted clothes. Those that did appeared to be predominantly in segments 4, 5 and 6 (sideline supporters, cautious participants, stalled starters) and used eBay or car boot sales. There was a perception that selling via eBay involved significant effort for little return unless the clothes were the more expensive branded items. This was even the case for clothes which had never been worn. Several participants suggested that selling clothes at car boot sales was at least enjoyable, but others responded that, rather than expending the effort, it was more convenient to give unwanted clothes to charity. Participants from different segments indicated that they shared or swapped clothes, usually with family members. Swapping with friends appeared to be more prevalent among females, and although some male participants said that they occasionally shared clothes with friends, this appeared atypical, with factors such as embarrassment coming into play. Children's clothes were often 'passed on' within and between families. Some parents organised informal groups for this purpose.

23.4 Conclusions and implications

The findings of this study offer implications for manufacturers, brands and retailers in the fashion industry, as well as having the potential to influence government policies towards sustainable clothing. The literature review and the Defra study show that there are various methods of improving sustainability in the fashion market that certain groups of consumers will respond positively towards. Many people in this study reported feeling powerless as individuals and consequently several suggested that the need to change behaviour might demand intervention by the government and industry, and that there is a need for reliable information as a prerequisite to bring about pro-environmental behaviour. The need for more information about the sustainability impacts of clothing interlocks with an apparent distrust of large companies and the possibility that suppliers may treat the sustainability agenda as a marketing ploy ('greenwash'). This distrust also shaded into a more general scepticism concerning global warming. However, respondents reported that they might have confidence in and be inspired by a national campaign to change behaviour led by a respected figurehead, with several participants describing the role of government as 'crucial' in order to change the 'system'. Participants also suggested that industry should accept responsibility alongside government. Various approaches to behavioural change began to emerge, including the following:

- More information (for example media, leaflets, Internet)

- Being inspired by a national campaign

- Having increased trust, arising from a reliable label and collaboration between government and industry regarding consistent goals

The findings indicate that sustainability issues should ideally be considered at the outset of the design process, rather than sustainability being something which is engineered in later, when it is difficult to make as much impact. Designers can take joint responsibility for reducing sustainability impacts, alongside technologists, buyers and marketers. Sustainability can be designed into clothes while retaining aesthetic appeal, for example by sourcing recycled fibres, fabric or componentry, to tempt consumers to buy them in preference to standard products with higher sustainability impacts. If sustainable fabrics are more expensive than average then design details may need to be minimised to reduce cost so that the product remains profitable and therefore viable for the company to produce/purchase; that is, financial sustainability needs to be considered as part of the triple bottom line (Elkington 2004). Designers, buyers and marketers can liaise with each other in order to communicate products' sustainable feature/s to consumers. This should be factual and informational, for example garment labels and in-store brochures, rather than being presented as promotional, since consumers may be resistant to this approach, yet it should be displayed prominently or made easily accessible in order to attract attention.

Instructions on maintaining and disposing of clothes can also be communicated to consumers, for example through labelling on or in garments (Dombek-Keith and Loker 2011). Information could also be provided online via company websites or social networking, promoted via brief weblinks printed on clothing labels. This can include, for example, information on washing, sewing and recycling. Retailers and educational institutions can collaborate to provide training for clothes maintenance, since consumers were found to lack these skills; for example short courses at colleges or universities could be promoted or partially sponsored by clothing retailers or brands. Designers, technologists and marketers in the fashion business could discuss the feasibility of renting out clothes or purchasing/accepting used clothes from customers for re-use or recycling, for example reselling 'vintage' items, since other companies have started to adopt this practice, thus demonstrating its feasibility.

Our key recommendation in terms of the design and manufacture of clothing is that companies should consider and take responsibility for the full lifespan of their products, rather than just the production and retailing stages, since the usage and disposal phases are potentially much longer, with greater negative impacts on the environment. Consequently, designing and engineering washability and durability into fashion products through astute selection of materials and styling, while taking disposal into account, are among the most effective methods which can be used to make clothing more environmentally sustainable.

References

Allwood, J.M., S.E. Laursen, C.M. de Rodriguez and N.M.P. Bocken (2006) *Well Dressed? The Present and Future Sustainability of Clothing and Textiles in the UK* (Cambridge, UK: Cambridge University Institute of Manufacturing).

Barnes, L., and G. Lea-Greenwood (2010) 'Fast Fashion in the Retail Store Environment', *International Journal of Retail & Distribution Management* 38.10: 760-72.

BBC Radio 4 (2010) 'Wasteful Disposal', You & Yours, broadcast 22 January 2010, www.bbc.co.uk/radio4/features/you-and-yours/unwanted-clothes, accessed 14 January 2012.

Belk, R.W. (1985) 'Issues in the Intention Behaviour Discrepancy', in J.N. Sheth (ed.), *Research in Consumer Behavior*, Vol. 1 (Greenwich, CT: JAI Press): 1-34.

Bianchi, C., and G. Birtwistle (2010) 'Sell, Give Away, or Donate: An Exploratory Study of Fashion Clothing Disposal Behaviour in Two Countries', *International Review of Retail, Distribution and Consumer Research* 20.3: 353-68.

Birtwistle, G., and C.M. Moore (2007) 'Fashion Clothing: Where Does it All End Up?', *International Journal of Retail and Distribution Management* 35.3: 210-16.

Blanchard, T. (2007) *Green is the New Black* (London: Hodder).

Carrigan, M., and A. Attalla (2001) 'The Myth of the Ethical Consumer: Do Ethics Matter in Purchase Behaviour?', *Journal of Consumer Marketing* 18.7: 560-78.

Connolly, J., and D. Shaw (2006) 'Identifying Fair Trade in Consumption Choice', *Journal of Strategic Marketing* 14: 353-68.

Cooper, T. (ed.) (2010) *Longer-lasting Products: Alternatives to the Throwaway Society* (Farnham, UK: Gower Publishing).

Co-operative Bank (2009) 'Ethical Consumerism Report', Co-operative Bank, www.goodwithmoney.co.uk/assets/Ethical-Consumerism-Report-2009.pdf?token=9d99f35136c2be9824aceaab78c52a2443123573|1350852397#PDFP, accessed October 2012.

Crane, A. (1999) 'Are You Ethical? Please Tick Yes □ Or No □: On Researching Ethics in Business Organizations', *Journal of Business Ethics* 20.3: 237-48.

Defra (2008) 'A Framework for Pro-Environmental Behaviours', Defra, www.archive.DEFRA.gov.uk/evidence/social/behaviour/documents/behaviours-jan08-report.pdf, accessed 7 January 2012.

Dombek-Keith, K. (2009) *Re-Fashioning the Future: Eco-Friendly Apparel Design* (Saarbrücken, Germany: VDM Verlag Dr. Müller).

Dombek-Keith, K., and S. Loker (2011) 'Sustainable Clothing Care by Design', in A. Gwilt and T. Rissanen (eds.), *Shaping Sustainable Fashion* (London: Earthscan): 101-18.

Domina, T., and K. Koch (1999) 'Consumer Reuse and Recycling of Post-Consumer Waste', *Journal of Fashion Marketing and Management* 3.4: 346-59.

Eckhardt, G.M., R. Belk and T.M. Devinney (2010) 'Why Don't Consumers Consume Ethically?' *Journal of Consumer Behaviour* 9: 426-36.

Elkington, J. (2004) 'Enter the Triple Bottom Line', in A. Henriques and J. Richardson (eds.), *The Triple Bottom Line: Does It All Add Up? Assessing the Sustainability of Business and CSR* (London: Earthscan): 1-16.

Ellis, N., and M. Higgins (2006) 'Recatechizing Codes of Practice in Supply Chain Relationships: Discourse, Identity and Otherness', *Journal of Strategic Marketing* 14 (December 2006): 387-410.

Fisher, T., T. Cooper, S. Woodward, A. Hiller and H. Goworek (2008) 'Public Understanding of Sustainable Clothing: A Report to the Department for Environment, Food and Rural Affairs', Defra, www.randd.defra.gov.uk/Default.aspx?Menu=Menu&Module=More&Location=None&Completed=0&ProjectID=15626, accessed 30 August 2011.

Fletcher, K. (2008) *Sustainable Fashion and Textiles: Design Journeys* (London: Earthscan).

Gibson, C., and E. Stanes (2011) 'Is Green the New Black? Exploring Ethical Fashion Consumption', in T. Lewis and E. Potter (eds.), *Ethical Consumption: A Critical Introduction* (London: Routledge): 169-85.

Gwilt, A., and T. Rissanen (eds.) (2011) *Shaping Sustainable Fashion* (London: Earthscan).

Ha-Brookshire, J.E., and N.N. Hodges (2009) 'Socially Responsible Consumer Behavior?: Exploring Used Clothing Donation Behavior', *Clothing and Textiles Research Journal* 27: 179-96.

Hustvedt, G., and M.A. Dickson (2009) 'Consumer Likelihood of Purchasing Organic Cotton Apparel: Influence of Attitudes and Self-Identity', *Journal of Fashion Marketing and Management* 13.1: 49-65.

Iwanow, H., M.G. McEachern and A. Jeffrey (2005) 'The Influence of Ethical Trading Policies on Consumer Apparel Purchase Decisions. A Focus on The Gap Inc.', *International Journal of Retail and Distribution Management* 33.5: 371-87.

Joergens, C. (2006) 'Ethical Fashion: Myth or Future Trend?' *Journal of Fashion Marketing and Management* 10.3: 360-71.

Joung, H.M., and H. Park-Poaps (2011) 'Factors Motivating and Influencing Clothing Disposal Behaviours', *International Journal of Consumer Studies*, DOI: 10.1111/j.1470-6431.2011.01048.x.

Kim, S., M. Littrell and J.L. Paff Ogle (1999) 'Social Responsibility as a Predictor of Purchase Intentions for Clothing', *Journal of Fashion Marketing and Management* 3.3: 207-18.

Klein, N. (2000) *No Logo* (London: Flamingo).

Low, W., and E. Davenport (2006) 'Mainstreaming Fair Trade: Adoption, Assimilation, Appropriation', *Journal of Strategic Marketing* 14: 315-27.

McDonough, W., and M. Braungart (2008) *Cradle to Cradle: Re-Making the Way we Make Things* (London: Vintage).

Micheletti, M. (2003) *Political Virtue and Shopping: Individuals, Consumerism, and Collective Action* (Gordonsville, VA: Palgrave Macmillan).

Morgan, L.R., and G. Birtwistle (2009) 'An Investigation of Young Fashion Consumers' Disposal Habits', *International Journal of Consumer Studies* 33: 190-98.

Park, H., and S.J. Lennon (2006) 'The Organizational Factors Influencing Socially Responsible Apparel Buying/Sourcing', *Clothing and Textiles Research Journal* 24.3 (July 2006): 229-47.

Rissanen, T. (2011) 'Designing Endurance', in A. Gwilt and T. Rissanen (eds.), *Shaping Sustainable Fashion* (London: Earthscan): 127-38.

Shaw, D., G. Hogg., E. Wilson, E. Shui and L. Hassan (2006) 'Fashion Victim: the Impact of Fair Trade Concerns on Clothing Choice', *Journal of Strategic Marketing* 14: 427-40.

Shove, E. (2003) 'Sustainability, System Innovation and the Laundry', Department of Sociology, Lancaster University, www.lancs.ac.uk/fass/sociology/papers/shove-sustainability-system-innovation.pdf, accessed October 2012.

Slater, K. (2003) *Environmental Impact of Textiles: Production, Processes and Protection* (Cambridge, UK: Woodhead Publishing Limited).

Tomolillo, D., and D. Shaw (2003) 'Undressing the Ethical Issues in Clothing Choice', *International Journal of New Product Development and Innovation Management*, June/July 2003: 99-107.

Ulasewicz, C. (2008) 'Fashion, Social Marketing and the Eco-Savvy Shopper', in J. Hethorn and C. Ulasewicz (eds.), *Sustainable Fashion: Why Now?: A Conversation Exploring Issues, Practices, and Possibilities* (New York: Fairchild).

Waste Online (2012) 'Waste at Home', Waste Online, www.wasteonline.org.uk/topic?topic=a0gC0000002RwLWIA0, accessed 7 January 2012.

Woodward, S. (2005) 'Looking Good, Feeling Right: Aesthetics of the Self', in D. Miller and S. Kuechler (eds.), *Clothing as Material Culture* (Oxford, UK: Berg).

Yates, L. (2008) 'Sustainable Consumption: The Consumer Perspective', *Consumer Policy Review* 18.4: 96-101.

Young. W., K. Hwang, S. McDonald and C.J. Oates (2010) 'Sustainable Consumption: Green Consumer Behaviour When Purchasing Products', *Sustainable Development* 18: 20-31.

Helen Goworek is Senior Lecturer in Marketing at Nottingham Business School. She previously worked in design and buying management roles in the clothing industry. Her research interests lie in sustainable fashion, retail buying, design and marketing. She teaches marketing, sustainability and design at undergraduate and postgraduate level.

Alex Hiller is Head of MSc Programmes at Nottingham Business School. His research interests centre on the role of ethics and its contribution to value in consumer behaviour, particularly in the purchase of clothing, and he teaches undergraduates and postgraduates in the fields of consumer behaviour, marketing ethics and services marketing.

Tom Fisher is Professor of Art and Design in the School of Art and Design at Nottingham Trent University. Tom's background is in fine art, design and sociology. He wrote his PhD on the role of plastic materials in consumption experiences, in the sociology department at the University of York.

Tim Cooper is Professor of Sustainable Design and Consumption at Nottingham Trent University. A social scientist, his research interests are multidisciplinary, embracing design, consumer behaviour, public policy and environmental ethics. He is contributing editor of *Longer Lasting Products* (Gower, 2010).

Dr **Sophie Woodward** is Lecturer in Sociology at the University of Manchester. She has carried out ethnographic research into women's wardrobes and has a continued interest in clothing as a form of material culture. She collaborates with Professor Daniel Miller in the Global Denim Project.

Index